W9-DFN-621

WOMEN IN THE SCIENTIFIC SEARCH:

An American Bio-bibliography, 1724-1979

by
PATRICIA JOAN SIEGEL
and
KAY THOMAS FINLEY

The Scarecrow Press, Inc.
Metuchen, N.J. & London
1985

Library of Congress Cataloging in Publication Data

Siegel, Patricia Joan.
    Women in the scientific search.

    Includes index.
    1. Science--United States--Bio-bibliography.
2. Women scientists--United States--Bibliography.
3. Women in science--United States--Bibliography.
4. United States--Bio-bibliography. I. Finley,
K. Thomas (Kay Thomas), 1934-   . II. Title.
Z7404.S57 1985   016.5092'2   84-20290
[Q141]
ISBN 0-8108-1755-1

pour notre petit amour

MOIRA ELIZABETH

CONTENTS

---

*Not included in <u>Notable American Women</u>.

PSYCHOLOGISTS

PREFACE

When grandmother says, "I hope Moira will not want to become a chemist in a laboratory surrounded by icky smells and messy concoctions," we see to what extent is engrained the traditional prejudice against women scientists. Beyond patronizing colleagues, fearful professional societies, and discriminatory recognition practices, there runs a current of feeling even among our educated and well-intentioned contemporaries that "nice girls" do not get involved in the nitty-gritty of scientific discovery. Theodore Zeldin, a British historian, said, "Marie Curie was helped by the fact that she was of Polish origin and foreign girls could do things in France which French girls, watched over by parents with pretensions, could not."

Yet there are numerous women who have given unstintingly of their talent, their time, and their energy to the scientific community with little reward for their struggles and achievements. We discovered this glaring lacuna while we were enjoying the renewal offered by that wonderful and essential tradition known as sabbatical leave. Interested in the history of science and of women, we spent some evening hours browsing in the library until the evidence of the neglect of women's contributions became so overwhelming that we metamorphosed into nightly sleuths.

A perusal of James McKleen Cattell's American Men of Science reveals that as early as the first edition in 1906 women were included, a fact too insignificant at the time to mention in the title. In the first seven editions (1906-1943), Cattell determined the thousand leading American men of science "to secure a group for scientific study." A star was awarded in the 12 principal sciences and the symbol "means that the subject of the biographical sketch is probably among the leading thousand students of science in the United States." The number awarded in each science is "approximately proportional to the total number of workers in that science." Although the starring system has been thoughtfully criticized, it certainly was a peer evaluation and indicates who American scientists thought were the leading workers in their field at the time.

This period, representing most of the first half of the twentieth century, produced 52 women recognized by their colleagues as important contributors to their discipline. The largest current effort to provide biographic and bibliographic data on women in the United States is certainly Notable American Women 1607-1950

and the fourth volume, Notable American Women: The Modern Period, published in 1971 and 1980 respectively. Correlation between
these two basic sources shows that just over half of the starred
women appear in Notable American Women (29 of 52). If the fact
that some were still living when the latter work was published, and
thus excluded, the overlap is good except for the field of zoology
where only three of 17 are found.

Other standard compilations of scientists and their works do
not show the same recognition of the importance of women scientists in the first half of the twentieth century. For example, the
excellent Biographical Dictionary of American Science, published
in 1979, includes only four of the 19 women selected by their peers
as distinguished contributors at the turn of the century. Fairness
demands notice that this work does include 14 other important wom-
en scientists and doesn't include the twentieth century, when women
scientists began to contribute in significant numbers. The 15-volume
Dictionary of Scientific Biography published the same decade names
seven American women, including three of the 52 who won stars.

The study of women in science is not a particularly recent
intellectual interest. In 1869 we find Lydia Ernestine Becker writing in The Contemporary Review, "On the Study of Science by Wom-
en." An important part of this long paper is the account of examinations given at the Royal College of Science for Ireland beginning
in 1855-1856 for the purpose of awarding prizes and medals in such
fields as geology, botany, zoology, chemistry, pure mathematics,
and laboratory work. In the thirteen years for which data are given,
women are found in the first three places in each field and in numbers far out of proportion to their distribution in the group taking
the examinations.

In the June 23, 1888, issue of The Woman's Journal, there
is a small note reporting that a Belgian lady, Mme. Renoz, has been
selected as the editor of La Revue Scientifique des Femmes. Thus,
it is not surprising that M. Rebière presented a Conférence entitled
Les Femmes dans la Science, published in 1894 and greatly expanded
in a second edition of 1897. American women, too, were making
recognized contributions to science and in The Chautauquan of 1898
and 1899 Mrs. M. Burton Williamson, soon to appear in the first
edition of American Men of Science, published a three-part paper,
"Some American Women in Science." Biographical sketches, photographs, and comments on the work of 44 women constitute a basic
source of information as the new century dawned.

References to women scientists appeared as parts of books
describing the contributions of women to the intellectual life in both
the nineteenth and early twentieth centuries; for example, W. A.
Newman Dorland in The Sum of Feminine Achievement published
in 1917 devotes a chapter to "Woman's Contribution to Science."
It was 1913 when John Augustine Zahm, writing under the nom de

plume H. J. Mozans, published <u>Woman in Science</u> treating both the
struggle for acceptance and biographical information for an extensive list of women scientists.

Recently, active scholarly interest in women scientists has
produced exciting results from such diverse environments as the
autumn 1978 issue of <u>Signs: Journal of Women in Culture and Soci-
ety</u> and the 1980 Symposium on <u>Women in the History of Science</u>
at Williams College. In our opinion three publications illustrate the
very best of current attempts to correct the neglect women scientists have suffered. The first is the superb study by Margaret W.
Rossiter, <u>Women Scientists in America: Struggles and Strategies
to 1940</u>. When we saw the title and began reading a review we
could see three years of work going out the window. It is our
sincere hope that our efforts complement hers, and that together
we can stimulate the great amount of research remaining.

The second promising activity is represented by the Association for Women in Mathematics which is using its <u>Newsletter</u> to present
solid, scholarly contributions to the history of women in science.
This is especially important since mathematics is so central to the
progress of science in general. Many of the papers found in this
publication reach far beyond any narrow definition of mathematics
and contribute to our understanding of a variety of scientific dis-
ciplines. It is a shame that collections of this valuable periodical
are so difficult to find.

The third and bottom line in this or any other scholarly discipline is the short paper resulting from hours, days, weeks, months,
years of digging. Finding these obscure gems, which are often
hidden in the back issues of little-known and barely-read journals,
such as alumnae bulletins and nonextant reviews, is pure scholarly
pleasure. How glad we were to find Jeanne E. Remington's study
<u>Katharine Jeannette Bush: Peabody's Mysterious Zoologist</u>. Per-
haps others will share her and our frustration and elation in the
search for truth about American women scientists.

Specifically, our purpose is that of any good bibliographer:
to provide a starting point for future work. From our own backgrounds we recognize the value of Hugo Paul Thieme's <u>La littérature
française du dix-neuvième siècle</u> and Friedrich Konrad Beilstein's
<u>Handbuch der organischen Chemie</u>, which provided a real impetus
for future work in nineteenth-century French letters and organic
chemistry. We started our research with the deceased women who
are found in one or more of the following sources: 1) <u>American
Men of Science</u> (first edition or starred), 2) <u>Notable American Wom-
en</u>, 3) <u>Biographical Dictionary of American Science</u>, and 4) the small,
but growing, number of biographical collections devoted to scientists
of both genders practicing a particular discipline. To this last
we have added the most exciting source of all, those women we discovered and are not found in any published collection. We have

evidence that our list is not exhaustive, but no one who pub-
lishes can ever wait until the job is done. The length of each biographical sketch is approximately proportional to the work left to
be done if one first understands that even the longest sketches
represent women for whom much remains to be learned and published. There are women in this collection who have everything
that Mme. Curie had except "good press." There are also women
here who represent the norm of practicing scientists; they worked
hard and produced useful results that promoted new research which
made their work out of date. There are also women who, for reasons that deserve study, ended their scientific career before they
even made a name among their contemporaries.

The bibliography is as complete as we have been able to make
it; we are certain this means it is very incomplete. It is our objective to concentrate on published studies of biography. The large
and important resources of correspondence, works about careers
for women in science, studies of institutions with which women scientists have been associated, and the professional bibliography of
these women have been presented only when they have been published and contain direct biographical references. There are two
distinct types of biographical dictionaries. We have included all
references to those which, like Dictionary of American Biography,
provide substantial biographical sketches and references. We have
cited those which, like American Men of Science, simply list biographical facts only when we were able to find no other published information. In general these materials are well presented in Women Scientists in America and to a less satisfactory degree in Notable American Women. We have made the greatest possible effort to present
accurate and complete citations and to make the nature and extent
of each item clear. Those few items we have not been able to see
are marked with an asterisk. Wherever we have found incorrect
information of fact or of implication, we have stated it as we have
found it with the sole intent of helping future scholars.

Four additional notes on style may be helpful. There are
a number of instances in which more than one woman is discussed
in a given work. Rather than repeat the full bibliographic citation
and most of the annotation each time, such works are fully described
in a general section and later referred to by item number. In those
cases where a particular woman is dealt with in more detail, a sup-
plementary annotation is included. There are instances in which
a woman appears many times in a book but without a single section
devoted to her biography. We employ "index" in the citation rather
than repeat the list of page numbers. We have, of course, checked
the accuracy of the index cited and provided any corrections needed.
Many of these women made contributions in more than one scientific
field. We have tried to place them in the section corresponding
to their chief interest as reflected in American Men of Science. In
general we have used this source to tentatively resolve conflicts
over dates, types of degrees, and professional affiliations. As

indicated in our annotation, the entries in that basic reference are most likely to have been proofread at least once by the woman herself.

One of the most troublesome problems in this work is deciding the proper name to use for a woman. We have tried to use a common-sense approach by listing her complete name at the head of each entry and then referring to her by the name she appears to have most commonly used. We are sure there are many examples of misusage which will come to light in the course of further research. A somewhat related type of problem is that of the proper sequence in which to present the women. We have elected the chronological approach by date of birth in an attempt to place the contributors in their historical perspective.

Material for this book has come from innumerable sources, some of which were very obscure. For their patience and persistence we are grateful to Mr. Robert Gilliam and Mrs. Norma Lawrence of the Interlibrary Loan Office of State University College, Brockport, New York. In addition, we thank heartily all those librarians, archivists and alumnae directors who responded so generously to our requests and who saved us miles of unaffordable travel. Thank you, too, Mr. Paul Hart, our student who solved some impossible problems for us while we were away from all American libraries.

We have met some truly fascinating women in the course of this study; it is our sincere hope that you will join us in making their acquaintance. As for Moira, we do not hope that she will be a chemist or even a scientist, only that she may be able to choose rationally what it is she does want to be.

P. J. S.
K. T. F.

GENERAL BIOGRAPHIES

1883

1. Hanaford, Phebe A. "Women--Scientists" in Daughters of America; or women of the century. Augusta, Maine: True and Company, ch. IX, pp. 250-270.
   Beginning with a section discussing, in the most optimistic
terms, the present and future role of women in science, the chapter
presents short biographical sketches of both known and unknown
women including Maria Mitchell, Almira Phelps, Erminnie Smith, and
Elizabeth Agassiz. The list of names would be a fine place to start
research on forgotten women of science. The chief deficiencies
are the brevity of most of the sketches and the lack of much in
the way of hard data concerning the women.

1891-1982

2. The National Cyclopaedia of American Biography. Various Editors. New York: James T. White. Volumes 1-61 (1982) and
   Current Volumes A (1930) through M (1978).
   A standard reference work in biography often criticized for
being too flattering to the subjects.

1897

3. Rebière, A[lphonse]. Les Femmes dans la Science. 2nd edition. Paris: Librairie Nony & Cie. In French. Reprinted:
   Cambridge, Massachusetts: MIT Press, 1974.
   A second and greatly expanded edition of Rebière's 1894 Conférence. Both works are international in scope but deal largely
with French women. The second edition pays more attention to
Americans, and the biographical detail is in general more extensive.
The treatment of Dorothea Klumpke, an American who made her
career in Paris, is described in great detail. There are also two
appendices which present quotations from many authors on the general subjects of women's capabilities in and contributions to science.
Reviews: Scientific American 78 (1898), p. 204. Popular Astronomy, 6 (1898), pp. 129-138, 211-228.

1898-1899

4. Williamson, Mrs. M. Burton. "Some American Women in

Science," The Chautauquan, 28 (ns 19) (November, 1898, January and February, 1899), pp. 161-168, 361-368, 465-473.
Photographs.
   Gives biographical detail on 44 American women from all fields
of science. Emphasis is on their scientific areas of interest. Many
excellent photographs. There is a lack of specific data concerning
dates and affiliations.

1901

5.   Stewart, Jane A. "Women Deans of Women's Colleges," The
     Chautauquan, 33 (August), pp. 486-492. Photographs.
   Discusses the role of women in an administrative capacity at
colleges devoted to women's education. Several women in science
were active in such positions. The article, in a manner not surprising for the time, takes a rather romantic view of the position
and what it promises for women in the future.

1906-1943

6.   Cattell, J[ames] McKeen, editor. American Men of Science.
     A biographical directory. New York: The Science Press, Edi-
     tions 1-7.
   In an effort to obtain a group of scientists for his studies
Cattell surveyed most of the scientific societies for names to be
included in what he hoped would be a "tolerably complete" list of
"those in North America who have carried on research work in the
natural and exact sciences." In addition to this survey he used
standard reference books, especially Who's Who in America, an analysis of contributions to scientific journals, and printed requests
in Science, The Popular Science Monthly, and The Nation. There
is no easy way of knowing which, if any, of the women suggested
their own name through this last method. About 10,000 names were
submitted, and each person was requested to send in a curriculum
vitae. Those not responding were pursued through the fourth request. As many as three proofs were sent out for confirmation
or revision. From this extensive editorial work 4,131 entries were
published in the first edition of 1906. This basic source of those
who were working scientists at the beginning of the twentieth century included 149 women, 19 of whom were awarded a star indicating that they were among the 1,000 most distinguished scientists
in North America. The method and criteria for awarding stars are
described in the Preface.

1906-1945

7.   The Carnegie Foundation for the Advancement of Teaching An-
     nual Reports.

Each year there is a section entitled "De Mortuis," which gives a brief biographical sketch of persons to whom a "retiring allowance" had been granted. For many of the less well publicized women these reports represent a valuable resource. A study of this early effort at a retirement plan for academics might be instructive.

1912

8. Logan, Mrs. John A. [Mary Simerson Cunningham Logan]. The Part Taken by Women in American History. Wilmington, Delaware: The Perry-Nalle Publishing Co. Reprinted: Arno, 1972.
A great number of biographies of varying lengths. There is no general section devoted to scientists, but they appear as "Educators and Women in Professions." Two important women, Calkins and Phelps (Almira), are found under "Playwrights and Authors." There is a long list of inventors (pp. 886-888) with no data other than city of residence and inventions.

1913

9. Mozans, H. J. [John Augustine Zahm]. Woman in Science: with an introductory chapter on woman's long struggle for things of the mind. New York: D. Appleton and Company, 452 pp. Reprinted: 1922 and 1974. Reviewed: Theodore Roosevelt. The Outlook, 106 (10 January 1914), pp. 93-95; Michael J. Crowe. "Who Was H. J. Mozans?" Isis, 68 (March 1977), p. 111; Deborah Jean Warner. Isis, 67 (1976), pp. 112-113.
As the subtitle promises, this detailed study of women in science begins with a long and sympathetic discussion of the obstacles faced by women from antiquity in their efforts to make a contribution worthy of their intellectual abilities. There follows a review of the various theses which have been advanced to support the supposed inferiority of women in intellectual areas; especially in scientific pursuits. The remaining three-quarters of the book is devoted to a survey of distinguished women and their accomplishments in each field of science. Mathematics, astronomy, physics, chemistry, natural sciences, medicine and surgery, archaeology, inventing, and women as inspirers and collaborators in science are included and surveyed from the earliest times to the beginning of the current century. (We have included all of the women discussed by Mozans.) A summary and an epilogue deal with the future of women in science. The work concludes with a short bibliography. This is truly a pioneering and inspiring work.

1914

10. Woman's Who's Who of America. John William Leonard, editor.

New York: American Commonwealth. Reprinted: Detroit:
Gale Research, 1976.
Provides basic biographical facts.

1917

11. Dorland, W. A. Newman. "Woman's Contribution to Science,"
    in The Sum of Feminine Achievement. A critical and analyti-
    cal study of woman's contributions to the intellectual progress
    of the world. Boston: Straford Company, ch. VI, pp. 140-
    151.
    Opens with a short paragraph attacking the argument that
women have not produced results as scientists. Following are short
sections devoted to different areas of science and medicine. He
names women workers and attempts to show how their contributions
exemplify certain patterns of development. Considers science in
its broadest definition.

1923

12. Anon. "Names of 12 Greatest of Our Living Women," The New
    York Times, 72 (6 May), pp. 1-11.
    Selected by a panel of distinguished men and women these are
the living American women who have given the greatest service to
humanity. Included are Anna [sic] Jump Cannon, Anna Botsford
Comstock, and Florence Rena Sabin. Gives a sketch of the accomplishments of each woman.

1924

13. The Biographical Cyclopaedia of American Women. 2 vols.
    Mabel Ward Cameron, editor. New York: Halvord. Re-
    printed: Detroit: Gale Research, 1974.
    Provides basic biographical data.

1928-1981

14. Dictionary of American Biography. 20 vols. and 7 supp.
    Various editors. New York: Scribner's.
    A high standard of scholarship is characteristic of these arti-
cles, but relatively few scientists are selected for this general reference work.

1931

15. Booth, Alice. "America's Twelve Greatest Women. Dr.

Florence Rena Sabin," Good Housekeeping, 92 (June), pp.
50-51, 198, 200, 202. Portrait.
This item applies only to Sabin. It is a long and detailed biographical sketch which deals with her career in surprising detail.
A popular, readable description which praises her highly, it is also
accurate.

1933

16. Anon. "Science. Best Women," Time, 21 (20 March), p. 36.
Photographs.
A popular report of the three women chosen from the fifth
edition of American Men of Science as "the leading women scientists
of the country and the equals of 247 topnotch men selected." Gives
brief descriptions of the scientific work and reaction to their selection for Ann H. Morgan, Ruth Benedict, and Libbie Hyman.

1935

17. Jaffe, Bernard. Outposts of Science. A journey to the workshops of our leading men of research. New York: Simon and
Schuster, index. Photographs.
Jaffe, an historian of science, and a fine writer, takes on the
nearly impossible task of trying to make sense for the layman of
the thousands of reports of research and their immeasurable impact
on our lives. His procedure, which he describes, was to determine the "eminent men" in each of the most important fields of current research. Using their biographies, he relates their roles in
the history of modern science. The plan sounds as difficult to carry out as the book. Jaffe did it! There is only one woman who
made it into this select group, but the important fact for the early
1930's is that there was one. Maud Slye's work in mouse cancer
receives a detailed treatment, but other women scientists are also
mentioned in connection with the work of their male counterparts.
There are suggestions for further reading.

1936

18. Carr, Emma Perry. "One Hundred Years of Science at Mount
Holyoke College," Mount Holyoke Alumnae Quarterly, 20, pp.
135-138. Photographs.
Perhaps the most important reason for the success Mount Holyoke has had in providing science education for women is their faculty. Carr presents brief sketches of the early leaders in the development of the College's programs.

1938

19. Knipp, Anna Heubeck, and Thaddeus P. Thomas. <u>The History</u>
     <u>of Goucher College</u>. Baltimore: Goucher College, index.
     Although not the earliest of the colleges devoted to providing
educational opportunity for women, Goucher has, for nearly a century, played an important role in that struggle. Excellent background reading on the development of the sciences as a part of
higher education for women and some all too brief insights on the
important women who were alumnae or faculty.

1940

20. <u>American Women 1935-1940: A Composite Biographical Diction-</u>
     <u>ary</u>. 2 vols. Durwood Howes, editor. Los Angeles: Richard
     Blank. Reprinted: Detroit: Gale Research, 1981.
     Provides basic bibliographic data.

1943

21. Yost, Edna. <u>American Women of Science</u>. Philadelphia:
     Frederick A. Stokes Company, 232 pp.
     Written in a style that should be informative and enjoyable
to readers of any age. Yost wishes to make a first effort toward
filling a general need of biographies of outstanding women. In the
foreword she expresses her surprise at the vast amount of work
done by American women scientists. The 12 women included are
cited under their individual entries in our work because these are
rather extensive and humane treatments. There is no bibliographic
material and technical questions are written in understandable language. The purpose of creating superior role models is well ful-
filled.

1944

22. Jaffe, Bernard. <u>Men of Science in America. The role of sci-</u>
     <u>ence in the growth of our country</u>. New York: Simon and
     Schuster, index.
     As in his earlier book (17) Jaffe tries to do the impossible
and comes close enough. By selecting the twenty men who were
the leaders in the development of American science and building
the story of that field around them, he achieves a certain balance.
He is especially careful to bring into the picture the host of other
men and women involved in the development of each discipline. The
contributions of women to each field are well presented, and his
criteria for selection, like those for the men, are sound.

1945

23.   Doolittle, Dortha Bailey.   "Women in Science," Journal of Chem-
      ical Education, 22 (April), pp. 171-174.
      In spite of the fact that this paper was published in a chemical
journal it reaches into many fields of science.   It deals largely with
American women, but does describe the work of several Europeans.
Most of the women mentioned are included in our work.   While the
amount of biographical detail is limited, the well-written sketches
pay special attention to the progress of science and show the breadth
of interest women have displayed and the fundamental nature of
many of their contributions.

1951

24.   Hogue, Mary Jane.   "The Contribution of Goucher Women to
      the Biological Sciences," Goucher Alumnae Quarterly, (Sum-
      mer), pp. 13-22.   Photographs.
      Goucher College has played an important role in the develop-
ment of women scientists reaching all the way back to the Baltimore College for Women.   Our work makes a large number of references to faculty and alumnae who have contributed in a variety
of scientific fields.   The title refers largely to medical biology, but
includes women in zoology, botany, and chemistry as well.   The
sketches are very informative, and several provide details which
are very difficult to obtain elsewhere.

1956

25.   Meigs, Cornelia.   What Makes a College?   A history of Bryn
      Mawr.   New York: Macmillan, 277 pp., index.
      As one of the most important women's colleges Bryn Mawr con-
tinues to play a central role in the education of talented female scientists and in the contribution of original scientific research.   This
book provides both vital background material on the growth of educational opportunity for women in the United States and specific
information on several distinguished teacher-scholars who served
on Bryn Mawr's faculty.   The emphasis is on their role in the development of the college, but there are also interesting glimpses
of their professional contributions.

1960

26.   Hawkins, Hugh.   Pioneer: A History of the Johns Hopkins
      University, 1874-1889.   Ithaca, New York: Cornell University
      Press, index.
      While it may be that the Johns Hopkins University was forced

to provide education for women, it is also true that several distinguished women scientists studied there, and Sabin became a member of the faculty. This well-written history provides important material concerning their careers.

1963-1976

27. Who Was Who in America. 6 vols. Chicago: A. N. Marquis.
    Provides basic bibliographic data.

1967

28. Anon. Idealism at Work. Eighty years of AAUW Fellowships.
    A report by the American Association of University Women,
    343 pp.
    Biographies and descriptions of the projects that won these
    AAUW Fellowships for the period 1956-1967. Although the book
    touches upon earlier history and achievements, there are two other
    works to be consulted for these years: Margaret E. Maltby's History of the Fellowships Awarded by the American Association of
    University Women 1888-1929 and Ruth W. Tryon's Investment in
    Creative Scholarship, which extends coverage to 1956. In the preface to Idealism at Work, Roettinger, Director of the AAUW Fellowship Program, states, "While this is chiefly a report on the accomplishments of the women who have held AAUW Fellowships, it
    is also a record of the achievement of the members who have made
    the program possible by their contributions and their work." The
    book is most valuable for the descriptions of the projects and their
    diversity.

1970-1980

29. Gillispie, Charles Coulston, editor in chief. Dictionary of Scientific Biography. (15 vols.) New York: Scribner's.
    This massive work published for the American Council of
    Learned Societies is an essential reference for the seven women
    lucky enough to be included. The biographies are well written
    and there are bibliographies of both their works and writings about
    them. One wonders how many of the men included are really more
    deserving of the space than their female counterparts who are not
    included.

1971-1980

30. Notable American Women 1607-1950 (3 vols., 1971) and Notable
    American Women: The Modern Period (1980). Edward T.
    James, editor. Cambridge, Massachusetts: Belknap Press
    (Harvard).

The major undertaking intended to provide scholarly information
on women in all phases of life along with bibliographical references
to their own work and writings about them. The biographies are
well done--readable, accurate and exciting. In many instances the
woman herself, both the personality and the professional, seems
to step right out of the book. The bibliography is not uniform.
There are too many errors; it is maddeningly incomplete in many
instances, and little guidance is provided. In spite of these problems this work is a most important reference, and we hope it will
be greatly expanded to include the large number of women who deserve such recognition.

1974

31. Rossiter, Margaret W. "Women Scientists in America Before
    1920," American Scientists, 62 (May-June), pp. 312-323.
    Photographs.
    An extensive study of women in science in nineteenth- and
early twentieth-century America. Gives abundant statistical data
and examples as she compares "the number, distribution and career patterns of the men" with their female counterparts. Includes
a lengthy discussion of education with particular attention given
to those colleges and universities that provided the leadership in
making equality for women a reality.

1975

32. Arnold, Lois. "Marie Curie Was Great, But ...," School
    Science and Mathematics, 75 (October), pp. 577-584.
    The article is largely about the failure of textbook authors to
use women either as participants or spectators in descriptions of
scientific work. However, a good number of women scientists are
mentioned by name and associated with a particular field. Gives
a useful orientation to the field.

1976

33. Kulkin, Mary-Ellen. Her Way. Biographies of women for young
    people. Chicago: American Library Association, index.
    A very nicely annotated bibliography of books about a few
women scientists which were written for young readers. It is a
shame that the young reader has been neglected by the lack of
material in this area.

34. Hypatia's Sisters. Biographies of Woman Scientists--Past and
    Present. Susan Schacher, coordinator. Seattle: Feminists
    Northwest.
    A series of sketches of women scientists from several fields
and times. The booklet grew out of a course entitled "Women &

Science" given at the University of Washington in the summer of
1975. There are some bibliographic references.

1977

35. Kadar, Agnes, and Barbara Shupe. "Science: A History of
     Woman's Work," Science Teacher, 44 (April), pp. 38-41.
     Photographs.
     An effort to provide science teachers with female role models
for younger students. Includes interesting notes about women from
a wide variety of scientific fields.

1978

36. Anon. "Women in Nineteenth-Century Science," Chemistry,
     51 (December), pp. 5-10. Photographs.
     A conversation between Deborah Warner, Curator of History
of Astronomy at The Smithsonian Institution, and Laura Riesenberg
of Chemistry concerning the exhibit honoring nineteenth-century
women in science. A few women are mentioned and placed in the
context of the early development of science in America.

37. Kohlstedt, Sally Gregory. "In from the Periphery: American
     women in science, 1830-1880," Signs, Journal of Women in Cul-
     ture and Society, 4 (Autumn), pp. 81-96. Photographs.
     Traces the rise of women in science in the first half of the
nineteenth century from their nearly invisible role to the beginning
of their true professional participation. Divides the three generations into "independents, disseminators and group coordinators,"
and illustrates how much the success of the women in the 1880's
depended upon the "persistent efforts of women who had worked
quietly in science throughout the century." Cites many names and
their specific contributions and provides detailed references to
sources. While the other articles in this special issue devoted to
women in science do not deal directly with biography, they represent an important effort and should be read by anyone interested
in this field of study.

38. Biographical Dictionary of American Educators 3 vols. John
     F. Ohles, editor. Westport, Connecticut: Greenwood Press.
     Many women scientists are included in brief but useful bio-
graphical sketches. There are references to other writings about
the subjects, but there are quite a few errors. The entries for
each woman are cited individually in our work.

39. Opfell, Olga S. The Lady Laureates. Women who have won
     the Nobel Prize. Metuchen, New Jersey: Scarecrow Press.
     Photographs.
     Thoughtful discussion of Nobel, the Prize, and the women who

have won it, followed by detailed chapter devoted to each woman.
Extensive bibliography and very human discussion of the person
as well as the scientist. The sketches of Cori and Mayer are annotated separately because of their extended nature.

1979

40. Biographical Dictionary of American Science: The seventeenth
    through the nineteenth centuries. Clark A. Elliott, editor.
    Westport, Connecticut: Greenwood Press.
    Well-written, brief sketches of the more prominent women scien-
    tists. Gives selected references to their works as well as works
    about them. Especially strong in its evaluation of the modern atti-
    tude about their work. Some of the entries contain only a few lines
    of personal data, and some women are mentioned only as the wife
    or mother of a male scientist.

41. Science, Sex and Society. Ann E. Kramer, Cherlyn S. Gran-
    rose and Jan B. Sloan, editors. The Project for the Advance-
    ment of Women in Science Careers. Women's Educational Equity
    Act Program. United States Department of Health, Education
    and Welfare. Newton, Massachusetts: Education Development
    Center.
    Developed as a readings book for classes dealing with women
    in science, much of this book concerns finding and getting a job.
    However, a part of the material consists of reprints of key topical
    papers, some of which contain biographical data and are difficult
    to obtain. See: Mitchell, Richards and Sabin.

42. Nobel, Iris. "Twentieth-Century Pioneers. Seven Scientists,"
    in Contemporary Women Scientists of America. New York:
    Julian Messner, ch. 1, pp. 9-17.
    As an introduction to her book, Nobel discusses briefly but
    adequately six of the women we are treating. She emphasizes their
    key role in paving the way and recognizes that there are many others
    equally deserving.

43. Tufty, Barbara. "Women in Science and Technology," in The
    Women's Book of World Records and Achievements. Lois Decker
    O'Neill, editor. New York: Anchor Press, Doubleday, ch.
    4, pp. 141-196. Photographs.
    Concentrates on the "first" of women scientists and engineers.
    Much of the material is in the last decade, for obvious reasons,
    but the last century is included. Some excellent photographs.

1980

44. Women in the History of Science. A Symposium. Victor E.
    Hill, chairman. Williamstown, Massachusetts: Williams Col-
    lege (25 January), 65 pp.

The unpublished transcript of the symposium sponsored by
Williams College and IBM. Deals with an international group of wom-
en, but includes many significant Americans. While in general we
are not citing unpublished material, these papers are too significant
to omit. An important perspective is the relationship of the women's
scientific achievements to a variety of themes in the humanistic tradition. There are excellent bibliographic references. This work should
be published.

45. Faunce, Patricia Spencer. Women and Ambition. A Bibliogra-
    phy. Metuchen, New Jersey: Scarecrow Press, sects. B2-
    B4, pp. 467-485.
    Concerned with writings about those who achieve or fail to
achieve in our society, but includes some interesting material related specifically to science, engineering, and mathematics. Not
a very complete bibliography which cites both major articles and
trivial notes without comment.

46. Levin, Beatrice S. Women and Medicine. Metuchen, New Jer-
    sey: Scarecrow Press. Photographs.
    Nicely written material on Cori and Sabin and, surprisingly,
an interesting mention of Bodley and Noether. Extensive bibliography. It is too bad that the important medical work of so many
women is missing.

47. Rossiter, Margaret W. "'Women's Work' in Science, 1880-
    1910," Isis, 71, pp. 381-398.
    The main theme of the development of scientific opportunities
for women does not suffer from the inclusion of a great deal of valuable biographical detail on the women themselves. While much of
this research also appears in Rossiter's book (49), there are details
which make this paper of continuing value.

1982

48. American Women Writers: A critical reference guide from co-
    lonial times to the present. 4 vols. Lina Mainiero, editor.
    New York: Frederick Ungar.
    Many women scientists were also writers, and it is pleasant
to see that their literary talent is appreciated alongside their scientific contributions. This important new effort presents women scientists from a quite different perspective. The sketches, though
brief, constitute an important resource.

49. Rossiter, Margaret W. Women Scientists in America: Strug-
    gles and strategies to 1940. Baltimore: The Johns Hopkins
    University Press, 439 pp. Photographs.
    A detailed analysis of the entire history of women in science
in America. This book contains the answers to many key questions
and asks enough new questions to last all of us who are interested

a lifetime. Unlike so many scholarly authors Rossiter is a writer;
she holds one's attention with the grace of a Dorothy Sayers and
never lets one doubt that she has all the evidence she needs to
back up every statement. If we seem a bit overawed by this work,
we are. We hope that others, like ourselves will take the chal-
lenge she offers and begin the research she so elegantly charts.
The much overused word "seminal" is appropriately applied to this
work. The wealth of carefully documented bibliography is as impressive as it is useful.

Reviews: Science (24 December 1982), p. 1299; The Chronicle
of Higher Education (2 February 1983), pp. 25-26; New York Times
Book Review (6 February 1983), p. 12; Chemical and Engineering
News (16 May 1983), p. 50.

ARCHAEOLOGISTS, ANTHROPOLOGISTS, ETHNOLOGISTS, AND FOLKLORISTS

GENERAL (See also 1129)

1889

50. McGee, Anita Newcomb. "The Women's Anthropological Society of America," Science, 13 (29 March), pp. 240-242.
    A discussion of the women who formed the group with emphasis on the leading figure, Tilly (Matilda) C. Stevenson. The idea that there should not be two separate organizations on the basis of sex is strongly put, as is the feeling that, for the moment, it is necessary. Most of the article is devoted to a presentation of typical papers read and the nature of the members' contributions.

1960

51. Mead, Margaret, and Ruth L. Bunzel. The Golden Age of American Anthropology. Selected and edited with introduction and notes by MM and RLB. New York: George Braziller, index.
    The editors selected the period 1880 to 1920 which represents the time from the formation of the Bureau of American Ethnology to the beginning of the post World War I generation of anthropologists from reorganized university departments. The book consists of less technical selections which are brief, yet convey a valid description of the author's point of view. Anthropologists who worked outside of North America have been omitted.
    Of special interest are the editors' introductions which provide important insights to the particular anthropologist and evaluation of her work. We present each of the women in her own section.

52. Lurie, Nancy Oestreich. "Women in Early American Anthropology," in Pioneers of American Anthropology. The uses of biography. June Helm, editor. Seattle, Washington: University of Washington Press, pp. 29-81 and unnumbered photographs.
    Traces the history of its subject from the formation of the Women's Anthropological Society in 1885 to the beginning of the era of women who were formally educated for the work. Each of the women is described in some detail, and her work is placed in the pattern of growth which the entire field underwent. There are important photographs of several of these women at work.

53. HARRIET ARNOT MAXWELL CONVERSE
     11 January 1836--18 November 1903
     In many respects Converse was not a scientist. This conclu-
sion is evident in her writings including <u>Myths and Legends of the
New York State Iroquois</u> where her style is imaginative and poetic
rather than being faithful to her sources. Such a shortcoming is
not surprising when one considers her complete lack of formal training and her earlier published contributions of literary essays and
poetry. Unlike many amateur scientists Converse deserves to be
included in a discussion of the rising professional spirit of latter
nineteenth-century anthropology. Her love of the Iroquois was
genuine, and they honored her for it. She spent a great part of
her life and fortune in supporting the causes of their well-being
and the preservation of their culture. In this work she was an
important collector of Indian relics. She not only spent her own
funds liberally, but was able to induce New York State and the
Onondaga Council to make significant gifts. Converse collections
in the New York State Museum, the American Museum of Natural
History and Harvard's Peabody Museum are of lasting scholarly value.
     Converse was born in Elmira, New York, where in 1796 her
grandfather had settled. He traded with the Indians in such an
honest manner that he became an adopted Seneca. Her father continued an active interest in the Seneca Tribe throughout his career
in country, state, and national office and also became an adopted
Seneca. The deaths of her first husband, George B. Clarke, and
her father left Converse with a substantial fortune. She married
an old friend, Franklin B. Converse, a writer who was interested
in Indian music. They happened to meet General Ely S. Parker,
an influential Seneca and Commissioner of Indian Affairs in the Grant
administration. Parker, convinced of the deep feeling Converse
had for the preservation of Indian culture, saw to it that she be
allowed to get as involved as she wished. As a result of her extremely successful work in defending Indian rights in both Albany
and Washington, she was made an honorary chief of the Six Nations.

                              1908

54. Parker, Arthur Caswell. "Introduction," in <u>Myths and Leg-
     ends of the New York Iroquois</u> by Harriet Maxwell Converse.
     Edited and annotated by Arthur Caswell Parker. New York
     State Museum Bulletin 125. Albany: University of the State
     of New York, pp. 14-30. Photograph. Reprinted: Port Wash-
     ington, New York: Ira J. Friedman, 1962.
     After a detailed analysis of the story-telling methods of the
Iroquois and the methods Converse used, Parker presents the basic
source of biographical information for her. Written by a "loving
friend and grateful student" it still offers a reasonably balanced
picture of her life and work. The book which follows is probably
her main written contribution and was assembled from her manuscripts after her death.

<u>1919</u>

55.   Parker, Arthur C[aswell]. <u>The Life of General Ely S. Parker.</u>
      <u>Last Grand Sachem of the Iroquois and General Grant's military</u>
      <u>secretary.</u> Buffalo: Buffalo Historical Society (Publication
      23), index.
         Parker and Converse corresponded extensively, and some of
      his letters to her are published here for the first time. There is
      a biographical sketch of her and specific references to research
      involving Parker's family and war service. Their close friendship
      and mutual respect are noted.

<u>1957</u>

56.   Eyres, Lawrence E. "YA-IE-WA-NOH (She Who Watches Over
      Us) Harriet Maxwell Converse," <u>Chemung County Historical</u>
      <u>Journal</u> (December), pp. 379-383.
         Much retelling of her life, but there are some new pieces of
      information. Emphasis on her Seneca names and their meaning.
      Describes her burial in some detail.

<u>1971</u>

57.   Fenton, William N. "Converse, Harriet Maxwell," <u>Notable</u>
      <u>American Women</u> (30), 1, pp. 375-377.
         Discusses her family background and the writing she did prior
      to becoming interested in the Iroquois. While recognizing her limi-
      tations Fenton points out that her collections are of lasting value
      to scholars. Good bibliography of her works and of writings about
      her collections.

58.   ERMINNIE ADELE PLATT SMITH
      26 April 1836--9 June 1886
         While raising four sons, Smith classified American mineral sam-
      ples for European museums and displayed a marked talent for the
      popularization of scientific subjects. In Jersey City she founded
      the Aesthetic Society, which held monthly meetings for the discus-
      sion of science, literature, and art. As an early female member
      of the American Association for the Advancement of Science, Smith
      took an active part and read papers before its annual meetings and
      became secretary of its Anthropology section. Her growing interest
      in anthropology and the Six Nations of the Iroquois Federation led
      Smith to become the first woman to carry out field work in ethnog-
      raphy. Her accurate observations were published by the Bureau
      of American Ethnology as <u>Myths of the Iroquois</u>. She began training
      native informants, a method used by later scholars with great suc-
      cess.

Smith graduated from Emma Willard's Troy (NY) Female Seminary in 1853 and later studied at the Universities of Strasbourg, Heidelberg and Freiberg. The range of her intellectual interests are evident in the fact that she studied both crystallography and German literature and graduated from the Bergakademie after pursuing the two year course in mineralogy. With financial support from the Smithsonian Institution she compiled a dictionary of the Iroquois language. This work, of over 15,000 words, remains unpublished, but is available to scholars at the Smithsonian. Smith was the first woman elected a fellow of the New York Academy of Sciences and was a member of the London Scientific Society. Much of her field work, in the United States and Canada, was with the Tuscarora by whom she was adopted and given the name "Beautiful Flower." Her name is attached to an undergraduate research prize in geology and mineralogy at Vassar College. (See also 1, 11.)

1880

59. Anon. "Revelations of Science," The New York Times 29 (29 August), p. 5.
Notes Smith's paper given at the Boston meeting of the American Association for the Advancement of Science the previous day. Says that Smith is "not only a good writer, but well-known in literary and scientific circles." Her paper is reprinted nearly in full.

60. Anon. "Science and Its Labors," The New York Times 29 (2 September), p. 3.
Notes her second paper at the meeting cited in item 59. Says she has made a long and earnest investigation of the Iroquois language. Gives a good summary of her purpose.

1883

61. Anon. Echoes of the Aesthetic Society of Jersey City. New York: Thompson & Moreau, Printers.
A volume containing articles on a variety of subjects, some of which were written by and for members of the Aesthetic Society which held its meetings at the home of its founder, Mrs. Erminnie A. Smith. In 1876 she invited a number of women to her home "to organize a society for mutual improvement." The name was chosen to reflect the Society's goals, "the cultivation and education of a taste for the beautiful in literature, science, and art." Mrs. Smith's own article, "Gems," relates the history and significance of precious stones.

1886

62. Anon. "Obituary. Mrs. Erminnie A. Smith," The New York Times 35 (10 June), p. 5.

Very brief, but notes that she started a class of ladies to study music, literature and the sciences and that they called themselves the Daughters of Aesthetics. Says she died of overwork.

1891

63. Anon. In Memoriam. Mrs. Erminnie A. Smith. Boston: Lee
    and Shepard. Printed for Private Circulation, 110 pp.
    A volume of prose and poetry of homage to Smith, founder
and supporter of the Aesthetic Society. Members of the Society
felt that it was the equivalent of the French Salon, and they particularly admired Smith's European manners and culture. She traveled
to the mines of Saxony and descended by "bucket many hundred
feet in the Harz Mountains." She also made contributions to our
knowledge of the aborigines. Smith's own shorter pieces about the
Iroquois Indians, whose language she spoke and whose customs she
understood, are also included. The Memorial Address delivered
at Vassar College on 9 June 1888 is reprinted here as are numerous
poems written by friends for this occasion. There are introductory
remarks by Sara L. Saunders-Lee and a photograph of the 1885
officers of the American Association for the Advancement of Science
taken in Ann Arbor, Michigan.

1935

64. W[alter] H[ough]. "Smith, Erminnie Adelle [sic] Platt," Diction-
    ary of American Biography (14), 17, p. 262.
    Short but interesting sketch in the careful manner of this
standard series. Notes her service on the staff of the Bureau of
American Ethnology of the Smithsonian Institution and her election
as a fellow (and the first woman) of the New York Academy of Sciences.

1971

65. Lurie, Nancy Oestreich. "Smith, Erminnie Adele Platt,"
    Notable American Women (30), 3, pp. 312-313.
    Places major emphasis on her work in anthropology saying
that it was she who introduced the technique of training native
informants which was used successfully by other workers. Gives
a reference to a published bibliography of her scholarly works.

1979

66. Anon. "Smith, Erminnie Adele Platt," Biographical Dictionary
    of American Science (40), p. 238.
    A sketch which places major emphasis on her scientific

interests. She was the first woman to do field work in ethnography.
There is a short, but useful, bibliography.

67. ALICE CUNNINGHAM FLETCHER
     15 March 1838--6 April 1923
     Fletcher's career is somewhat unusual in that most of her early
efforts were devoted to working for the rights of Indians, especially with regard to their security in land holdings. She had read
widely, but wished to see firsthand the ways of Indian life. In
about 1881 she went to Nebraska to live with the Omahas and was
deeply disturbed by the conditions she found. The Indians themselves were afraid, with good reason, that the government would
dispossess them and they appealed to Fletcher for aid. During
the course of her highly successful crusade to obtain fair treatment for the Indians, she won their confidence and began to make
an extensive collection of data and relics. These efforts also won
for her respect in Washington, and she carried out several demanding
assignments, seeing that the provisions of legislation were put into
effect.
     In addition to the studies resulting in what is probably her
most important single volume, The Omaha Tribe, she worked among
the Sioux, Winnebago, Pawnee, and Nez Percés. These labors resulted in forty-six monographs in addition to her shorter published
pieces. She became especially interested in Indian music and began
the difficult task of transcribing hundreds of songs of the Plains
Indians. Since she was not trained in music, she sought the collaboration of Edwin S. Tracy and John C. Fillmore, the Director
of the Milwaukee Music School, but it was her sharp ear and extraordinary memory that resulted in the preservation of this cultural
treasure.
     Considering the demands of her efforts in service and scholar-
ship it is remarkable that she was also active in the women's movement as a charter member and vice-president of the Women's Anthropological Society until 1899 when the Anthropological Society
of Washington admitted its first women members. Fletcher became
president of that Society in 1903. Her professional activities and
honors include vice-president of the American Association for the
Advancement of Science; president of the American Folk-Lore Society; founder and charter member of the American Anthropological
Association; and member of the editorial board of the American
Anthropologist. (See also 4, 8, 9, 11, 32.)

                              1890

*68. [Biographical sketch], Woman's Tribune (4 January).

1892

*69.   [?], New England Magazine, ns 6 (April).

1896

*70.   [Interview], Buffalo [New York] Courier (31 August).

1921

71.   Parkman, Mary R[osetta]. "A Campfire Interpreter. Alice
      C. Fletcher," in Heroines of Service. New York: The Cen-
      tury Co., pp. 210-231. Reprinted from 1917 edition. Photo-
      graph.
      Written for younger readers, the long sketch of Fletcher is
less sentimental than most. Places great emphasis on her interest
in music and the mutual respect that developed between her and
the Indians.

1923

*72.   [Obituary], Washington Evening Star (7 and 8 April).

73.   Anon. "Alice Cunningham Fletcher," The Southern Workman,
      52 (May), pp. 212-213.
      Obituary which presents a concise, well-balanced picture of
her.   Mentions she was a supporter of the Hampton Institute.

74.   Hough, Walter. "Alice Cunningham Fletcher," American
      Anthropologist, ns 25 (April-June), pp. 254-258. Reproduc-
      tion of an 1888 crayon drawing.
      Treats all of the professional aspects of her career and contains
a partial bibliography of her writings. The author obviously thinks
highly of her.

75.   Lummis, Charles F. "In Memoriam. Alice C. Fletcher," Art
      and Archaeology 16 (July-August), pp. 75-76. Photograph.
      Highly personal and nearly poetic tribute from her colleague
in the Archaeological Institute of America.

76.   LaFlesche, Francis. "Alice C. Fletcher," Science, 58 (17
      August), p. 115.
      Written by her adopted son and collaborator, this brief obitu-
ary offers an important eye-witness view of the woman.

*77.   [Obituary], Buffalo [New York] Courier (31 August).

1931

78. F[rederick] H. M[artens]. "Fletcher, Alice Cunningham,"
     Dictionary of American Biography (14), 6, pp. 463-464.
     Standard biographical sketch with special attention to her pub-
lications, many of which are cited. Has high praise for her in both
scientific and humanitarian work.

1960

79. B[unzel], R[uth] L. The Golden Age of American Anthropol-
     ogy (51), pp. 227-228.
     Discusses her relationship with Francis LaFlesche and their
studies of the Indians of the Southern Plains.

1971

80. Wilkins, Thurman. "Fletcher, Alice Cunningham," Notable
     American Women (30), 1, pp. 630-633.
     A fine example of the biographical sketch at its best. Well-
balanced and sympathetic, every aspect of her life and career are
discussed within the limits of the short space available. Excellent
bibliography.

81. ANNIE AUBERTINE WOODWARD MOORE
     27 September 1841--22 September 1929
     Combining her interest and skill in music with a love of lit-
erature and talent in language, Moore translated a number of German and French novels. When she had completed a translation of
the Nibelungenlied, the manuscript was reviewed by Rasmus B.
Anderson, professor of Scandinavian languages at the University
of Wisconsin. He recognized the talent displayed in the work and
invited her to join him in Madison. After learning the Norwegian
language she and Anderson collaborated in the translation of a large
quantity of the contemporary literature of Norway.
     In addition to playing an active role, along with Anderson,
in making Norwegian literature known in America, Moore became
the first American to make a serious study of Scandinavian music.
After 1880 she continued translating, gave many lecture-recitals,
and published extensively. In the years 1900 to 1912 she taught
at the Madison Musical College and was the literary critic for the
Wisconsin State Journal.

1929

82. Anon. "Mrs. A. W. Moore Dies; Author and Composer,"

The New York Times, 79 (24 September), p. 32.
Describes Moore as the friend of several prominent musicians
and one of the first to deliver illustrated musical talks. Notices
that she wrote under the nom de plume Auber Forestier and that
she did translations and editorial work.

83. Hustvedt, Lloyd. "Moore, Annie Aubertine Woodward," Notable American Women (30), 2, pp. 572-573.
Traces the development of her interest in music and describes
precisely her role in the various projects. Refers to most of her
works and relates them to the times in which they were collected
and published.

84. LUCY McKIM GARRISON
    30 October 1842--11 May 1877
    A musician and teacher of particular note, Garrison grew up
in an atmosphere of deeply felt antislavery sentiment. In 1862 she
went with her father to the Sea Islands off the South Carolina coast
and became the only Northern musician to record the songs of the
freed slaves. Although it was among the very early collations of
slave music and perhaps the first to give it a sympathetic treatment,
its publication did not receive attention and was abandoned after
only two parts.
    Garrison, supported by her husband, became active in the
New York weekly, the Nation. In this setting she was an active
participant in the collection of Negro music. Along with William
F. Allen and Charles P. Ware she is author of Slave Songs of the
United States. This large work continues to be regarded as an
important source in American music.

1963

85. Epstein, Dena J. "Lucy McKim Garrison, American Musician,"
    Bulletin of the New York Public Library, 67 (October), pp.
    529-546. Portrait from the Sophia Smith Collection facing p.
    529.
    Drawn from the McKim papers (New York Public and Cornell
University Libraries) and Garrison's own book, this study would
be an excellent beginning for a full biography. A carefully documented analysis of her most important works complements extensive
background on her family. Extensive and well-chosen quotations
from her correspondence.

1971

86. Epstein, Dena J. "Garrison, Lucy McKim," Notable American
    Women (30), 2, pp. 23-24.

Describes in fine detail the circumstances that led to her interest in the music of the former slaves. A clear presentation of the
difficulties involved in seeing this important work published and
the role played by her husband.

87. SARA YORKE STEVENSON
     19 February 1847--14 November 1921
     Born in Paris, France, Stevenson grew up in the midst of an
exciting intellectual society where she gained a deep affection for
archaeology. With her family in Mexico from 1862 until 1867, she
gathered material for an important book, Maximilian in Mexico.
     After her marriage to Cornelius Stevenson of Philadelphia in
1870 she remained active in her study and research of antiquities.
Perhaps her most enduring contribution is the role she played in
the development of the Museum and Department of Archaeology at
the University of Pennsylvania. She was instrumental in obtaining
large collections which she personally classified, catalogued, and
displayed.
     In addition to these heavy responsibilities in Philadelphia she
went to Rome in 1897 and Egypt in 1898 at the request of the University and the American Exploration Society. She published a
number of scholarly papers on various aspects of Egyptian archaeological research along with some more popular articles. Insurance
and Business Adventures in the Days of Shakespeare and in Those
of William Penn has been republished and translated.
     Stevenson's activities were not restricted to archaeology; she
was the first president of the Equal Franchise Society of Pennsylvania. As president of the Civic Club, concerned with the improvement of Philadelphia, she was influential in the growth of many
more such clubs. She was chairman of the French war relief committee and was awarded academic palms as Officier d'Instruction
Publique in 1916 and made a Chevalier du Legion d'Honneur in 1920.
Academic honors were also granted Stevenson for her scholarly efforts. In 1894 she became the first woman lecturer on the Harvard
calendar when she spoke at the Peabody Museum. In that same
year she received the first honorary degree presented to a woman
by the University of Pennsylvania. She was elected to membership
in the Archaeological Institute of America, the American Philosophical Society, the American Association for the Advancement of Science, and the American Oriental Society. She held elective office
in these and other scholarly and civic organizations. (See also
4, 9, 11.)

1935

88. A[nna] L. L[ingelbach]. "Stevenson, Sara Yorke," Diction-
     ary of American Biography (14), 17, pp. 635-636.
     Mentions her accomplishments as a hostess and lists her chief

publications. In addition to noting her scientific work and the recognition she received, the sketch provides some information about
her other public service interests. Short bibliography.

1906

89.   Anon. "Stevenson, Sara Yorke," The National Cyclopaedia
       of American Biography (2), 13, p. 83. Etching.
       Nearly all about her scientific career; a list of titles of her
publications completely without bibliography.

1978

90.   Meyerson, Martin, and Dilys Pegler Winegrad. Gladly Learn
       and Gladly Teach. Franklin and his heirs at the University
       of Pennsylvania, 1740-1976, ch. 10, pp. 117-129. Photo-
       graph.
       A very modern history of a university; tells the story with
readable text and many excellent photographs. Pays special attention to the importance of women in the growth and evolution of
the physical and intellectual plant. Stevenson is the dominant figure in the story but several other important women are included.
Good notes are included.

91.   MATILDA COXE EVANS STEVENSON
       12 May 1849--24 June 1915
       In 1879 Stevenson accompanied her husband on an expedition
to collect specimens and report on the archaeological remains in
the Western Territories. In the company of ethnologists F. H. Cush-
ing and J. K. Hillers, the Stevensons lived for six months at the
Zuñi pueblo in New Mexico. As she aided her husband in the preparation of reports and published a paper on the Zuñi, her interest
in anthropology grew until, encouraged by the eminent British
scholar Edwin B. Tylor, she began to contribute significant research on all phases of pueblo culture.
       At the same time as Stevenson was establishing herself as an
important figure in American anthropological research, she played
a key role in opening opportunities for women in that science. She
was the founder and first president of the Women's Anthropological
Society of America. This organization was disbanded in 1899 when
the Anthropological Society of Washington admitted all of its members and the American Anthropological Association invited female
charter members.
       Important recognition came in 1888 when she took her deceased
husband's place in the Bureau of American Ethnology and completed
their joint work. Stevenson was an especially important figure in
that she was more acute than others of her time in realizing that

Indian society was changing rapidly and that its culture must be recorded or lost forever. Modern evaluations of her contribution recognize the importance of her timely preservation of so much of the pueblo culture. (See also 8, 11, 50.)

1915

92.   Anon.   "Noted Ethnologist Dead," The New York Times, 64
      (25 June), p. 11.
      Served the Smithsonian Institution for 26 years in the Bureau of American Ethnology. Notes that she worked with her husband, but also indicates her own authorship. The author notes that their work for peace among the Indians through the Smithsonian was said to have been a greater force than the cavalry.

93.   Anon.   [Obituary].   Science, 42 (9 June), p. 50.
      Notes her death and twenty-five years of service with the Bureau of American Ethnology.

*94.   [Obituary].   Washington Evening Star (25 June).

1916

95.   Holmes, W[illiam] H.   "In Memoriam.   Matilda Coxe Stevenson,"
      American Anthropologist, ns 18 (October-December), pp. 552-559.   Portrait.
      Several quotations from her publications and close attention to her skill in winning the confidence of the people with whom she worked.   A section is devoted to her husband.   Her publications are listed with full bibliography, but they are almost certainly incomplete.

1929

96.   Anon.   "Stevenson, Matilda Coxe," The National Cyclopaedia of American Biography (2), 20, pp. 53-54.
      Stresses her active life in seeking knowledge about the Indians and gives an extended list of her writings with year of publication.

1960

97.   B[unzel], R[uth] L.   The Golden Age of American Anthropology (51), pp. 152-155; 203-206.
      The first reference places Stevenson and her husband in the newly organized Bureau of American Ethnology under John Wesley Powell.   The second gives a somewhat more detailed picture of her work.

<u>1971</u>

98. Lurie, Nancy Oestreich. "Stevenson, Matilda Coxe Evans,"
     <u>Notable American Women</u> (30), 2, pp. 373-374.
     A nicely balanced sketch of the career of a dedicated woman
researcher. Makes it clear that her contributions are most notable
for the large amount of useful data collected and that she played
a role in establishing the best methods for field work among the
Indians. Describes her part in the efforts to secure women professional acceptance in anthropology.

99. ZELIA MARIA MAGDALENA NUTTALL
     6 September 1857--12 April 1933
     Nuttall, one of an important group of archaeologists who
showed the extent and significance of the pre-Columbian history
of Mexico, was self-taught and extremely productive. Her interest
in Mexican civilization began early when her mother gave her the
nine-volume work entitled <u>The Antiquities of Mexico</u>. She traveled
extensively throughout her life and always had a keen eye for valuable and neglected information.
     Two important aspects of Nuttall's contribution to archaeology
were her ability to discover forgotten documents and to understand
the significance of artifacts uncovered in excavations. In Florence
she found evidence for the manuscript which bears her name as
<u>Codex Nuttall</u>. In the process of searching for quite unrelated
material in the National Archives of Mexico she recognized important
new information on the exploits of Sir Francis Drake. She followed
this trail through libraries and archives in America, Britain, and
on the continent. She was the first to recognize and to demonstrate
through her studies that the archaic culture of Mexico is much older
than had been thought.
     Nuttall, an active and forceful person, had several loud dis-
putes with other scholars and even renounced, for a period of time,
the honorary professorship she held at Mexico's National Museum.
She was also widely honored and respected. In addition to numerous other professional memberships she was an honorary special
assistant at Harvard's Peabody Museum for 47 years. She received
this appointment when her very first paper in 1886 attracted the
attention of F. W. Putnam, the distinguished American anthropologist. (See also 4, 9, 11.)

<u>1933</u>

100. Anon. "Necrology: Zelia Nuttall," <u>Bulletin of the Pan Ameri-</u>
      <u>can Union</u>, 67 (July), pp. 603-604.
      Emphasizes her work to bring about closer cultural ties be-
tween the United States and Mexico.

101. Tozzer, Alfred M. "Zelia Nuttall," American Anthropologist,
      ns 35 (July-September), pp. 475-482. Portrait facing p. 475.
      Very extensive treatment of her career with good balance
in pointing out her most important contributions as distinguished
from those more widely acclaimed. Provides a large and well-documented bibliography of her published works.

102. Means, Philip Ainsworth. "Notes and Comment. Zelia Nut-
      tall: An Appreciation," The Hispanic American Historical Re-
      view, 13 (November), pp. 487-489.
      Written by her student, this article provides important ma-
terial about her personality and especially about her home in Mexico.

                              1966

103. Parmenter, Ross. "Glimpses of a Friendship Zelia Nuttall
      and Franz Boas," in Pioneers of American Anthropology (52),
      pp. 83-147. Three photographs in the preceding, unnumbered
      section.
      A truly important source of detailed information concerning
the place held by Nuttall in the developing field of American anthropology. Parmenter skillfully weaves the sparse but fascinating material in their correspondence into a quite reasonable description
of a long and important friendship. There are extensive and well-
chosen quotations from the letters and the entire article is fully
documented. Essential reading for Nuttall and her role in anthropology.

104. Parmenter, Ross. "Nuttall, Zelia Maria Magdalena," Notable
      American Women (30), 2, pp. 640-642.
      An excellent, brief treatment of her entire life in the same
careful but readable style of item 103. Describes her activities
in various areas and points out the importance of her contributions
to the highly successful efforts to discover the pre-Columbian history of Mexico and Central America. Clarifies the importance of
her discoveries of two major codices and contrasts them with her
theoretical speculations. Good bibliography.

105. CORNELIA HORSFORD
      25 September 1861--24? November 1944
      Educated in private schools of Cambridge and Boston, Hors-
ford continued her father's archaeological research following his
death. Her studies centered on Iceland, Greenland, Vinland, and
the British Isles. In the mid-1890's she sent out archaeological
expeditions to Iceland and Great Britain. Most of her published
articles deal with the Norse discovery of North America, a subject
in which she conducted and directed several research projects.

An honorary vice-president of the London Viking Club, Horsford was also active in a number of professional societies; the National Geographic Society, the Irish Text Society and the Iceland Antiquity Society. (See also 11.)

1904

106. Anon. "Horsford, Cornelia," The Twentieth Century Biographical Dictionary of Notable Americans. Rossiter Johnson, editor in chief, vol. 5, pages unnumbered. Boston: The Biographical Society. Reprinted: Gale Research Co., 1968.
Very brief outline of her work in archaeology with a list of some books and dates of publication.

107. Anon. "Horsford, Cornelia," in Biographical Cyclopaedia of American Women (13), 1, pp. 168-169.
Somewhat longer sketch but mostly a description of her ancestry. A great deal of space is given to her father. Concludes with a fairly detailed bibliography of her works.

108. NATALIE CURTIS BURLIN
26 April 1875--23 October 1921
After beginning a career as a concert pianist, Burlin turned to the task of preserving Indian, Negro, and African songs which she felt were rapidly disappearing. At the time she began, few studies of this music were being conducted, and her work is important in spite of some shortcomings and the efforts of later students. She was genuinely interested in the people she studied, and The Indians' Book also contains records of Indian poetry, folklore, and religious beliefs.
An important side effect of her work was to change a government policy of prohibiting the singing of native songs by the Indians. President Theodore Roosevelt, a family friend, assisted her and wrote a dedication for her first book. Burlin was only 46 when, after speaking at an international art congress in Paris, she was killed in an accident.

1921

109. Aldrich, Richard. "Music: Good and Bad New Works," The New York Times, 71 (6 November), sect. 6, p. 4.
A very laudatory note saying she was a good musician, but that her contribution to the preservation of Indian and Negro music will be of greater value. Calls her ardent and authoritative. A very brief note of her death appeared on page 13 of this paper on 29 October 1921.

110. Anon. "Natalie Curtis Burlin," The Outlook, 129 (23 Novem-
      ber), pp. 458-459.
      Brief, but rather detailed column. Burlin was a frequent
contributor to The Outlook. Also contains a tribute by Dr. Gregg,
the principal of Hampton Institute.

1926

111. Anon. "Natalie Curtis," Southern Workman, (March), pp.
      127-140. Photograph.
      Presents the text of a memorial address by Elbridge L. Adams,
some other tributes and details of the meeting held in Curtis' honor,
31 January 1926. A scholarship and a bronze statuette were presented in her memory.

1971

112. Kurath, Gertrude. "Curtis, Natalie," Notable American Women
      (30), 1, pp. 420-421.
      Points out that very few people had an interest in the music
of either Indians or Negroes at the time Curtis began her studies.
Her expectation that the music of the Indian would be lost rapidly
did not occur, and later work has made some of her shortcomings
apparent. Hers was, however, a pioneering effort, and the music
she transcribed is still of value.

113. ELSIE CLEWS PARSONS
      27 November 1875--19 December 1941
      Parsons' extremely productive career included scholarly re-
search, publications, and popularly written books. In these activities she showed deep concern for the effect society has on the
individual. She was especially harsh on the efforts society makes
to keep women in a subordinate position. In her earlier years she
was an active radical, and throughout her life as well as in her
writings she showed herself to be a nonconformist.
      In 1915 she made a rather abrupt change in her professional
life. While in the Southwest she became interested in the Indian
folklore and began a lifetime of extended field studies among the
Zuñi, Hopi, Taos, Tewa, Laguna, and other tribes. Over the years
she produced a large number of important treatises and over a hundred scholarly articles. In addition to her studies of Indian cultures, Parsons studied the folklore of a variety of cultural types
including French- and Portuguese-speaking people along the Eastern Coast and the Caribbean. Always her research methods demanded the careful transcription of extensive amounts of data.
      All of Parsons' education was at Columbia University (AB,

Barnard College, 1896; AM, 1897; PhD, 1899). Her stature was
acknowledged by her presidency of the American Folklore Society
(1918-1920), the American Ethnological Association (1923-1925), and
the American Anthropological Association (1940-1941). (See also
48.)

1941

114. Anon. "Dr. Elsie Parsons, Ethnologist, Dies," The New York
      Times, 91 (20 December), p. 19.
      Contains a good deal of material on her family background.
Notes her 21 books, presidency of the American Anthropological
Association, and extensive field trips.

1942

115. Boas, Franz. "Obituary. Elsie Clews Parsons," Science,
      95 (23 January), pp. 89-90.
      Similar in tone and content to his other memorial (116), but
a good addition by one who was in a position to make an assessment of her accomplishments. Contributes some useful personal
insights.

116. Boas, Franz. "Elsie Clews Parsons, Late President of the
      American Anthropological Association," The Scientific Month-
      ly, 54 (May), pp. 480-482. Photograph.
      High praise coupled with an evaluation of the human being
written by one of the leaders in the formation of modern anthropology. Boas saw her as "disdainful of all selfish pettiness and
truthful in thought and action."

1943

117. Reichard, Gladys F. "Elsie Clews Parsons," Journal of
      American Folklore, 56 (January-March), pp. 45-56, addenda
      p. 136.
      Stresses the breadth of her interests and her brief though
significant teaching career. Deals with only a small part of her
large body of published work, selecting those books which represent the plan and mind of the author. Parsons once told the author
that she hated to leave out any part of the data she collected since
she thought of her work as a mosaic. Provides an extensive bibliography.

118. Spier, Leslie, and A[lfred] L. Kroeber. "Elsie Clews Par-
      sons I and II," American Anthropologist, ns 45 (April-June),
      pp. 244-251, 252-255.
      Both of these memorials discuss the nature and significance

of Parsons' work and give some attention to analyzing her motivation. The articles complement one another. Spier concentrates more on the technical details, sequence, and organization of her research, while Kroeber is more concerned with the personality of the research- er. It is clear that both writers thought very highly of the person and her accomplishments.

1950

119. Reichard, Gladys F. "The Elsie Clews Parsons Collection," Proceedings of the American Philosophical Society, 94 (June), pp. 308-309.
     Describes the notebooks, unfinished manuscripts, paintings, pra{-}ersticks, etc., which make up this large and valuable collec- tion. Describes the work to be done and provides some biographi cal information.

1960

120. B[unzel], R[uth] L. The Golden Age of American Anthro- pology (51), pp. 546-547.
     In spite of its brevity this is a valuable contribution in pro- viding a personal touch in the interpretation of Parsons' work.

1971

121. Boyer, Paul S. "Parsons, Elsie Clews," Notable American Women (30), 3, pp. 20-22.
     Shows the nonconformist in Parsons and stresses her inter- est in the question of women being kept in subjection. Deals with her love of field work and the exceptional nature of her entire ca- reer for a woman born in a well-to-do family.

1978

*122. Keating, Barbara. "Elsie Clews Parsons: Her Work and Influence in Sociology," Journal of the History of Sociology, 1, pp. 1-9.

123. Goldfrank, Esther S. Notes on an Undirected Life: As one anthropologist tells it. Flushing, New York: Queens College Press, pp. 21-35 and index.
     An unusual biography of Franz Boas, written by his long- time secretary, student, and colleague, it draws extensively on his correspondence. The brief section devoted to Parsons is sup- plemented with many references elsewhere in the book. Carefully documented and contains extensive bibliography.

1982

124. Franklin, Phyllis. "Elsie Worthington Clews Parsons," _Amer-
      ican Women Writers_ (48), 3, pp. 345-347.
      Speaks of Parsons' career as being divided into parts: 1)
Speculative sociology and 2) Anthropology after meeting Franz
Boas. Claims that while she was greatly respected and praised
in her lifetime she has received little attention since her death.
Some references.

125. RUTH FULTON BENEDICT
      5 June 1887--17 September 1948
      A most complicated person, Benedict graduated from Vassar
College (AB, 1909) and went to live with her mother after a trip
to Europe. She did charitable work, taught at a girls' school,
drifted into marriage, attempted to write a book, and finally in 1919
enrolled in the New School for Social Research. Here she became
excited by anthropology and received her doctorate from Columbia
University in 1923.
      Since childhood Benedict had been partially deaf, a handicap
which made field work especially difficult for her. She did publish
some Indian folklore, but her annual appointment as a lecturer at
Columbia held no great promise. After she and her husband had
separated and she had been promoted to assistant professor in 1931,
she began to develop a concept which led to an important book,
Patterns of Culture. During World War II Benedict worked in the
Office of War Information on several countries including Japan. She
was involved in the new methods developed for the study of complex
societies from a distance. After the war she went to Japan to complete _The Chrysanthemum and the Sword: Patterns of Japanese_
Culture. This important work brought to her and Columbia a huge
program of "Research in Contemporary Cultures." She was still
only an associate professor in spite of heading this massive research
program and being elected president of the American Anthropological Association. Recognized as America's leading anthropologist,
Columbia finally appointed her full professor in the last year of
her life. (See also 16, 28, 43, 48, 1223.)

1942

126. Kerr, Adelaide. "Women in Science: Dictators and Anthro-
      pology, Dr. Ruth Benedict Looks into the Problem," _New York_
      Post (6 June), p. 17. Photograph.
      One of a series of articles introducing readers to women who
are working in a wide variety of scientific fields. Discusses Benedict's research and books in a friendly and informative manner.
Many quotations.

<u>1949</u>

127. Mead, Margaret, and Mary E. Chandler. "Ruth Fulton Bene-
     dict 1887-1948," <u>American Anthropologist</u>, 51 (July-September),
     pp. 457-468. Photograph.
     Mead, a contemporary and close associate of Benedict, writes
with a great deal of knowledge and understanding of this most complex person. A careful development of the difficult path which
led her to anthropology is followed by a concise outline of her principal works. Major emphasis is placed on the way her own personality influenced her research and writing. An abbreviated list of
her honors in followed by Chandler's long bibliography.

128. Lee, Dorothy. "Ruth Fulton Benedict (1887-1948)," <u>Journal
     of American Folklore</u>, 62 (October-December), pp. 345-347.
     Photograph.
     Benedict served as editor of this <u>Journal</u> from 1925 to 1939,
and this issue was dedicated to her. The detailed analysis of her
work given here is obviously written by a person who admired her
greatly. The major theme is the breadth of influence shown by
Benedict's work.

129. Barnouw, Victor. "Ruth Benedict: Apollonian and Dionysian,"
     <u>University of Toronto Quarterly</u>, 18 (April), pp. 241-253.
     An important biography by one of Benedict's students. A
most unusual type of intellectual biography. The student criticizes
his teacher severely in one sense, but concludes, "It may sound
paradoxical, in the light of what has gone before, but I think that
Ruth Benedict made a very great contribution to present-day anthropology.... It takes courage to stick to the important issues, and
Ruth Benedict had that courage."

<u>1959</u>

130. Mead, Margaret. <u>An Anthropologist at Work: Writings of
     Ruth Benedict</u>. Boston: Houghton Mifflin, 583 pp. Re-
     printed: New York: Avon, 1973.
     Although not a biography in the usual sense, this carefully
selected and edited collection is indispensable in any study of Benedict.

<u>1971</u>

131. Fleming, Donald. "Benedict, Ruth Fulton," <u>Notable Ameri-
     can Women</u> (30), 1, pp. 128-131.
     A longer biographical sketch than most in this series. Flem-
ing traces Benedict's life and career in general but pays special
attention to the inner life she developed as a child. Especially

concerned with the doubts and fears she experienced in her young
adulthood.

1974

132. Mead, Margaret. Ruth Benedict. New York: Columbia Uni-
      versity Press, 180 pp. Photographs.
      As Benedict's literary executor Mead is in an unusually strong
position to study all of the relevant data for a detailed analysis
of a most complex personality. Mead also has the advantage of having known and worked with Benedict for most of their professional
careers. The product is a most readable and lively biography in
spite of the degree of technical details. There are many quotations
from unpublished journals as well as from Mead's earlier study (130).
More than half of this book (pp. 79-176) consists of selected writings of Benedict. These were chosen to modernize the work of
130. There is a short, critically selected bibliography.

1978

133. Goldfrank, Esther S. Notes on an Undirected Life: As one
      anthropologist tells it. Flushing, New York: Queens Col-
      lege Press, pp. 35-40 and index.
      A revealing picture of the relationship of Benedict with her
teacher, Franz Boas, told by his secretary, student and colleague.
Carefully documented, including a relevant bibliography.

134. Collins, June M. "Benedict, Ruth Fulton," Biographical Dic-
      tionary of American Educators (38), 1, p. 111.
      Gives substantial biographical detail in a limited space. Ref-
erences are well written and cover a broad range of sources.

1979

135. Briscoe, Virginia Wolf. "Ruth Benedict. Anthropological
      Folklorist," Journal of American Folklore, 92, pp. 445-476.
      The subtitle is a phrase Benedict used to describe herself,
yet this paper is the first attempt to explore and evaluate her impact on the field of folklore. Drawn from her unpublished papers
at Vassar, this article is a rather technical analysis of her work.
Concludes that a great deal of work remains to be done using Benedict's ideas about cultural context.

1982

136. Kahn, Miriam. "Ruth Benedict," American Women Writers
      (48), 1, pp. 134-137.

A more detailed sketch than is common in this series. Lists her nom de plume, Anne Singleton, and stresses the importance of her writing beyond the field of anthropology. Mentions her poetry. Several unusual references.

GENERAL (See also 873, 1163)

1891

137. Singleton, Esther. "Women as Astronomers," The Chautauquan, 14, pp. 340-342.
Presents the work of a number of notable American women astronomers in the context of their dedication to science. The earlier part of this paper (pp. 209-212) deals only with European women.

1892

138. Reed, Helen Leah. "Women's Work at the Harvard Observatory," New England Magazine, ns 6, pp. 165-176. Photographs. Reprinted: Farmer, Lydia Hoyt. What America Owes to Women. The National Exposition Souvenir (1893). Buffalo: Charles Wells Moulton, ch. 28, pp. 271-280.
Provides an insight to the tone of the end of the century by blending women's accomplishments, the new emphasis on photographic astronomy, and the special talent women possess in this developing field. Most of the prominent women and some lesser names are presented.

1898

139. Davis, Herman S. "Women Astronomers," Popular Astronomy, 6 (May and June), pp. 129-138, 211-220 and 220-228.
Gives biographical sketches of women astronomers from the earliest times. The American women are found in the third part subtitled, "Contemporary." In effect, this long and interesting paper is a review of Rebière's book, Les Femmes dans la Science (3). Davis concludes, "In spite of the frequency of trivial errors, of which the above are illustrations, the very excellence of the book as a whole, however, is the main justification for some mention of them, that the next edition, which presumably must appear in a few years may be free of these and all similar errors."

1904

140. McKenney, Anne P. "What Women Have Done for Astronomy

in the United States," Popular Astronomy, 12 (March), pp.
171-182.
Gives biographical sketches of most of the chief women astronomers of the period along with some who are lesser known. A
valuable source.

1927

*141. [Todd, Mabel L.] "Women Astronomers at Harvard," Harvard
       Alumni Magazine, 29, pp. 420-422.

1931

142. Bailey, Solon I. The History and Work of the Harvard Ob-
      servatory. New York: McGraw-Hill, index.
      A major history of the Harvard Observatory written by a long-
time member of the staff. The tone is a bit stiff and the work heavy
with technical data, but the women appear to be given full credit
for their accomplishments.

1969

143. Shapley, Harlow. Through Rugged Ways to the Stars. New
      York: Scribner's, index.
      An autobiography by the Observatory's fifth director. Reads
well and provides a point of view quite different from Bailey (142),
but the women receive very little space.

1971

144. Jones, Bessie Zaban, and Lyle Gifford Boyd. The Harvard
      College Observatory. The first four directorships, 1839-
      1919. Cambridge, Massachusetts: Belknap Press (Harvard),
      ch. 11 and index. Photographs.
      The authors are intent on making this large scale history
"portray something of the human qualities of the men and women
who were closely involved." They have done this difficult job while
retaining most of the valuable dry facts. The chapter title, "A
Field for Women," is a bit misleading in that Jones and Boyd do
not segregate them. On the contrary, the women are given credit
as important members of the team. The material is well illustrated
and has excellent documentation.

1979

145. Warner, Deborah Jean. "Women Astronomers," Natural

History, 88 (May), pp. 12-26. Photographs.

Within a small space Warner does a remarkably comprehensive job of examining not only the contributions made by women to the field of astronomy but the vital questions associated with careers for talented women. Marriage-career problems, the role of women's colleges, and women in professional societies are discussed. As usual, only such big names as Pickering at Harvard appear, but short articles do have limitations. One might hope Warner would follow this up with a more extensive treatment and some new faces.

1983

146. Whitman, Betsey S. "Women in the American Mathematical Society Before 1900," Association for Women in Mathematics Newsletter, 13 (July-December), pp. 10-13, 7-9, [n.p.].

A fine example of meeting one of the most pressing needs in the scholarship of women in science. Whitman has done the drudgery and produced a readable account of some interesting women crying for further study. Since many of the teachers of mathematics were also teaching and doing research in astronomy, there is much information here in both fields.

147. MARIA MITCHELL
1 August 1818--28 June 1889

Mitchell was the first American woman scientist to win international recognition and is one of the very few scientists to be known by people outside of her field. This unusual situation results from her success as a teacher and from her early and moderate efforts for women's rights. Because her work came so early (mid-nineteenth century) and at a time when new discoveries in astronomy were arousing interest in nonacademic as well as academic circles, she received much more public attention than is usual for scientific accomplishment. Even though this acclaim was richly deserved, she herself had doubts when Matthew Vassar offered her one of the largest telescopes in the country.

When she arrived in Poughkeepsie for the opening of Vassar Female College in September 1865, she had discovered a comet, received a gold medal from the King of Denmark, and become the first woman elected to the American Academy of Arts and Sciences and the American Association for the Advancement of Science. In spite of her lack of a college education and her own doubts she was an extraordinary teacher. Her ability to stimulate talented students is clear from the number of young women who began their studies under her direction and went on to distinguished scientific careers. In large measure Vassar's success and its excellent reputation can be attributed to her presence on its first faculty.

She continued her research at Vassar and made important contributions to our knowledge of sunspots and the surfaces of

Jupiter and Saturn. Of special significance was her involvement
of her students directly in her scientific work. She also played
a role in the growing movement to obtain opportunities for women
to gain an education and enter scientific careers on an equal basis
with men. She founded the Association for the Advancement of
Women and served as its president for two years. In addition to
other honors Mitchell was the first woman elected to the American
Philosophical Society and to be inducted into the Hall of Fame. (See
also 1, 4, 8, 9, 11, 35, 36, 37, 40, 41, 43, 140.)

1889

148. Anon. "Obituary. Maria Mitchell," The New York Times,
      38 (29 June), p. 5.
      A little more on her early life than is usual. Discusses her
problem about priority in the discovery of the comet bearing her
name.

149. Anon. "Maria Mitchell," Boston Evening Transcript, 16th
      year (28 June), p. 1.
      Says that she contributed greatly to the success of Vassar
College which she served for a quarter of a century. Mitchell was
prominently identified with the movement to improve the lot of women
in the United States.

150. Spofford, Harriet Prescott. "Maria Mitchell," The Chautau-
      quan, 10 (ns 1) (November), pp. 181-185.
      Probably written to inspire the young, this article makes her
seem too good to be believed, but it is in the pattern of its time
and does at least admit that she was something of a radical and
that in her youth she was not beautiful. Even if a bit over-glori-
fied, this picture provides a glimpse of Maria Mitchell as seen by
her female contemporaries.

151. Anon. "Notes. Miss Maria Mitchell," The Observatory, 12
      (August), pp. 332-333.
      Brief note of her death with reference to her discovery of
seven comets and the honors which came to her. In the "Correspondence" section of the next issue (September 1889), Lewis Swift
points out that she discovered only one comet and that it was with
a three-inch telescope rather than the naked eye.

152. Anon. "Obituary. Maria Mitchell," The American Journal of
      Science, 3rd series, 38, p. 172.
      Notes that she was elected a member of the American Academy
of Arts and Sciences of Boston early in her career.

1890

153. Whitney, Mary W. "Maria Mitchell," The Sidereal Messenger,

9 (February), pp. 49-51. Photograph.
    As Mitchell's successor and former student, Whitney writes
with great feeling and with firsthand knowledge. After covering
the high points of her career she stresses Mitchell's influence as
a teacher.

154.   [Mitchell, Henry]. "Maria Mitchell," American Academy of
       Arts and Sciences, Proceedings, 25 (27 May), pp. 331-343.
       A most valuable article since it concentrates heavily on her
youth and work with her father. The author, who says he is "the
spokesman of others, of Trustees, and Faculty, and students of
the College she served so faithfully," does describe her teaching
and research at Vassar, but emphasizes her early life. Mentions
her association with the Academy and relates an interesting anecdote.

                                    1891

155.   Whitney, Mary W. "Life and Work of Maria Mitchell, L.L.D.,"
       Papers Read Before the Association for the Advancement
       of Women. Eighteenth Women's Congress, Toronto, Canada,
       October, 1890. Fall River, Massachusetts: Privately printed,
       pp. 12-28.
       Greatly amplifies the brief obituary (153) written earlier.
Mitchell played an important role in the development of this organization, both as its president and in the collection of information
on women working in science. This biographical sketch, which is
longer than most, was written by a former student, colleague and
Mitchell's successor. It contains important insights and details not
obtainable elsewhere.

                                    1893

156.   Wood, Frances Fisher. "Sketch of Maria Mitchell," in What
       America Owes to Women. The National Exposition Souvenir.
       Lydia Hoyt Farmer, editor. Buffalo: Charles Wells Moulton,
       ch. 27, pp. 264-270.
       A nice sketch of Mitchell which deals with her personality
and is more believable than most. Makes a point of her bluntness,
caustic tongue, and summary manner. Refreshing.

                                    1896

157.   Kendall, Phebe Mitchell. Maria Mitchell. Life, letters, and
       journals. Boston: Lee and Shepard, 293 pp. Reprinted:
       Freeport, New York: Books for Libraries Press, 1971.
       Her sister's tribute in the form of sequential quotations from
Mitchell's papers. Written in the stilted language of the times and
with a desire to say only favorable things about a deceased loved

one. It remains a good source for the chronology of Mitchell's own
thoughts.

1897

158.   Anon.   "Mitchell, Maria."   The National Cyclopaedia of Amer-
       ican Biography (2), 5, pp. 236-237.   Ink sketch.
       Discusses her European tour and her salary argument at Vas-
sar.   Refers to most of the standard details.

1912

159.   Babbitt, Mary King.   Maria Mitchell as Her Students Knew
       Her.   An address by Mary King Babbitt.   Poughkeepsie, New
       York, 32 pp.
       Miss Babbitt, a student of Mitchell in her later years, has
written about the teacher-scholar and the devoted Vassar faculty
member in a way that illustrates Mitchell's personal attitudes and
philosophy of science.   "'Did you learn that from a book, or did
you observe it yourself?' she would ask.   Where books were so numerous and so easy of access, and where it was so much more con-
venient to use authors' eyes than our own, she insisted upon our
using our own....   In summing up what she felt we ought to demand of ourselves in the way of systematic and logical work, she
told us, 'The entrance to astronomy is through mathematics.   You
must make up your mind to steady and earnest work.   You must
be content to get on slowly if only you get on thoroughly.   The
phrase "popular science" has in itself a touch of absurdity--that
knowledge which is popular is not scientific.'"

1934

160.   C[aroline] E. F[urness].   "Mitchell, Maria," in Dictionary
       of American Biography (14), 13, pp. 57-58.
       The author is two generations later than her subject but holds
a deep respect for the work done by that pioneer.   Brief, but its
emphasis on Mitchell's early intellectual development is important.

1949

161.   Wright, Helen.   Sweeper in the Sky.   The Life of Maria Mit-
       chell.   First Woman Astronomer in America.   New York: Mac-
       millan, 246 pp.
       A well-written, readable biography which reflects the author's
careful research.   She has acquired an understanding of Nantucket
and its meaning for Mitchell.   A good narrative bibliography explains
in detail where Wright obtained her information.

1970

162. Stoddard, Hope. "Maria Mitchell," in Famous American Women.
New York: Crowell, pp. 295-304. Photograph.
A modern sketch with all of the standard data but well written and much less stiff than earlier works. Places more emphasis
on her teaching and introduces some of her most revealing quotations.

1971

163. Merriam, Eve. "Maria Mitchell (1818-1889). Astronomer,"
in Growing up Female in America. Ten lives. New York:
Dell, pp. 83-101.
A brilliant refutation of any lingering arguments that women
cannot contribute to this or that field of human activity. In the
words of the women themselves, in this case Mitchell's diary, one
lives the day by day reality of hard work and success. Skillfully
done.

164. Wright, Helen. "Mitchell, Maria," Notable American Women
(30), 2, pp. 554-556.
An excellent shorter version of Wright's full biography,
(161). Important comment on her as a teacher and on her work
with the Association for the Advancement of Women.

1974

165. Hoffleit, Dorrit. "Mitchell, Maria," Dictionary of Scientific
Biography (29), 9, pp. 421-422.
Standard career information but well presented in a limited
space. Notable that she is included.

1976

166. Anon. "Maria Mitchell, Astronomer, 1818-1889; U.S.A.,"
Hypatia's Sisters (34), pp. 31-34. Likeness.
A biographical sketch which catches certain essential aspects
of Mitchell's philosophy in spite of the fact that it centers the attention it pays to her interest in causes for women's rights.

1978

167. Peltzman, Barbara Ruth. "Mitchell, Maria," Biographical Dictionary of American Educators (38), 2, pp. 905-906.
Brief and accurate.

168. Kohlstedt, Sally Gregory. "Maria Mitchell: The Advancement of Women in Science," New England Quarterly, 51 (March), pp. 39-63.
Carefully documents the early efforts to show the high quality of scientific work done by women. A beginning toward a much needed study of the Association for the Advancement of Women. Mitchell played an important role in this group both as president and committee member collecting and publishing the accomplishments of women in science.

1979

169. Anon. "Mitchell, Maria," Biographical Dictionary of American Science (40), p. 182.
Describes her early work with her father and notes that she was the first woman to be recognized for her work in astronomy. A good review of Mitchell's life, followed by a short bibliography.

170. SARAH FRANCES WHITING
23 August 1847--12 September 1927
The founder of Wellesley College, Henry F. Durant, desired to have an all-female faculty. The area of physics, however, which remained a required course until 1893, presented a serious problem: where to find a female physics teacher. He chose Whiting, who at that time was teaching classics and mathematics at the Brooklyn Heights Seminary for girls. She had studied natural philosophy, Latin, Greek, and mathematics with her father and had taken an AB degree at Ingham University in Le Roy, N.Y. With Durant's assistance she was allowed to spend two years as a guest in the first laboratory for teaching physics in this country--that of E. C. Pickering at MIT. After another two years of selecting, ordering, and installing the required equipment, Whiting opened at Wellesley the second such laboratory. One year later Pickering, who had become director of the Harvard Observatory, introduced Whiting to the exciting possibilities of applying physics, especially spectroscopy, to the study of the heavens. For two decades she dreamed of an observatory at Wellesley and taught applied physics using a celestial globe and a portable four-inch Browning telescope.
As this record suggests Whiting was a teacher, and most of her publications are in the area of science education; for example, she is the first to have introduced day-time laboratory work in astronomy. Her success as a teacher is clear from the number of students she inspired to productive careers and is a direct result of her constant efforts to obtain the very latest research results and introduce them to her classes. She visited Europe frequently, and her studies in the leading laboratories of the day resulted in exciting lectures illustrated with current research techniques.

Through her influence the Whitin Observatory was designed and
opened under her direction in 1900. She received an honorary
ScD from Tufts College in 1905. (See also 9, 43.)

1912

171. Anon. [Resignation] Science, 36 (30 August), pp. 271-
      272.
      Reports that Whiting will resign her position as professor
of physics and continue as professor of astronomy and director of
the observatory. Notes that she was the first woman physics student at the Massachusetts Institute of Technology and that her physics laboratory at Wellesley was one of the first in the country.

1927

*172. [Obituary]. Boston Herald.

173. Cannon, Annie J. "Sarah Frances Whiting," Science, 66 (4
      November), pp. 417-418.
      Written by her former student who had now become an inter-
nationally respected astronomer, this memorial combines all of the
feeling for an admired friend with the deep respect one feels for
an influential teacher.   The facts are here, but it is the tone that
is important.

174. Cannon, Annie J. "Sarah Frances Whiting," Popular Astronomy,
      35 (December), pp. 539-545. Photographs.
      A continuation and amplification of her earlier article (173).
Cannon again stresses the teacher who pioneered the use of labo-
ratory instruction in physics and astronomy. Vivid glimpses of
Whiting's social life.

1971

175. Anslow, Gladys A. "Whiting, Sarah Frances," Notable
      American Women (30), 3, pp. 593-595.
      More information on her early life and her visits to Europe.
The extent to which she went to provide the most up-to-date scientific material for her students is clearly described.

1979

176. Anon. "Whiting, Sarah Frances," Biographical Dictionary
      of American Science (40), p. 273.
      Only a few lines listing some dates; of little use.

177. MARY WATSON WHITNEY
      11 September 1847--20 January 1921
      Whitney was remembered by her fellow students and colleagues
at Vassar College as "distinguished in a broad range of subjects
and having sound judgement and progressive ideas." She graduated from Vassar (AB, 1868; AM, 1872) and studied at the University of Zurich from 1873-1876.
      In 1881 Maria Mitchell invited her student to return to Vas-
sar as a private assistant, and in 1888 Whitney succeeded her as
professor of astronomy and director of the Observatory. Until her
retirement in 1910 Whitney not only exceeded the high standards
expected in her teaching responsibilities but introduced an ambitious
program of research at the Observatory. By that time she had produced over 100 publications and was being recognized as an important contributor to the field. Her students were in great demand
by the leading institutions of astronomical research.
      In a number of ways Whitney worked for the cause of women's
education. She was a founder and first president of the Vassar
Alumnae Association, a member of the Association for the Advancement of Women and a charter member of the American Astronomical
Society. While she was refused membership in the Astronomische
Gesellschaft, ten years later two of her students won a prize of 100
marks offered by that organization for the calculation of the orbit
of comet 1826 II. (See also 9, 138, 140, 146.)

                              1922-1923

178. Furness, Caroline E. "Mary W. Whitney," Popular Astrono-
      my, 30 and 31 (December and January), pp. 597-608, 25-35.
      Photographs.
      These two papers are much more than a memorial tribute.
In them Furness, the third generation of distinguished teacher-
scholars of astronomy at Vassar College, goes well beyond describing her teacher's career. She outlines clearly the role played by
both Vassar and these remarkable women in the growth of scientific
opportunity for women. A great deal of American astronomical research of the period is also presented. A vital source for research
in areas other than women in science.

                               1936

179. C[aroline] E. F[urness]. "Whitney, Mary Watson," Diction-
      ary of American Biography (14), 20, pp. 163-164.
      The restrictions of space make this sketch so much less im-
pressive than her earlier work (178), but it is well written and explains Whitney's role at Vassar.

1971

180.   Wright, Helen. "Whitney, Mary Watson," Notable American
        Women (30), 3, pp. 603-604.
        Well-balanced summary of her career with more emphasis on
her scientific contributions.

1979

181.   Anon. "Whitney, Mary Watson," Biographical Dictionary of
        American Science (40), p. 274.
        Only a few lines listing some dates; of little use.

182.   MARY EMMA BYRD
        15 November 1849--30 July 1934
        After earning an AB degree at the University of Michigan
(1878), Byrd taught high school for four years and studied at the
Harvard Observatory for one year. From 1883 to 1887 she taught
at Carleton College and served as first assistant in its Observatory.
Byrd moved to Smith College in 1887 as director of the observatory
and the first professor of astronomy. She rose to the rank of full
professor in 1898. In 1906 she protested the acceptance of Rockefeller and Carnegie Foundation grants by resigning and becoming
head of the Astronomical Department at the Normal College of the
City of New York.
        Byrd's principal research interest was the application of pil-
lar micrometers to the problem of determining the position of comets.
She collaborated with Whitney of Vassar to determine both the latitude and longitude of the Smith College Observatory. It was in teaching that she found her greatest satisfaction. Her method was to go
out of doors and observe. She published two manuals for this purpose.
        In 1904 Carleton College recognized Byrd with an honorary
PhD. She was a member of the Astronomical and Astrophysical Society of America, the Pacific Astronomical Society, and the British
Astronomical Association. (See also 9, 138, 140, 146.)

1906

*183.   [Her resignation]. Boston Globe (7 May).

184.   Anon. "Miss Mary E. Byrd's Resignation," Popular Astron-
        omy, 14 (August and September), pp. 447-448.
        A news note about her devotion to principle. Some family
background, references to her publications and other brief biographical data are given.

1934

185. Hoblit, Louise Barber. "Mary E. Byrd," Popular Astronomy, 42, pp. 496-498.
Supplements the sparse biographical information, but is especially important in its emphasis on the high moral character she displayed throughout her life. Helps to understand her leaving a promising career over a matter of principle.

186. ELLEN AMANDA HAYES
23 September 1851--27 October 1930
Hayes earned the AB degree at Oberlin College (1878) and accepted a faculty position at Wellesley College. She became professor of mathematics in 1888. She soon became interested in aplied mathematics. From 1904 until her retirement in 1916 she was professor of astronomy and applied mathematics.
Her students were involved in the computation of the orbit of comets and with her, they determined the latitude of the Whitin Observatory. Hayes wrote both technical and popular books and articles dealing with mathematics and astronomy. Outside of scientific circles she has been cited as a promising author. Her book Letters to a College Girl, published in 1909, sold well, and after her retirement she completed a historical novel, The Sycamore Trail. Hayes was also a radical, a socialist, and perhaps a communist. She was a member of the American Association for the Advancement of Science, the Astronomical and Astrophysical Society of America, and a founding member of the History of Science Society. (See also 140, 146.)

1931

187. Anon. "Ellen Amanda Hayes," Oberlin College Necrology for the Year 1930-31.
Provides facts about Hayes as a writer in addition to her scientific career. Quotation from The Wellesley Townsman of 30 October 1930 praises her knowledge, leadership, and sincere interest in others.

188. Gordon, Geraldine. "Ellen Hayes, 1851-1930," The Wellesley Magazine, 15 (February), pp. 151-152. Photograph.
Says her vigorous, independent spirit sometimes made her a difficult colleague. Talks about her paper, The Relay. She published it to give publicity to certain movements and facts which she saw as incorrectly presented in the press.

*189. Brown, Louise. Ellen Hayes: Trail Blazer, np (1931?).

190.   WILLIAMINA PATON STEVENS FLEMING
       15 May 1857--21 May 1911
       Few scientists have had greater need of genius and perse-
verance than Fleming. With a public school education obtained in
her native Scotland and alone in America after a failed marriage,
she entered domestic service in the home of Edward C. Pickering,
the new director of the Harvard College Observatory. Pickering
is said to have been so upset over an inefficient assistant that he
invited his maid to do the work.
       At this particular time the application of spectroscopy to the
classification of stars was just beginning, and Pickering saw the
need for a massive program of stellar photography. For 30 years
Fleming and Pickering worked together, and what began as the "Pickering System" quickly became recognized as the "Fleming-Pickering
System" of classification. From her first routine clerical tasks Fleming quickly demonstrated an extraordinary talent for original research. Her discovery that all variable stars show spectral emis-
sion lines was a new and useful research tool. She published a list
of 222 such stars along with the necessary set of comparison stars
which allowed accurate determination of their magnitude. At the
time of her death 28 novae were known, ten of which she had discovered. Pickering acknowledged the fact of their collaboration,
and they signed reports jointly as early as 1890. Fleming was also
a first-rate administrator and skillfully supervised the work of a
large staff of young women "computers" who by 1910 had examined
and catalogued nearly 200,000 photographic plates.
       This massive and important work brought many honors to Flem-
ing. In 1898 she became the first woman to be given an official appointment by the Harvard Corporation. She received honorary memberships in the Société Astronomique de France and the Sociedad
Astronómica de Mexico (along with a gold medal). She was the first
American woman (sixth overall) elected to the Royal Astronomical
Society and a charter member of the Astronomical and Astrophysical Society. (See also 9, 11, 32, 40, 43, 138, 140.)

                                    1911

191.   W.T.L.   "Obituary. Mrs. Fleming," British Astronomical As-
       sociation Journal, (May), p. 395.
       Notes her elections as an honorary member in 1906 and the
importance of her work in star classification.

192.   Rolston, William E.   "Mrs. W. P. Fleming," Nature, 86 (1
       June), pp. 453-454.
       Says that her death represents "an almost irreparable loss."
Recounts her large collection of discoveries in 1910 and shows his
amazement with the quite un-British remark, "Not a bad haul of discoveries for one year!"

193.   Cannon, Annie J.   "Mrs. Fleming," Scientific American, 104
       (3 June), p. 547.

A most sympathetic view by her colleague. Attempts to show the human side of Fleming without failing to remark in wonder at the vastness of her contribution to astronomy.

194. Cannon, Annie J. "Williamina Paton Fleming," Science, ns 33 (30 June), pp. 987-988.
Similar to her other memorial article (193), but with a bit more emphasis on her methodology.

195. Archenhold, F. S. "Williamina Fleming," Das Weltall [Berlin], 11 (15 July), pp. 310-311. In German.
Takes most of the material from Pickering's comments about her. Gives some details of her methods and cites her accomplishments.

196. Pickering, Edward C. "Williamina Paton Fleming," Harvard Graduates Magazine, 20 (September), pp. 49-51. Photograph.
As her supervisor and collaborator, Pickering says, "she occupied one of the most important positions in the Observatory." Reviews the effort involved in being a supervisor and her contributions which were little recognized outside of the Observatory. Outlines on the basis of firsthand knowledge, the extent and significance of her scientific work.

197. Cannon, Annie J. "Minor Contributions and Notes. Williamina Paton Fleming," Astrophysical Journal, 34 (November), pp. 314-317.
Similar to earlier published memorials (193, 194). Stresses her confidence in the evidence of the photographs when others were skeptical.

1912

198. H. H. T. [Obituary]. Royal Astronomical Society Monthly Notices, 72 (February), pp. 261-264.
Points out that she is one of five women elected to Honorary membership. Has high praise for the large amount of careful work she carried out and the equally large original scientific contributions which resulted from it. Extraordinary note: "... [In] putting her work alongside that of others, it would not be unjust to remember that she left her heavy daily labours at the observatory to undertake on her return home those household cares of which a man usually expects to be relieved."

199. Thompson, Grace Agnes. "Williamina Paton Fleming," New England Magazine, 48 (December), pp. 458-467. Photograph.
This long and well-written study presents a valuable picture of the environment in which Fleming worked. It is detailed in its treatment of Pickering's development of plans for making maximum use of the new science of photography. Describes rather fully

Fleming's work, but also relates her skill as a homemaker. This
point occurs in nearly all of the tributes to her.

1931

200. R[aymond] S. D[ugan]. "Fleming, Williamina Paton Stevens,"
      Dictionary of American Biography (14), 6, pp. 462-463.
      Brief and standard treatment, but authoritatively written in
a readable style. Some bibliography.

1971

201. Hoffleit, Dorrit. "Fleming, Williamina Paton Stevens," Notable
      American Women (30), 1, pp. 628-630.
      Treats all of the aspects of her career and life in a concise
manner. Especially strong on Pickering's role at Harvard and in
her work. Good bibliography.

202. Gingerich, Owen. "Fleming, Williamina Paton," Dictionary
      of Scientific Biography (29), 4, pp. 33-34.
      Deals well with her scientific work and still gives useful per-
sonal data. Bibliography is more informative than usual.

1978

203. Gordon, Anne. "Williamina Fleming: 'Women's Work' at the
      Harvard Observatory," Women's Studies Newsletter, 6 (Spring),
      pp. 24-27.
      Discusses the recurrent theme of women making a unique and
possibly feminine contribution in astronomy. Most of the other Harvard "computers" are mentioned.

1979

204. Anon. "Fleming, Williamina Paton," Biographical Dictionary
      of American Science (40), p. 93.
      Gives a few dates and is of little use.

205. DOROTHEA KLUMPKE ROBERTS
      9 August 1861--5 October 1942
      Klumpke was born in San Francisco where she received her
earliest education. Her mother recognized the talents of three of
her daughters and sought equal educational opportunities for them
in the schools of Germany and Paris. All three young ladies remained in Paris where they attained remarkable professional success.

After obtaining her baccalaureate in science and mathematics, Klumpke was admitted to the Paris Observatory as its first woman student. She submitted a mathematical thesis concerning the rings of Saturn, and according to the eminent mathematician Gaston Darboux, who happened to be the chairman of her examination committee, she defended it brilliantly. She was the first woman to be awarded a doctoral degree by the Faculté des Sciences of the University of Paris.

As the first woman member of the staff of the Paris Observatory, Klumpke became director of the bureau of measurements. Her skill in French, German, and English made her much sought after as a lecturer, and she was asked to translate the scientific memoirs of foreign astronomers who attended conferences often held in Paris. She published a number of scientific studies in the Bulletin Astronomique and was the only woman member of the Société Astronomique de France. Klumpke also wrote, for American readers, a dramatic account of one of her balloon ascents.

In 1901 she married the distinguished Welch astronomer Isaac Roberts. They collaborated in some studies, and after his death she published Celestial Atlas and Supplement as a memorial.

The work of Klumpke is particularly notable in that she was not only an able computer, but an acute observer. She was elected to membership in many astronomical societies in France, America, Britain, and Germany for the merit of her work was widely recognized. The Institut de France made her an Officier de l'Académie, and the French government presented her the cross of the Legion d'Honneur. She was also awarded prizes for particular scientific contributions such as that of the Académie des Sciences in 1893 and the Prix des Dames by the Société Astronomique de France in 1897. (See also 3, 4, 9, 140.)

1893

206. Anon. "General Notes. Miss Dorothea Klumpke," Popular Astronomy, 1 (March), p. 336.
Says that she received her Doctor of Science degree. Expresses interest in the fact that the French papers urged their readers not to be surprised at a young lady being talented in the exact sciences.

1894

207. Rebière, A[lphonse]. Les Femmes dans la Science (3), pp. 70-71. Expanded in the 2nd edition, 1897, pp. 154-159. In French. Photograph.
Describes her work and the excellence of her thèses. Gives some bibliography of her works and writings about her career. Recently part of this work has been translated into English (214).

1900

208. Klumpke, Dorothea. "A Night in a Balloon. An Astronomer's
      Trip from Paris to the Sea in Observation of Leonids," The
      Century Magazine, 60 (June), pp. 276-284.
      Autobiographic article written for an American audience. There
are a few biographical notes by the editor, but it is the literate tone
and excitement conveyed by the author that are important. The
ascent failed to realize its objectives for reasons spoken of in a footnote, but see item 210.

209. Vorst, Bessie van. "The Klumpke Sisters," The Critic, 37
      (September), pp. 224-229.
      Discusses the family of three talented young American women
who, together with their equally remarkable mother, have made highly notable careers in Paris.

1903

210. Roberts, Dorothea Klumpke. "General Notes. Mrs. Dorothy
      [sic] Klumpke Roberts Observed the Leonids from a Balloon,"
      DeLisle Stewart, translator. Popular Astronomy, 11, pp. 220-
      222.
      A large portion of her report of a second and successful bal-
loon ascent; first published in Spanish [Bulletin of the Astronomical
Society of Mexico, March, 1903].

1913

211. Mozans, H. J. Women in Science (9), pp. 193-194.
      Reports Klumpke's brilliant thesis defense and her growing
career in Paris.

1942

212. Anon. "Mrs. Dorothea Roberts," The New York Times, 92
      (6 October), p. 23.
      A notice which deals mostly with her family.

1944

213. Anon. "Roberts, Dorothea Klumpke. The National Cyclo-
      paedia of American Biography (2), 31, pp. 405-406.
      Provides data on her honors and memberships as well as the
usual personal and professional information.

1983

214. Kenschaft, Lori, translator and editor. Les Femmes dans la Science (3), section on Klumpke (207). Association for Women in Mathematics Newsletter, 13 (September-October), pp. 10-12. Photograph.
Translation of this part of Rebière's important work.

215. MARY PROCTOR
1862--unknown
Proctor was born in Dublin, Ireland, and received most of her education in London where she graduated from the College of Preceptors. Perhaps her most important education was from her father, whose interest in astronomy and writing became his daughter's passion. After her family moved to America, Proctor studied at Columbia University and began writing. At that time her father was editor of Knowledge, and with his guidance she wrote a series of articles on comparative mythology. She wrote a large number of articles and several books dealing with popular astronomy.
In addition to her writing Proctor began in 1893 to lecture on astronomy. Her first public appearance was at the Chicago World's Fair where she was led to believe the audience would be made up of young children. She arrived with a carefully prepared lecture entitled "Goblins from Starland" and appropriate illustrations only to find the hall filled with adults. Her impromptu lecture received favorable reviews in the Chicago papers. Continuing her public career, she gave hundreds of talks in a large number of countries.
Proctor did some work in astronomy, but it was mostly in the form of observation of important celestial events. Her major contribution lies in her popularization of astronomy, especially for children. She was elected a fellow of the American Association for the Advancement of Science in 1898 and was a member of several national astronomical societies. (See also 4, 9, 11.)

1907

216. Anon. "Proctor, Mary," The National Cyclopaedia of American Biography, (2), 9, pp. 282-283.
About the most complete biographical data in print of this widely published author. Provides the same basic story as the several biographical dictionaries in which Proctor is listed but gives more detail of her lecturing career. Is also more specific as to titles and dates of publication of several of her books.

217. ANNIE JUMP CANNON
11 December 1863--13 April 1941

In a life of dedication and productivity difficult to compre-
hend, Cannon analyzed and classified the spectra of nearly 400,000
stars. Of perhaps even greater importance was her effect on the
system itself. Her modifications rendered it both simpler and more
elegant. After graduating from Wellesley College (BS, 1884), she
returned to her home in Dover, Delaware, and a quiet society life
of parties, music, and travel. When her mother died in 1893 she
returned, first to Wellesley and then to Radcliffe, as a special student in astronomy. In 1896 she joined the Harvard College Observatory where, under the direction of E. C. Pickering, a group of outstanding women were making silent but remarkable contributions to
the literature of stellar spectra.

From the beginning of her work Cannon was more than a mere
collector and classifier of data. Her observations, both with the
telescope and from photographic plates, led to the discovery of approximately 300 variable stars and five novae. This research represents an impressive scientific contribution, but it is in the Henry
Draper Catalogue and Extentions (1918-1949) that she showed the
true magnitude of her skill and dedication. Harlow Shapley, a more
recent director of the Harvard Observatory, described her work
as "a structure that probably will never be duplicated in kind or
extent by a single individual." As William Crach Bond Astronomer,
she became one of the first women to receive an appointment from
the Harvard Corporation, just 17 years after she became the first
woman to receive an honorary doctorate from Groningen and 13 years
after Oxford presented her with its first honorary doctoral degree
given to a woman. Cannon was at one time the only woman member
of the Royal Astronomical Society and one of the few women ever
elected to the American Philosophical Society. (See also 9, 11, 12,
23, 32, 35, 36, 42, 43, 140.)

1929

218.   Anon. "Dr. Annie J. Cannon," Scientific American, 140
       (February), p. 103. Photograph.
       Cites her as the most eminent woman astronomer. Doesn't
say, but may be in connection with her selection by the League of
Women Voters as one of the 12 leading American women.

1931

219.   Anon. "Award of Gold Medals to Dr. Annie J. Cannon and
       Professor Henry B. Bigelow," Science, 74 (25 December), pp.
       644-645.
       Recounts the ceremony at the awarding of the National Acad-
emy of Sciences' Henry Draper Medal. The director of the Harvard
Observatory, Harlow Shapley, read the selection committee's report
which consisted of a lengthy account of her outstanding research
contributions. Notes that this is the first time the Medal has been
awarded to a woman.

1932

220. J. M.   "The Award of the Draper Medal to Dr. Annie J. Can-
      non," The Scientific Monthly, 34 (April), pp. 378-379. Photo-
      graph.
      Shorter presentation but in the same tone as (219).

1941

221. Anon. "Annie J. Cannon, 77; Noted Astronomer," The New
      York Times, 90 (14 April), p. 17.
      An unusually long obituary with a detailed biography. Cen-
ters attention on her numerous honors but also quotes her on several aspects of her life and work.

*222. [Obituary]. Morning News [Wilmington, Delaware] (14 April).

223. Anon. "Dr. Annie Jump Cannon," The New York Times, 90
      (15 April), p. 22.
      An editorial tribute containing high praise for Cannon.

224. Gaposchkin, Cecilia Payne. "Obituary. Annie Jump Can-
      non," Science, 93 (9 May), pp. 443-444.
      A true memorial by one great astronomer to another. Quite
aside from the recitation of publications and honors, Gaposchkin
makes her colleague and friend a fully alive human being. The final comment is illustrative, "Perhaps the greatest tribute that I can
pay to her memory is to say that she was the happiest person I have
ever known."

225. Anon. "Doctor Annie Cannon, Famous Astronomer, Dies,"
      Equal Rights, 27 (May), pp. 41, 43.
      This official organ of the National Women's Party carries a
tribute to a fellow member. A nontechnical presentation, much of
it is in her own words. Concludes with one of her most famous quotations, "My success, if you would call it that, lies in the fact that
I have kept at my work all these years. It is not genius, or anything like that, it is merely patience."

226. Brück, H. A. [Obituary of Cannon], Observatory, 64 (May),
      pp. 113-115.
      A note on page 59 announces Cannon's death and the obituary
says her name will forever be linked with the great Henry Draper
Catalogue. She was, at the time of her death, the only Honorary
Member of the Royal Astronomical Society.

227. Waterfield, R. L. "Obituaries. Dr. Annie J. Cannon,"
      Nature, 147 (14 June), p. 738.
      Along with the standard biographical material this obituary
makes the point that she was a skilled observer in addition to her

better-known work in the classification of spectra. Also points out
that she played an active role in promoting opportunity for women.

228. Campbell, Leon. "Annie Jump Cannon," Popular Astronomy,
        49 (August), pp. 345-347. Photograph facing p. 345.
        Evaluates Cannon's work as "of the first rank.... The as-
tronomical world will not soon forget Annie J. Cannon. She has
left an indelible mark in the minds and hearts of all." Stresses,
as do most of the articles about her, the pleasure she took in
friends, travel, and life in general.

229. Anon. "Cannon, Annie J[ump], Current Biography, p. 132.
        Notes her selection as one of the 12 "greatest living Ameri-
can women" by the National League of Women Voters in 1929.

230. Shapley, Harlow. "In Memoriam," The Telescope, 8 (May-
        June), pp. 52-54. Photographs.
        Biographical notes taken from the text of his remarks at the
memorial service for Cannon.

231. Payne-Gaposchkin, Cecilia H. "Miss Cannon and Stellar Spec-
        troscopy," The Telescope, 8 (May-June), pp. 62-63.
        Gives Cannon great praise for her work on the Draper Cata-
logue. Says that she "was not a theorist and never published a
controversial word or a speculative thought. Where she found chaos
she left cosmos."

232. Cannon, Annie Jump. "The Story of Starlight," The Tele-
        scope, 8 (May-June), pp. 56-61.
        The text of a radio broadcast made by Cannon which reveals
something of her personality and philosophy.

1942

233. Shapley, Harlow. "Obituary Notices. Annie J. Cannon (1863-
        1941)," The American Philosophical Society Yearbook, 1941.
        Philadelphia: By the Society, pp. 362-364.
        An obituary written by the director of the Observatory during
the last 20 years of Cannon's long career, it is especially meaningful. The bulk of it is devoted to the text read at the Harvard memorial service. Says that there is to be a Memorial Volume in the
Draper Catalogue and a memorial room at the Harvard Observatory.

1943

234. Yost, Edna. American Women of Science (21), pp. 27-43.
        Two major aspects of Cannon's person stand out in Yost's
treatment: her nearly incomprehensible productivity and her warmth
as a human being.

235. Cannon, Annie J., and Margaret Walton Mayall. The Annie
Jump Cannon Memorial Volume of the Henry Draper Extension.
Annals of the Astronomical Observatory of Harvard College.
Cambridge, Massachusetts: By the Observatory, 112, p. 1.
The preface is a short tribute to Cannon.

1964

236. Gingerich, Owen. "Laboratory Exercises in Astronomy--
Spectral Classification," Sky and Telescope, 28 (August), pp.
80-82. Photograph.
Uses Cannon's work, at least a tiny portion of it, to introduce students to the most modern work in astronomy. Good historical and philosophical introduction. Some biographical material.

1971

237. Gingerich, Owen. "Cannon, Annie Jump," Dictionary of Scientific Biography (29), 3, pp. 49-50.
A factual sketch notable only in that she is included.

238. Hoffleit, Dorrit. "Cannon, Annie Jump," Notable American
Women (30), 1, pp. 281-283.
While presenting all of the basic data on this remarkably productive person, Dorrit also succeeds in making her a very human
character. Her love of people is clear from several notes like her
annual egg-rolling contest for observatory children.

239. Jones, Bessie Zaban, and Lyle Gifford Boyd. The Harvard
College Observatory (144), pp. 403-409 and index. Photograph.
Fairly standard material, but written in an especially interesting manner. Presents her more in the context of the work rather
than as an individual super-star.

1973

240. Margaret W. Mayall. "Cannon, Annie Jump," Dictionary of
American Biography (14), supp. 3, pp. 130-131.
Brief but nicely balanced. Presents each phase of Cannon's
life and career in proportion. Better than usual bibliography. A
good place to read a short summary.

241. ANTONIA CAETANA DE PAIVA PEREIRA MAURY
21 March 1866--8 January 1952
After graduating from Vassar College (AB, 1887) with honors

in several subjects and having come under the influence of Maria
Mitchell, Maury went to the Harvard Observatory. At that time the
director, E. C. Pickering, was interested in adding great amounts
of new data to the system he and Williamina Fleming had developed
for the spectral classification of stars. Maury, however, found
greater detail in the spectra and began to establish her own system.

The inevitable conflict between Pickering and Maury led to
her finally leaving Harvard in 1896, not to return until 1918. However, during the eight years prior to her departure she had conducted what is now recognized as her most creative research. Pickering discovered the first spectroscopic binary, a double star which
cannot be detected by visual means; Maury calculated its period and
then discovered the second such star system. Her new system of
stellar classification allowed for small differences in the width and
distinctness of the lines of the photographic spectra and proved just
the needed data allowing Ejnar Hertzsprung, a Danish astronomer,
to demonstrate the existence of dwarf and giant stars.

Maury lectured and taught at various schools until she returned to Harvard. She continued her work on spectroscopic bi-
naries including some very complex systems. After her retirement
in 1935 she continued to visit frequently to check the latest spectra. The significance of her early studies are now widely recognized, and she received the Annie J. Cannon Prize in 1943. Her
association with Harvard was happier after the 1920 appointment of
Harlow Shapley as director. (See also 9, 23, 43, 138.)

1931

242. Bailey, Solon I. The History and Work of the Harvard Ob-
        servatory (142), pp. 152-157 and index.
     Rather technical, but describes clearly the relationship of
the work of Maury and Cannon.

1952

243. Hoffleit, Dorrit. "Antonia C. Maury," Sky and Telescope,
        11 (March), p. 106. Photograph.
     A brief obituary but representative of the various aspects
of her career in nontechnical language.

1971

244. Jones, Bessie Zaban, and Lyle Gifford Boyd. The Harvard
        College Observatory (144), pp. 236-238, 395-400, and index.
        Photograph.
     Very personal account of the important but elusive career
of Maury at Harvard. Says she was the most original of the wom-
en at Harvard.

245. Gingerich, Owen. "Maury, Antonia Caetana De Paiva Pereira,"
Dictionary of Scientific Biography (29), 9, pp. 194-195.
Brief but interesting for its long quotation describing Hertz-
sprung's evaluation of the importance of Maury's work.

1980

246. Hoffleit, Dorrit. "Maury, Antonia Caetana De Paiva Pereira,"
Notable American Women (30), 4, pp. 464-466.
Especially strong work on the relationship between Maury and
Pickering. Treats both parties fairly and shows her eventual justi-
fication in modest tones. Good presentation of the other aspects
of her life and career as well.

247. HENRIETTA SWAN LEAVITT
4 July 1868--12 December 1921
During her senior year at Radcliffe College (AB, 1892) and
in the following year Leavitt took two courses in astronomy. With
this limited background she began, in 1895, as a volunteer in the
Harvard Observatory. She was appointed to the permanent staff
in 1902 and later became chief of a department.
The principal work at this time was the determination of the
brightness of stars or their photographic magnitude. This work
required meticulous care and extraordinary patience. The director
of the observatory, E. C. Pickering, assigned Leavitt the task of
comparing 46 stars near the North Pole on 299 photographic plates
in order to establish a standard for further work. This work and
several supplements were published by 1926 and used until 1940.
More recent work has required newer standards established by modern instrumental methods, but the need for them was first suggested
by Leavitt's discovery that fainter stars are redder than brighter
stars.
Another measure of Leavitt's contribution to astronomy is the
number of variable stars she discovered. Of the 2,400 known in
her lifetime, about half of them were her discoveries. However,
her most important scientific contribution resulted from her study
of the Cepheid variable stars in the Magellanic Clouds. She noted
that the brighter variables have longer periods and determined that
the apparent magnitude decreased linearly with the logarithm of the
period. This period-luminosity relationship has become the key to
determining interstellar distances and the size of the universe. (See
also 9, 35, 43.)

1921

*248. [Obituary]. Boston Transcript, (13 December).

1922

249. Bailey, Solon I. "Henrietta Swan Leavitt," Popular Astron-
      omy, 30 (April), pp. 197-199.
      Written by her colleague at the Harvard Observatory, this
piece is remarkable in that it fails to make any mention of the
period-luminosity law for which she was later nominated for a Nobel
Prize. Stresses her great industry in carrying out Pickering projects.

1931

250. Bailey, Solon I. The History and Work of the Harvard Ob-
      servatory, (142), pp. 140-145, index.
      Presents several technical descriptions of various projects on
which Leavitt worked. It is surprising that the research which led
to her nomination for the Nobel Prize receives only a statement added at the end of her biographical sketch. "She first noted, in connection with her research on the variables in the Magellanic Clouds,
the important fact that the length of period bears a definite relation
to the absolute magnitude."

1935

251. Jaffe, Bernard. Outposts of Science (17), pp. 490-493.
      In connection with his discussion of "Galaxies," Jaffe makes
a good presentation of Leavitt's development of the period-
luminosity law and shows how important it became in other studies.

1936

252. Anon. "Leavitt, Henrietta Swan" The National Cyclopaedia
      of American Biography (2), 25, pp. 163-164.
      Material on her family and a longer than usual description
of her scientific contributions.

1969

253. Shapely, Harlow. Through Rugged Ways to the Stars (143),
      pp. 53, 91.
      Points out that some of his most important work depended
critically on Leavitt's. Also relates some of her other studies to
those of Cannon.

1971

254. Hoffleit, Dorrit, "Leavitt, Henrietta Swan," Notable

American Women (30), 2, pp. 282-283.
Points out the undramatic character of her work and the con-
sequent lack of attention she received. Acknowledges the fundamental nature of her contributions. Of special interest is Hoffleit's
point that, like most scientists, her own work led to the progress
which rendered it obsolete.

1973

255. Gingerich, Owen. "Leavitt, Henrietta Swan" in Dictionary
      of Scientific Biography (29), 8, pp. 105-106.
      Concentrates on her scientific career and makes a point of
her most basic discovery, the period-luminosity law. Notes that
her contemporaries were much more impressed by her discovery of
2,400 variable stars.

1976

256. Mitchell, Helen Buss. "Henrietta Swan Leavitt and the Ce-
      pheid Variables," The Physics Teacher, 14 (March), pp.
      162-167. Drawing from photograph.
      Inspired by the lack of role models for women in science,
Mitchell traces Leavitt's career in some detail. A very large amount
of scientific data is presented at a level appropriate for the intended
student audience. Shows some of the uses to which her period-
luminosity law has been put. Makes an attempt to sketch out some
of her personal life.

257. CAROLINE ELLEN FURNESS
      24 June 1869--9 February 1936
      Furness graduated from Vassar College (AB, 1891) and Co-
lumbia University (PhD, 1900). While at Vassar she was greatly
influenced by Mary Whitney, who in 1894 invited Furness to return
as an assistant in the Observatory. Together they began a program of research in the observation of comets and minor planets.
Following the completion and publication of her doctoral thesis, Furness and her students extended the work to a catalogue of 408 stars
within 2° of the North Pole which was published in 1905. Beginning
in 1909 Furness collaborated with Whitney in her studies of variable
stars. In 1911 she was appointed both acting director of the Observatory and associate professor.
      She was especially interested in the use of photography in
astronomical research, and students under her direction were actively engaged in the research. Furness edited Observations of Variable Stars Made at Vassar College (1901-1912) and in 1916 she was
made Maria Mitchell Professor of Astronomy. She was elected a fellow of the Royal Astronomical Society in 1922. (See also 23, 140.)

258.   Makemson, Maud W.   "Caroline Ellen Furness," Publications
       of the Astronomical Society of the Pacific, 48, pp. 97-100.
       Photograph.
       Well-balanced sketch which discusses Furness' scientific in-
terests, her personal life and her interests in her students and wom-
en's opportunities in general.

1937

259.   Anon.   "Caroline Ellen Furness," Monthly Notices of the
       Royal Astronomical Society, 97, pp. 272-273.
       Discusses mostly her scientific work but comments that "Miss
Furness enjoyed the reputation of being in the front rank of the
teaching profession." Notes that she was elected a Fellow of the
Society on 9 June 1922.

260.   CECILIA HELENA PAYNE-GAPOSCHKIN
       10 May 1900--7 December 1979
       The writer of her obituary for the Royal Astronomical Soci-
ety called Payne-Gaposchkin "probably the most eminent woman astronomer of all time." She collaborated with her husband in the
direction of 29 assistants making more than one and a quarter million observations of variable stars for what has become the standard reference for such stars to the tenth magnitude. They have
presented the most complete picture of the structure and evolution
of our Galaxy in Variable Stars and Galactic Structure and The Galactic Novae. Later this extraordinary couple made two million visual estimates of variable stars in the two Magellanic Clouds.
       After she completed her undergraduate degree at Cambridge
University (BA, 1923), Payne became the first to earn a doctorate
in astronomy from Radcliffe College (1925). Her thesis has been
called "the most brilliant ever written in astronomy." In this first
original work she used Harvard's enormous collection of stellar spectra to establish the amount of the chemical elements found in the
cosmos. It was several years before astronomers realized that her
study correctly demonstrated the very great abundance of hydrogen
and helium present in the Universe.
       Payne-Gaposchkin was elected to a number of the leading sci-
entific societies, including the American Philosophical Society, the
American Academy of Arts and Sciences, the American Astronomical Society, and the Royal Astronomical Society. She was the first
woman to become, through the normal paths of academic advancement, professor and chairman of a department at Harvard University. (See also 23, 28, 43.)

1941

261. Science, ns 93 (9 May), pp. 443-444. See item 224. This
reference is sometimes presented in such a fashion as to suggest that it is about Payne-Gaposchkin.

1942

262. Carey, Frank. "Career in the Cosmos, Mrs. Gaposchkin a
Noted Astronomer," New York Post (5 June), p. 11. Photograph.
Discusses her work and her fame. Is most interesting for
the part about her avocations, for example, she is still trying to
get her first detective story published.

1947

*263. Scientific Monthly, 64 (March), p. vi. Photograph.

1956

264. Stafford, Jane. "Careers Ahead. Science Careers for Wom-
en," Independent Woman, 35 (August), pp. 4-6, 30. Photograph.
The first of a series of articles about careers for women.
While Payne-Gaposchkin is featured, there is relatively little biographical material and a number of other women are discussed.

1957

265. Anon. "University Women Honor Astronomer," The New York
Times, 106 (27 June), p. 34.
Presented an award in conjunction with the 75th anniversary
of the American Association of University Women. It was made for
the purpose of "broadening our understanding of the ages and life-
times of stars and stellar systems."

266. Anon. "Harvard Astronomer Wins 1957 Achievement Award,"
Journal of the American Association of University Women, 51
(October), pp. 15-17. Photograph.
Commentary on the lecture delivered by Payne-Gaposchkin
the day following the award cited above (265). Quotations from
her text along with some biographical material. Mention of the
award presentation and the completion of the AAUW history.

267. Anon. "Payne-Gaposchkin, Cecilia (Helena)," Current Biography Yearbook, pp. 421-423. Photograph.

A good biographical sketch with more than the usual detail.
Her personal and professional life are described in a warm and readable manner. Quite a few specific references are given to her lectures and writings.

1969

268. Shapley, Harlow. Through Rugged Ways to the Stars (143),
      pp. 95-96.
      A brief but important glimpse of the respect Shapley had for
Payne-Gaposchkin. Says she "was and is a genius type of person."

1971

269. Jones, Bessie Zaban, and Lyle Gifford Boyd. The Harvard
      College Observatory (144), pp. 193, 409, 413.
      The authors claim Payne-Gaposchkin is "Unquestionably the
most distinguished recipient [of the Edward C. Pickering Astronomical Fellowship for Women]," yet we find a near total lack of attention paid her in their otherwise splendid book.

1982

270. Gingerich, Owen. "Obituaries. Cecilia Payne-Gaposchkin,"
      The Quarterly Journal of the Royal Astronomical Society, 23,
      pp. 450-451.
      All of the high points of a distinguished career are men-
tioned here, but there is still a bit of the warm human being.
Better than the usual obituary. Concludes with the fine quotation
of her advice to young people, especially young women, "Do not
undertake a scientific career in quest of fame or money. There
are easier and better ways to reach them. Undertake it only if
nothing else will satisfy you; for nothing else is probably what you
will receive."

BACTERIOLOGISTS

(See also 1020)

271. ANNA WESSELS WILLIAMS
     17 March 1863--20 November 1954
     In the very first year of her career Williams isolated a strain
of the diphtheria bacillus which made possible the widespread immunization of children and subsequent near irradication of diphtheria. Her initial success may appear to have been a stroke of
luck, but her continued and important contributions to our understanding of this infectious disease and others is evidence that work,
not luck was responsible. She is also known for her work in the
diagnosis and treatment of rabies.
     Williams earned a diploma from the New Jersey State Normal
School in Trenton (1883) and an MD at the Woman's Medical College
of New York (1891). In 1894 she began as a volunteer in the di-
agnostic laboratory of the New York City Department of Health.
Along with William H. Park, the founder of the first municipal laboratory to apply bacteriology to the problems of public health, she
worked until her mandatory retirement in 1934 to realize the growth
of this pioneering institution. Through no fault of his own, Park
often overshadowed his colleague in the credit given their joint
work. Williams shared authorship with Park in many research publications and writings for the layperson. Her independent research
results provide an additional measure of the significance of her contribution. She was the coauthor of the second through the eleventh
editions of the highly successful text Pathogenic Microorganisms Including Bacteria and Protozoa. They also wrote the first attempt
to reveal their fantastic microscopic world to the non-scientist:
Who's Who Among the Microbes.
     In addition to her scientific work, Williams played a key role,
again with Park, in making possible the rapid growth of the Research Laboratories. She became assistant director in 1905 and for
nearly thirty years developed the smooth organization and team work
which characterized its growth in stature and productivity. The
significance of her contributions were recognized, and she was the
first woman to be elected to office in the laboratory section of the
American Public Health Association. (See also 954, 955.)

1941

272. Oliver, Wade W. The Man Who Lived for Tomorrow. A bi-
      ography of William Hallock Park, MD. New York: Dutton,
      index.

A long and detailed biography of Park, the guiding force in
New York City's efforts to make bacteriological diagnosis a basic
method in public health, especially in the control of diphtheria.
The story of Park and Williams was intertwined from the earliest
days of the laboratory. They began in 1894 when she isolated the
famous Park-Williams diphtheria No. 8, a strain of diphtheria bacillus which is a uniquely strong and constant producer of toxin. A
great many technical references are given.

Williams spoke at the dedication, 6 October 1936, of the new
research laboratory named for Park. Part of her comments is especially revealing: "I have been asked by one in authority to speak
for three minutes, on the work of the women in our laboratory. I
refused, not because of the three minutes, but because in all my
40 years' experience in these laboratories I never had to consider
women as women in the work; it was always the worker, man or
woman."

1954

273. Anon. "Anna W. Williams, Scientist, Is Dead," The New York
     Times, 104 (21 November), p. 86.
     Says Williams is one of the country's outstanding bacteriolo-
gists. Together with Park she developed a useful rabies test and
isolated the Williams strain of diphtheria bacillus. Cites her honors
and talks about the celebrated case of her forced retirement.

1971

274. Robinton, Elizabeth D. "Williams, Anna Wessels," Notable
     American Women (30), 3, pp. 737-739.
     Describes in detail both Williams' scientific work and her
contributions to the development of the New York City Laboratories.
Is especially good in pointing out her leadership in making the laboratory personnel function as a team. Makes clear the relationship
between Park and Williams.

1974

275. Robinton, Elizabeth D. "A Tribute to Women Leaders in the
     Laboratory Section of the American Public Health Association,"
     American Journal of Public Health, 64 (October), pp. 1006-
     1007.
     Discusses the first six women to play significant roles in
health science laboratory work. Devotes quite a bit of space to
Williams, since she was the first to chair the Laboratory Section.

276. KATHERINE ELIZA GOLDEN BITTING
      29 April 1869--15 October 1937
      Studied at Purdue University (BS, 1890; MS, 1892) and was
employed as botanist by the United States Experiment Station at La-
fayette, Indiana. In 1890 Golden joined the Purdue faculty and was
promoted to assistant professor in 1901. Her appointment was first
in botany, but was changed to biology as her interests shifted toward biochemistry and bacteriology. She was particularly interested
in fermentation and enzymes and published a number of articles and
monographs alone and in collaboration with other scientists.
      After having married another Purdue professor, Arvill Wayne
Bitting, in 1904, she taught only one more year. The Bittings entered the field of food preservation where they worked together and
became widely respected. During World War I they both joined the
quartermaster corps and directed the food supply and planning branch
for the United States Army. They received honorary doctorates
from Purdue University in 1935. (See also 4.)

                              1937

277. Anon. "Mrs. A. W. Bitting, '90," Purdue Alumnus, 25 (No-
      vember), p. 14. Photograph.
      Obituary with a fairly complete outline of her life.

                              1940

278. Anon. "The Katherine Golden Bitting Collection on Gastron-
      omy," Report of the Librarian of Congress, 1940, pp. 255-
      256.
      Her library, which represents an important collection in this
field of food chemistry, was presented to the Library of Congress
by her husband as a memorial. This report describes the collection and gives very useful biographical details.
      We are indebted to Keith Dowden of the Purdue Univer-
sity Libraries Special Collections for his assistance.

279. MARY HEFFERAN
      24 June 1873--20 July 1948
      Hefferan was educated at Wellesley College (AB, 1896; AM,
1898) and at the University of Chicago (PhD, 1903). She remained
at Chicago serving as curator of the Bacteriological Museum and
taught in the Department of Bacteriology until 1910. She was interested in the agglutinative relations of nonpathogenic organisms,
red chromogenic organisms, and proteolytic enzymes. Her research
publications appeared in the Journal of Infectious Diseases and several European journals. It seems that sometime during the First
World War Hefferan made a dramatic change of career. In 1913 she

was a bacteriologist in Grand Rapids, Michigan, and in 1919 she
was director of the Blodgett Home for Children in that city. Her
obituary speaks of her as a social work pioneer and only mentions
her scientific training.

1948

280. Anon. "Social Work Pioneer Here Dies at Home," Unidenti-
      fied [Grand Rapids, Michigan?] newspaper clipping from Wel-
      lesley College Archives (21 July), pp. 1?, 3, 7. Photograph.
      A long sketch which emphasizes her many social and civic
contributions. "Among her friends it was known that she turned
from what might have been a brilliant career in science to assume
duties she felt more urgent."
      We are indebted to Wilma R. Slaight, Archivist of Wellesley
College; Daniel Meyer, Assistant Archivist, and his collaborator,
Richard Popp, of the University of Chicago for their assistance.

281. ALICE CATHERINE EVANS
      29 January 1881--5 September 1975
      The importance of Evans' work in relating the disease brucel-
losis to unpasteurized milk was seriously retarded by several factors. A woman without a doctoral or a medical degree (BS, Cornell
University, 1909; MS, University of Wisconsin, 1910) was trying to
convince physicians and veterinarians that they should collaborate
with one another. Her studies, reported in 1917, showed that three
organisms isolated from diseased cattle, goats, and pigs were nearly
identical and were common in the milk of healthy cows. While the
idea was not well received, she further demonstrated, on the basis
of worldwide examination of samples, that the new genus Brucellae
consisted of several strains which could be distinguished serological-
ly. In spite of confirmation by others, some scientists continued
to resist her conclusions.
      The disease, which is very difficult to diagnose, became wide-
ly recognized by the late 1920's, and in the next decade the pas-
teurization of milk reduced its occurrence in the United States.
Evans was the first woman elected president of the Society of American Bacteriologists and was a delegate to the First (Paris, 1930)
and Second (London, 1936) International Congress of Microbiology.
In 1934 she received an honorary MD from the Women's Medical College of Pennsylvania and in 1936 an honorary ScD from Wilson College. (See also 954, 955.)

1929

282. Kruif, Paul de. "'Before you Drink a Glass of Milk.' The
      story of a woman's discovery of a new disease." Ladies Home

Journal, 46 (September), pp. 8-9, 162, 165-166, 168-169.
Photograph. Reprinted: Men Against Death. New York:
Harcourt, Brace, ch. 5, 1932.
   A popular but extraordinarily well-written account of both
the person and her work. The great difficulties she had to overcome are clearly presented along with the importance of the work
for science and society in general.

1943

283. Anon. "Evans, Alice C(atherine)," Current Biography Year-
     book, pp. 198-200. Photograph.
     Perhaps a little dramatic, but a generally well-written account
of Evans' work. Pays much attention to her scientific work, in nontechnical language, and too little to her education and personal life.

1944

284. MacKaye, Milton. "Undulant Fever," Ladies Home Journal,
     61 (December), pp. 23, 69-70.
     A popular plea for not drinking raw milk. The coverage of
Evans' work is quite adequate.

1971

285. O'Hern, Elizabeth M. "Evans, Alice Catherine," Notable
     American Women (30), 1, pp. 219-221.
     A careful and full account of her life and work. Without a
large amount of highly technical detail the elements of Evans' research and the difficulty of its being accepted are made clear.
Makes important comments on her personality.

1973

*286. O'Hern, Elizabeth M. "Alice Evans, Pioneer Microbiologist,"
      American Society for Microbiology News, (September).

1975

287. Anon. "Alice Evans, Who Found Cause of Undulant Fever in
     Man, Dies," The New York Times, 124 (7 September) p. 51.
     Calls her a "pioneer bacteriologist who discovered the similar-
ity between bacteria which cause abortion in cows and undulant fever in man." Says she was the first woman elected president of
the Society of American Bacteriologists. This date has sometimes
been reported as 8 September.

288.   Anon.   "Alice Evans, 94, Bacteriologist, Dies," The Washing-
       ton Post, 98 (8 September), p. B4.
       Obituary citing the internationally known bacteriologist who
identified the organism causing undulant fever.   Traces her career
in some detail, including her long tenure at the United States Public Health Service.

289.   Anon.   "Dr. Alice Evans Dies at 94, Joined PHS in 1918;
       Among 1st Women to Pick Med. Research Career," United
       States. National Institutes of Health, Record, (23 September),
       p. 3.   Photograph.
       Brief review of the facts of her life with notes about her ca-
reer being something of a pioneering effort and her establishment
of a scholarship fund at Federal City College.

1976

290.   Eddy, Bernice E.   "Obituary: Alice Catherine Evans,"
       American Society for Microbiology News, 42, pp. 166-168.
       Photograph.
       Cites her scientific accomplishments, but pays more attention
than most to her personal life.   Refers particularly to her independent spirit.

1977

291.   O'Hern, Elizabeth M.   "Alice Evans and the Brucellosis Story,"
       Annali i Sclavo Rivista di Microbiologia e di Immunologia, 19
       (February), pp. 12-19.   In English with an Italian summary.
       Tells in some detail, but with a minimum of technical language,
the full story of Evans' study of milk as a carrier of brucellosis.
Especially good in presenting the difficulties she had in gaining acceptance of her work and her eventual victory.

292. FANNY RYSAM MULFORD HITCHCOCK
    7 February 1851--25 September 1936
    Hitchcock earned a PhD at the University of Pennsylvania in
1894 but does not appear to have held any professional positions.
She was interested in both biological and chemical topics ranging
from iron ores to the diseases of the pineapple plant. These interests are also illustrated by her membership in the Chemical Society,
the Mathematical Society, and the Torrey Botanical Club. She was
a fellow of the New York Academy of Sciences. (See also 872.)

293. Hitchcock is cited in American Men of Science, 1906-1921.
    We are indebted to Francis James Dallett, Archivist of the Uni-
versity of Pennsylvania, for his assistance.

294. MARTHA BUNTING
    2 December 1861--unknown
    After her graduation from Swarthmore College (BL, 1881),
Bunting studied at the University of Pennsylvania, Woods Hole,
Johns Hopkins University, and Bryn Mawr College (PhD, 1895).
She held teaching positions in several schools, including Goucher
College, Girls' High School,Philadelphia, and Wadleigh High School,
New York City. In 1912 she became Carnegie Research Assistant
in physiology at the University of Pennsylvania. Her broad tech-
nical interests included the origin of sex cells and studies of cork
tissue. Her work appeared in the literature.

295. Bunting is cited in American Men of Science, 1906-1910; Who
    Was Who in America, 4, p. 135.

296. GWENDOLEN FOULKE ANDREWS
    26 June 1863--1936?
    Andrews prepared for Bryn Mawr College with studies at Mr.
and Mrs. L. M. Johnson's School in Philadelphia. At Bryn Mawr
she attended a special course in 1888-1889. The 1908 register of
students notes that she was a "hearer in biology." She was married to Professor Ethan Allen Andrews and they were living in Baltimore at that time. In addition to an active interest in the structure of protoplasm, which she published as The Living Substance,
and articles in the American Journal of Morphology, she studied
educational psychology of children.

297.   Andrews is cited in <u>American Men of Science</u>, 1906-1921.
        We are indebted to Lucy Fisher West, College Archivist of
Bryn Mawr College for her assistance.

298.   ESTHER FUSSELL BYRNES
        3 November 1867--1 September 1946
        All of Byrnes' collegiate education was at Bryn Mawr College
(AB, 1891; AM, 1894; PhD, 1898). After teaching at Vassar and
Bryn Mawr she moved to the Girls' High School of Brooklyn.
        The field of marine science attracted Byrnes, whose studies
of maturation and fertilization, limb muscles and limb regeneration
in amphibia were considered important. In 1926 she was granted
sabbatical leave to tutor the Princesses of the Japanese Royal Family. Upon her return to Brooklyn, she taught for an additional
four years before her retirement in 1932.

                                1946

299.   Anon. "Dr. Esther Byrnes, a Science Teacher," <u>The New</u>
        <u>York Times</u>, 95 (5 September), p. 27.
        Gives her memberships and notes that she was chairwoman
of the section on biology of the New York State Science Teachers
Association and a fellow of the New York Academy of Science.
Also strong on her work in Japan.

300.   Anon. "Recent Deaths. Esther Fussell Byrnes," <u>School and</u>
        <u>Society</u>, 64 (14 September), p. 185.
        Notice of her education and professional positions.

301.   DAISY MAUDE ORLEMAN ROBINSON
        6 November 1869--12 March 1942
        In the first edition of <u>American Men of Science</u> (1906), Rob-
inson is listed as having an interest in biology and medicine. Although she had a most colorful career, she does not seem to have
ever had more than an avocational interest in biology. Nothing
is known of her early life or education. She received her medical
education at Columbia University (MD, 1890) and studied for two
years at the University of Zurich before returning to Columbia to
take further graduate work (MS, 1894).
        In the First World War she joined the medical corps of the
French Army and transferred to the American army when the U.S.
entered the war. She was decorated by both nations. After the
war she worked in the New York State Department of Health and
later the United States Public Health Service. She served for a
short time as Acting Surgeon-General. She retired in 1938.
        Her scientific interests, as she lists them, were medical in

nature and include the ill effects of Röntgen rays, the diagnosis
and treatment of herpes zoster, and the Noguchi system in serum
diagnosis of syphilis.

1942

302. Anon. "Dr. Daisy Robinson, A Noted Surgeon," The New
      York Times, 91 (14 March), p. 15.
      Notes her war service and private practice in dermatology.
Says she was the widow of Dr. Andrew Rose Robinson, who was
one of the founders of the Polyclinic Hospital in Washington. A
fairly complete review of her career.

303. WILHELMINE MARIE ENTEMAN KEY
      22 February 1872--31 January 1955
      Enteman was educated at the University of Wisconsin (AB,
1894) and the University of Chicago (PhD, 1901). She taught biology at the New Mexico Normal University from 1903 and studied
the variation and coloration of plants and the social behavior of
wasps.

304. Enteman is cited in American Men of Science, 1906.
      We are indebted to Bernard Schermetzler, Archivist of the
University of Wisconsin-Madison; Daniel Meyer, Assistant Archivist,
and his collaborator, Richard Popp, of the University of Chicago,
for their assistance.

GENERAL (See also 442, 1403)

1955

305. Ewan, Joseph. "San Francisco as a Mecca for Nineteenth-
    Century Naturalists," in A Century of Progress in the Nat-
    ural Sciences. 1853-1953. San Francisco: California Acad-
    emy of Sciences, pp. 1-63.
        Provides a fine picture of the environment in which several
    important women botanists played their part. There are helpful
    bibliographies of writings about them.

306. SOPHIA HENNION ECKERSON
    unknown--19 July 1954
        A family-oriented person, Eckerson spent some years of her
    early womanhood helping her younger brothers in their chosen
    fields of medicine and art. Then she enrolled in Smith College
    where she received her BA in 1905 and MA in 1907. She continued
    her studies and obtained her PhD from the University of Chicago
    in 1911. Although it was rare for a woman to be on the staff at
    Chicago, she was a member of the faculty until 1920.
        Invited as a plant microchemist by Washington State Univer-
    sity, she spent a semester there in 1914, and in 1919 she worked
    with the Bureau of Plant Industry, United States Department of
    Agriculture, in Washington, D.C. Upon leaving Chicago in 1921,
    she returned to the USDA to work in the Cereals Division and went
    to the University of Wisconsin until 1923. When the Boyce Thomp-
    son Institute was founded in 1924, she became a charter member
    and remained there until she retired in 1940.
        The greatest influence in her life was her teacher, William
    Francis Ganong, and as his disciple Eckerson herself became known
    for her superb teaching and for her assistance to students. She
    prepared a textbook called Outlines of Plant Microchemistry for her
    classes in plant physiology. It was designed to teach the metabolic
    processes in plants. Modesty and desire for perfection prevented
    her from ever publishing it. Others, however, have recognized
    her methods which have found their way into later textbooks. Her
    work with nitrates, cellular membranes, fungi, starch grains, and
    nutritive minerals was significant enough to earn her the chairman-
    ship of the physiological section of the Botanical Society of America,
    an elected post held almost exclusively by men. Her achievements

also won her recognition as a starred scientist in American Men of Science in the 1938 edition, a distinct honor for a woman. She died in Pleasant Valley, Connecticut, after an enjoyable retirement.

1954

307. Pfeiffer, Norma E. "Sophia H. Eckerson, Plant Microchemist," Science, 120 (19 November), pp. 820-821.

A short but revealing memorial tribute. Helpful and important considering that respect for Eckerson is relatively recent. This account of her life appears to be the only extant one. Makes her seem a very attractive person.

308. JANE COLDEN FARQUHAR
27 March 1724--10 March 1766

Known by posterity as Jane Colden because she married late in life, she is actually the first American woman to gain recognition in any field of science. Her father, Cadwallader Colden, was a significant figure in eighteenth-century botany and his daughter worked with, and learned from, him at a very early age. Through her father she and her work were known to several European botanists, including Linnaeus. She mastered his system of plant classification when her father translated it from the Latin, and this more than any other aspect of her career seems to have won her widespread recognition.

It is only certain that she wrote one published work, but there may, in fact, be others. She drew and described in English nearly 400 local plants and exchanged seeds and plants with other botanists. The original manuscript is in the British Museum, and a portion of it was published in 1963. Modern evaluations of her work vary, but in general her descriptions are considered excellent --full, careful, and evidently taken from living specimens. Her drawings on the other hand are considered very poor. It is quite possible that the drawings which were praised in her lifetime have been lost. She first identified the gardenia in honor of her friend, the American naturalist Alexander Garden. (See also 40.)

1861

309. Anon. "Biographical. The Colden Family," Newburgh Telegraph and Weekly News, (25 April), p. 6.

This article traces the history of the entire family and mentions Jane as "being celebrated [like her father] for her Botanical knowledge." The article cited in the Dictionary of American Biography under the name S. W. Eager was not found.

1895

310. Britten, James. "Biographical Notes, VIII--Jane Colden and
     the Flora of New York," Journal of Botany, 33, pp. 12-15.
       While doing research on another early American botanist,
Britten discovered Colden's work at the British Museum. He discusses the nature and quality of her drawings.

1907

311. Vail, Anna Murray. "Jane Colden, an Early New York Bot-
     anist," Torreya, 7 (February), pp. 21-34.
       This little article is particularly interesting in that it may
be the first serious attempt at scholarship in the field of women
scientists. Vail, who is herself one of the elusive characters of
the early twentieth-century scene, presents the biographical details and asks important questions about Britten's earlier paper (310).
Much of the significant correspondence is quoted and woven into
the story.

1930

312. M[arion] P. S[mith]. "Colden, Jane," Dictionary of American
     Biography (14), 4, pp. 288-289.
       Well-written, brief account of her life and work. The article
provides several important quotations about her. Some useful bibliography, but see item (309).

1961

313. Humphrey, Harry Baker. "Jane Colden. 1724-1766," in Mak-
     ers of North American Botany. New York: Ronald, pp. 53-
     54.
       Recognizes that "her career as a botanist is worthy of note."

1962

314. Hollingsworth, Buckner. "Jane Colden, 1724-1766. Ameri-
     ca's First Woman Botanist," in Her Garden Was Her Delight.
     New York: Macmillan, pp. 23-34.
       A readable and very human account of Colden and her rela-
tionship with her father. Discusses the botanical world of the
eighteenth century and presents many details of Colden's work.
Hollingsworth admits nevertheless that "as a woman, though, Jane
remains entirely anonymous."

1965

315. Eifert, Virginia S. "Jane Colden, First Woman Botanist,"
in Tall Trees and Far Horizons. Adventures and discoveries
of early botanists in America. New York: Dodd, Mead, ch.
4, pp. 49-62.
Avoids all of the pitfalls of pseudo-scholarship and presents
an attractive yet authoritative picture of Colden and her place in
early American botany. This article reads like a story and, of
course, had to be pieced together from the fragments. Still, one
is aware of the soundness of the thought and the essential correctness of the view presented.

1970

316. Stearns, Raymond Phineas. Science in the British Colonies
of America. Urbana, Illinois: University of Illinois Press,
pp. 565-567 and index.
Describes, in her father's words, the interest and skill
Colden displayed in applying the Linnaean system to botany in
America. Stearns says that her collections are of historical rather
than practical interest because of their lack of flowers and root
structure. He also points out that it is likely she attracted so much
attention because she was a woman rather than as a result of her
scientific work.

1971

317. Hindle, Brooke. "Colden, Jane," Notable American Women
(30), 1, pp. 357-358.
Brings together the little that is known of the facts of Colden's life and deals well with her scientific contribution. Good
treatment of her renown in international botanical circles.

1979

318. Anon. "Colden, Jane," Biographical Dictionary of American
Science (40), pp. 58-59.
A fine sketch of Colden's contribution and life. A bibliog-
raphy.

319. CLARISSA TUCKER TRACY
12 December 1818--15 November 1905
A noted teacher at Ripon (Wisconsin) College, Tracy began
her work when the college was founded and remained there as

Professor Emerita until her death. She was originally employed
as "matron of the boarding department." Her education was typical of the times--gathered here and there as she taught to pay for
her own studies at a variety of academies and seminaries.

Also typical were her teaching responsibilities covering the
entire liberal arts spectrum: algebra, English literature and composition, Latin, and botany. In spite of these demands, to say
nothing of those of housekeeper, Tracy along with her students
published the largest list of flora of the region then available.
Based on thirty years of field work, Plants Growing Without Cultivation in Ripon and the Near Vicinity represented not only a very
modern teaching method, but also a carefully conducted and valuable
research contribution. She was remembered by her students and
colleagues for her great organizational ability and her genuine understanding as a teacher.

                                1908

320.   Merrell, Ada Clark. Life and Poems of Clarissa Tucker Tracy.
       Chicago: R. R. Donnelley & Sons, 150 pp. Photograph.
       A rich source of biographical detail written at Tracy's re-
quest by her long-time student and friend. There is little direct
reference to her scientific work and no bibliography. Stresses her
personal piety and example and her large contribution to the success of Ripon College. There are frequent quotations from her
speeches and writings; many of her poems are printed in full and
there is an ample collection of appreciative statements from students
and friends.

                                1975

321.   Brown, Victoria. "Clarissa Tucker Tracy," in Uncommon
       Lives of Common Women. The missing half of Wisconsin his-
       tory. Madison: The Wisconsin Feminists Project, pp. 22-
       23. Photograph.
       A modern treatment of her life which retains the best of the
earlier emphasis on her strength of character and devotion to her
work.

                                1979

322.   Anon. "Tracy, Clarissa Tucker," Biographical Dictionary
       of American Science (40), p. 252.
       A summary of her career. There are dates for her educa-
tional background and a good discussion of her scientific contribution. Some bibliography.

323. LYDIA WHITE SHATTUCK
        10 June 1822--2 November 1889
        After having completed her studies at Mount Holyoke Seminary
(1851), Shattuck became a member of the faculty and remained there
until her retirement as professor emerita in 1889. She was the first
and most important exponent of the model of scientific education
established by the school's founder, Mary Lyon. In addition to
botany, her first love, she had a genuine interest in chemistry
and also taught physics, physiology and astronomy.
        Shattuck was one of 50 persons (15 women) selected for the
short-lived but important Anderson School of Natural History at
Penikese Island. There she came in contact with Louis Agassiz,
the founder, and other foremost naturalists. She was a long-time
friend and correspondent of Asa Gray. In fact, her "publications,"
consisting of the exchange of information and specimens, were typical of contemporary botanists.
        Mount Holyoke, under Shattuck's leadership and with the aid
of her students, built an impressive herbarium and botanical garden. In addition to her ability to inspire students she was recognized by her contemporary, C. A. Young of Princeton, who characterized her "attainments as a botanist and student of natural history [as] remarkable for the time ... there were very few women
in the country who could be ranked with her." She traveled widely, always increasing her store of knowledge to be passed on to
her students. Mount Holyoke named a science building in her honor.

                                    1890

324. Anon. Memorial of Lydia W. Shattuck. Boston: Beacon Press,
        46 pp. Photograph.
        Basic biographical source which contains the text of the ser-
mon at her funeral, a biographical sketch, views of her as a teacher and scholar, and tributes by many colleagues, students, and
friends.

                                    1940

325. Cole, Arthur C. A Hundred of Mount Holyoke College. The
        Evolution of an Educational Ideal. New Haven: Yale Univer-
        sity Press, pp. 156-158. Photograph.
        This work is the complete history of Mount Holyoke from its
founding as a female seminary in 1837 under the courageous leadership of Mary Lyon to the large and important institution it had
become in 1940. The beginnings and development of its science
departments are succinctly recalled. Shattuck, her assistant Susan
Bowen, and her student Cornelia Clapp, who was soon to be her
colleague, are all included. A lovely photograph of Shattuck.

1971

326.   Haywood, Charlotte. "Shattuck, Lydia White," Notable
       American Women (30), 3, pp. 273-274.
       Places emphasis on her central role in the early growth of
science at Mount Holyoke, but also points out her active and important development of contacts with the scientific world outside
of the college.

1979

327.   Anon. "Shattuck, Lydia White," Biographical Dictionary of
       American Science (40), p. 234.
       A good presentation of Shattuck's scientific contribution.
Some bibliography.

328.   KATE FURBISH
       19 May 1834--6 December 1931
       Following a public school education, Furbish took drawing
courses in Portland (Maine) and Boston. She also studied in Paris,
but French literature rather than science. Her interest in botany,
which had begun under her father's influence when she was 12,
did not really manifest itself until about 1860 when she attended
a series of lectures by George L. Goodale, later a professor at Harvard.
       Her ambition was to prepare drawings of all native plants
of Maine excepting grasses, sedges, trees, and ferns, and in this
she was quite successful. For 35 years she roamed the difficult
regions of the state collecting, classifying, and making the most
delicate and accurate watercolor pictures. These drawings in 16
large folio volumes were and continue to be appreciated both for
their botanical significance and their artistic statement.
       In 1897 Merritt L. Fernald, another Harvard botanist, named
a plant she had discovered in her honor, saying she was the "distinguished artist-botanist ... who, through her undaunted pluck
and faithful brush, has done more than any other to make known
the wonderful flora of the 'Garden of Maine.'" In addition to her
"Illustrated Flora," which she presented to Bowdoin College, other
results of her activities are available to students. These resources
include 4,000 sheets of dried plants in Harvard's Gray Herbarium
and 182 sheets of ferns in the Portland Society of Natural History.
(See also 40, 43.)

1924

329.   Coburn, Louise H. "Kate Furbish, Botanist," Maine Natural-
       ist, 4 (15 November), pp. 106-109. Photograph.

Written by her long-time friend and fellow botanist, this obituary gives helpful personal insights on her attitudes about her work.

1931

330.   Anon.   "Miss Kate Furbish Oldest Resident and Noted Botanist Dies," Brunswick [Maine] Record (10 December).
Gives details of her funeral and the high points of her education and career.

1939

331.   Anon.   "Kate Furbish," Bulletin of the Josselyn Botanical Society of Maine, no. 7, unnumbered.   Photograph.
Carries this dedication: "To Miss Kate Furbish a Founder and ex-President of the Josselyn Botanical Society of Maine.   A pioneer in the botanical exploration of this State, a woman whose exquisite, lifelike and accurate paintings of the wild flowers of Maine stand as a worthy memorial of her enthusiasm, industry and devotion."   Short biography.

1971

332.   Schwarten, Lazella.   "Furbish, Kate," Notable American Women (30), 1, pp. 686-687.
Concentrates on her devotion to her work and the high regard professional botanists had for it.   Especially good description of the rugged country in which she worked and was inspired.

1977

333.   Saltonstall, Richard, Jr.   "Of Dams and Kate Furbish," Living Wilderness, 40 (January), pp. 42-43.   Photograph.
Uses the environmental issue of a proposed dam to introduce excellent, modern biographical treatment of Furbish.   The plant named for her has become an endangered species and played a key role in preventing the construction.   Contains a reproduction of her drawing of the plant named for her.

334.   Cole, John.   "The Woman Behind the Wildflower That Stopped a Dam," Horticulture, 55 (December), pp. 30-35.   Photograph.
Full biographical sketch of Furbish worked into a report of the role the plant named after her played in the environmental issue.   Several excellent reproductions of her watercolors of Maine plants.

1979

335.   Anon.   "Furbish, Kate," Biographical Dictionary of American
       Science (40), p. 97.
       Adequate outline of her life and contributions.   Good list of
her works.

336.   SUSAN MARIA HALLOWELL
       25 August 1835--29 December 1911?
       She spent her professional life as professor of natural his-
tory at Wellesley College from its foundation in 1875 until her retirement in 1902.   Hallowell spent most of her summers engaged
in study at Harvard or at European laboratories and museums.   She
was chiefly interested in histological and physiological botany.

1911

337.   Anon.   "Scientific News and Notes," Science, ns 34 (29 De-
       cember), pp. 911-912.
       Note of her death and long service at Wellesley College.

338.   MARY KATHARINE LAYNE CURRAN BRANDEGEE
       28 October 1844--3 April 1920
       Educated as a physician (MD, University of California, 1878),
Brandegee was drawn to botany through materia medica although
she was interested in several areas of biology.   With her early associations in the California Academy of Sciences she helped to build
its herbarium and became its curator in 1883.   This position was
especially important in the then lively growth of botanical collections and classification in the Western United States.   There was
a strong movement to break away from the older, dominating,
Eastern establishment.
       A widow in 1889, she married Townshend Stith Brandegee,
and for 35 years they shared a deep interest in the collection and
classification of western plants.   In addition to their joint collection of over 75,000 specimens, given to the herbarium of the University of California, they established a series of Bulletins at the
Academy and later the journal Zoe.   This latter publication provided the necessary means for amateur and professional observers
to make their findings accessible.   Although their planned flora
of California was never written, the huge collection and its careful classification represent a valuable research contribution.   (See
also 4, 40, 305.)

1926

339. Setchell, William Albert. "Mary Katharine (Layne) (Curran) Brandegee. 1844-1920," in University of California Publications in Botany, 13, pp. 165-177.
A basic source of biographical data on Brandegee following the important account of her husband and collaborator. Includes a brief autobiographical sketch and an extensive bibliography of her work, written primarily by John Hendley Barnhart.

1932

340. Jones, Marcus E. "Katherine [sic] Brandegee," Desert Plant Life, (August and September), pp. 41 and 51.
A rather folksy account by a friend of the Brandegees, full of the flavor of the person and the times. Provides information not otherwise available and asks questions that deserve further study.

1933

341. Jones, Marcus E. "Mrs. T. S. Brandegee," Contributions to Western Botany, 18, pp. 12-18. Photograph.
More in the same tone of item (340). Jones points out that he is "not ... attempting biographies, my aim is to mirror to you the person as he appeared to me." Again, a wealth of detail impossible to duplicate.

342. Ewan, Joseph. "A Bibliogeographical Guide to the Brandegee Botanical Collection," American Midland Naturalist, (May), pp. 772-789.
This article is largely a study of their travels intertwined with their collection, but it also contains valuable biographical data. See especially Ewan's thoughtful annotations of the writings of others about the Brandegees.

343. Jaeger, Edmund C. "Bold Kate Brandegee ... Pioneer California Woman Botanist," Calico Print, (March), pp. 8-9, 32-33. Photograph.
Another sketch by a contemporary spiced with several stories and quotations. Another impossible piece to duplicate and valuable in spite of its undoubtedly biased viewpoint.

1971

344. Dupree, Hunter, and Marian L. Gade. "Brandegee, Mary Katharine Layne Curran," Notable American Women, (30), 1, pp. 228-229.

　　　　Excellent description of her work at the California Academy
of Sciences. Especially good in relating her efforts to organize
the collection and the role she played in making the botanists of
California independent. Remarks on her involvement in the founding
of publications.

1979

345.　Anon.　"Brandegee, Mary Katharine Layne Curran,"
　　　　Biographical Dictionary of American Science (40), p. 39.
　　　　A condensed outline of her educational and professional career and a detailed description of her scientific contributions. A
limited bibliography.

346.　FLORA WAMBAUGH PATTERSON
　　　　15 September 1847--6 February 1928
　　　　A specialist in the taxonomy of fungi, Patterson studied at
Antioch College, Cincinnati Wesleyan College (AM, 1883), Radcliffe
College, and Iowa State University (AM, 1895). She served the
United States Department of Agriculture in various capacities ris-
ing to mycologist in charge of the herbarium of the Bureau of Plant
Industry. Her publications include several monographs as well as
scientific articles. (See also 4, 8, 11.)

1928

347.　Galloway, Beverly T.　"Flora W. Patterson, 1847-1928,"
　　　　Phytopathology, 18 (November), pp. 877-879.
　　　　She served for 25 years with the Bureau of Plant Industry
of the United States Department of Agriculture. Her active mind
developed interests beyond her field, and she was a helpful and
able advisor. Gives some personal information and a bibliography.

1929

348.　Charles, Vera K.　"Mrs. Flora Wambaugh Patterson,"
　　　　Mycologia, 21 (January-February), pp. 1-4. Photograph.
　　　　This memorial article is much more personal than item 347.
Says that Patterson was a particularly valuable colleague because
of her wide knowledge of the most modern trends in science. A
bibliography.

349.　CORA HUIDEKOPER CLARKE
　　　　9 February 1851--2 April 1916

Following a private school education, Clarke attended classes at various Boston institutions, including the Horticultural School for Women, the Bussey Institute, and the Boston Society of Natural History. In 40 years of study devoted to the relationship of parasitic insects on plants she contributed a great deal to the understanding and treatment of insect-galls. She studied summers at Harvard University and wrote a number of articles and monographs on insects, mosses, and seaweeds. Clarke played an active role in the "Study at Home Society," an early attempt to promote educational opportunity for women. (See also 4.)

1910

350. Anon. "Miss Clarke Is Winning Fame as 'Plant Doctor,'" Boston Sunday Post, (9 January), p. 40. Photograph.
Describes her interests in the action of parasites on plants and especially her efforts to develop methods of restoring the plants. Several quotations from an interview with her.

1916

351. Anon. "Scientific Notes and News," Science, ns 43 (9 June), p. 815.
Note of her death which mentions her being a fellow of the American Association for the Advancement of Science.

352. Anon. "Cora H. Clarke," Psyche, 23, p. 94.
Obituary giving a fairly complete account of her life and a number of specific references to her publications. Deals with her scientific accomplishments and indicates that several species were named in her honor. Surprisingly detailed for such a short piece.

353. HENRIETTA EDGECOMB HOOKER
12 December 1851--13 May 1929
Hooker exerted an important influence on her Alma Mater, Mount Holyoke College (AB, 1873), where she taught botany for 35 years. She studied at the Massachusetts Institute of Technology, and the Universities of Chicago, Berlin, and Syracuse (MA and PhD, 1889).
During her years at Mount Holyoke, Hooker studied the morphology and embryology of Cuscuta. She served as chairwoman of the Department of Botany from 1884 until her retirement (1908) and was promoted to full professor in 1904.

354. Anon. "De Mortius. Henrietta Edgecomb Hooker," (7).
Brief obituary given all who had received retiring allowances from the Carnegie Foundation. Gives facts of her education and professional positions.

355. CLARA ETON CUMMINGS
      13 July 1855--28 December 1906
      While affiliated with Wellesley College for much of its history,
in addition to having been a student there in 1876, Cummings does
not appear to have ever taken any academic degree. She is said
to have shown such a marked talent for the study of botany, especially the identification of cryptogamic flora, that she was retained as a permanent member of the department. Beginning as
curator of the museum in 1878 she rose to the rank of Hunnewell
Professor of Botany in 1905. In the following year her title was
changed to Hunnewell Professor of Cryptogamic Botany, in recognition of her achievement of distinction in that field of specialization.
      In many extended field trips Cummings made a collection of
mosses and lichens of New England, California, Alaska, and Europe.
In collaboration with other botanists she published a rather extensive series of studies of these plants. She was an associate editor
of The Plant World.

                              1907

356. Anon. "Scientific Notes and News," Science, ns 25 (11 Jan-
      uary), pp. 77-78.
      Somewhat longer obituary than is usual for this periodical.
Describes her long tenure at Wellesley as well as the details of her
academic advancement.

357. KATE OLIVIA SESSIONS
      8 November 1857--24 March 1940
      A powerful force in the introduction of new nursery stock
to California, Sessions was also important for her popularization
of horticulture. Following her graduation from the University of
California at Berkeley (PhB, 1811), she taught in primary and
secondary schools. Then in 1885 she opened a nursery and flower
shop in San Diego. Her lease, which required her to make annual
plantings in the area, resulted in the now famous Balboa Park.
      Sessions traveled extensively and worked closely with out-
standing botanists of the day to discover and import the most beautiful and drought-resistant varieties of plant materials. It is well
established that she was the first to introduce a large number of
what are today the most abundant and enjoyed of California trees
and plants. In some cases her collecting trips produced scientific
results, but it was in the beautification of her state that she ex-
celled. To this end she also worked with architects in designing
gardens for the greatest artistic and horticultural benefit. She
also conducted adult education classes in garden and landscape design.
      Sessions' contributions were recognized during her lifetime
in the form of tree plantings. More recently an elementary school

and a memorial park have been named in her honor by Pacific Beach, California, her home from 1923 to her death. (See also 305.)

1939

358. Anon. "Two Meyer Medals Awarded During 1939. Kate Sessions and David Fairchild cited for plant introduction achievements," Journal of Heredity, 30 (December), pp. 531-533. Photograph.

Presentation of the medal, "in recognition of her distinguished service to American horticulture." Review of her career with emphasis on the introduction of species new to the San Diego area. Sessions was the first woman to receive this medal.

1943

359. T. D. A. Cockerell. "Kate Olivia Sessions and California Floriculture," Bios, 14 (December), pp. 167-179. Photographs.

The story of Sessions' life as told largely through the reminiscences of friends and associates. Many of the articles about her projects are cited, especially in California Gardens.

1950

360. Payne, Theodore. "History of the Introduction of Three California Natives," El Aliso, 2 (15 March), pp. 109-114.

An interesting account, written by a nurseryman, concerning the origin and development of certain shrubs. Corrects a number of errors and misunderstandings about them.

1952

361. Moran, Reid. "Brandegee Itineraries," Madroño, 11 (July), pp. 258-259.

In the section entitled "Cape Region, September to November, 1902," Sessions is reported to have made a trip with Brandegee to the area of San José del Cabo.

1961

362. Padilla, Victoria. "Kate Olivia Sessions," in Southern California Gardens. An Illustrated History. Berkeley: University of California Press, pp. 167-173. Photograph.

A nicely written biographical sketch which stresses Sessions' unique contributions to the appreciation of native and imported

plants in California. Says that "The San Diego garden that does
not have a plant introduced or popularized by Miss Sessions is most
unusual." Tells of her collecting trips and scientific work as well
as her nursery business.

1971

363. Mathias, Mildred E. "Sessions, Kate Olivia," Notable American
     Women, (30), 2, pp. 262-263.
     Information on her early life and education, but most of the
article deals with her beautification efforts. List of the many species she made popular in the San Diego area.

364. ELIZABETH GERTRUDE KNIGHT BRITTON
     9 January 1858--25 February 1934
     Britton graduated from Hunter College (then Normal College)
in 1875 where she remained until 1885, first as a critic teacher in
the model school and later as assistant in natural science. Her
interest in botany was already well developed when she married
Nathaniel Lord Britton in 1885. She had joined the Torrey Botanical Club and had published her first scientific paper on albinism
in plants.
     Her husband, a geologist at Columbia College, had become
so interested in botany that he moved to that department the year
following their marriage and became known internationally in his
own right. The Brittons shared their field work completely, making
numerous expeditions to the West Indies where she added to the
knowledge of mosses through observation and collection. Her efforts to develop the moss collection at Columbia met with great success, and by various means, including the purchase of important
collections, it became a large and important research tool. During
the 1890's the Brittons suggested the establishment of the New
York Botanical Garden and they both successfully promoted its foundation. Nathaniel became the first director-in-chief in 1896, and
together they carried out those responsibilities for more than 33
years.
     Britton was a very productive research worker with 346 arti-
cles, many of them on bryology, the study of mosses. As editor
of the Bulletin of the Torrey Botanical Club, she gained a reputation for her sharply critical reviews of what she considered careless
scientific work. As she grew older Britton became an important
voice in the effort to educate the public on the preservation of our
natural wildflowers. Though some of her pure science colleagues
deplored this waste of her talent and energy, it marks an early
recognition of the need to safeguard one of our most beautiful
natural resources. Britton was one of the founders and the first
president of the Sullivant Moss Society, which later became the
American Bryological Society. (See also 4, 11.)

1934

365. Howe, Marshall A. "Elizabeth Gertrude Britton," <u>Journal
      of the New York Botanical Garden</u>, 35 (May), pp. 97-104.
      Photograph.
          A detailed coverage of her career which places special empha-
      sis on the role she and her husband played in the foundation of
      the New York Botanical Garden. It is followed by the text of a
      Memorial and Resolution from the Advisory Council of the Garden
      in appreciation of her service.

1935

366. Grout, A. J. "Elizabeth Gertrude (Knight) Britton," <u>The
      Bryologist</u>, 38 (January-February), pp. 1-3. Photograph.
          The study of mosses was Britton's specialty, and she was
      a central figure in the formation of this journal. The memorial
      was written by a former student. He makes no secret of the fact
      that she was outspoken, but her hasty remarks "could never ob-
      literate the memory of her kindness to me and my wife while I was
      her student."

367. Barnhart, John Hendley. "The Published Work of Elizabeth
      Gertrude Britton," <u>Bulletin of the Torrey Botanical Club</u>,
      62 (January), pp. 1-17.
          The author explains that an excellent biography has been
      published (365), which he does not wish to duplicate, but this
      article does contain some additional biographical detail. Essential
      for a study of Britton, it includes a nearly complete bibliography
      of her 346 signed publications, and they are indexed.

1936

368. Anon. "Britton, Elizabeth Gertrude Knight, <u>The National
      Cyclopaedia of American Biography</u> (2), 25, p. 89.
          Traces her career and gives a detailed account of her activ-
      ities in the development of research opportunities and means of pub-
      lication for the community of botanists in New York.

1940

369. Anon. "Mrs. Britton Honored in Dedication of Plaque by New
      York Bird and Tree Club in Wild Flower Garden," <u>Journal
      of the New York Botanical Garden</u>, 41 (June), pp. 129-137.
          Describes the all-day program in honor of Britton including
      the dedication of the plaque and beginning of a fund to help pro-
      tect wild flowers.

370. Gager, C. Stuart. "Elizabeth G. Britton and the Movement for
      the Preservation of Native American Wild Flowers," Journal
      of The New York Botanical Garden, 41 (June), pp. 137-142.
      Aside from her research in the mosses, Britton was interested
in the environment, especially with regard to protecting wildflowers
from extinction. This was the natural result of the Brittons' work
with the New York Botanical Garden in which she was an active
participant. Her early recognition of the importance of ecology
brought her credit, but also the complaint that she should be using
her time more productively. Article outlines her endeavors to promote ecological awareness.

371. Barnhart, John Hendley. "Elizabeth Gertrude Knight Britton
      as a Scientist," Journal of The New York Botanical Garden,
      41 (June), pp. 142-143.
      While Britton was active in the fight for the protection of
the natural beauty represented by wildflowers, she did not give
up her work in science. A brief description of some of her interests.

                                1961

372. Humphrey, Harry Baker. "Elizabeth Gertrude Knight Britton.
      1858-1934," in Makers of North American Botany. New York:
      Ronald, pp. 38-39.
      A reasonably complete sketch of her major contributions.
Limited bibliography of articles about her.

                                1971

373. Steere, William Campbell. "Britton, Elizabeth Gertrude
      Knight," Notable American Women (30), 1, pp. 243-244.
      Shows her work as an independent person, not as Mrs.
Nathaniel Britton. Good treatment of the criticism she received
for her work in wild flower preservation. Bibliography.

                                1979

374. Anon. "Britton, Elizabeth Gertrude Knight," Biographical
      Dictionary of American Science (40), pp. 41-42.
      In the eight lines she received, there is nothing one cannot
find in other biographical sources.

375. HARRIET LATHROP MERROW
      8 September 1858--unknown
      Merrow studied at Wellesley College (BS, 1886; AM, 1893)

and at the University of Michigan (1893-1894). She taught at the
Rhode Island College of Agriculture and Mechanical Arts where she
became especially interested in parasitic fungi. Following her retirement in 1920 she traveled in Europe and to Jamaica where she
spent a month working at the tropical laboratory at Cinchona. In
1925 she reported to her class reunion that she was still an active
member of the Botanical Society of America. She was probably still
a member of the Society for Plant Morphology and Physiology.

376. Merrow is cited in American Men of Science, 1906-1921.
        We are indebted to Wilma R. Slaight, Archivist at Wellesley
College, for her assistance.

377. ALICE EASTWOOD
        19 January 1859--30 October 1953
        Eastwood was one of a group of important botanists working
in California around the turn of the century. Before moving still
further west she made important collections and discoveries in the
Colorado mountains. This work was published at her own expense
as A Popular Flora of Denver, Colorado in 1893.
        She was invited to join Katharine Brandegee at the California
Academy of Sciences and later succeeded her as curator of the herbarium, in which position she remained for the rest of her life.
She increased the Academy's collection by over 340,000 specimens
in spite of the 1906 San Francisco earthquake and fire. Eastwood
deserves the bulk of the credit for saving a valuable collection from
complete ruin by that disaster. She was also responsible for the
redevelopment of the Academy's important botanical library.
        In addition to acting as editor to various journals at different
times, Eastwood founded and edited Leaflets of Western Botany,
which represented an important outlet for the active research then
taking place in the western United States. Her articles, which num-
bered over 300, include both scientific reports and efforts to make
botany more widely appreciated. She was a leader in the movement
to promote public awareness of the importance of saving native species. Eastwood was widely recognized as a distinguished scholar by
her contemporaries. She was honorary president of the Seventh
International Botanical Congress (Stockholm, 1950) and was starred
in every edition of American Men of Science, an indication that her
peers recognized her as one of the 1,000 most important scientists.
(See also 4, 305.)

1905

378. Wallace, Alfred Russel. My Life. A Record of Events and
        Opinions. London: Chapman & Hall, pp. 180-184.
        A brief description of the trip he took with Eastwood to
Gray's Peak in July 1887.

1949

379. Abrams, Leroy. "Alice Eastwood--Western Botanist," *Pacific Discovery*, 2 (January-February), pp. 14-17. Photographs.
      The author, who met Eastwood while he was a student at Stanford, has written an article which, though popular in tone, represents a most important tribute to a nonacademic. In the author's words, "she has interested more people in plants and plant life than has any other person in California or the West." Especially striking photographs of Eastwood at a young and a mature age.

380. Valjean, Nelson. "Alice Eastwood, Hardy Perennial," *Nature Magazine*, 42 (October), pp. 361-362. Photographs.
      Now that Eastwood is 90 she takes a taxi the five miles to work each day and has a short nap after lunch. There are some wonderful quotations and a great deal of descriptive material on the 1906 San Francisco fire.

1953

381. Wilson, Carol Green. "The Eastwood Era at the California Academy of Science," *Leaflets of Western Botany*, (28 August), pp. 58-64.
      A detailed and very readable presentation of Eastwood's enormous influence on the botanical collection at the California Academy. Especially good treatment of her role in saving the most essential items in the earthquake.

382. Wilson, Carol Green. "A Partial Gazetteer and Chronology of Alice Eastwood's Botanical Explorations," *Leaflets of Western Botany*, (28 August), pp. 65 ff.
      From the files of the California Academy of Science and Eastwood's notebooks Wilson has assembled a most valuable view of the extensive collecting trips. This material is vital to any attempt to understand Eastwood's importance.

383. Reitter, Victor, Jr. "Horticulture and the California Academy of Science," *Leaflets of Western Botany*, (28 August), pp. 79-84.
      Eastwood was to a large extent the Academy in botany, and no article with this title could fail to be about her contribution. Reitter, a nurseryman, is especially interested in her role in making people aware of the importance of botanical knowledge to the complete enjoyment of plants. He reviews her activities and expresses confidence that they are "beginning to bear fruit."

384. Sexton, Veronica J. "Books and Botany," Leaflets of Western
      Botany, (28 August), pp. 85 ff.
      Deals well with Eastwood's work in restoring the library of
the California Academy of Science after the 1906 fire.

385. Anon. "Alice Eastwood, Noted Botanist, 94," The New York
      Times, 103 (31 October), p. 17.
      Recounts her career and especially her many honors.

1954

386. Howell, John Thomas. "Alice Eastwood. 1859-1953," Taxon,
      3 (May), pp. 98-100. Photograph.
      An obituary by her friend and colleague. Rather complete
review of her career with a reference to her published bibliography.

387. Howell, John Thomas. "Memorials and Correspondence. Alice
      Eastwood, 1859-1953," Sierra Club Bulletin, 39 (No. 6), pp.
      78-80.
      With its emphasis on her interest in the out-of-doors and
her support of the principles of the Sierra Club, this obituary represents a nice complement to the others by Howell (386, 388).

388. Howell, John Thomas. "I Remember, When I Think ...,"
      Leaflets of Western Botany, 7 (26 August), pp. 153-164.
      Highly personal reminiscence of Eastwood's long-time friend
and collaborator. Anecdotes presented here are never to be found
again. Especially strong on her delight in disregarding small social
conventions.

389. Dakin, Susanna Bryant. The Perennial Adventure. A tribute
      to Alice Eastwood. 1859-1953. San Francisco: California
      Academy of Sciences, 48 pp. Photograph.
      An extended tribute drawn from the full-length biography
by Wilson (390). The essay is well written and informative, and
this work is especially important because it contains such memora-
bilia as her bookplate, a very early photograph, the text of her
high school valedictory, and a reprint of one of her early papers.

1955

390. Wilson, Carol Green. Alice Eastwood's Wonderland: The ad-
      ventures of a botanist. San Francisco: California Academy
      of Sciences, 222 pp.
      A biography in nontechnical language, written by a well-
informed admirer. Many warm, personal stories gathered by the
author through extensive interviews with Eastwood during the last
year of her life. This first-person account is richly supplemented

by material from Eastwood's partially completed <u>Memoirs</u>. Includes
a brief foreword by the director of the California Academy of Sciences.

1957

391. Cantelow, Ella Dales, and Herbert Clair Cantelow. "Biographi-
      cal Notes on Persons in Whose Honor Alice Eastwood Named
      Native Plants," <u>Leaflets of Western Botany</u>, 8 (January), pp.
      83 ff.
      A most unusual kind of bibliography, but one which is quite
correct for Eastwood, who delighted in saying, "I count my age
by friends, not years--and I am rich in friends."

1958

392. Kearney, Thomas H. "Botanists I Have Known," <u>Leaflets
      of Western Botany</u>, 8 (November), pp. 275-280.
      Published after the author's death from notes he made for
a talk some years earlier. Highly personal views of a number of
famous botanists. Includes a mention of Eastwood's invitation to
him to join the Academy after he retired and moved to California.

1962

393. Hollingsworth, Buckner. "Alice Eastwood. 1859-1953.
      Botanist--Scholar--Adventurer," in <u>Her Garden Was Her De-
      light</u>. New York: Macmillan, pp. 126-138.
      A full account of the great California botanist's life and ac-
complishments. Eastwood appears as a modern woman of great physical and intellectual strength. Without a college degree of any kind,
she was acknowledged as an international authority on the botany
of the western United States. The struggles of her childhood and
the productivity of her professional life are described in detail as
are the dangers she braved seeking and classifying the variety
of plants found in the western mountains.

1971

394. Ewan, Joseph. "Eastwood, Alice," <u>Notable American Women</u>,
      (30), 1, pp. 216-217.
      Very readable account of an extraordinary career so difficult
to describe in a few words. Good on her breadth of interest and
activity. Bibliography is outstanding in coverage but weak in detail.

395. FLORENCE MAY LYON NORTON
      6 March 1860--unknown
      Lyon taught in various high schools in Michigan between stud-
ies at the University of Michigan (1879-1882 and 1886-1887). She
then enrolled at the University of Chicago where she took both undergraduate and graduate degrees (SB, 1897; PhD, 1901). Following a year as instructor in botany at Smith College she returned
to Chicago as an associate in botany. Her scholarly interests were
with seed plants and morphology. She married Strong Vincent Norton sometime prior to 1921 and she left Chicago in 1906.

396. Norton is cited in American Men of Science, 1906-1921.
      We are indebted to Daniel Meyer, Assistant Archivist, and
his collaborator Richard Popp, of the University of Chicago for
their assistance.

397. CARRIE MATILDA DERICK
      1862--10 November 1941
      Born in Quebec, Canada, and educated at McGill University
(AB, 1890; AM, 1896), Derick became the first woman to be a member of the staff at McGill. She conducted research in plant morphology, physiology, and genetics at Woods Hole and the Universities of London and Bonn. Her professional career extended from
her first appointment as demonstrator in botany (1891) to professor emerita (1929).
      Derick had research interests in the nuclear changes in grow-
ing seeds and the differences observed between resting and active
cells. In addition to her scholarly work she was an active feminist
and for many years was the president of the Montreal Suffrage Association.

1941

398. Anon. "Obituary. Dr. Carrie M. Derick," The New York
      Times, 91 (11 November), p. 23.
      Notice citing her feminist activities. Says she was the first
woman appointed at McGill.

399. ANNA MURRAY VAIL
      7 January 1863--unknown
      Vail studied botany privately, mostly in Europe. She be-
came the librarian of the New York Botanical Garden and associate
editor of the Bulletin of the Torrey Botanical Club. Her chief interest was in taxonomy.

400. Vail is cited in American Men of Science, 1906-1921.

401. MARGARET CLAY FERGUSON
      20 August 1863--28 August 1951
      While a special student at Wellesley College (1888-1891),
Ferguson so impressed Susan Hallowell, professor and head of the
department, that she was asked to return as an instructor in 1893
in spite of having no academic degree. In 1896 she went to Cornell University (BS, 1899; PhD, 1901) where her thesis set the
standard for future research in the life history of plants.
      From 1901 until her formal retirement in 1932 Ferguson served
Wellesley as teacher and administrator. Under her direction the
department became a leading undergraduate center for plant sciences. In addition to her scholarly contributions she made an important educational one by emphasizing the necessity of studying
other sciences, especially chemistry, and their relationship to botany. She was also responsible for introducing greenhouse experi-
mentation as an integral part of undergraduate study. Her design
of a building was implemented by Wellesley and named for her in
honor of her work.
      In spite of the heavy demands of teaching and administra-
tion she continued to pursue an active research program even six
years after her retirement. Following her early studies of func-
tional morphology and cytology of the native pine she began to make
important genetic studies. Using the genus Petunia she first demonstrated its usefulness in the study of higher plant genetics. Her
work which helped to revise the taxonomy of the varieties, showed
that there is no Mendelian inheritance for flower color or pattern
in these plants. The importance of this work was recognized when
she became the first woman president of the Botanical Society of
America (1929) and a fellow of the New York Academy of Sciences
(1943).

                                1932

402. Hart, Sophie Chantal. "Margaret Clay Ferguson," The Wel-
      lesley Magazine, (June), pp. 408-410. Photograph.
      Written by a former student on the occasion of Ferguson's
formal retirement from Wellesley. Makes a major point of her vitality, both physical and intellectual.

                                1947

403. Creighton, Harriet B. "The Margaret C. Ferguson Green-
      houses," The Wellesley Magazine (February), pp. 172-173.
      Photograph.
      Written by the chairman of the department of botany at
Wellesley College, the article goes well beyond its limited title and
deals extensively with Ferguson's career in research and teaching.

1952

404. Creighton, Harriet B. "Margaret Clay Ferguson," Wellesley
      Alumnae Magazine (January), p. 106.
      This obituary in fact deals in a thoughtful, if brief, fashion
with the entire history of botany at Wellesley. This is natural since
Ferguson's influence was so great over a period of more than 30
years. The outline for a fine biography.

1971

405. Hirsch, Ann M., and Lisa J. Marroni. "Ferguson, Margaret
      Clay," Notable American Women (30), 1, pp. 229-230.
      A well-written study of Ferguson which gives full attention
to her several different research interests as well as her important
contributions to teaching.

406. JULIA WARNER SNOW
      30 August 1863--24 October 1927
      Snow cooperated with the United States Fish Commission in
their biological survey of the Great Lakes by studying plankton
and microscopic forms of freshwater algae. She was educated at
Cornell University (BS, 1888; MS, 1889) and the University of Zurich (PhD, 1893). After teaching at various schools and colleges
she joined the faculty of Smith College. She was promoted to associate professor of botany in 1906. She remained an active member of the faculty until her death. Following her doctoral work
at Zurich she made her way from Constantinople to Russia alone,
an unheard of undertaking for a woman in the 1890's. Her friends
knew her as a rather timid person, but at the same time she continued her worldwide travels. She was especially fond of the Orient
and became quite an authority on the art and architecture of China
and India. (See also 4.)

1927

407. Anon. "Julia W. Snow: In Memoriam," Smith Alumnae Quar-
      terly (November).
      The text of a tribute given by Mrs. Bernard in chapel some-
time after Snow's death on 24 October. Reviews her education and
pays particular attention to her travels.

408. Anon. "Obituaries. Julia W. Snow '88," Alumnae News (8
      December).
      Brief review of Snow's education and service at Smith. Makes
a point of her extraordinary trip to Russia.

409.   Anon.   "Prof. Julia Warner Snow of Smith College Is Dead"
        and "Dean Pays Tribute to Prof. J. W. Snow," unidentified
        newspaper clippings in the Smith College Archives.
        Obituary tributes which review Snow's education, travels
and contribution to Smith.
        We are indebted to Eleanor M. Lewis, Research Associate at
Smith College, and Kathleen Jacklin, Archivist at Cornell University, for most of this information about Snow.

410.   ISABEL SEYMOUR SMITH
        22 October 1864--19 January 1948
        While studying at Oberlin College (AB, 1901) and the Uni-
versity of Chicago (SM, 1905), Smith taught high school in Fre-
mont (Ohio) and botany at Oberlin.   In 1903 she joined the faculty
of Illinois College as an instructor and rose to the rank of full professor in 1909.   In 1927 she retired and returned to Oberlin where
she served as curator of the herbarium and the botanical laboratory.
She was a member of the Illinois Academy of Science and served
as its vice-president in 1919.   Her botanical interests centered on
the native trees of her home state.

411.   Smith is cited in American Men of Science, 1906.
        We are indebted to Ray English, Head Reference Librarian
at Oberlin College, for his assistance.

412.   IDA AUGUSTA KELLER
        11 June 1866--unknown
        A specialist in plant physiology, Keller received her educa-
tion at the Universities of Pennsylvania (1884-1886) and Zurich (PhD,
1890).   After a year of further study at the University of Leipzig
she taught botany at Bryn Mawr College as she had prior to her
graduate study.   In 1893 Keller joined the faculty of the Philadelphia High School for Girls where she became head of the Departments of Chemistry and Botany.   In addition to a number of scientific articles published mostly in the Proceedings of the Academy
of Natural Sciences, she was the coauthor of the Handbook of the
Flora of Philadelphia and Vicinity.   She was an active member of
a number of professional societies and held elective offices.
        We are indebted to Lucy Fisher West, Archivist at Bryn Mawr
College, and Francis James Dallett, Archivist at the University of
Pennsylvania, for their assistance.

413.   JOSEPHINE ELIZABETH TILDEN
        24 March 1869--15 May 1957
        After completing her undergraduate education at the Univer-

sity of Minnesota (BS, 1895), Tilden was appointed to an assistantship in botany. She received her MS degree in 1897 and rose through
the academic ranks to professor in 1910, the rank at which she
retired in 1937.

During her career at Minnesota she conducted research in
phycology and published a number of important works on algae.
At the time of her death her first book, Minnesota Algae, published in 1910, was still a widely used technical reference work.
As early as 1895 she began a bibliography of published work on
algae which was widely distributed. Her final book, The Algae
and Their Life Relations, was published in 1935 and 1937 and represents the first American effort to summarize the known characteristics of these important marine and freshwater plants. She played
an important role in the development of standard methods of drawing algae for publication.

Her colleagues recalled her as being "a considerate teacher
who invariably communicated much of her great personal enthusiasm
for her subject" to generations of students. One rare example of
her dedication is found in the 1934-1935 expedition when she led
ten graduate students during an entire academic year traveling from
the Red Sea to Australia and San Francisco collecting algae. She
was honored as a delegate to the First Pan-Pacific Scientific Congress in Honolulu (1920) and to similar Congresses in Melbourne
and Sidney (1923) and Tokyo (1926).

1957-1958

414. Anon. "Josephine Elizabeth Tilden. 1869-1957," University
of Minnesota Senate Minutes, pp. 33-34.

A memorial, introduced and adopted as a resolution by the
Faculty Senate. Gives excellent biographical details and portrays
a genuine feeling of admiration by her colleagues.

We are indebted to Carol Christensen and Lois G. Hendrick-
son, Library Assistants in University Archives of the University
of Minnesota, for their assistance.

415. MARY AGNES MEARA CHASE
20 April 1869--24 September 1963

Chase has no academic degrees nor formal training of any
kind, yet, as a result of her intelligence, curiosity, and energy
she made major contributions to the systematic study of grasses
in the western hemisphere. She and her husband worked together,
during their short but happy marriage, on the School Herald. After his untimely death she held a variety of jobs in an effort to
repay their debts, and during those hard times she acquired a
deep interest in botany. She learned wherever and from whom-
ever she could and began to display marked talent in the description and drawing of grasses.

For over 60 years Chase served the United States Department of Agriculture in the Division of Forage Plants. In 1936 she
became principal scientist in charge of systematic agrostology and
senior botanist. When she made her last collecting trip in 1940
over 12,200 plants, mostly grasses, had been added to the National Herbarium. These specimens included many completely new
grasses among the 4,500 she brought from Brazil and made the herbarium a unique research tool. She was the author of 70 research
publications and wrote the popular First Book of Grasses in 1922.

Chase was well known for her activities in various reform
movements including women's rights, prohibition, and socialism.
At one time she was jailed and forcibly fed. She received many
honors, including a certificate of merit from the Botanical Society
of America, a medal for service from Brazil, and an honorary DSc
from the University of Illinois. The Smithsonian Institution made
her its eighth honorary fellow, and she was unanimously elected
a fellow of the Linnaean Society.

1956

416.   Hillenbrand, Liz. "87-Year-Old Grass Expert Still Happy
       with Subject," The Washington Post and Times Herald, 79
       (30 April), p. 7. Photograph.
       After being retired for 17 years Chase still works every
day. An extensive personal interview in which she says she would
rather talk about grass than herself. "Grass is much more interesting. If it were not for grass the world never would have been
civilized."

1958

417.   Furman, Bess. "Grass Is Her Liferoot," The New York Times,
       107 (12 June), p. 37. Photograph.
       An excellent biographical sketch on the occasion of Chase's
honorary DSc from the University of Illinois. Tells the wonderful
story of her first interest in grass when her grandmother told her
that grass didn't have flowers.

1959

418.   Fosberg, F. R., and J. R. Swallen. "Agnes Chase," Taxon,
       8 (June), pp. 145-151. Photograph.
       A biographical sketch follows a short tribute to Chase on the
occasion of her 90th birthday. Both of these praise her exceptional work in the classification of grasses and her assistance to
younger workers. Includes a complete bibliography of her publications.

419. Carmichael, Leonard. "Foreword," in First Book of Grasses, by Agnes Chase. 3rd edition. Washington, D.C.: Smithsonian Institution, pp. v-ix.
A biographical sketch by the Secretary of the Smithsonian in the newest edition of Chase's best-known book. Says it will be widely read by young students and others generally interested in the botany of grasses. Praises her long and valuable service to the Smithsonian and American botany.

1963

420. Anon. "Mrs. Agnes Chase, Botanist Is Dead," The New York Times 113 (26 September), p. 35. Photograph.
Calls her "Dean of experts in the study of grasses." She claims that her career began when her grandmother told her that grass doesn't have flowers and she insisted it does. Chase was active in reform movements and always found time to help sincere students.

1971

421. Stieber, Michael T. "Chase, Mary Agnes," Notable American Women, 1, pp. 146-148.
In addition to a full review of her scientific career Stieber pays unusual attention to her personal life and political views. A very helpful and interesting article.

1978

422. Anon. [Portrait of Chase], Taxon, 27, pp. 373-374.
Fairly extensive footnote giving an outline of her career and most significant publications.

1979

423. Stieber, Michael T. "Manuscripts Produced and/or Annotated by Agnes Chase Pertinent to Grass Collections at the Smithsonian Institution," Huntia, 3, pp. 117-125.
The author has done a careful bit of scholarship on the useful research tools produced by Chase following her trips to Europe. The breadth of her own research is quite clear and the Index of Botanists compiled by Stieber indicates the range of her interests and knowledge of her subject.

424. YNES ENRIQUETTA JULIETTA MEXIA
24 May 1870--12 July 1938

Mexia showed ability in natural science at the University of California where she studied from time to time, but never completed a degree. She was happiest out in the field, removed from civilization, and the numerous specimens she collected, dried, and described were a major contribution to the clarification of earlier and incomplete records.

On each of her trips to remote regions of Mexico, Brazil, Peru, Bolivia, Argentina, and Chile she studied the people and animals in addition to the flora. Her contribution must also include the basic information she obtained in these fields of science. Still, it was the botanical results that make the most impressive record. For example, in 1927 she returned from western Mexico with 1,600 items, in sets of 15 specimens, including a new genus and approximately 50 new species. Again, in 1932 she obtained 3,200 items in sets of about 20 specimens.

The most distinguished botanists of the day were vocal in their praise of her skill as well as her energy. Several plants were named for her, including the genus Mexianthus mexicanus, which Harvard's Benjamin L. Robinson selected in the hope that "its cheerfully alliterative appellation will be easily remembered and will keep in mind your noteworthy service in exploration." After her Brazilian expedition of 1932 Edwin B. Copeland said the 300 ferns included in the 3,200 samples mentioned earlier were such "as we rarely see from the tropics, including in every specimen a practically complete representation of the features of the plant." In reference to that same trip Joseph Grinnell, a noted ornithologist, wrote, "My own eyes grew big as I looked at the birds she had collected."

1930

425. Spencer, Marjorie. "Botanical Quests of a Woman in Latin America. Mrs. Ynes Mexia Takes to the Field, in Brazil," Pan American Magazine (April), pp. 389-391. Photograph.

A popular article, but all the same an exciting, readable account of her adventures and the importance of her contributions to science. A not too subtle plea for women to take an interest in science.

1932

426. Anon. "Notes and News. Mrs. Ynes Mexia," Madroño, 2 (October), p. 77.

A brief, but useful, report of her rather extensive collecting trip up the Amazon and over the Andes. Notice of her lectures on the trip.

1935

427. Bracelin, Mrs. H. P. "Itinerary of Ynes Mexia in South America," Madroño, 3 (October), pp. 174-176.
A description and a detailed list of her points of collection and the collection numbers for an expedition to Brazil and Peru in the period 1929-1932. Also includes a list of the institutions where sets of the collections may be seen.

1937

428. Anon. "U.C. Scientist Back from Trip into South America for Plants," The San Francisco News (6 March), p. 3. Photograph.
Brief but dramatic account of her latest jungle foray. Caption on photographs is interesting: "Woman Botanist Longs for 'Quiet Jungle.'"

1938

429. Bracelin, Mrs. H. P. "Ynes Mexia," Madroño, 4 (October), pp. 273-275. Photograph.
An obituary with details of her ancestry, scientific career, and specific notes on her expeditions and publications.

430. Bracelin, N. Floy. "Ynes Mexia," Science, 88 (23 December), p. 586.
Brief note as an obituary with a partial list of her expeditions and numbers of specimens. Notes that several species and one genus were named for her.

1941

431. Goodspeed, T. Harper. Plant Hunters in the Andes. New York: Farrar and Rinehart, pp. 13, 153.
Not a lengthy treatment, but interesting in that it shows the nature of some of her travels and the people with whom she was associated. The author gives her special praise for the confidence she had won from the natives.

1957

432. Anon. "Biographical Notes. Mexia, Ynes," Leaflets of Western Botany, 8 (January), pp. 95-96.
Brief and belated obituary which contributes little.

<u>1971</u>

433. Ewan, Joseph. "Mexia, Ynes Enriquetta Julietta," <u>Notable</u>
      <u>American Women</u> (30), 2, pp. 533-534.
      Very well-written account of Mexia's life and career. This
article makes exciting reading and presents all of the facts without being stuffy. Good bibliography.

434. EMMA LUCY BRAUN
      19 April 1889--5 March 1971
      Braun must be ranked as one of the pioneer ecologists in
addition to her contributions to the taxonomy of the vascular plants.
All of her collegiate education was at the University of Cincinnati
(AB, 1910; AM, 1912; PhD, 1914) where she taught from 1910 until
1948. Her early retirement provided the freedom for field research
which produced important contributions for the rest of her life.
In all she wrote approximately 180 articles and four books. At the
time ecology was just coming to be recognized as a scientific discipline, and Braun played a major part in that very modern innovation.
      In several areas she provided the foundation for future work.
For example, 25 years of field study involving over 65,000 miles
of travel resulted in <u>Deciduous Forests of Eastern North America</u>.
Modern prediction of future ecological change of hardwood forests
is based on this seminal publication. In addition to this and other
important publications Braun organized the Ohio Flora Committee
within the Ohio Academy of Science. For this and other efforts
to bring together the scholar and the public she became the first
woman president of that society and the Ecological Society of
America.

<u>1971</u>

435. Anon. "Necrology. E(mma) Lucy Braun," <u>The Ohio Journal</u>
      <u>of Science</u>, 71 (July), pp. 247-248.
      A brief obituary with a good representation of the standard
facts of career, accomplishments and honors.

<u>1973</u>

436. Stuckey, Ronald L. "E. Lucy Braun (1889-1971), Outstand-
      ing Botanist and Conservationist: A Biographical Sketch,
      with Bibliography," <u>The Michigan Botanist</u>, 12 (March), pp.
      83-106. Photographs.
      An impressive study of Braun's career. This is not really
a sketch at all, but the beginning of a full biography. There are
extensive quotations from reviews of her works and citations when

she received honors. The nature and amount of her research support and her research associates are discussed. This piece is an
example that might well be followed in the future.

1978

437. Peskin, Perry K. "A Walk Through Lucy Braun's Prairie,"
      The Explorer, 20, pp. 15-21. Photographs.
      A more popular account of Braun's career with emphasis on
her concern for the preservation of the natural beauty and vitality of the wilderness. An important article seeking to reach those
who will not read the more detailed, scientific accounts.

1980

438. Stuckey, Ronald L. "Braun, Emma Lucy," Notable American
      Women (30), 4, pp. 102-103.
      Using his superb earlier article (436), Stuckey manages to
abridge the piece without losing the essence of the subject. Good
detail is presented without becoming dry. The bibliography could
stand more detail.

GENERAL (See also 292, 821, 1168, 1187)

1975

439. Houlihan, Sherida, and John H. Wotiz. "Women in Chemistry Before 1900," Journal of Chemical Education, 52 (June), pp. 362-364.
    Points out that the first two known chemists were female perfumers in Mesopotamia in approximately 2000 B.C. Notes the outstanding women chemists in the eighteenth and nineteenth centuries and mentions growing opportunities for women chemists in education. Touches briefly on male attitudes.

1976

440. Miles, Wyndham D., editor. American Chemists and Chemical Engineers. Washington, D.C.: American Chemical Society, 544 pp.
    A series of biographical sketches similar to those being presented here, but with much more limited and unannotated bibliography.

441. Roscher, Nina Matheny. "Women Chemists," Chemtech, 6 (December), pp. 738-743. Photographs.
    Discusses the changes observed in career patterns of women who have received the Garvan Medal of the American Chemical Society. There is a limited amount of biographical information, but the women and their careers are related to changing attitudes toward women in chemistry.

442. RACHEL LITTLER BODLEY
    7 December 1831--15 June 1888
    As a young collegian at the Wesleyan Female College in Cincinnati (diploma, 1849) and later as a member of its faculty (1849-1860), Bodley had special interest in both chemistry and botany. From 1860 to 1862 she studied at the Polytechnic College in Philadelphia.
    Her first original scientific work was in botany, and she collected and classified a large plant collection in her three years at the Cincinnati Female Seminary. At the Philadelphia Female (later

Women's) Medical College in 1865 she continued her interest in botany
in spite of holding the first chair of chemistry. An active program
of summer trips greatly enhanced her collection, especially of sea
plants. These activities, along with many special lectures, resulted
in Bodley's election to the Academy of Natural Sciences of Philadelphia in 1871 and the New York Academy of Sciences in 1876.

A botanist first, perhaps, but her interest and activity in
chemistry were equally notable. She gave six invited lectures on
"Household Chemistry" at the Franklin Institute. It was her suggestion that American chemists honor the centennial of Joseph Priest-
ley's discovery of oxygen by meeting at his American home in North-
umberland, Pennsylvania, in 1874. The American Chemical Society,
of which she was a charter member and vice-president, was founded
as a direct result of that meeting.

She became dean of the Woman's Medical College in 1874 and
served for 14 years. During her tenure the College grew in stature, and many of its graduates became successful physicians. She
made the first carefully documented study of women who combined
productive careers with marriage. In 1879 the College presented
her an MD in recognition of her significant influence. (See also
40, 46.)

1873

*443. American Chemist, 4, p. 5 (1873-1875).

1888

444. Bolton, Sarah K. "Rachel Littler Bodley," in Successful
      Women. Boston: D. Lothrop, ch. 8, pp. 149-174. Picture.
      Reprinted: Plainview, New York: Books for Libraries Press,
      1974.
      Presents much biographical information without an excess of
the high moral tone typical of the late nineteenth-century biographer.

445. Anon. "In Memoriam," The Woman's Journal, 19 (23 June),
      p. 199.
      A rather long biographical sketch, taken from the Philadel-
phia Ledger, constitutes this obituary. Provides useful contemporary views as well as facts about her. A strong tone reflects her
fight for women's rights.

1949

446. Alsop, Gulielma Fell. "Rachel Bodley. 1831-1888," Journal
      of the American Medical Women's Association, 4 (December),
      pp. 534-536. Photograph.
      A detailed biographical sketch which cites her as a chemist-

scientist and underlines her work with the Women's Medical College.

447.   Alsop, Gulielma Fell.   "Bodley, Rachel Littler," Notable
       American Women (30), 1, pp. 186-187.
       Excellent picture of the woman with strong emphasis on her
varie: interests and administrative work.   Little is said about her
scientific interests and accomplishments.

1976

448.   Miles, Wyndham D.   "Rachel L. Bodley.   1831-1888," Ameri-
       can Chemists and Chemical Engineers, (440), p. 38.
       A sketch of her academic career with a special note of her
early role in the American Chemical Society.   A few references are
given.

1978

449.   Dirkes, M. Ann.   "Bodley, Rachel Littler," Biographical Dic-
       tionary of American Educators (38), 1, p. 145.
       A brief but well-balanced account of Bodley's career.   Limited
references are given.

1979

450.   Anon.   "Bodley, Rachel Littler," Biographical Dictionary of
       American Science (40), pp. 33.
       An outline of her career which gives a great deal of informa-
tion in a short space.   A useful bibliography.

1980

451.   Levin, Beatrice S.   Women and Medicine (46), p. 149.
       Describes Bodley's survey of the careers of graduates of the
Woman's Medical College of Pennsylvania in 1881.

452.   RACHEL LLOYD
       1839--7 May 1900
       One of the first women to become a professional chemist,
Lloyd made important contributions as a teacher and published several substantial papers on the synthesis of acrylic acid derivatives.

Her most important contribution was to the development of the sugar
beet industry in the United States. As an assistant chemist at the
Nebraska Agricultural Experimental Station, she directed elaborate
series of systematic experiments which ultimately demonstrated that
with careful farming the surgar beet could be a profitable crop in
any part of the State. In 1977 Nebraska ranked eighth in the nation, producing over one million tons of sugar valued at almost
thirty-seven million dollars.

In addition to these activities Lloyd was also a full-time member of the faculty at the University of Nebraska. She taught a
very heavy load of lecture and laboratory courses and was promoted
to full professor in 1888. She was remembered by her students
as a great teacher, advisor, and counselor.

Lloyd studied at private schools and the Harvard Summer
School, but apparently took no undergraduate degree. She earned
a PhD from the University of Zurich in 1886. Her dissertation
concerned the high temperature chemistry of aromatic compounds,
and she may be the first American woman to have earned a doctorate in chemistry.

1969

453. Manley, Robert N. Centennial History of the University of
      Nebraska, 1869-1969. Lincoln, Nebraska: University of Ne-
      braska Press, pp. 111, 130, 140.

Manley says, "a brilliant woman professor, Rachel Lloyd, who
joined the faculty in 1888, presided over the Chemical Laboratory."
Discusses her work with the sugar beet and pays special attention
to the shameful way the university treated her, and men as well,
in the matter of retirement salary. A very nicely written, modern, university history.

1982

454. Tarbell, Ann T., and D. Stanley Tarbell. "Dr. Rachel Lloyd
      (1839-1900): American Chemist," Journal of Chemical Education,
      59 (September), pp. 743-744.

Lloyd was discovered by the Tarbells while they were writing a history of organic chemistry in the United States. A recognition of the importance of this totally forgotten chemist. Fully
documented and smoothly written.

455. Peterson, Glenda. "Rachel Lloyd Made Beet Crop Success,"
      Sunday Journal and Star [Lincoln, Nebraska] (24 October).

Detailed account of Lloyd and her contributions to Nebraska.
Recognizes the importance of the work done by the Tarbells (454).
Especially strong on the high regard her colleagues had for her
during her lifetime. Suggestion that others took credit for her
work deserves study.

We are indebted to Joseph Svoboda, University of Nebraska Archivist, for this article and other assistance.

456. ELLEN HENRIETTA SWALLOW RICHARDS
      3 December 1842--30 March 1911
      An early graduate of Vassar College (AB, 1870), she was the first woman to take a degree at the Massachusetts Institute of Technology (BS, 1873); this same year she received an MA from Vassar. Affiliated with MIT until her death, Richards conducted pioneering studies in several fields. It is not an overstatement to claim that she was a major figure in the early development of sanitary chemistry, ecology, and home economics. She assisted her husband, the founder of MIT's metallurgical and mining engineering laboratories, and was the first woman elected to the American Institute of Mining and Metallurgical Engineers. In his biography her husband is quoted as saying that her work didn't earn the doctorate she desired because "the heads of the department did not wish a woman to receive the first DS in chemistry."
      Though Ellen Richards was first of all a scientist, her role in the development of educational and career opportunities for women is significant and must be recognized. She represents the approach of accepting the established female role without protest and at the same time doing work of such obvious merit that even the least generous observer must praise it and recognize its creator. Smith College awarded her an honorary ScD in 1910. (See also 4, 8, 9, 23, 33, 35, 36, 41, 767, 768.)

1897

457. Anon. "Richards, Ellen Henrietta (Swallow)," The National Cyclopaedia of American Biography (2), 7, p. 343.
      Short presentation of her life and career up to this time. Rather general on her scientific contributions.

1911

458. Anon. "Mrs. Ellen H. Richards Dead," The New York Times, 60 (31 March), p. 11.
      A brief note on her education and long (40 years) service at MIT. Says that she was president of the Home Economics Association and that her influence in developing scientific studies among women was large.

459. Anon. [Remarks on her death], Science, 33 (7 April), pp. 523, 686.
      Says that she was well known for her contributions to sanitary engineering and requests that materials be sent to Hunt who is writing a biography (468).

460. Talbot, H. P. "Mrs. Ellen H. Richards. 1842-March 13,
      1911," The Journal of Industrial and Engineering Chemistry,
      3 (May), pp. 352-353.
      Reviews her education and the many fields she worked in
during her lifetime. Notes her work on behalf of women and families of limited means. Says that she and her husband often enter-
tained students in their home.

461. Howe, Elizabeth M. "Ellen H. Richards," Vassar Miscellany
      (May), pp. 575-580.
      A very nicely written biographical sketch without the usual
sentimentality of a memorial. Includes a poem, "In Memoriam. Ellen H. Richards" by Laura E. Richards, and an appeal for material
to be used in the projected biography by Caroline L. Hunt (468).

462. Anon. "Memorials to Mrs. Richards." The Technology Re-
      view (June), p. 334.
      Brief notice of the biography by Caroline L. Hunt (468) and
the creation of the Ellen H. Richards Research Fund.

*463. [Obituary]. The Journal of Home Economics (June).

*464. [Obituary]. Technology Review (July), pp. 365-373. Photo-
      graph.

*465. [Memorial issue with bibliography]. The Journal of Home
      Economics (October).

                                1912

466. Anon. "Memorial to Mrs. Ellen H. Richards," Science, 35
      (2 February), pp. 176-177.
      The third annual meeting of the Home Economics Association
of Greater New York took the form of a tribute to Richards. The
first speaker, Margaret Maltby, is quoted in part as saying she
was "the prophet, the scientist and the practical optimist."

467. Anon. "Memorial to Mrs. Richards," Vassar Miscellany (April),
      pp. 13-15.
      Notice of efforts to design a suitable memorial and a report
of the Endowment Committee which proposes a fund to support "an-
nually a lecturer of distinction who shall give to the students of
Vassar College a lecture or lectures along the line of Mrs. Richards'
interest in the development of Euthenics, or the science of right
living. "

468. Hunt, Caroline L. The Life of Ellen H. Richards. Boston:
      Barrows, 329 pp.
      Written just after Richards' death, this biography contains
an indispensable store of thoughts, quotations, and remembrances
of her friends, students, and associates. Her husband sponsored

and contributed to the project. Much of Richards' diary (Vassar, 1868-1870) is reproduced along with extensive quotations from her writings and letters. These basic sources add much flavor and significance to this study. Treats Richards' importance in the fields of home economics, ecology, sanitation, and the women's movement.

469. Talbot, H. P. "The Life of Ellen H. Richards [a review],"
       Science, 36 (15 November), pp. 677-678.
       This is a book review (468), but it goes into such detail
that it constitutes an important biographical sketch in itself. Talbot has high praise for Hunt's work.

*470. Talbot, Marion. "Mrs. Richards' Relation to the Association
       of Collegiate Alumnae," Journal of the Association of Colle-
       giate Alumnae, 5, pp. 302-304.

                                1929

471. Anon. "In Memory of Ellen H. Richards," Journal of Home
       Economics, 21 (June), pp. 403-412.
       A detailed account of the dedication exercises which took
place at the Massachusetts Institute of Technology on 3 December 1928. The full record of speeches by associates of Richards at various stages of her life constitutes a source of personal detail of great value in spite of its highly formal tone.

                                1931

472. Barrows, Anna. "Recollections of Ellen H. Richards," Jour-
       nal of Home Economics, 23 (December), pp. 1124-1127.
       Twenty years after Richards' death the author presents some
remarks on her life and writings. The note includes a long letter Richards wrote to one of her friends from undergraduate days at Vassar. This text provides helpful autobiographical notes.

                                1935

473. M[arion] T[albot]. "Richards, Ellen Henrietta Swallow,"
       Dictionary of American Biography (14), 15, pp. 553-554.
       Good brief review of Richards' life which touches on all of
the varied aspects of her career. Written by a colleague in the home economics movement who understandably claims her leadership in that area to be her greatest achievement. Some useful bibliography.

1936

474. Richards, Robert Hallowell. <u>Robert Hallowell Richards. His
     Mark</u>. Boston: Little, Brown, ch. 10 and index.
     In his autobiography Richards is lavish in praise of his first
wife and the genuine collaboration in their life together at MIT.
He presents many personal and professional details that could only
come from such a unique source. Her extensive contributions to
his professional activities, as well as her own great scientific and
humane accomplishments, are dealt with in detail. While he admits,
"I am not a man of letters," he succeeds in reaching his goal, "to
tell young people, simply and briefly, the story of a happy and
not uneventful life." One should say two happy and not uneventful lives.

1942

475. MacLeod, Grace. "Reminiscences of Ellen H. Richards,"
     <u>Journal of Home Economics</u>, 34 (December), pp. 705-709.
     Written by one of Richards' students nearly 50 years later,
this article is full of firsthand examples drawn from a variety of
situations. Mostly based on a student-teacher relationship, the
material selected brings out the full personality and contribution
of this remarkable woman.

1943

476. Yost, Edna. <u>American Women of Science</u> (21), pp. 1-26.
     Emphasis is on Richards' many accomplishments, difficulties
and, especially, her cheerful acceptance of male prejudice. A fine
example of the difficult task of showing both the professional and
personal life and spirit.

1963

477. Stern, Madeleine B. "The First Woman Graduate of M.I.T.
     Ellen H. Richards, Chemist. 1873," in <u>We the Women. Ca-
     reer firsts of nineteenth-century America</u>. Wood engravings
     by John de Pol. New York: Schulte Publishing Co., ch.
     6, pp. 118-144.
     Richards' life and career told in interesting detail and in a
most readable manner. There is a description of her education at
Vassar and the development of an interest in applied chemistry.
The several aspects of her long and distinguished career at MIT
are each described and illustrated. She is presented as a person
of boundless energy and with determination to make the studies
of the laboratory an important force in the improvement of human
life. Richards' charming and healthful home receives full notice.

1971

478.   James, Janet Wilson.   "Richards, Ellen Henrietta Swallow,"
        Notable American Women (30), 3, pp. 143-146.
        Much longer than most of the sketches in this series, but
necessary for so extensive a career. Pays full attention to each
phase of Richards' work and portrays the total woman as well. The
bibliography is partial, but does indicate the material to be found
in each entry.

1973

479.   Clarke, Robert. Ellen Swallow: The Woman Who Founded
        Ecology. Chicago: Follett, 276 pp. Reviewed: New Re-
        public (November, 1973); Science (September, 1974); The
        Saturday Evening Post, 246 (October, 1974).
        Although, as the title suggests, this biography relates chief-
ly to Richards' early appreciation of the importance of the environment, Clarke has covered a much broader area. He deals with his
subject in a most sympathetic and intelligent manner. It might be
noted that the reviews vary widely in their evaluation.

1974

480.   Rosen, George. "Ellen H. Richards (1842-1911), Sanitary
        Chemist and Pioneer of Professional Equality for Women in
        Health Science," American Journal of Public Health, 64 (Au-
        gust), pp. 816-819.
        Based on the biographical information in Hunt's book (468).
The author describes Richards' work with the unsuccessful New
England Kitchen and the very successful Woman's Laboratory at
MIT. She advanced the health of communities and the position of
women.

1976

481.   Costa, Albert B. "Ellen Henrietta Swallow Richards. 1842-
        1911," American Chemists and Chemical Engineers (440), pp.
        405-406.
        A good sketch of her life centering on her as a chemist.
Useful bibliography.

482.   H[enrietta] W[exler]. "Ellen Swallow Richards. First Lady
        of Science," American Association of University Women Jour-
        nal, 70, p. 12.
        A biographical note attached to an article on the new posi-
tion of women in science.

483. Anon. "Ellen Swallow. Chemist, environmentalist. 1842-
       1911; U.S.A.," in Hypatia's Sisters (34), pp. 40-45. Portrait.
       A most readable account of Richards' life and career. Nice,
indirect treatment of the fact that she suffered the prejudice without complaint and went about her extraordinarily productive business.

1978

484. Ridley, Agnes Fenster. "Richards, Ellen Henrietta Swallow,"
       Dictionary of American Educators (38), 3, pp. 1094-1095.
       A sketch which outlines the high points of her extensive ca-
reer. Ridley gives a surprisingly long list of her books with publication dates. Abbreviated but useful bibliography.

1979

485. Anon. "Richards, Ellen Henrietta Swallow," Biographical
       Dictionary of American Science (40), p. 216.
       Only a few lines giving nothing of real interest aside from
the fact that she is included at all.

486. HELEN CECILIA DeSILVER ABBOTT MICHAEL
      23 December 1857--29 November 1904
       A talented pianist, Abbott studied music in Paris and in her
native Philadelphia during the period 1875-1881. Her interest in
science was aroused by a copy of Helmholtz's Optics, and she studied privately hoping to prepare for a medical career. Toward the
end of her life she did complete the MD and actually established
a free hospital where she practiced for a short time.
       Between these two careers, which were filled with promise
in spite of their brevity, Abbott did pioneering work in chemotax-
onomy--the application of chemistry to plant morphology. Modern
writers on this subject have made it clear that she was the first
to express the basic concept and to support it with detailed laboratory studies. The results of her research were not only published in scientific journals, but presented by her in well-attended
public lectures. Newspaper reviews of these presentations recognized her as a forceful and talented speaker on such difficult
topics as "The Chemical Basis of Plant Forms."
       Abbott studied traditional chemistry with one of America's
most distinguished chemists, Arthur Michael, whom she married in
1888. She collaborated with her husband on several research problems and later published a series of papers dealing with crotonic
acid derivatives. Little is known about their marriage, which lasted
only a short time.
       Throughout her life Abbott had a deep interest in art, litera-

ture, and philosophy. She wrote some poetry and criticism and lectured on a number of literary topics. A person of remarkably broad talents she represented a new model for young women eager to grow intellectually as the new century opened.

1907

487. Dole, N[athan] H[askell]. "Biographical Sketch," in Helen Abbott Michael. Studies in Plant and Organic Chemistry and Literary Papers. Cambridge, Massachusetts: Riverside Press, pp. 3-107. Photograph.
      This article is more than a biographical sketch. Much of the material is taken from Michael's fragmentary autobiography. Source for what little is known of her short life. Is most notable for all of the questions it leaves half-answered. Further work is called for on this intriguing woman.

1963

488. Alston, Ralph E., and B. L. Turner. Biochemical Systematics. Englewood Cliffs, New Jersey: Prentice-Hall, pp. 45-46, 67, 354.
      Gives Abbott credit for her very early recognition of the importance of chemical analysis in systematic morphology. Cites three of her early papers.

1974

489. Gibbs, R. Darnley. Chemotaxonomy of Flowering Plants, vol. 1. Montreal: McGill-Queen's University Press, pp. 11-12.
      A note in which the author says, "Helen C. de S. Abbott must have been a remarkable woman, writing as she did on chemotaxonomy in the 1880s."

1982

490. Tarbell, Ann Tracy, and D. Stanley Tarbell. "Helen Abbott Michael: Pioneer in Plant Chemistry," Journal of Chemical Education, 59 (July), pp. 548-549.
      The Tarbells relate the importance of Abbott's chemistry, but of greater interest is their recognition that here is a truly remarkable person. As she grew older, "she wrote and presented critical papers on travel, drama, and poetry which revealed her keen mind, broad culture, desire for women's freedom, and her flowing literary and poetic style." Here is a subject for study which should represent a high point in someone's scholarly career.

491. MARY FRANCES LEACH
      22 March 1858--9 April 1939
      Leach studied at Mount Holyoke College and returned there
as professor of chemistry (1893-1900) after earning a BS at the
University of Michigan in 1893. She also studied in Europe at the
Universities of Göttingen and Zurich before completing the PhD at
Michigan in 1903.
      At Western College for Women, where she was professor of
chemistry and hygiene (1907-1923), her interests centered on the
chemistry of nitrogen and bacteria.

492. Leach was cited in American Men of Science, 1906-1921.
      We are indebted to Elaine D. Trehub, Mount Holyoke College
History Librarian, for assistance in the form of a valuable, but
unidentified obituary clipping dated August 1939 and to Lauralee
A. Ensign, Alumni Records Operations Manager of the University
of Michigan, for several important records.

493. ELIZABETH ALLEN ATKINSON
      7 October 1868?--27 February 1956
      After earning a PhD at the University of Pennsylvania in
1898, Atkinson served as an assistant demonstrator in chemistry
at the Woman's Medical College of Pennsylvania for three years.
She was associated with the Philadelphia Clinical Laboratory (1901-
1907) where she worked on the analysis of metals.
      We are indebted to Francis James Dallett, Archivist of the
University of Pennsylvania, for his assistance.

494. MARTHA AUSTIN PHELPS
      13 February 1870--15 March 1933
      After receiving her education at Smith College (BS, 1892)
and Yale University (PhD, 1898), Austin taught at various schools
in New England. From 1901 to 1904 she taught science at Wilson
College. In 1904 she married Isaac King Phelps with whom she collaborated and published a number of articles in the American Journal of Science. She was interested in the quantitative analysis of
several elements, especially the use of double ammonium phosphates
in magnesium, zinc, and cadmium. She became one of the earliest
women scientists employed by the Bureau of Standards when she
served as an analyst in 1908-1909.

495. Phelps is cited in American Men of Science, 1906-1921.
      We are indebted to Eleanor M. Lewis, Research Associate of
the Smith College Archives, for an important, but apparently unpublished obituary of Phelps.

496. MARY BIDWELL BREED
        15 September 1870--15 September 1949
        Breed was educated at Bryn Mawr College (AB, 1894; AM,
1895; PhD, 1901). She won the European Fellowship and became
the first woman to participate in scientific work at Heidelberg where
she worked in Victor Meyer's laboratory. Her research involved
both inorganic and organic chemistry, and she taught at several
private schools. However, her most notable contributions were as
a college dean, especially at the Margaret Morrison College of the
Carnegie Institute of Technology. By the time she retired in 1929
she had played a central role in raising the standing of this institution from a trade school to that of a fully qualified college.

1949

497. Anon. "Miss Mary Breed, Retired Educator," The New York
        Times, 98 (16 September), p. 28.
        A brief description of Breed's career with special emphasis
on her role as an academic administrator.

498. Anon. [Obituary], School and Society, 70 (24 September),
        p. 206.
        Notice which remarks about her being the first woman to
work in Victor Meyer's Heidelberg laboratory.

499. MARY ENGLE PENNINGTON
        8 October 1872--27 December 1952
        It is hard to imagine a more diversified set of careers than
those of Mary Pennington. In 1890 she entered the University of
Pennsylvania and in two years had completed the requirements for
a BS. The University refused to grant her that degree, but allowed her to continue her studies and awarded her a PhD in 1895.
She studied an additional two years and moved to Yale for another
year of physiological chemistry.
        In 1898 her home city had nothing to offer a young woman
chemist so Pennington opened the Philadelphia Clinical Laboratory
and became recognized for the high quality of her analyses. She
was appointed a lecturer at the Woman's Medical College of Pennsylvania and head of the city health department's bacteriology laboratory. Her interest in food preservation may have been formed
while in this position since she was conducting early studies of im-
pure milk.
        In 1907 Pennington was appointed a bacteriological chemist
in the Bureau of Chemistry of the United States Department of Agriculture. She was made chief of the Food Research Laboratory
in 1908. In these positions, obtained by taking the civil service
examination as M. E. Pennington and being appointed before Washington officials knew she was a woman, she carried out a series

of significant studies. These efforts led to methods of processing, storing, and shipping food that greatly increased its quality and availability. Her work on rail shipment in refrigerator cars became nationally known.

After this life full of service in private business, teaching, and government service, Pennington became director of research and development of the American Balsa Company. Three years later she set up her own consulting office in New York City. Her clients called on her expert knowledge and involved her in travel amounting to as much as 50,000 miles a year until her death in 1952. (See also 23, 32, 35, 634, 954.)

1940

500. Pierce, Anna. "American Contemporaries. Mary Engle Pennington. An Appreciation," Chemical and Engineering News, 18 (10 November), pp. 941-942. Photograph.
      Written in conjunction with the awarding of the Garvan Medal of the American Chemical Society. This longer biographical sketch contains several important quotations and describes in some detail Pennington's contributions in the food preservation area.

1941

501. Heggie, Barbara. "Profiles: Ice Woman," New Yorker, 17 (6 September), pp. 23-30. A sketch.
      There are a number of excellent quotations in this interview which deals more with the personal side of her life, including a description of her apartment. Reports that Pennington is said to have read very little outside of her field of science.

1943

502. Yost, Edna. American Women of Science (21), pp. 80-98.
      Yost places great emphasis on Pennington's practical approach to the solution of real problems. On the one hand, she is the person who rolls up her sleeves and tries, while on the other, she is the scholar who maintains the highest standards of scientific accuracy. The extraordinary breadth of her accomplishments is fully noted.

1946

503. Goff, Alice C. Women Can Be Engineers (634), pp. 183-214.
      Written by a woman who is herself an engineer, the book is clearly an attempt to promote the study of engineering by women. The attempt is well carried out, and Goff presents many outstanding

examples. Pennington is followed through a long series of her most
famous cases; in each instance she is shown as a completely capable
person who can meet each problem with a practical solution based
on the best scientific work.

1952

504. Anon. "Mary Pennington, Engineer, 80, Dead," The New
      York Times, 102 (28 December), p. 48.
      An expert on refrigeration of perishable foods, she devised
many of the methods used to store and transport them. She was
interested in science education for women.

1953

505. Anon. "Necrology. Mary E. Pennington," Chemical and En-
      gineering News, 31 (5 January), p. 87. Photograph.
      An outline of her career with a note that she was the 1940
winner of the Garvan Medal and one of the earliest women to join
the American Chemical Society.

506. Anon. "Dr. Mary Pennington Dies," American Egg and Poul-
      try Review (January), p. 60.
      A note about her work with special emphasis on her associa-
tion with the poultry industry. Says that she was one of the five
honorary life members of the Institute of American Poultry Industries.

507. Anon. "Dr. Mary Engle Pennington," Ice and Refrigeration
      (February), p. 58. Photograph.
      A rather long obituary and memorial article which traces
Pennington's career. Emphasizes her numerous activities in the
area of refrigeration and gives an impressive list of her professional memberships and honors.

508. Anon. "Nunc Dimittis. Mary Engle Pennington," Poultry
      Science, 32 (April), p. 363.
      Says that she was the first poultry research worker and that
she developed methods which helped to maintain high quality of
eggs, poultry, and fish during storage and transport.

509. Anon. "Mary Engle Pennington. October 8, 1872--December
      27, 1952," Refrigerating Engineering (February), p. 184.
      Photograph.
      An obituary with special mention of her long service and
membership in the American Society of Refrigerating Engineers.
Also lists her other professional memberships and honors. Gives
a good outline of her contributions in the field of food preservation.

1976

510. Bishop, Ethel Echternach. "Mary Engle Pennington. 1872-
1952," American Chemists and Chemical Engineers (440), pp.
386-387.
  A readable account of Pennington's career which shows the
great variety of projects in food preservation which she undertook.

1980

511. Wiser, Vivian. "Pennington, Mary Engle," Notable American
Women (30), 4, pp. 532-534.
  Devotes some of her limited space to each of Pennington's
careers. A readable and well-balanced account. Bibliography is
cited without commentary.

512. FLORENCE JACKSON
  3 August 1872--December 1952
  An instructor in chemistry at Wellesley College from 1899 to
1908, Jackson was born in England and studied at Smith College
(BS, 1893; AM, 1902). She was interested in qualitative tests for
metals.
  Sometime around 1910 Jackson made a rather striking career
change. For reasons that we do not know she left chemistry and
established a strong career in college personnel work. In a 1939
biographical dictionary she lists herself as a vocational lecturer
at large. A typed biographical sketch from the Smith College archives (1938) gives a list of 59 colleges and universities which she
had visited one or more times. This same document states her present occupation as Associate in the Personnel Bureau, Wellesley College. Other partially identified documents give some insight to her
services which seem to be concerned with what we should call career counseling. Jackson's work in the practical matters of planning
and developing a career for young women in the first quarter of
the century certainly deserves further study.

513. Jackson was cited in American Men of Science, 1906-1910.
  We are greatly indebted to Eleanor M. Lewis, Research Associate of the Smith College Archives, and Wilma R. Slaight, Archivist of Wellesley College, for their assistance.

514. ADELIN(E) ELAM SPENCER
  31 December 1872?--19 December 1937
  There is some doubt of the year of Spencer's birth since it
appears as 1870-1872 in the few documents we have been able to
see. We have chosen 1872, found in American Men of Science,

since this is the only one she is likely to have proofread. The possible terminating "e" of her first name is found in just that manner on a Cornell University alumni association card.

After graduating from Newcomb College and Tulane University (AB, 1890; AM, 1894), Spencer continued her education at Cornell University (MS, 1896). She returned to Newcomb as instructor in chemistry after having spent a brief period as a science teacher in Monroe, Louisiana. As she progressed through the academic ranks, her interests shifted toward geology. In 1913 she became instructor in geology; in 1916, assistant professor of chemistry; and in 1934, professor of geology. She retired as professor emerita of geology in 1936. In addition to these interests she was obviously a keen observer of nature in general. On one of her geology field trips she discovered a new species and genus of sea urchin as a minute fossil.

1938

515. Anon. "Adelin Elam Spencer," Cornell Alumni News (17 February).
     Relates a few facts of her career, in particular her discovery of a new species of sea urchin.

516. [Typed obituary]. Tulane University Archives.
     Review of Spencer's education and her service to Newcomb College. Notes that she was a member of the first class. Gives her date of birth as 31 December 1870.

517. Anon. "Adelin Spencer, Retired Newcomb Teacher Is Dead," [unidentified publication] (11 January).
     Review of her career with details of funeral and notice of her sea urchin discovery. Says she was actively interested in rights of women and the underprivileged.

518. Spencer is cited in American Men of Science, 1906-1910.
     We are indebted to Kathleen Jacklin, Archivist of Cornell University, and Doris H. Antin, University Archivist of Tulane University, for their assistance in finding the documents cited.

519. ANN HERO NORTHRUP
     21 April 1875--24 April 1949
     Hero studied chemistry at Vassar College (AB, 1896; AM, 1897). She taught at the Pratt Institute until 1903 when she joined the Tulane University faculty where she became professor in 1905. She married a Tulane law professor, Elliott Judd Northrup, in 1914 and they taught together until 1926. From that date until the time World War II became obviously unavoidable, they made their home in Europe. Northrup had long had an interest in the

German language and is noted for her translation of three important
books by eminent German chemists. These years in Europe between
the Wars as viewed by a chemist and a lawyer would make fascinating reading. A resolution of the Newcomb faculty at the time of
her death also makes Northrup an intriguing subject: "She was
a person of strong convictions and of some prejudices.... Her in-
dividuality marked her as a unique figure on the Newcomb faculty."

<u>1949</u>

520. [Newcomb College Faculty]. "Resolution on the Death of
      Mrs. Ann Hero Northrup." (26 May).
      Gives details of her education and service to the College.
A great many points of obvious interest for future study.

521. Hero is cited in <u>American Men of Science</u>, 1906-1910 and un-
      der her married name in 1921.
      We are indebted to Doris Antin, University Archivist of Tu-
lane University; Lisa Browar, Curator of Rare Books and Manuscripts of Vassar College; and Terri O'Shea, Vassar College Alumni
Association for their assistance.

522. DOROTHY ANNA HAHN
      9 April 1876--10 December 1950
      At Mount Holyoke College where she taught organic chemis-
try for 25 years, Hahn established a major research effort in the
synthesis of cyclic polypeptides called hydrantoins. These molecules, related to the proteins, required the application of both
skillful organic chemical technique and the newly developed methods
of ultraviolet spectrophotometry. Hahn and Emma P. Carr, then
chairman of the department, collaborated in this work. Of far
greater significance than the thirty papers she published in the
progress of these studies was the fact that she was able to complete them with the assistance of undergraduate students and only
a very limited number of master's degree candidates.
      Hahn's education was obtained over a long period of time and
in a number of laboratories. She began her training at Bryn Mawr
College (AB, 1899) and concluded it at Yale University (PhD, 1916).
In the years between she studied at the University of Leipzig with
Arthur Hantzsch and at Bryn Mawr with E. P. Kohler. Studies
with these distinguished men, in addition to her year at Yale with
Treat B. Johnson, gave her both the spirit and the background
for her deep belief in the necessity of combining teaching with research.
      In addition to this extraordinary research productivity Hahn
also was the coauthor of three important reference books and a translation and expansion of a German textbook of organic chemistry.
She also had an active interest in industrial chemistry which not

only contributed to her awareness of important new developments,
but made it possible for Mount Holyoke to obtain needed facilities
and scholarships. Many of her students remembered her skill in
inspiring them and her warm friendship.

1941

523.   Austin, Janet Evans. "Retirement in June. Dorothy A.
       Hahn, Mount Holyoke Alumnae Quarterly (August), p. 55.
       Photograph.
       Written by one of Hahn's students, the article is rich in
praise of her skill and dedication as a teacher and gives an impressive account of her research activities. There is a good outline of her academic career and professional positions.

1950

524.   Anon. "Deaths. Dorothy A. Hahn," Science, 112 (29 De-
       cember), p. 798.
       An obituary which mentions her most important book-length
publications and pays tribute to her research work with students.

1951

525.   Renfrew, Alice G. "Dorothy A. Hahn, Scientist and Teach-
       er," Mount Holyoke Alumnae Quarterly (February), p. 153.
       Pays special attention to her extensive research activities
and the role played by her students in that work. Also provides
insights to the woman's personality.

1971

526.   Renfrew, Alice G. "Hahn, Dorothy Anna," Notable American
       Women (30), 2, pp. 108-109.
       Longer, but written in the same fine manner as her obituary
(525), this sketch gives a fairly detailed outline of Hahn's career
with references to her major publications. Interesting material on
her activities outside of chemistry.

527.   IDA WELT
       23 April 1876?--1950
       Born in Vienna, Austria, Welt studied at Vassar College (AB,
1891) and then at the University of Geneva, Switzerland (BS, 1895;
PhD, 1896). She taught at the Girls' High School of New York
City following five years in various posts at Geneva. At some

point she returned to Vassar where she was a member of the faculty
for many years, but the records there, which give her year of birth
as 1871, are very incomplete. She returned to Geneva where she
died in 1950. In addition to her several articles in the chemical
literature concerning physiological chemistry she wrote an often
cited article dealing with the accomplishments of Jewish women in
science [Hebrew Standard, 50 (5 April, 1907)]. Certainly, this
is a woman deserving greater attention.

528. Welt is cited in American Men of Science, 1906-1910.
    We are indebted to Lisa Browar, Curator of Rare Books, and
Terri O'Shea, of the Alumnae Association, both of Vassar College
for their assistance in at least making a start in the study of Welt's
career.

529. EMMA PERRY CARR
    23 July 1880--7 January 1972
    Carr is so closely linked with Mount Holyoke College and the
application of the graduate education technique of student involvement in research, it would be impossible to think of them separately. She began her 65-year association with the college in 1899 when
she studied there for two years and served as an assistant in chemistry for three. Following a year at the University of Chicago (BS,
1905) she returned for three years as an instructor before completing her education at Chicago (PhD, 1910).
    The years between 1913 and her retirement in 1946 were ones
of great productivity. She served as professor and chairman of
the department and built a program which integrated teaching and
research which has rarely been approached. In addition to heavy
administrative duties she was considered an extraordinarily fine
teacher at all levels. But it was in the development of an ambitious
research program for undergraduates and a limited number of master's degree candidates that Carr won deserved recognition. Under
her guidance Mount Holyoke became one of the first American research centers to make use of ultraviolet spectrophotometry to determine the structure of complex organic molecules. She spent several periods at leading European universities learning these new
techniques. At a later period she and her students began making
fundamental contributions to the understanding of the causes of
selectivity of absorption of such radiant energy by studying simple
and very specific structures.
    Carr was widely recognized for the significance of her con-
tributions and appointed to a number of important scientific commissions. She received four honorary degrees and was the first Garvan Medal winner when that award was created by the American
Chemical Society to recognize the work of women chemists. (See
also 23, 43, 563.)

1942

530.   Anon.   "Carr, Emma Perry," National Cyclopaedia of American
       Biography (2), F, pp. 364-365.
       Outline of the highlights of Carr's career with a bit of inter-
esting information on her family and avocational interests.

1938

*531.   Journal of Industrial and Engineering Chemistry, 16 (10 May),
        pp. 263-264.

1946

532.   Hallock, Grace Taber, editor.   "Emma Perry Carr. Professor
       Emeritus of Chemistry," Mount Holyoke Alumnae Quarterly,
       30 (August), pp. 53-55.   Photograph.
       A composite portrait made up of sketches written by eight
alumnae, former students and a colleague of Carr.   Presents all
of the biographical data, but, more importantly, is rich in details
of the person as seen by those who studied with her.   Pays special attention to her career as a teacher.

1957

*533.   Burt, C. Pauline.   "Emma Perry Carr," Nucleus, 34 (June
        1957), pp. 214-216.   Photographs.

1959

534.   Anon.   "Carr, Emma P(erry)."   Current Biography Yearbook,
       pp. 55-57.   Photograph.
       An outline of Carr's life and career with several quotations
from other articles about her.   Written in nontechnical language,
the article emphasizes the innovation of her teaching methods and
the importance of her research, both of which were notable contributions to the science of her time.   Some references.

1972

*535.   [Obituary].   Holyoke [Massachusetts] Transcript-Telegram
        (8 January).

536.   Anon.   "Dr. Emma P. Carr, 91 Chemist at Holyoke," The
       New York Times, 121 (8 January), p. 32.
       Developed a group research technique which allowed her to

become a pioneer in the field of absorption spectra. The laboratories at Mount Holyoke were dedicated in her honor in 1955.

537. Anon. "In Memoriam. Emma Perry Carr," Mount Holyoke
     Alumnae Quarterly, (Spring), pp. 23-25.
     Includes the text of the tribute delivered by George B. Hall
at a memorial service. The personal insights of her colleagues are
here as well as the standard biographical information.

1976

537. Atkinson, Edward R. "Emma Perry Carr. 1880-1972,"
     American Chemists and Chemical Engineers (440), pp. 66-
     67.
     Important details on Carr's influence on the growth of chem-
istry at Mount Holyoke. Emphasis on her effective use of research
in teaching and the importance of that research to chemistry in
general.

1980

539. Verbrugge, Martha H. "Carr, Emma Perry," Notable American
     Women (30), 4, pp. 136-138.
     Good background on Carr's education and career with an es-
pecially well-written, nontechnical presentation of her scientific research. Describes the growth of her international reputation and
its influence on Mount Holyoke College. Good bibliography.

540. AGNES FAY MORGAN
     4 May 1884--20 July 1968
     Morgan was one of the pioneers in the development of home
economics as a scientific discipline. Her work in nutrition and biochemistry, which concerned practical problems dealing with vitamins
in food, was both substantial and significant. When she began her
career, these fields were so new that she later said research was
necessary so that she would have something to teach. As a teacher
she made heavy demands on her students but was considered fair
in dealing with them.
     She began her studies at Vassar College, but completed all
of her work at the University of Chicago (BS, 1904; MS, 1905; PhD,
1914). Prior to her doctoral work she taught at several colleges
and married. Her husband encouraged her to return to Chicago
for that degree, and he moved with her to Berkeley when she was
offered a position at the University of California in 1915.
     At California Morgan quickly became chairman of the new de-
partment of Household Science and Arts. She remained active in
the development of what became one of the foremost departments

of home economics until her death. In spite of her fine record in
teaching and research she was proudest of the administrative work
which led to the establishment of this department and played a major role in the growth of the science of home economics. She won
the Garvan Medal of the American Chemical Society (1949) and the
Bordon Award from the American Institute of Nutrition (1954). She
was called upon many times by political bodies to study the practical implications of nutrition.

1941

*541.   Anon. The Progress of Science, a Review of 1941, The Grolier
        Society, p. 260. Photograph.

1949

542.   Anon. "Garvan Medal to Agnes Morgan," Chemical and En-
        gineering News, 27 (28 March), p. 905. Cover photograph.
        Says that the medalist taught the first scientific nutrition
course at the University of California. Gives a list of research
accomplishments with emphasis on her studies of the interrelation-
ships between the vitamins and hormones.

1950

*543.   Anon. "Report of Committee on Faculty Research Lecture,
        1950-51," University of California [Berkeley] Faculty Bulle-
        tin, 20 (November), p. 41.

1954

*544.   Anon. "Our Distinguished Faculty," California Monthly, 44
        (May), p. 21.

1967

545.   Anon. "Agnes Fay Morgan--Her Career in Nutrition," in
        "Landmarks of a Half Century of Nutrition Research. A
        symposium honoring Doctor Agnes Fay Morgan's fiftieth anni-
        versary at the University of California," The Journal of Nu-
        trition, 91, supp. 1, pt. 2 (February), pp. 1-3.
        A biographical sketch which emphasizes Morgan's contribu-
tion to nutrition and the University of California. Traces her academic career and mentions some of her honors. This special issue
includes her closing remarks (pp. 65-67), which are autobiographical.

1968

546. Anon. "Dr. Agnes Morgan, Nutritionist, Dies," The New York Times, 117 (23 July), p. 36.
A pioneer in the developing science of nutrition had been a member of the Berkeley faculty since 1915. She published 30 papers since her "retirement" in 1954. Lists her major interests, including vitamin analyses and the effect of heat on the nutritional value of food.

547. Todhunter, E. Neige. "Biographical Notes from History of Nutrition. Agnes Fay Morgan, May 4, 1884--July 20, 1968," Journal of the American Dietetic Association, 53 (December), p. 599.
Calls Morgan "one of the great pioneers in research and teaching of the modern science of nutrition." Reviews her scientific contributions and her many honors.

548. Anon. "Deaths. Agnes Fay Morgan," Chemical and Engineering News, 46 (5 August), p. 158. Photograph.
Notice of her death which lists some of her most important research contributions and honors.

1969

*549. Okey, Ruth; Barbara Kennedy Johnson; and Gordon MacKinney. Agnes Fay Morgan, 1884-1968, In Memoriam. Berkeley: University of California (May).

550. Okey, Ruth. "Agnes Fay Morgan (1884-1968)--A Biographical Sketch," The Journal of Nutrition, 104 (September), pp. 1102-1107. Photograph.
Writes in detail about Morgan's career, mentions her honors, and says she was a leader in promoting the cause of education for women.

1976

551. Gorman, Mel. "Agnes Fay Morgan. 1884-1968," American Chemists and Chemical Engineers (440), pp. 348-349.
Well-written summary which points out her role as an inspiration to young women. Excellent bibliography.

1977

552. Emerson, Gladys A. "Agnes Fay Morgan and Early Nutrition Discoveries in California," Federation Proceedings, 36 (May), pp. 1911-1914.

Describes her major research accomplishments and makes clear the nature and extent of her collaboration with other scientists. There is much personal biographical information.

1980

553.   Raacke, I. D.   "Morgan, Agnes Fay," Notable American Women (30), 2, pp. 495-497.
Nicely written biographical sketch which describes the elements of her career and also points out her interest and skill as an administrator.   Good bibliography.

554.   GRACE MEDES
9 November 1886--31 December 1967
Although her PhD (Bryn Mawr College, 1916) was in zoology, Medes spent nearly 50 productive years in the field of physiological biochemistry.   At the University of Minnesota Medical School in 1924 she discovered the metabolic disorder tyrosinosis.   The condition was later found to be less rare than had been originally thought and a symposium to discuss it was held in her honor at Oslo, Norway, in 1965.

Following her studies at Vassar College (AB, 1904; AM, 1913) she taught at Vassar and Wellesley Colleges.   From 1932 until her retirement in 1956 she worked at the Lankenau Hospital Research Institute in Philadelphia.   Medes contributed to the understanding of cysteine metabolism and later, with the availability of carbon isotopes, to fatty acid metabolism.   This later work played an important role in the eventual discovery of acetyl coenzyme A. She also participated in the earliest studies of the metabolism of fatty acids in cancer cells.

Even after her retirement she worked as a visiting scientist at the Fels Research Institute of Temple University.   Her final paper appeared just a short time before her death.   She was awarded the Garvan Medal by the American Chemical Society in 1955.   (See also 955.)

1955

555.   Anon.   "Grace Medes.   Garvan Medal," Chemical and Engineering News, 33 (11 April), p. 1515.   Photograph.
A note of the presentation of the Garvan Medal of the American Chemical Society.   Cites several of her most important research contributions.   Interesting comment on the lack of research support for her early work.

1976

556. Bishop, Ethel Echternach. "Grace Medes. 1886-1967,"
      American Chemists and Chemical Engineers (440), pp. 330-
      331.
      While giving the biographical data this brief article is most
important for the personal recollections of the author which contribute to a fuller picture of Medes' life.

557. ETHEL MARY TERRY McCOY
      10 February 1887--23 May 1963
      Educated at the University of Chicago (AB, 1907; PhD, 1913)
Terry served on its faculty until 1927. She published a number
of studies concerning oxidation and stereochemistry. After her
marriage she collaborated with her husband, Herbert N. McCoy,
on an introductory textbook and laboratory manual. The McCoys
moved to California in 1927. For the next 11 years she returned
to Chicago each Spring where she worked as a research associate.

1964

*558. Robertson, G. Ross. Herbert Newby McCoy, 1870-1945. Los
       Angeles: Privately printed.

1976

559. Eichelberger, Lillian. "Ethel Mary Terry," American Chemists
      and Chemical Engineers (440), pp. 470-471.
      A review of her work with some attention to the collaboration
with her husband. Important personal insight to her philosophy
of life and work.

560. MARY LURA SHERRILL
      14 July 1888--27 October 1968
      As a faculty member and chairman of the Department of
Chemistry, Sherrill served Mount Holyoke College for 44 years.
Her belief in and ability to administer group research activities led
the faculty and students to make important scientific contributions
in spite of limited resources. Most notable is her work with Emma
P. Carr on the ultraviolet spectroscopy of unsaturated hydrocar-
bons and her World War II syntheses of novel antimalarial drugs.
      Sherrill was educated at Randolph-Macon Woman's College
(BA, 1908?; MA, 1909) and the University of Chicago (PhD, 1923).
She received an honorary DSc from the University of North Carolina in 1948 and the Garvan Medal from the American Chemical Society in 1947.

1947

561. Anon. "Mary Lura Sherrill," Chemical and Engineering News,
      25 (21 April), pp. 1119, 2811.
      Describes the winner of the Garvan Medal as a born teacher.
A brief review of her career with emphasis on her work with the
physical structure of molecules and their dipole moments.

1957

*562. Crawford, J. V. [Mary Lura Sherrill], Nucleus, 34. Photo-
       graphs.

563. Sherrill, Mary L. "Group Research in a Small Department,"
      Journal of Chemical Education, 34 (September), pp. 467-468.
      Photograph.
      A biographical sketch is given at the presentation of the
Norris Award to Sherrill and Carr. The article is also useful, for
it describes the research with undergraduates for which both wom-
en are so justly famous.

1976

564. Atkinson, Edward R. "Mary Lura Sherrill. 1888-1968,"
      American Chemists and Chemical Engineers (440), p. 436.
      Describes her long career at Mount Holyoke and her research
work with students in close collaboration with Emma Perry Carr.

565. MARY LETITIA CALDWELL
      18 December 1890--1 July 1972
      After completing her undergraduate education at Western Col-
lege for Women (AB, 1913), Caldwell taught there for four years
and began her graduate work at Columbia University (PhD, 1921).
She remained at Columbia as the sole woman member of its senior
faculty and the only woman to be promoted to full professor (1948).
In addition to her teaching responsibilities she was advisor to the
graduate students, managed the details of graduate financial support, and served as secretary to the department.
      Caldwell's research was in the purification and study of the
important enzyme group known as amylases. The methods developed
in her research group, which included 18 doctoral students, have
proven to be of lasting scientific and commercial importance. Using
these highly purified enzymes, she and her collaborators were able
to show that alpha amylases, isolated from different sources, varied
in the mechanism of their action. They were the first workers to
crystallize pancreatic amylase. Caldwell was awarded the Garvan
Medal of the American Chemical Society in 1960 and an honorary
DSc by Columbia in 1961. (See also 43.)

1960

566.   Anon.   "Garvan Medal.   Dr. Mary L. Caldwell," Chemical
       Engineering News, 38 (18 April), p. 86.   Photograph.
       Describes her research in the carbohydrate enzymes which
won her the Garvan Medal.   Also notes her effective, and freely
given, assistance to graduate students.

1972

567.   Anon.   "Mary L. Caldwell of Columbia Dies," The New York
       Times, 121 (2 July), p. 20.
       Enzyme expert taught chemistry for 41 years and was de-
voted to her research.   She won the Garvan Medal in 1960 for her
work in the study of starch-splitting amylases.

1976

568.   Daly, Marie M.   "Mary Letitia Caldwell.   1890-1972,"
       American Chemists and Chemical Engineers (440), pp. 62-
       63.
       Very readable, personal view of Caldwell.   Both her research
and her notable service to Columbia are well described.

569.   CLARA MARIE DE MILT
       8 May 1891--10 May 1953
       De Milt's early education in chemistry, history, and English
at Newcomb College of Tulane University (BA, 1911; MS, 1921) gave
her an excellent background for her later important contributions
to the history of chemistry.   She was most interested in biography
and specialized in seventeenth- through nineteenth-century France.
Her studies of the work of Auguste Laurent showed clearly the importance of this neglected scientist.   One author has said that if
his so-called extreme ideas had been accepted by French chemists,
atomic weights would have come into use at least ten years earlier.
       In 1920 she began teaching at Newcomb and remained there
until her death with the exception of 1924-1925 when she completed
her doctoral work at the University of Chicago.   Although de Milt
taught, wrote and directed students' research in the history of
chemistry she, along with student collaborators, contributed stud-
dies in organic chemistry.   She published this work as well as three
laboratory manuals.   In addition to teaching and scholarly activities
she served as department chairman from 1941 to 1949.

1953

570.   Anon.   "Necology.   Clara M. de Milt," Chemical and

Engineering News, 31 (31 August), p. 3570.
A notice with a list of professional positions.

571.   Anon. "Recent Deaths. Clara Marle [sic] de Milt," School
       and Society, 77 (23 May), p. 334.
       A notice of her death which lists her teaching positions.

1954

572.   Scott, John Mark. "Clara Marie DeMilt (1891-1953),"
       Journal of Chemical Education, 31 (August), pp. 419-420.
       Photograph as frontispiece.
       A memorial which has high praise for her industry and great
enthusiasm for science. Her interests beyond history and biography
and her skill as a teacher are noted and a partial bibliography of
her publications and those of her students is given.

1964

573.   McConnell, Virginia F. "Clara de Milt, Historian of Science,"
       Chymia. Annual Studies in the History of Chemistry, 9, pp.
       201-215. Photograph.
       Written by her student and successor, this paper is not only
a tribute, but a careful examination of the principal research areas
in which de Milt made important contributions. Of significance is
the discussion of de Milt's philosophy about science. Cites the resolution made by her colleagues upon her death, "Chemistry was a
living and magnificent thing for her and had to be shown to her
students as such." A probably complete bibliography of her publications and those finished under her direction is given.

1976

574.   McConnell, Virginia F. "Clara Marie de Milt," American
       Chemists and Chemical Engineers (440), pp. 116-117.
       An abridged version of item 573. Retains the personal fla-
vor and leaves out the detailed philosophical analysis.

575.   LOUISE KELLEY
       10 October 1894--12 November 1961
       Kelley taught at Goucher College for 39 years following the
awarding of her PhD by Cornell University in 1920. She served
this college and the American Chemical Society in administrative
roles. For her contributions to the National Defense Research Committee during and following World War II, she was one of nine women
to receive the President's Certificate of Merit.

In addition to her active teaching and administrative work Kelley was assistant editor of the Journal of Physical and Colloid Chemistry and Chemical Reviews from early in her career until its end. She was the coauthor (1st edition, 1932) and sole author (2nd edition, 1943) of an important textbook, Organic Chemistry. Her contributions to Goucher College were recognized both by the college (DSc, 1959; lecture hall named for her, 1968) and by the profession (Manufacturing Chemists Association award, 1959). (See also 19.)

1961

*576.   [Obituary]. Boston Globe (13 November).

*577.   [Obituary]. Batimore Sun (14 November).

*578.   [Obituary]. Baltimore News Post (14 November).

1976

579.   Webb, James L. A. "Louise Kelley," American Chemists and Chemical Engineers (440), pp. 269-270.
    A nicely rounded account which presents Kelley's career involving research, teaching, administration, and editing. Lists her several honors.

580.   GERTY THERESA RADNITZ CORI
    15 August 1896--26 October 1957
    The first American woman and the third woman ever to win a Nobel Prize, Cori graduated from the Medical School of the German University of Prague (MD, 1920). In that same year she married Carl Cori with whom she shared a lifetime of fruitful biochemical research and ultimately the Nobel Prize in 1947.
    The Coris came to the United States in 1922 and joined the staff of what was to become Roswell Park Memorial Institute in Buffalo, New York. Here, in addition to their routine duties associated with the study of malignant diseases, they collaborated on the first of a long series of studies of normal carbohydrate metabolism. In this and other laboratories they were made to feel that their work together was not appreciated by the heads of research. The pressures on them as a couple were a heavy burden and the lack of recognition in the face of first-rate scientific work a severe disappointment, but they persevered and showed that the mechanism then believed to account for glucose metabolism was fundamentally wrong. Their work not only demonstrated the true intermediate but the enzyme responsible for the key step. It wasn't until she won the Nobel Prize that Cori obtained a full professorial position. (See also 32, 35, 39, 42, 43, 46, 956, 957.)

<u>1947</u>

581. Anon. "Physiology or Medicine 1947. Presentation Speech
      by Professor H. Theorell, Head of the Biochemical Nobel De-
      partment of the Royal Caroline Institute," in <u>Nobel Lectures.</u>
      <u>Physiology or Medicine</u>. London: Elsevier, 1964, pp. 179-
      185.
      The speech in which the winners of the Nobel Prize are pre-
sented to the King is actually a review of their work on a not too
technical level. In this case, since they shared the work with Bernardo Houssay, the contributions of all three are mentioned and
related one to another. Lectures given by the recipients and their
biographical sketches follow the speech (pp. 207-209).

582. Anon. "Drs. Cori, St. Louis, Get Nobel Prize as Husband-
      Wife Chemist Team," <u>The New York Times</u>, 97 (24 October),
      pp. 1, 20.
      A popular account including a statement of the citation and
the amount of the award. The Coris are the third married couple
to win the Prize. On page 20 there is a separate article in which
they explain their work with emphasis on the importance of the synthesis of the enzyme. There are some personal notes about them.

583. Anon. "Medicine. The Winners," <u>Time</u>, 50 (3 November),
      p. 81. Photograph.
      News release reporting the award of the Nobel Prize without
much of interest.

584. Anon. "Cori, Carl F(erdinand) and Cori, Gerty T(heresa
      Radnitz)." <u>Current Biography Yearbook</u>, pp. 135-137.
      Photograph.
      Good review of their lives making it plain that they were
really a fine team. Interesting quotations from other scientists about
the nature of their work and their methods.

<u>1948</u>

585. Anon. "Medical Woman of the Month. Dr. Gerty T. Cori,"
      <u>Journal of the American Medical Women's Association</u>, 3 (Sep-
      tember), p. 372. Photograph.
      Biographical facts with major attention given to her having
won the Garvan Medal of the American Chemical Society.

<u>1953</u>

586. Anon. "Guest Speaker Mid-Year Meeting 1953. Gerty T.
      Cori, MD," <u>Journal of the American Medical Women's Associ-</u>
      <u>ation</u>, 8 (October), p. 340. Photograph.
      A notice of her selection and a few biographical facts.

1956

587. Houssay Bernardo A. "Carl F. and Gerty T. Cori," Bio-
      chimica et Biophysica Acta, 20, pp. 11-16. Photographs.
      A very warm and personal biographical sketch by the man
who shared the 1947 Nobel Prize with the Coris. Describes their
work and its importance and provides a year by year list of the
most significant discoveries made by them.

1957

588. Anon. "Dr. Gerty T. Cori, Biochemist, Dead," The New
      York Times, 107 (27 October), p. 86. Photograph.
      Outline of life and career with special emphasis on the work
leading to the Nobel Prize. Long list of other honors.

1958

589. Doisy, E. A. "Gerty Theresa Cori (1896-1957)," American
      Philosophical Society Yearbook, 22, pp. 108-111.
      Some personal data, but mostly a detailed description of her
research with her husband. Good and not too technical presentation of their work.

590. Ochoa, Severo, and Herman M. Kalckar. "Gerty T. Cori,
      Biochemist," Science, 128 (4 July), pp. 16-17.
      An interesting joint approach to developing the multifaceted
career of Cori. The two authors present quite different pictures
of her work following a brief introduction to the educational background of both husband and wife. First, there is a concentration
on their joint work which led to the Nobel Prize. The second part
deals with her work mostly following 1947. High praise for their
efforts in each case.

1959

591. Yost, Edna. "Gerty Theresa Cori (1896-1957)," in Women
      of Modern Science. New York: Dodd, Mead, pp. 1-16.
      Photograph.
      As in her earlier book (21) Yost is simply trying to make
available more biographical material on women scientists. She obviously finds the stories of these women fascinating and conveys
her enthusiasm to the reader. The work leading to the Nobel Prize
is presented in an understandable manner, but it is the attention
to the person of Gerty Cori that is most impressive. Yost writes
with empathy for her subject, and she has a flair for making their
professions and their personalities come alive.

1969

592. Cori, Carl F. "The Call of Science," in Annual Review of
      Biochemistry, 38, pp. 1-20.
      An autobiographical article which tells of their collaborative
research as only he could. Details of the emotional and human side
of their lives are related to the progress of their research. A vital
source of information.

1971

593. Fruton, Joseph S. "Cori, Gerty Theresa Radnitz," Dictionary
      of Scientific Biography (29), 3, pp. 415-416.
      An outline of her education followed by a description of the
years of work leading to the Nobel Prize. Mentions her later work
and gives a bibliography of some of her publications and several
articles about her.

1976

594. Cori, Carl F. "Gerty Theresa Cori. 1896-1957," American
      Chemists and Chemical Engineers (440), pp. 94-95.
      Largely taken from his autobiography (592). Brief but con-
tains more than just facts. Exhibits a most understanding attitude
concerning the difficulties she faced.

1978

595. Opfell, Olga S. "Cycle of Courage. Gerty Cori," in The
      Lady Laureates. Women Who Have Won the Nobel Prize (39),
      pp. 183-193, 255. Photograph.
      Discusses the research work leading to the Nobel Prize, but
also adds some personal interpretation. The entire story of their
joint careers is well told. There is a short bibliography.

1980

596. Levin, Beatrice S. Women and Medicine (46), pp. 136-139.
      Photograph.
      Using extensive quotations from Rosalyn Yalow, the second
woman to win the Nobel Prize in medicine, we obtain a view of the
Coris from a fellow scientist. The remarks are too brief and the
author adds little detail. Long bibliography, but not all devoted
to Cori.

597. Parascandola, John. "Cori, Gerty Theresa Radnitz," Notable
      American Women (30), 4, pp. 165-167.

Nicely done biographical sketch with less emphasis on the Nobel Prize and the details of the scientific work leading to it. Emphasis is on her life and the difficulties a woman faces when she and her husband are trying to follow their careers together. Bibliography.

598. JANE ANNE RUSSELL WILHELMI
9 February 1911--12 March 1967
Russell was interested in the metabolism of carbohydrates, as were the Coris, and for a while she collaborated with this extraordinary team. By the time she had completed her education at the University of California at Berkeley (BA, 1932; PhD, 1937), she had published six papers on the relationship of pituitary hormones to these processes. During her career at Yale University, which lasted until 1950, she continued to develop these interests and made some fundamental contributions. In spite of her growing stature, as indicated by the Ciba Award for hormonal studies in 1946, she received little academic reward and moved with her husband to Emory University as an assistant professor.

At Emory Russell expanded her research to include nitrogen metabolism and showed that growth hormones are not only necessary for growth per se, but also for the prevention of protein breakdown. In all she published more than 70 research papers and received wide recognition for her accomplishments. She was appointed to important scientific boards by the National Institutes of Health, the National Research Council, and the National Science Foundation. She shared the Upjohn Award of the Endocrine Society with her husband and was elected to the editorial board of the American Physiological Society. She was finally made a full professor two years before her death.

1967

599. Long, C. N. H. "In Memoriam: Jane A. Russell," Endocrinology, 81 (October), pp. 689-692.
A detailed biographical memoir which seems to emphasize the number of her publications. There is also an interesting note about her ability to design a simple experiment which would get at some important point. Nice material on the happy life she shared with her husband and her talents and interests outside of the laboratory.

1980

600. Raacke, I. D. "Russell, Jane Anne," Notable American Women (30), 4, pp. 610-611.
A well-balanced description of her career and accomplishments. Places special emphasis on the difficulty she had in winning recog-

nition for her work. Presents her as a woman with interests and skills beyond her obvious talents in science. Notes her honors and influence in science-policy making.

(See also 681, 1379)

601. ALMIRA HART LINCOLN PHELPS
15 July 1793--15 July 1884
Raised in an inquisitive family with wide-ranging interests, Phelps studied at home and in a number of academies, institutes, and female seminaries. Of these the most famous and intellectually important was that of her sister, Emma Willard's Troy New York Female Seminary. Phelps also taught there and at a number of schools in New England. It was just after the death of her first husband, James H. Lincoln, that she went to the Troy faculty, and it was there that she published her first, most successful book, Familiar Lectures on Botany.
When her sister went to Europe, Phelps became acting principal of the Seminary and increased her growing reputation as an educator. While caring for the two younger children of her new husband, John Phelps, her own two daughters, and bearing two additional children, Phelps continued her writing career. In 1838 she became the principal of a short-lived seminary in West Chester, Pennsylvania. After two years at the Rahway (New Jersey) Female Institute, she moved by invitation to the Patapsco Female Institute. In all of these positions she had the full support of her husband.
Under her direction, until 1856, Patapsco became a well-known institution which lived up to her goal of turning out "good women rather than fine ladies." Her books played a major role in the movement to bring science into the standard course of study. While she did so much to support educational opportunity for women, she also strongly opposed woman's suffrage and took an active stand against it. In 1859 she became the second woman to be elected to the American Association for the Advancement of Science. (See also 1, 8, 23, 37, 40, 48, 718.)

1868

602. [Barnard, Henry]. "I. Educational Biography. Mrs. Almira Lincoln Phelps," Barnard's American Journal of Education, 17 (September), pp. 611-622(?).
A detailed review of Phelps' education and career. Places special emphasis on her writing and describes her thoughts about the place of science in the curriculum for young ladies. Includes a brief bibliography of her works. The pages of this article have

been given in several later biographies as 611-622, but we were
only able to find information on Phelps through page 620.

1884

603. Anon. "A Noted Teacher's Death," The New York Times,
      33 (16 July), p. 5.
      An obituary with some family background; devoted mostly
to her career as an educator and writer.

1909

604. Anon. "Phelps, Almira (Hart) Lincoln," The National Cyclo-
      paedia of American Biography (2), 11, p. 359.
      Entry giving family background and a list of her books with
publication dates.

1914

*605. Galpin, Ruth. Mrs. Almira Hart Lincoln Phelps. Privately
      printed.

1934

606. T[homas] W[oody]. "Phelps, Almira Hart Lincoln," Dictionary
      of American Biography (14), 14, pp. 524-525.
      Woody, an authoritative writer on women's education in the
United States, says, "her career was noteworthy for her popularization of the sciences as fit subjects for girls' education." Gives
a list of her books with publication dates and a brief review of her
career.

1936

607. Bolzau, Emma Lydia. Almira Hart Lincoln Phelps Her Life
      and Work. Philadelphia: University of Pennsylvania, 534
      pp. Photograph.
      A doctoral dissertation which is the definitive biography of
Phelps. A remarkably modern treatment which not only reads well,
but is fully documented. The extensive bibliography is nicely sub-
divided into primary sources (mostly correspondence), newspaper
accounts, and secondary works.

1937

608. Weeks, Mary Elvira, and F. B. Dains. "Mrs. A. H. Lincoln

Phelps and Her Services to Chemical Education," Journal of
Chemical Education, 14, (February), pp. 53-57. Photograph.
The authors discuss in detail Phelps' writings in the area of
chemistry and point out their strengths and weaknesses in the context of the time. They say, "her principal contributions to chemical literature were: a translation of a French dictionary of chemistry (1830), 'Familiar Lectures on Chemistry' (1838), and 'Chemistry
for Beginners' (1834)." They suggest that her methods of teaching, with experiments and practical examples, were very modern.

1971

609. Rudolph, Frederick. "Phelps, Almira Hart Lincoln," Notable
American Women (30), 3, pp. 58-60.
Traces Phelps' career and presents her personal life well
integrated with her teaching, administration and writing. Sees her
as a person having strong convictions and a genuine love of science. Little bibliography.

1976

610. Miles, Wyndham D. "Almira Hart Lincoln Phelps. 1793-1884,"
American Chemists and Chemical Engineers (440), pp. 389-
390.
An excellent evaluation of the chemical writings of Phelps
along with an outline of her career.

1978

611. Tomera, Audrey N. "Phelps, Almira Hart Lincoln," Biographical Dictionary of American Educators (38), 3, p. 1027.
The facts about Phelps' career and writing with a good, but
highly abbreviated, bibliography.

1979

612. Anon. "Phelps, Almira Hart Lincoln" Biographical Dictionary
of American Science (40), p. 204.
Reviews her education and teaching career; lists her major
contributions and gives a short bibliography.

1982

613. Kohlstedt, Sally Gregory. "Almira Hart Lincoln Phelps,"
American Women Writers (48), 3, pp. 379-381.
Author believes that she was an imaginative, successful edu-
cator and a prolific writer. Phelps intended to educate and elevate

young women and also wrote in a popular, melodramatic mode.
"Herself the model of the self-determination she taught, Phelps
helped establish the possibility for women's public and political
roles."

614. LUCRETIA CROCKER
      31 December 1829--9 October 1886
      Although she was never a practicing scientist, Crocker un-
doubtedly did more to advance scientific appreciation and understanding than any other single person. She was a superb classroom teacher herself with a natural ability to inspire students.
Her writing and service on various commissions made important contributions to the introduction of science in the schools of New England and beyond.
      Crocker graduated from the State Normal School in West New-
ton, Massachusetts, in 1850 and taught there for four years. Her
appointment in geography and mathematics reflected a lifelong emphasis on those subjects although she influenced the entire field of
natural science education. She joined the faculty of Antioch College, but after only two years she decided that her calling was
not in college teaching and returned to Boston. It was the influence
of the noted Harvard naturalist Louis Agassiz that brought about
Crocker's major intellectual focus. Her successful efforts to improve
science teaching and to achieve wider public appreciation of science
began when she attended his lectures. She worked with a number
of distinguished women in the development of such important intellectual programs as the Society to Encourage Studies at Home.
      As a member of the Boston School Committee, after a fight
to win the seats to which she and five other women had been
elected, she was then elected to the Board of Supervisors where
she served until her death. With the full support of leading scientists at Harvard and the Massachusetts Institute of Technology
Crocker was able to insist on the best technical materials and highest standards in the Boston schools. She was especially influential
in raising standards for the preparation of science teachers. In
1880 she was elected to the American Association for the Advancement of Science. (See also 40.)

                              1886

615. Anon. "Lucretia Crocker," Boston Evening Transcript
      (11 October), p. 1.
      An obituary which stresses her involvement with the Boston
school board. Presents a few brief remarks on her relationship with
the teachers and her scientific interests.

616. L. M. P. "In Memoriam. Lucretia Crocker," The Woman's
      Journal, 17 (23 October), p. 341.

A longer tribute which discusses in particular Crocker's character traits. Important for understanding her personal goals and attitudes.

617. Cheney, Mrs. Ednah Dow. Memoirs of Lucretia Crocker and Abby W. May. Boston: Privately printed, pp. 1-57.
The combined memorial to two of the women who struggled to be seated on the Boston school board is both a biographical sketch and a series of tributes to them. Especially important for Crocker are the remarks of Professor Hyatt read before the American Association for the Advancement of Science on 20 October 1866 (pp. 9-12).

1971

618. Green, Norma Kidd. "Crocker, Lucretia," Notable American Women (30), 1, pp. 407-409.
A balanced factual account which also underscores the cultural vision of Crocker's efforts.

1979

619. Anon. "Crocker, Lucretia," Biographical Dictionary of American Science (40), pp. 66-67.
A brief account of her career with special emphasis on the associations she formed with the leading Boston scientists.

620. LUCY LANGDON WILLIAMS WILSON
18 August 1865--3 September 1937
Wilson was educated as a biologist at the State Normal School in Castleton, Vermont (1878), and Philadelphia (1881). She continued her education at the University of Pennsylvania (PhD, 1897) and studied at Cornell, Chicago, and Harvard Universities as well as at the Woods Hole Marine Biological Laboratory.
From 1892 until just prior to her death she taught and held administrative positions at various Philadelphia schools, including Temple University. Wilson was especially interested in methods of teaching natural sciences to school children. She employed individualized and laboratory methods and made studies of new techniques being developed in Europe and South America. Many of her travels abroad included lectures at international conferences; she won a gold medal at the 1900 Paris Exposition. Wilson was the author of a large number of books and articles describing methods and making materials available to school teachers.

1941

621. Anon. "Wilson, Lucy Langdon Williams," The National
      Cyclopaedia of American Biography (2), 29, pp. 206-207.
      Discusses her family background, her education, and career.
Gives a good list of her books with their publication dates. Mentions her memberships and honors.

1978

622. Kohut, Sylvester, Jr. "Wilson, Lucy Langdon Williams,"
      Biographical Dictionary of American Educators (38), 3, pp.
      1411-1412.
      Much detail is included in a limited space. Some unusual
bibliographic items.

623. CATHERINE BRIEGER STERN
      6 January 1894--8 January 1973
          In recent years the "new math" has received a great deal
of criticism from educators, scientists, and parents. However, it
is the excesses to which it has been subjected rather than the basic
principles which have been deplored. Stern's work was nearly a
quarter of a century in advance of the widespread application of
the idea of learning basic principles rather than simply memorizing
facts. With her own children she began to develop an interest
in early education. She studied the Montessori method and during
the 1920's and 1930's she conducted a kindergarten, an after-school
club, and a teacher-training institute in her home in Breslau, Germany.
          It was in Breslau where Stern was born and educated, first
at the Mädchen Gymnasium and later at the University of Breslau
(PhD, 1918). Her doctoral work was in physics and mathematics,
but she also had talent in language and literature. She was fluent
in French, produced plays, and wrote poetry. These skills in language arts other than mathematics also played a part in her work
since she was deeply interested in children's reading as well as
their mathematics. She developed methods of rather similar construction which were suitable to both areas.
          In 1932 and 1933 she produced two important books in which
she discussed the theory behind her teaching experience and the
practical aspects of conducting her kindergarten. Since 1919 she
and a fellow university student, Rudolf Stern, had been married
and sharing a full and happy life, but these days were rapidly drawing to a close for everyone, especially European Jews. The Sterns,
like so many others, came to the United States through Canada
in 1938. She continued her work, partly at the New School for
Social Research with Max Wertheimer, the Gestalt psychologist, and

partly in her experimental Castle School. A number of important books, which all stressed the basic concept of letting young children explore basic concepts in reading and mathematics in place of rote learning, appeared in the 1940's and 1950's. She published <u>Children Discover Arithmetic</u> in 1949 and with her daughter, Toni Stern Gould, <u>Children Discover Reading</u> in 1965. Of special importance was her development of such tools as blocks of different lengths and slots in which they could be fitted. Such devices are important in helping children to see numbers and the operations of arithmetic in concrete form. This and other aspects of her work have been used with success in the field of special education.

1973

624. Anon. "Catherine B. Stern, Teacher, Author, 79," <u>The New York Times</u>, 122 (9 January), p. 42.
        Contributed to the modern theory of teaching elementary mathematics and reading. Stern developed visual materials and wrote several books. She was the founder and research director of the Castle School.

1977

625. Anon. "Stern, Catherine (Kathe Brieger)," <u>The National Cyclopaedia of American Biography</u> (2), 57, p. 661.
        Describes her methods and lists her major publications. Gives some personal information.

1980

626. Troxel, Richard D. "Stern, Catherine Brieger," <u>Notable American Women</u> (30), 4, pp. 659-660.
        A well-written description of her life and the development of her teaching methods. Relates her own growth to that of her scientific interests and places both in the evolving context of current psychological thought.

627.   SUSANNA PHELPS GAGE
       26 December 1857--5 October 1915
       Gage was educated at Cornell University (PhB, 1880) and the
following year married Simon H. Gage. She wrote a number of articles on the structure of muscles and the comparative morphology
of the brain and nervous system. One author has said that her
writings "have been quoted by some of Europe's leading anatomists." She won a star in the second edition of American Men of
Science (1910) as one of the 1,000 most distinguished American scientists. For one so highly respected by her peers it is sad that
nothing appears to have been written concerning her life and work.
(See also 4.)

                                1915

628.   Anon. [Death notice], Science, 42 (15 October), p. 523.
       Earned her PhB at Cornell University in 1880 and was well
known for her work in comparative anatomy.

                                1917

629.   Anon. "Memorial to Susanna Phelps Gage," Science, 45 (26
       January), pp. 82-83.
       Her husband and son gave Cornell $10,000 to be used to
support research in physics. This gift was in recognition of the
fact that she was the first woman to take laboratory work in physics at Cornell. The department responded, "It is notable and grati-
fying evidence of the unity of the scientific spirit that this fund
for the promotion of physics is established in memory of one whose
life was given to biology."

630.   MARY JANE ROSS
       29 January 1877--15 July 1964
       Ross was for the most part a practicing physician after 1909,
but prior to that date she worked in embryology with a special interest in the development of the stomach glands.
       She was educated at Cornell University (AB, 1898; PhD, 1902)
and did further graduate work at the University of Pennsylvania
(AM, 1900). Her medical education was at the Johns Hopkins University (MD, 1902). She was resident pathologist at St. Luke's

Hospital, New Bedford, Massachusetts from 1907 to 1909.

In 1909 Ross moved to Binghamton, New York, where she was engaged in general practice and obstetrics until her retirement in 1949. She established the first well-baby clinic in that city in 1914 and was honored by the Medical Society of the State of New York as the outstanding general practitioner of 1953.

1954

631. Anon. "State Medical Society Honors Dr. Mary Ross of Binghamton," **Post Standard [Binghamton?]** (11 May).

A notice of the award as outstanding general practitioner of 1953 with several important pieces of biographical information. Emphasis is on her role in delivering over 5,000 babies, including successive generations of the same family.

632. Anon. [Ross Award]. New York Herald Tribune (11 May). Photograph.

Brief caption to photograph showing Ross receiving her award as the outstanding general practitioner of 1953.

1964

633. Anon. "Woman Doctor, 87, Dies in Binghamton." Unidentified clipping in the Cornell University Archives.

Notes that at her retirement she was the oldest practicing physician in Broome County and says she studied at Columbia ([sic] Cornell?) University.

We are indebted to Kathleen Jacklin, Archivist of Cornell University, for her assistance in learning about Ross's career.

GENERAL (See also 499, 1187)

1946

634. Goff, Alice C. <u>Women Can Be Engineers</u>. Youngstown, Ohio:
Privately printed, pp. 227.
   Goff, who was herself a "structural engineer," has written
a valuable book about women's contributions to engineering and
related fields.   World War I, she believes, helped women engineers
to become recognized, and in 1946 she says, "The war (World War
II) is certain to result in notable gains for women engineers and
scientists, because war speeds up forces that have long been in
operation."   The essays provide a personal biographical sketch and
concise explanations, which the nonspecialist can understand, of
their work and/or their publications.

635. LILLIAN EVELYN MOLLER GILBRETH
   24 May 1878--2 January 1972
   One of the founders of scientific management, Gilbreth also
represents an extraordinary example of the possibility of combining a career with marriage and family.   She is best known through
the book and movie <u>Cheaper by the Dozen</u>, but her actual professional accomplishments are far more remarkable than any fiction.
The Gilbreths, she and Frank, were a team in everything they did;
they and their large family lived the organized and humane life they
taught.   In the context of the turn-of-the-century world it would
have been hard to imagine a less likely couple.   Her studies at Berkeley (BLitt, 1900; MLitt, 1902) in English literature seem to have
little in common with the self-made builder with a flair for inventing
equipment and techniques for the improvement of efficiency.   With
their rapidly growing family her contribution was at first largely
in the editing of his writing and correspondence.   Soon they began
to use their home as a model laboratory in the constant search for
the "one best way" to carry out each task.   They taught management groups at home in addition to their travels, university lectures, industrial consultations, and writing demanded by this new
and growing field.
   Gilbreth was able to complete a PhD in psychology at Brown
University (1915).   Her major contribution both personally and in
their joint work became the appreciation of human qualities in the
application of time and motion studies.   At first there was a lack

of sympathy for this theme on the part of a profit-seeking, industrial community, but as a result of her modest, persuasive presentation, her studies were recognized as an important method in modern management.

Frank Gilbreth died in 1924, and until she was in her eight-
ies Lillian continued to teach, develop, and apply the methods they
began together. She held teaching positions at several colleges
and universities; most notably at Purdue where she became professor of management in 1935. At Purdue she helped establish the
Time and Motion Study Laboratory and made important contributions to the School of Home Economics. She is probably best remembered for her research and her efforts to aid the disabled and
handicapped. (See also 23, 1223.)

1931

636. Fleischman, Doris E., editor and compiler. An Outline of
Careers for Women. A practical guide to achievement. Garden City, New York: Doubleday, pp. 166-173.
This chapter is divided into a biographical sketch of Gilbreth
which lists her children's names and a few of her publications, and
an important essay about industrial engineering written by Gilbreth herself. The article is largely autobiographical since she
and her husband created so much of the theory and practice of
this emerging field.

1935

637. Anon. "Interesting People: Homemaker. Dr. Lillian Moller
Gilbreth," American Magazine, 119 (March), p. 37. Photograph.
A nearly full-page picture of Gilbreth with a statement describing her active life as a professional and a mother.

638. Anon. "Women in Business. III. Lillian M. Gilbreth,"
Fortune, 12 (September), p. 82. Photograph.
A feature series dealing with women in management. Gives
a few facts associated with her career.

1940

639. Anon. "Women Honor Mrs. Gilbreth as an Engineer," New
York Herald Tribune, 100 (27 March), p. 17. Photograph.
A pioneer in industrial psychology receives a life membership in the Engineering Woman's Club. The text of the citation
is reprinted. There is an especially fine quotation from the president of the Newark College of Engineering who says society expects a woman to achieve and still carry out all of the duties of
running a home.

640. Anon. "Gilbreth, Lillian Evelyn," Current Biography Year-
     book, pp. 336-337. Photograph.
     Gives her background, writings, and honors, but also re-
lates her career to her personal life and especially her family. Some
useful references are included.

1943

641. Yost, Edna. American Women of Science (21), pp. 99-121.
     The treatment of Gilbreth is unusually sensitive since she
was a close friend, and Yost is an important biographer of this
unusual husband-wife team. Major emphasis in dispelling the common belief that efficiency must dehumanize people.

642. Bragglotti, Mary. "Silhouette. She Had So Many Children
     ...," The New York Post (19 June), p. 7. Photograph.
     An interview with many quotations about careers, children,
and coping.

1946

643. Goff, Alice C. "Lillian Moller Gilbreth," in Women Can Be
     Engineers (634), pp. 116-132.
     Essay gives details concerning the various projects the Gil-
breth family studied as a family. While it is fairly complete in the
biographical facts of Gilbreth's life and career, it is more important for its representation of the methods they used in the development of management theory. The basic point of their home as happy
and efficient is clear.

1948

644. Anon. "1948 A.W.A. Award Presented to Management Engi-
     neer," Personal and Guidance Journal, 27 (December), p. 214.
     Award given by the American Woman's Association, "for dis-
covering, recognizing, and formulating [with her husband and their
associates] the laws of human motion which in industry are accepted
today as fundamental." This journal is often cited as Occupations.

1949

645. Yost, Edna. Frank and Lillian Gilbreth, Partners for Life.
     With a foreword by A. A. Potter. New Brunswick, New Jer-
     sey: Rutgers University Press, 360 pp.
     A fascinating biography of two unusual individuals whose
marriage seemed totally unlikely. A shy, retiring girl who loved
poetry and music and took a Master's Degree in English at Columbia

wedded a former bricklayer become engineer, ambitious contractor, and avid researcher in the techniques of management. He wanted a total partnership, and at the beginning of their honeymoon he started her apprenticeship, "First I want to teach you about concrete and masonry." Yost reviews the evolution of this partnership and reveals the extraordinary talent and courage exhibited by Lillian Gilbreth after her husband's death. How she became the "First Lady of Engineering" and raised 12 children without much help and how she promoted Frank's work in the scientific management of motion are feats few could accomplish. This book could be enjoyed by teens and adults.

1951

646. Anon. "Gilbreth, Lillian (Evelyn) M(oller)," in Current Biography Yearbook, pp. 233-235. Photograph.
      This biography, which supersedes the earlier version (640), provides the same basic information, but updates it. With the growth and development of Gilbreth's career this is a necessary addition. New references are provided.

1959

647. Clymer, Eleanor, and Lillian Erlich. "Lillian Gilbreth, Engineer," in Modern American Career Women. New York: Dodd, Mead, pp. 1-11. Photograph.
      A nicely told story for the younger reader. The work of the Gilbreths is treated as a part of their life together, and the questions of career and family seem to have appropriate answers. This is not a technical work and no bibliography is given.

1970

648. Gilbreth, Frank B., Jr. Time Out for Happiness. New York: Thomas B. Crowell, 254 pp.
      A delightful book by Frank and Lillian's eldest son who, he says, took much of his material from Edna Yost's biography of his parents (645) and from his "mother's privately printed book, The Quest of the One Best Way." Anecdotal, humorous, and personal, this work also reveals how the Gilbreths were able to help the handicapped through their motion studies and reviews the history of the long "feud" between the Frederick W. Taylor and the Frank Gilbreth systems of "scientific management." The difficult period of his mother's early widowhood is treated with empathy without being sentimental.

649. Stoddard, Hope. "Lillian Gilbreth," in Famous American Women. New York: Thomas Y. Crowell, pp. 193-200. Photograph.

In a short space Stoddard seems to capture the professional
engineer and professional homemaker. The central ideas of scientific management and the close collaboration of the Gilbreths are
nicely described. There is a short bibliography.

1972

650.   Krebs, Albin. "Dr. Gilbreth, Engineer, Mother of Dozen.
        Family and Career," The New York Times, 121 (3 January),
        p. 30. Photograph.
        An obituary notice followed by a long article which touches
on most of the events of Gilbreth's career. Attention is given to
her great capacity for work and her total faith in the new work
she and her husband were doing together. Several highly personal
stories of their lives and work. The 12 children are brought into
the story and their roles in family projects clearly shown. A very
nice piece of newspaper writing.

651.   Anon. "Memorial Services for First Lady of Engineering,"
        Society of Women Engineers Newsletter, 18 (January), pp.
        1-3. Photographs.
        Detailed sketch of Gilbreth's life and most significant contri-
butions written by her admiring colleagues. Cites her many accomplishments and honors. A message from Olive Salembier asks
for private contributions to the Lillian Moller Gilbreth Scholarship
Fund as a mark of respect.

652.   Potter, Andrey A. "Reminiscences of the Gilbreths," Purdue
        Alumnus (February), pp. 4-6.
        Written by a long-time friend and colleague of the Gilbreths,
this sketch provides a great deal of personal insight to their methods and motivations. Clearly Potter has admiration for them as
scientists, but she also found them both to be the finest examples
of people who know how to enjoy life fully.

653.   May, Elizabeth Eckhardt. "Lillian Moeller [sic] Gilbreth.
        1878-1972. Pioneer in the Rehabilitation of the Handicapped
        Homemaker," Journal of Home Economics, (April), pp. 13-
        16. Photographs.
        A number of examples are given of Gilbreth's efforts to de-
vise equipment and techniques to help homemakers with physical
handicaps. The cordial relationship between the Gilbreths and the
American Home Economists Association is described.

1980

654.   Cowan, Ruth Schwartz. "Gilbreth, Lillian Evelyn Moller,"
        Notable American Women (30), 4, pp. 271-273.
        Shows the large variety of projects in which the Gilbreths

engaged and the energy she displayed in carrying on after his death.
Cites specific examples to illustrate the balance between his scientific and her human strengths. The warmth of their family life
and the intensity of their professional career is beautifully told.
A good, but limited bibliography.

655. EDITH CLARKE
    10 February 1883--29 October 1959
    Although her relatives were opposed, Clarke determined to
obtain an education and enrolled at Vassar College (AB, 1908).
Three years of teaching at a private school and a college convinced
her that the future lay in engineering. The correctness of this
judgment was clear to her after courses at the University of Wisconsin and a summer job at American Telephone and Telegraph.
The solution of mathematical equations proved so interesting that
she remained with AT&T for six years.
    During World War I Clarke studied at the Massachusetts Institute of Technology and received the first master's degree in electrical engineering granted a woman by that school (MS, 1919). When
World War I ended, only unprofessional positions were open to a
woman engineer, and she decided to travel. She spent the next
year (1921-1922) teaching physics at the Constantinople Woman's
College, but engineering still called, and she returned to General
Electric.
    Employment conditions had now improved enough to give Clarke
the opportunity to display her ability. Over the next 23 years she
worked on the design of large power stations. She was especially
productive in the development of calculating devices that allowed
the prediction of system reactions to extraordinary events without solving the same sets of equations over and over again. Her publications were widely recognized for their high merit. She was the
first woman to be elected a fellow of the American Institute of
Electrical Engineers and received two prizes from that professional
society. After her retirement she had one more teaching appointment when she was invited by the University of Texas to be a professor of electrical engineering. For the next nine years she conducted an active program of graduate student research and publication.

1941

656. MacLennan, Nancy. "Women Inventors Steal the Show at G-E
    Party," The Bridgeport [Connecticut] Post, (24 March).
    Photograph.
    Clarke and the physicist Katharine Blodgett are quoted on
science and engineering, opportunities for women, their inventions,
and a variety of other topics at an annual General Electric Company
meeting in Bridgeport. A bit sensationalized, but good reading all
the same.

1946

657. Goff, Alice C. "Edith Clarke," in Women Can Be Engineers
      (634), pp. 50-65.
      Combines some background and personal information with a
detailed but not too technical discussion of several of Clarke's most
important publications. Emphasizes that she is at home with the
use of mathematics and urges young women not to be afraid of that
subject which is so essential to an engineer.

1948

658. Early, Dudley. "Miss Edith Clark [sic]: Fate Placed Her
      on the Path of Fame," Austin [Texas] American-Statesman
      (10 October). Photograph.
      A folksy style, but still a tribute to Clarke as "probably"
the only woman professor of electrical engineering in the nation.
Lists some of her accomplishments and quotes her on women in engineering and their problems with mathematics. Caption of photograph says "Mrs. Clarke."

659. Anon. "No Time to Retire. Teaching Opens New World to
      Woman, 65," The Dallas [Texas] Morning News (12 Decem-
      ber), p. 22. Photograph.
      Talks about her change from industry to academia after 26
years of research at General Electric. Also mentions her work in
Turkey at the Constantinople Women's College.

1956

*660. The New York Times, (19 February).
      Nothing could be located corresponding to this reference
from Notable American Women (661).

1980

661. Rockefeller, Terry Kay. "Clarke, Edith," Notable American
      Women (30), 4, pp. 151-153.
      Good review of her career at General Electric, but very lit-
tle on the years in Texas. Treats the difficulties faced by a
woman engineer.

662. IRMGARD FLÜGGE-LOTZ
      16 July 1903--22 May 1974
      Born in Germany and educated at the Hanover Technische
Hochschule (diplom ingenieur, 1927; doctor, 1929), Flügge-Lotz

carried out some of her most important studies at the Aerodynamische Versuchsanstalt in Göttingen. This work on the lifting force of wings of various shapes continued to be recognized as a fundamental contribution throughout her lifetime. It was also at Göttingen that she met and married Wilhelm Flügge, with whom she collaborated during their entire careers.

Both Flügge and Flügge-Lotz were denied any real career opportunities because of their anti-Nazi sentiments and on account of her sex. They were invited by Hermann Göring, noted for his emphasis on talent even at the expense of political impurity, to positions at the Deutsche Versuchsanstalt für Luftfahrt, the central aeronautics research institute. By maintaining the delicate balance between good science and bad politics, they survived the war and came to Stanford University following a year of research in Paris. The next 20 years in California were productive ones with her publications exceeding 50 technical papers and two important books. She was finally promoted to full professor in 1960 after becoming an international authority on automatic control theory. As Stanford's first woman engineering professor and the second woman fellow of the American Institute of Aeronautics and Astronautics she was honored for her lifetime of fundamental contributions. (See also 43.)

1969

663. Anon. "'A Life Full of Work'--The Flügges," Stanford Engineering News (May), unnumbered. Photograph.

Personal views of their lives and careers at the time of their retirement from active teaching. The Flügges show no trace of bitterness at the effects political events had on their work and lives.

1973

664. Anon. "Awards, Honorary Degree. Irmgard Flügge-Lotz," Stanford Engineering News (November), unnumbered. Photograph.

Notice of her being the recipient of an honorary DSc from the University of Maryland. Gives the full citation, which "recognizes her many years of engineering accomplishments in the field of aerodynamics and guidance control."

1974

665. Spreiter, John R.; Milton D. Van Dyke; and Walter G. Vincenti. "Memorial Resolution, Stanford University. Irmgard Flügge-Lotz. 1903-1974." 3 pp.

A biographical sketch by her colleagues on the occasion of her death. Some specific comments about her research interests and a deeply felt respect and admiration for her.

666. Anon. "Irmgard Flügge-Lotz--'A Life Full of Work,'" <u>Stan-</u>
      <u>ford Engineering News</u> (May), unnumbered. Photograph.
      Reviews her career. When asked why she became an engineer
she said, "I wanted a life that would never be boring."

667. Anon. "Prof. Irmgard Flügge-Lotz Dies; Taught Engineering
      at Stanford," <u>The New York Times</u>, 123 (23 May), pp. 44.
      The first woman to hold a full professorship at Stanford and
the first woman chosen a fellow of the American Institute of Aeronautics and Astronautics. Recounts the academic difficulties in
Nazi Germany.

1975

668. Spreiter, John R.; Milton D. Van Dyke; and Walter G. Vin-
      centi. "In Memoriam, Irmgard Flügge-Lotz, 1903-1974," <u>IEEE</u>
      <u>Transactions on Automatic Control</u>, AC-20 (April), pp. 183a-
      183b. Photograph.
      A careful review of her education and professional career.
The major theme is her research on automatic control, but her other
contributions are noted. After she retired from teaching she continued to carry out research of significance to the space program.

1980

669. Hallion, Richard P. "Flügge-Lotz, Irmgard," <u>Notable American</u>
      <u>Women</u> (30), 4, pp. 241-242.
      Presents the education and career development pattern of
a young scientist between the World Wars in Europe in an excellent
manner. A long, but not too technical, discussion of her research
interests and publications is equally well written. A good bibliography.

670. AUGUSTA ROBINSON PINNEY
     birth and death dates unknown
     Pinney is included in each of the first three editions of
American Men of Science (1906-1921) and uses the title Mrs. From
1868 to 1888 she taught at Miss Robinson's School for Young Ladies
(possibly in Springfield, Massachusetts), where she lists her address. Her scientific interests are suggestive of a very modern
concept in our concern for ecology--bugs that are useful in keep-
ing down injurious insects. She was a member of the American
Association for the Advancement of Science and the Zoology and
Botany Clubs of Springfield.

671. MARGERETTA HARE MORRIS
     3 December 1797--29 May 1867
     Nothing is known of her education and very little of her
life, most of which she appears to have spent in Germantown,
Pennsylvania, with her mother and unmarried sister. She was ac-
quainted with a number of scientists and prepared illustrations for
some botanical papers. Her own studies of the Hessian fly and
the seventeen-year locust were published in the leading scientific
journals of the day and represent an important contribution, particularly for agriculture. Morris may also have studied the relationship of fungi to plants. She was the first woman to be elected
to the Philadelphia Academy of Natural Sciences when she was made
an honorary member in the late 1850's. (See also 37, 40.)

1898

*672. Moon, Robert C[harles]. The Morris Family of Philadelphia.
      Philadelphia: R. C. Moon, 2, pp. 399-404, 581-583.

1967

673. Graustein, Jeannette E. Thomas Nuttall Naturalist. Explora-
     tions in America. 1808-1841. Cambridge, Massachusetts:
     Harvard University Press, pp. 374, 454.
     Morris made illustrations for a publication of interest to Nut-
tall, and the evidence suggests she had known him for several
years. He was a member of the committee which judged her first
paper for the American Philosophical Society.

674. Wainwright, Nicholas B., editor. A Philadelphia Perspective.
     The diary of Sidney George Fisher covering the years 1834-
     1871. Philadelphia: The Historical Society of Pennsylvania,
     pp. 107-108, 286, 328.
     Fisher makes two brief references to Morris, nearly 19 years
apart, but they are very interesting reading. In 1840 he is full
of praise for her study of the Hessian fly, saying she will merit
the gratitude of the nation if her inferences, which appear to him
conclusive, are correct. In 1859 he says, she "is an old maid ...
and has published some papers on supposed or real discoveries
about the Hessian fly."

1979

675. Anon. "Morris, Margaretta Hare," Biographical Dictionary
     of American Science (40), pp. 185-186.
     About her life and scientific contributions. Says her dis-
coveries had significance for agriculture. Good bibliography of
her works and writings about her.

676. CHARLOTTE DE BERNIER SCARBROUGH TAYLOR
     1806--26 November 1861
     Taylor graduated from a private school in New York City
and appears to be self-taught in science. Her studies of insects,
mostly associated with cotton and wheat, were careful and made
with magnifying glasses but not a compound microscope. At least
19 papers on entomological subjects are known, but since she published them in literary magazines (e.g., Harper's New Monthly)
rather than scientific journals she is often recognized as a writer
rather than a scientist. For the time she had an unusual awareness of the ecological relationship of insects and agriculture.
Through her studies of insect habits and her publications she urged
the informed control of pests.

1871

677. Allibone, S. A[ustin]. A Critical Dictionary of English Lit-
     erature and British and American Authors. Philadelphia:
     J. B. Lippincott, 3, p. 2342.
     Simply states that her book, Scenes from Plantation Life,
is in preparation, but important in that she was considered an
author worth noting.

1899

678. Anon. "Taylor, Charlotte de Bernier," in The National

Cyclopaedia of American Biography (2), 2, p. 164. Pen and
ink sketch.
    Mostly about her fine manners and great social charm but
does refer to her use of the microscope, "for six and eight hours
at a time." Lists some of her scientific and popular books and articles.

1936

679. R[ichard] H. S[hryock]. "Taylor, Charlotte de Bernier,"
     Dictionary of American Biography (14), 18, pp. 319-320.
         Good overall view of Taylor's life with more emphasis on her
     scientific writing. Evaluates their worth and the probable cause
     of their being so little recognized. Says there is little evidence
     that her work had much effect on later scientific activities. Some
     helpful bibliography on her articles published in magazines.

1979

680. Anon. "Taylor, Charlotte De Bernier Scarbrough,"
     Biographical Dictionary of American Science (40), p. 247.
         Review of her life and scientific interests in highly abridged
form. Gives a list of her writings with helpful bibliography.

681. ANNA BOTSFORD COMSTOCK
     1 September 1854--24 August 1930
         From her childhood Comstock was surrounded by nature for
     which she felt a strikingly early kinship. She was a true natural-
     ist, and her most important contributions are in her efforts to make
     the beauty of nature clear to all, especially children. After some
     limited education and a year of teaching she enrolled in languages
     and literature at Cornell University. After she met John H. Com-
     stock, a young faculty member in entomology, she left college but
     continued to be active in natural science. She gained stature as
     an illustrator of her husband's books and eventually became one
     of the first four women elected to the Society of the Sigma Xi and
     the third woman elected to the American Society of Wood-Engravers.
     Her husband was strong in his support of her career, and she
     completed her degree at Cornell (BS, 1885).
         In 1895 she was appointed to the Committee for the Promo-
     tion of Agriculture in New York State. Over the years until about
     1926 she carried out a vigorous program of lecturing and writing
     in an effort to improve farming methods by teaching children the
     scientific approach to nature appreciation. In a poll taken in 1923
     she was recognized as one of America's 12 greatest living women.
     In 1899 she became the first woman to obtain a professorship at
     Cornell, and while this was withdrawn for a time for political

reasons, she was again promoted in 1920. In 1930, just prior to
her death, she was awarded an honorary doctorate by Hobart College of Geneva, New York. It is said that she, more than anyone
else, was instrumental in recruiting pioneers in the field of nature
study. (See also 4, 12, 37, 40, 48.)

1924

682.   Sawyer, Ruth. "What Makes Mrs. Comstock Great," The
       Woman Citizen, ns 9 (20 September), pp. 8-9, 28. Photo-
       graph.
       A lengthy interview after which the author evaluates the
reasons for Comstock's selection as one of America's 12 greatest
living women in 1923. Sawyer, a novelist and long-time friend,
also talked with former teachers, current colleagues, Professor Comstock and Mrs. Comstock, collecting various views of her career
and reasons for her success. The results make interesting reading
and form a warm and human picture of a fine naturalist and splendid teacher.

1930

683.   Anon. "Anna Botsford Comstock," Nature Magazine, 16 (Oc-
       tober), p. 207.
       A review of Comstock's education and teaching career. Gives
a partial list of her writings and some of her honors. Says it would
be hard to accurately estimate the extent of her influence in nature
study.

1931

684.   Essig, E[dward] O[liver]. A History of Entomology. New
       York: Hafner Publishing, pp. 577, 861. Reprinted: 1965.
       Photograph.
       Essig's very demanding selection criteria results in Com-
stock being the only woman included in this detailed study which
is largely devoted to the western United States, especially California. The following legend appears under her photograph: "wife
of Prof. J. H. Comstock, ably assisted him in his entomological work
and also made a national reputation in entomological illustration and
engraving and in nature study." Her birth date is included in
his Tabular Progress of Entomology.

685.   Howard, L. O. "John Henry Comstock," in "A History of
       Applied Entomology (Somewhat Anecdotal)," Smithsonian Mis-
       cellaneous Collections, 84, pp. 57-61.
       An important contribution to our appreciation of the relation-
ship between John and Anna and the unique role she played at

Cornell. "She mothered generations of young students who came
to her husband's department for study, and gave them an insight
into home and social life that made their stay at Cornell very pleasant."

1932

686. Anon. "Comstock, Anna Botsford," The National Cyclopaedia
of American Biography (2), 22, p. 11. Photograph.
Emphasizes her work with her husband and reviews her
academic career. Gives a good list of her publications with year
of publication. Mentions some of her honors.

1946

687. Needham, James G. "The Lengthened Shadow of a Man and
His Wife, I and II," Scientific Monthly, 62 (February and
March), pp. 140-150, 219-229. Photograph.
This history of the department of entomology at Cornell University by the long-time colleague of the Comstocks is really the
life story of them as they built the department from nothing. The
first part deals mostly with John Comstock, but also treats their
meeting and marriage. The second part of the paper is nearly all
about her career and provides a great deal of firsthand information. The intimacy of their shared lives and the magnitude of their
contribution are very clear.

1950

688. Wanamaker, John. "The Story of a Rolltop Desk," Nature
Magazine, 43 (October), pp. 429-430. Photograph.
Using the structure of Comstock's favorite old-fashioned desk,
Wanamaker creates an interesting and informative picture of the
manner of her work. The neat pigeonholes and their labels are
a useful frame in which to describe the orderly and productive mind
and hand which used them.

1953

689. Comstock, Anna Botsford. The Comstocks of Cornell: John
Henry Comstock and Anna Botsford Comstock. Glenn W. Herrick
and Ruby Green Smith, editors. Ithaca, New York: Comstock Publishing, 286 pp. Photographs.
A source of detailed biographical data with obvious emphasis
on John Comstock. In spite of this limitation, Anna Comstock sup-
plies a great deal of otherwise unavailable personal information concerning her life and career. A most readable and vital account
with excellent photographs but limited bibliography.

690. Vinal, William Gould. "The Science Janus," School Science
      and Mathematics, 53 (May), pp. 345-357, especially 353-355.
      Making a plea for a balance between the specialist and the
generalist in science departments, Vinal offers Comstock as an example of the very best of generalists. In addition to his purpose
of comparison, the author gives a good biographical sketch. The
general theme is continued in a later paper, but does not refer
to Comstock.

                                1971

691. Mallis, Arnold. "John Henry Comstock (1849-1931) and Anna
      Botsford Comstock (1854-1930)," in American Entomologists.
      New Brunswick, New Jersey: Rutgers University Press, pp.
      126-138. Photograph.
      Devotes a good amount of space to her and makes clear the
closeness of her relationship with her husband. Gives less attention to her nature study work, but is important for its detail of
the entomological contributions.

692. Jacklin, Kathleen. "Comstock, Anna Botsford," Notable
      American Women (30), 1, pp. 367-369.
      A balanced account of the life shared by the Comstocks.
Gives a nice, artistic feeling about a woman who combined the best
of science, poetry and art in her career. A useful bibliography.

                                1975

693. Smith, Edward H. "The Comstocks and Cornell: In the Peo-
      ple's Service," Annual Review of Entomology, vol. 21, pp.
      1-25.
      A detailed and well-documented biography of both John and
Anna. The main theme is his work in entomology, but his relationship with his wife and their ties to Cornell during a period of growth,
make this a valuable source for her life as well.

                                1978

694. Barr, Bonnie B. "Comstock, Anna Botsford," Dictionary of
      American Educators (38), 1, p. 293.
      A brief review of Comstock's career with emphasis on her
nature study publications and some notice of her books. A comment about her honors and a limited bibliography.

                                1979

695. Anon. "Comstock, Anna Botsford," Biographical Dictionary
      of American Science (40), p. 60.

A few lines giving nothing of interest beyond the fact that
she is listed at all.

696. Talbot, Bruce. "Anna Comstock Nature Study Pioneer," The
      Conservationist (January-February), pp. 14-17. Photographs.
      A short but very readable biographical sketch which shows
the early and important influence Comstock had in promoting an
appreciation of nature. Mentions other aspects of her career and
presents beautiful reproductions of some of her engravings.

1982

697. Kohlstedt, Sally Gregory. "Anna Botsford Comstock," Ameri-
      can Women Writers (48), 1, pp. 389-391.
      Comstock's work, unlike much of the natural history writing
of the period, was accurate. The tone was popular, and yet the
substantive content was scholarly. She was a key figure at Cornell and in the nature study movement. She also wrote one novel,
Confessions of a Heathen Idol (1906) under the pseudonym Marion
Lee.

698. ELIZABETH GIFFORD PECKHAM
      19 December 1854--3 January 1940
      A specialist in entomology of the spiders and wasps, Peck-
ham began her scientific education at Vassar College (AB, 1876;
AM, 1889). After her marriage in 1880 to George W. Peckham they
collaborated in studies of certain species of spiders. Their work
was published by the Natural History Society of Wisconsin. After
her husband's death in 1914, she continued her education at Cornell University (PhD, 1916).

699. Peckham is cited in American Men of Science, 1906-1921.
      We are indebted to Lisa Browar, Curator of Rare Books, and
Terri O'Shea, Alumnae Association, both of Vassar College, for their
assistance in locating some useful information.

700. MARY ISABEL McCRACKEN
      1866--29 October 1955
      McCracken spent her entire academic life at Stanford Univer-
sity where she enrolled at the advanced age of 34 after teaching
in the public schools of Oakland, California for a full decade. In
her senior year (AB, 1904), she joined the staff as an assistant
in physiology and entomology. Her graduate education (MA, 1905;
PhD, 1908) was obtained while she continued her teaching duties.
She retired as professor emerita in 1931.
      In research McCracken had a broad range of interests and
tied much of the work directly to her teaching; for example, she

kept bees in a special demonstration hive. She made a fairly extensive study of silkworms and published several articles as a result. As a research associate of the California Academy of Sciences (1931-1942) she developed her longstanding interest in birds and their relationship to insects.

Her colleagues and former students praised her work as a teacher. She was recognized for her skill in interesting students in the subject of entomology and for insisting on the mastery of fundamentals. She took a personal interest in her students and often helped them emotionally and financially.

1931

701. Vickery, Robert K. "Dr. Isabel McCracken," Stanford Illustrated Review, 32 (June), pp. 412-413. Photograph.

A former student writing at the time of McCracken's retirement praises her for the interesting manner of her presentation of entomology. Also comments about the thorough grounding students received in economic entomology from her. Says that she hopes to use her new freedom to complete the analysis and writing of several research projects in which she has collected data for years.

1955

702. Wiggins, Ira L.; Arthur C. Giese; and Siemon Muller, "Memorial Resolution, Stanford University. Mary Isabel McCracken. 1866-1955," Unpublished, undated, 2 pp.

The text of the comments of her colleagues at the time of her death. Generally positive, but lukewarm in regard to her research productivity.

703. Anon. "In Memoriam, 1955. McCracken," Stanford Review, 57 (December), p. 28.

Obituary giving the facts of her education and academic career. Mentions her work at the California Academy of Sciences with the wild bee collection. She is reported to have worked closely with two of her more famous colleagues, David S. Jordan and Vernon Kellogg, in what was apparently an important experimental course entitled "bionomics."

704. Anon. "Dr. Isabel M. McCracken, Early Farm Zoologist, Dies," unidentified newspaper clipping.

A nice article which claims she was one of the pioneers at Stanford and cites her role as a founder of the Palo Alto Junior Museum. Most of the material is taken directly from the other obituary articles.

We are indebted to Linda J. Long, Manuscripts Specialist, Stanford University Archives, for this material.

GENERAL (See also 738, 1403)

1978

*705.   James. Preston E., and G. J. Martin.   The Association of
American Geographers.   The First 75 Years.

706.   ZONIA BABER
24 August 1862--unknown
A graduate of the University of Chicago (SB, 1904), Baber
taught geography in various Chicago schools.   She was a member
of several professional organizations including the Chicago Geographical Society, which she served as president.   At the 50th anniversary celebration of this society Baber was recognized for having put forward the original suggestion for its formation.   At that
time she was 86 and professor emerita, having been associate professor of the teaching of geography and geology at Chicago from
1901 to 1921.

1947

707.   Steyskal, Irene.   "Geografic [sic] Society Will Observe Its
50th Anniversary," Chicago Sunday Tribune (15 February).
Notes that Baber made the first suggestion that the Society
be formed.   She, now 86 years old, is to be honored at the banquet.   We are indebted to Daniel Mayer, Assistant Archivist of the
University of Chicago, and his associate Richard Popp for their
assistance.

708.   ELLEN CHURCHILL SEMPLE
8 January 1863--8 May 1932
After her undergraduate education at Vassar College (AB,
1882), Semple returned to her home to teach in a private school.
Her interests soon led to extensive reading in history and a growing awareness of social and economic problems.   While on a European trip she made the decision to study geography at the University of Leipzig with Friedrich Ratzel.   Based upon her reading
and a written examination, she took a graduate degree at Vassar

(MA, 1891) and went to Leipzig. In spite of university rules for-
bidding women, she won the attention of Ratzel and some of his
colleagues who permitted her to attend their lectures that year and
again in 1895.

In a pattern which continued throughout her career she rode
into the backcountry of Kentucky to study the influence of geographic isolation on the life of the people. Her first article appeared in 1901 and attracted widespread attention among her colleagues. Future articles continued to receive favorable discussion
in geographic circles. In 1904 she presented a paper at the International Geographical Congress in Washington and in 1905 before
the Royal Geographical Society of London. She was also invited
to give courses at the universities of Oxford and Chicago.

Her second and most important book, Influences of Geographic
Environment, on the Basis of Ratzel's System of Anthropo-Geography,
had been requested by her former professor. In fact, it went beyond his work and presented much of her original thought. This
publication was immediately recognized as a contribution of great
importance. However, as in most fields, fashion of scholarship in
geography changed during the latter part of her life. Her deter-
ministic position lost ground to the philosophy of the individual's
freedom to choose from a variety of options in life. However, there
can be little doubt of the importance of Semple's role in stimulating
research and writing among American geographers.

In 1921 she joined the new graduate department of geography
at Clark University and was promoted to full professor in 1923.
The significance of her work was recognized in the honorary LLD
she received from the University of Kentucky (1923), the Cullum
Medal of the American Geographical Society (1914), the gold medal
presented by the Geographic Society of Chicago (1932), and her
election as the first woman president of the Assocation of American
Geographers in 1921. (See also 8, 11, 48.)

1932

709. Whitbeck, R. H. "Ellen Churchill Semple," The Geographi-
      cal Review, 22, pp. 500-501.
      A memorial which calls Semple "America's most outstanding
anthropogeographer." Reviews briefly her most notable books and
notes her constant contributions to the literature. "Her more than
thirty years of industrious devotion to her chosen field have left
their distinctive impress upon geography in the United States."

710. Atwood, Wallace W. "An Appreciation of Ellen Churchill Sem-
      ple, 1863-1932," Journal of Geography, 31 (September), p.
      267.
      A short tribute by the first director of the graduate pro-
gram in geography at Clark University, who says, "she became
an inspiration to the entire group ... a faculty of specialists."
Has high praise for her research and leadership in general.

1933

711. Colby, Charles C. "Ellen Churchill Semple," Annals of the
     Association of American Geographers, 23 (December), pp.
     229-240. Photograph.
     A detailed biography of Semple calling her, "the greatest
anthropogeographer in the world." A section is devoted to her
education, including a discussion of the importance of the time between her degrees at Vassar. An analysis of each of her important
works and of their influence on geographic thought follows. A bibliography of her publications.

1954

712. Gelfand, Lawrence. "Ellen Churchill Semple: Her Geographi-
     cal Approach to American History," The Journal of Geography,
     53 (January), pp. 30-41.
     A detailed analysis and criticism of Semple's methods as ap-
plied especially to history. Even though the author finds many
shortcomings, he also carefully points out the cases where her
methods are useful. He gives her full credit for the importance
of her work in stimulating research and writing in American geography. There is much straight biographical material here as well.

1962

713. Wright, John K. "Miss Semple's 'Influences of Geographic
     Environment,' Notes Toward a Bibliobiography," The Geo-
     graphical Review, 52 (July), pp. 346-361.
     A most interesting project in which the author attempts to
write the biography of Semple's book. Some of this paper is rather
technical, but the central idea is fairly clear. The question deals
with how the book gained its great reputation and then lost it and
the even more difficult problem of whether it deserved to fall out
of favor. Even if the analysis gets difficult, this paper is an important part of understanding Semple since she was so totally committed to the concepts expressed in the book under discussion.

1971

714. Anon. "Semple, Ellen Churchill," Notable American Women
     (30), 3, pp. 260-262.
     Since most of the published biography of Semple deals with
her published work and/or influence as a geographer, it is important to have this more broadly based sketch. It is especially strong
in its description of her education in the United States and Europe.
Deals well with her professional career including her other studies.

1982

715. Brooker-Gross, Susan R. "Ellen Churchill Semple," American Women Writers (48), 4, pp. 56-57.
A brief but nicely balanced sketch which makes Semple's strengths and limitations clear. Good bibliography.

716. ALICE FOSTER
1872--1962
A specialist in the geography of Spain and Mexico, Foster was educated at the Universities of Iowa (AB, 1918) and Chicago (SM, 1921; PhD, 1936). Her doctorate, at the age of 63, came as the climax of a lifetime of productive teaching and scholarship. During her long association with Chicago she published several textbooks and research articles in the leading scientific periodicals. She was especially interested in the field of geography in education and served as president of the National Council of Geography Teachers in 1941. That group presented her with their Distinguished Service Award in 1947.

1963

717. Harris, Chauncy D. "Alice Foster. 1872-1962," Journal of Geography, 62 (February), p. 77.
A short memorial article which praises her studies of Spain and Mexico. A special notice of her efforts in the field of geography teaching.

GENERAL (See also 58, 514)

1977

718. Arnold, Lois Barber. "American Women in Geology. A historical perspective," Geology, 5 (August), pp. 493-494.
As an introduction to the symposium "Women and Careers in Geoscience," this paper outlined the names of women geologists beginning with the educator-naturalists like Phelps and Agassiz and continuing to the mid-twentieth century. An important overview without much detail.

1979

719. Wallace, Jane H. "Women in the Survey," Geotimes, 24 (March), p. 34.
Presents the names of women who have been associated with the United States Geological Survey from 1879 and discusses their treatment. Too brief, but important.

1982

720. Elder, Eleanor S. "Women in Early Geology," Journal of Geological Education, 30 (November), pp. 287-293. Photographs.
A series of well-written, but all too brief sketches of most of the leading American women in geology at the beginning of the present century. There is coverage of earlier women, especially in France, who had some interest and influence. A very good start and well-documented.

721. MARY EMILEE HOLMES
10 April 1849--unknown
Holmes combined her interests in paleontology and zoology when she taught at her alma mater, Rockford College (AB, 1868). Her graduate education was obtained at the University of Michigan (AM, 1887; PhD, 1888). After 11 years at Rockford she served various Presbyterian mission societies and became the editor and proprietor of the Freedmen's Bulletin. For her "original scientific investigation and discovery," she was the first woman elected a fellow of the Geological Society of America.

722.   Holmes is cited in <u>American Men of Science</u>, 1906-1910; <u>Who Was Who in America</u>, 1, pp. 581-582.

723.   JENNIE MARIA ARMS SHELDON
       29 July 1852--unknown
       Sheldon studied as a special student at the Massachusetts Institute of Technology for at least two years between 1877 and 1881 and as a special laboratory student at the Boston Society of Natural History during that same period. From 1878 until she married in 1897 she taught zoology and geology in the Boston schools. She was an assistant to Alpheus Hyatt at the Natural History laboratory for 25 years.
       With her husband in Deerfield, Massachusetts, she continued to study and publish books and articles dealing with the clays of the Connecticut valley, the invertebrata, and historical subjects. She worked to establish the Naples Table for the promotion of laboratory research by women. (See also 4.)

724.   Sheldon is cited in <u>American Men of Science</u>, 1921; <u>Woman's Who's Who of America</u>, p. 738.

725.   FLORENCE BASCOM
       14 July 1862--18 June 1945
       Bascom was born in the period of a raging Civil War. Her father was a professor of moral philosophy and a powerful pulpit orator. Such circumstances would seem to all but forbid the development of an outstanding scientific career. Yet Bascom not only became a leading figure in American scientific education and research, but did so, surprisingly, in the field of geology. In the 1880's she introduced the microscopic study of minerals in the United States and, in spite of her unofficial status, became the first woman awarded a doctorate by Johns Hopkins University (1893) and the first American woman to obtain a doctorate in geology. Her earlier education was nothing short of unbelievable since at the University of Wisconsin, where her father was president, she received four degrees (AB and BL, 1882; BS, 1884; AM, 1887).
       In 1895 Bascom began a career at Bryn Mawr College which represented a brilliant continuation of her struggles and successes over the next 33 years. Even in this center of awareness of women's need for broad intellectual opportunity, geology was openly considered inappropriate as a career. Building a major department with a respected research reputation could only be accomplished by a person of extraordinary talent, stamina, and conviction. Lack of administrative enthusiasm, an emotional obstacle in itself, meant inadequate space, funds, and faculty. Bascom became accepted as a leader among American geologists, and Bryn Mawr produced the majority of female geologists well into the 1930's.

One of her several notable students, Eleanora Bliss Knopf, stresses the importance of character and adherence to high standards as central to Bascom's teaching and scholarship. In small class es she demanded the very best of both intellectual and physical commitment from herself and her students. The thought of delaying the start of a day's field work beyond seven a.m. for the sake of a better breakfast was unthinkable. After a full day on horseback or horse and buggy she would spend the evening in drafting and map work. The winter months, too, demanded that every moment not devoted to teaching be spent in the laboratory or writing reports. It was universally agreed that this dual rigor in research and teaching made Bascom the legendary figure she became to scientists and people of the countryside in which she worked.

Bascom's impressive contributions to petrology, the application of microscopic techniques to geology, began at Wisconsin in the mid 1880's and became apparent at Hopkins. Knopf assures us that Bascom's doctoral dissertation placed her among the foremost American petrographers. The importance of her work and its future potential were recognized immediately when in 1896 she became the first woman assistant on the United States Geological Survey. In that position and later, promoted to geologist, she made detailed studies of the Piedmont in Maryland, Pennsylvania, and part of New Jersey. Publications, which contribute impressively to understanding that complicated area, appeared as parts of the Geological Survey Folios and Bulletins from 1909 through 1938. Over all she published forty titles, all displaying the vigor and incisiveness found in her lectures and conversation.

The honors that came to Bascom also reflect her pioneering professional position among American women in science. After being the second woman elected a fellow of the Geological Society of America (1894), she was the first woman to be elected to its Council (1924) and to serve as its vice-president. It has been incorrectly stated that she was a member of the National Academy of Sciences.

Bascom retained her professional devotion to the last. Her health failed in the late 1930's while she was completing aerial studies of a region of Pennsylvania. She died, an inspiration to her colleagues and students, in the New England she loved. (See also 4, 25, 36, 43.)

1895

726.   Anon. [Appointment], American Geologist, 15 (May), p. 336.
       A note saying that Bascom has been appointed at Bryn Mawr.

1900

727.   Thwaites, Reuben Gold, editor. The University of Wisconsin.
       Its history and its alumni with historical and descriptive
       sketches of Madison profusely illustrated. Madison,

Wisconsin: J. N. Purcell, p. 300. Photograph facing p. 300.

A biographical sketch with a complete list of her publications to that date.

1925

728. Bascom, Florence. "The University in 1874-1887," Wisconsin Magazine of History, 8 (March), pp. 300-308.

A beautiful autobiographical essay of her years at the University of Wisconsin. Indispensable firsthand account of the happy circumstances of her early collegiate education.

1937

729. Anon. "Eminent Woman Geologist Honored at Luncheon Given in Washington," New York Sun, 105 (29 December), p. 10. Photograph.

A long article describing Bascom's accomplishments in the most glowing terms. Gives an account of her discoveries and honors. Especially good in discussion of her teaching and advising students.

1945

730. Anon. "Florence Bascom, Geologist, is Dead," The New York Times, 94 (20 June), p. 23. Photograph.

A brief review of her education and teaching career.

731. Ogilvie, Ida H. "Obituary. Florence Bascom. 1862-1945," Science, 102 (28 September), pp. 320-321.

Written by a former student, the obituary gives a fairly long account of Bascom's career with special emphasis on her teaching and scholarship. Errs in saying she was the first fellow of the Geological Society of America and a member of the National Academy.

732. Ogilvie, Ida H., and Howard L. Gray. "Florence Bascom," Bryn Mawr Alumnae Bulletin (November), pp. 12-13. Photograph.

Personal information combined with a detailed treatment of the development of the department of geology at Bryn Mawr written by two people who knew and admired her.

1946

733. [Bryn Mawr Faculty Committee]. "Resolution on the death of Professor Bascom," Minutes of the Faculty (25 March), unnumbered.

Read by Professor Wyckoff, this is both a review of her career and a statement of the high regard in which she was held by her colleagues.

734. Knopf, Eleanora Bliss. "Memorial of Florence Bascom," American Mineralogist, 31 (March-April), pp. 168-172. Photograph.
Knopf, one of Bascom's many talented students, writes in a reserved manner, but one full of respect and admiration for her teacher. The central theme is of her high intellectual demands of herself and of her students; the result of her father's influence and her New England background in general. A detailed bibliography of her writings.

1971

735. Rosenberg, Carroll S. "Bascom, Florence," Notable American Women (30), 1, pp. 108-110.
A balanced picture of Bascom as a teacher and scholar. Gives information of her problems in developing the department of geology at Bryn Mawr. Errs in saying she was the first woman fellow of the Geological Society of America.

1973

736. Watson, Edward H. "Bascom, Florence," Dictionary of American Biography (14), supp. 3, pp. 37-39.
Good biographical sketch of her education and career with somewhat more attention paid to the research activities. Also presents some personal characteristics. Errs in saying she was the first woman fellow of the Geological Society of America.

1975

737. Arnold. Lois. "Florence Bascom and the Exclusion of Women from Earth Science Curriculum Materials," Journal of Geological Education, 23 (September), pp. 110-113. Photograph (cover).
The article makes a good case for the discrimination against women in earth science through the image presented by the current teaching materials. Lists many women scientists and gives a substantial biography of Bascom. Actually there is little new material, but it underscores the need for including women. The error of Bascom being the first woman fellow of the Geological Society of America is continued.

738. ELIZABETH FLORETTE FISHER
26 November 1873--25 April 1941

Before graduating from the Massachusetts Institute of Technology (BS, 1896), Fisher began teaching at Wellesley College. She taught both geology and geography until poor health forced her retirement in 1926. From 1912 she lectured on geography at Harvard University and was the first woman to teach there for such a long period of time. Fisher's extensive studies of river terraces and oil fields gained for her recognition as one of the few American women qualified in the rugged life of the field geologist. Her Resources and Industries of the United States was widely used as a textbook and reference work.

1930

739. Anon. "Fisher, Elizabeth Florette," The National Cyclopaedia of American Biography (2), C, p. 208. Photograph.
Brief sketch outlining her education and research. Cites one of her publications.

1941

740. Anon. "Miss Elizabeth F. Fisher," The New York Times, 90 (3 May), p. 15.
An obituary which cites her long service at Wellesley and the fact that she wrote several books and articles on rivers and conservation.

741. CARLOTTA JOAQUINA MAURY
6 January 1874--3 January 1938
In addition to teaching at Barnard College (1909-1912) and the Huguenot College, Cape of Good Hope, South Africa (1912-1915), Maury served the Brazilian government and the Royal Dutch Shell Petroleum Company as a paleontologist. She studied at Radcliffe College and the University of Paris before completing degrees at Cornell University (PhB, 1896; PhD, 1902). She wrote extensively on various subjects in paleontology and, in 1916, organized an expedition to the Dominican Republic.

1938

742. Anon. "Miss C. J. Maury, Paleontologist," The New York Times, 87 (4 January), p. 23.
Describes her family background and the extent of her work with the government of Brazil. Points out that she did important industrial work in addition to teaching.

743. IDA HELEN OGILVIE
      12 February 1874--13 October 1963
      The founder of Barnard College's department of geology, which
in 1903 was one of the first in an American woman's college. Ogilvie
studied under Bascom at Bryn Mawr College (AB, 1896 or 1900)
and completed her education at Columbia University (PhD, 1903).
In addition to her teaching and administrative duties Ogilvie conducted geological studies in such diverse locations as Maine, New
York, California, and Mexico. She was the third woman elected
a fellow of the Geological Society of America and served the New
York Academy of Sciences as vice-president. She had an interest
in agriculture, especially cattle breeding, as well as petrology, paleontology, and glacial problems.

                              1963

744. Anon. "Dr. Ida Ogilvie of Barnard Dies, First Geology Chair-
      man Was 89," The New York Times, 113 (15 October), p.
      39.
      A fairly complete outline of her career with some interesting
and unusual notes about her view of the future of women in geology
and her other interests. States incorrectly that she was the second
woman to be elected a fellow of the Geological Society of America.

                              1964

745. Wood, Elizabeth A. "Memorial to Ida Helen Ogilvie," Bulletin
      of the Geological Society of America, 75 (February), pp. P35-
      P39. Photograph.
      Traces her career and gives a great deal of information about
her personal characteristics. She had many interests beyond her
duties as administrator, teacher, and scholar. After World War
I she confined her professional activities to teaching.

746. ANNA ISABEL JONAS STOSE
      17 August 1881--27 October 1974
      Stose was educated at Bryn Mawr College (AB, 1904; AM,
1905; PhD, 1912) where she and her classmates Eleanora Bliss Knopf
and Julia Gardner were influenced by Florence Bascom. Following
college she was a geologist with the Maryland and Pennsylvania geological surveys (1919-1937), the Virginia Geological Survey (1926-
1945), and the United States Geological Survey (1930-1954). In
each of these professional positions she made outstanding contributions to our understanding of Appalachian geology.
      Her numerous and exact observations in the field, particu-
larly in those areas that were completely uncharted until her time,

constituted a geological picture which played a key role in later
studies. Stose was often accused, fairly, of carrying her inter-
pretations too far, based on the actual observations. She was accused, unfairly, of being unwilling to change her mind about in-
terpretations once she had published them. She had a deserved
reputation for being impetuous and for saying exactly what was
on her mind.

On balance it must be admitted that although she was controversial and there were imperfections in her work, many of her
once disparaged theories have ultimately proven to be close to the
mark and the vital starting point for subsequent modification and
elaboration. The literature clearly demonstrates that she did not
hold to old ideas in the face of new and convincing evidence. In
later years several of her former collaborators on various surveys
recognized that her contributions were much more important than
their earlier disagreements. She was elected a fellow of the Geological Society of America in 1922.

1977

747. Dietrich, R. V. "Memorial to Anna I. Jonas Stose. 1881-
     1974," Geological Society of America. Memorials, 6, pp. 1-
     6. Photograph.
     Deals with her entire career and takes pains to discuss the
allegations of her unwillingness to change her mind and demonstrates them to be unfounded. Introduces some of her poetry and
in general shows the breadth of her cultural interests. A selected
bibliography of her writings and those carried out under her direction.

748. JULIA ANNA GARDNER
     26 February 1882--15 November 1960
     Throughout her career Gardner was interested in the mol-
lusks found in sedimentary and other rock. After completing her
education at Bryn Mawr College (AB, 1905; AM, 1907) and The
Johns Hopkins University (PhD, 1911) she continued this area of
research with the United States Geological Survey. During World
World I she served in France where, with the Red Cross, she was
injured in the line of duty near Rheims.

Following the war she joined the USGS as a staff member.
She rose to associate geologist in 1924 and geologist in 1928. Most
of her work at this time was in Texas and northeastern Mexico.
The results of these studies were of special importance to the growing petroleum industry. Her publications in the period prior to
World War II established her as an international authority in paleontology. In that war, as in the first, she played an active role
working with the Military Geology Unit of the USGS. She developed
an interest in the geology of the islands of the western Pacific and

studied their fossils while taking part in the geological mapping
of the area. Gardner was active in professional organizations and
promoted the international exchange of data and specimens. At
her retirement in 1952 she received the Distinguished Service Award
from the Department of the Interior and was serving as president
of the Paleontological Society. The following year she was elected
a vice-president of the Geological Society of America.

1961

749. E. B. K. "In Memoriam. 1905. Julia Gardner, A.B., M.A.
'07," Bryn Mawr Bulletin, (Winter), p. 23.
    Obituary giving the most basic biographical data and facts
about her career.

750. Sayre, A. Nelson. "Julia Anna Gardner (1882-1960)," Bulletin of the American Association of Petroleum Geologists, 45
(August), pp. 1418-1421. Photograph.
    A readable biographical sketch with a large amount of inter-
esting information about the person as well as the geologist. Does
full justice to her work in geology and describes her important work
during World War II.

751. Wilson, Druid. "Julia Anna Gardner. 1882-1960," The Nau-
tilus, 75 (July), pp. 122-123.
    A survey of her most important contributions calling them,
"foundation stones and bench marks in Coastal Plain stratigraphy
and paleontology." Mentions her encouragement of Japanese scientists after World War II.

1962

752. Ladd. Harry S. "Memorial to Julia Anna Gardner (1882-1960),"
Proceedings Volume of the Geological Society of America Annual Report for 1960 (February), pp. 87-92.
    Long biographical paper with refreshing quotations from
Gardner. Detailed treatment of each area of her work as well as
a good deal of human interest material. Includes a bibliography
of her works.

1980

753. Nelson, Clifford M., and Mary Ellen Williams. "Gardner,
Julia Anna," Notable American Women (30), 4, pp. 260-262.
    A nicely balanced account of Gardner's career which treats
each of the several quite different aspects in a firm and enjoyable
manner. The facts do not get in the way of making this sketch
one you will remember.

754.   ELEANORA FRANCES BLISS KNOPF
       15 July 1883--21 January 1974
       Under the guidance of Florence Bascom and in the company
of Julia Gardner and Anna Stose, Knopf received a sound education in geology and chemistry at Bryn Mawr College (AB and AM,
1904; PhD, 1912). She had studied at the University of California
at Berkeley and accepted a postdoctoral fellowship at The Johns
Hopkins University some years later.
       Her first professional position was as a geologic aide for the
United States Geological Survey. The very next year, in addition
to her fairly routine assignment, she reported a Pennsylvania de-
posit of the mineral glaucophane which to that time was thought
to be found only on the Pacific coast. She was promoted to assistant geologist in 1917. Following her marriage to Adolph Knopf
in 1920 she worked privately at Yale and lectured at Harvard. She
accepted assignments from the USGS, as a full geologist, until 1955.
When her husband received an appointment at Stanford University
in 1951 she became a research associate in the geology department.
They made studies of several locations in the Rocky Mountains until
his death in 1966.
       One of her most important works concerned Stissing Mountain,
a complex region on the New York-Connecticut border. There had
been disagreement concerning its geological nature since the 1840's,
and Knopf received widespread recognition for her studies. One
very significant outcome of this work occurred when, searching
for new techniques to apply in the study, she translated the works
of Bruno Sander on the use of texture, grain orientation, and optical properties of minerals in understanding geologic history. Her
application of these techniques and the publication of Structural
Petrology brought her well-deserved attention. She held a number
of important posts in the Geological Society of America and the National Research Council. Bryn Mawr presented her with a citation
for outstanding research and writing in 1960.

                                  1974

755.   Anon. "Prominent Geologist Dies at 90," Tribune [Redwood
       City, California], (23 January).
       Obituary summarizing her work. Concentrates on the last
years at Stanford University.

                                  1977

756.   Rodgers, John. "Memorial to Eleanora Bliss Knopf. 1883-
       1974," Geological Society of America. Memorials, 6, pp. 1-4.
       Photograph.
       A nicely written tribute which combines the scientific with
the human sides of this talented woman. Relates a bit of the Bryn
Mawr years which produced such a group of outstanding geologists.
Gives a selected bibliography of her writings.

1980

757. Aldrich, Michele L. "Knopf, Eleanora Frances Bliss," Notable
      American Women (30), 4, pp. 401-403.
      Describes her work in collaboration with her husband as well
as that conducted independently. Good detail of the development
and application of techniques she imported.

758. WINIFRED GOLDRING
      1 February 1888--30 January 1971
      Except for her education and two years of teaching at Wel-
lesley College (AB, 1909; AM, 1912) Goldring spent her entire life
in and around Albany, New York. She began as a temporary "scientific expert" at the New York State Museum and by 1916 had begun her own research on the paleontology of sea lilies from the
middle of the Paleozoic era. At a time when the field of paleobot-
any was attracting a great deal of scientific interest she made the
Albany collection world-recognized. She received a permanent appointment as associate paleontologist in 1920, and her most important monograph, The Devonian Crinoids of the State of New York,
was published in 1923. Goldring never looked for an academic appointment and disliked lecturing, but she had a natural talent for
educational materials. Her handbooks and especially her exhibi-
tions were widely copied and considered models for teaching. She
wrote some popular books which served well both as college texts
and as introductions for the layman. She also frequently worked
with graduate students studying some aspect of New York geology.
      In 1939 Goldring became the first woman to be appointed State
Paleontologist. Two years earlier she had received an honorary
doctorate from Russell Sage College; a second degree was presented
by Smith College in 1957. She was the first woman elected president of the Paleontological Society (1949) and vice-president of the
Geological Society of America (1950).

1971

*759. Fisher, Donald W. "Memorial to Winifred Goldring. 1888-
       1971," Geological Society of America. Memorials 3 (November),
       pp. 96-102.

1980

760. Kohlstedt, Sally Gregory. "Goldring, Winifred," Notable
      American Women (30), 4, pp. 282-283.
      A very well-written biographical sketch. This article pays
much more attention to the human qualities of Goldring, without
neglecting the significance of her scientific work. Especially good
job on her public service and assistance to students.

761. TILLY EDINGER
      13 November 1897--27 May 1967
      Like so many scientists of her generation who were born and
educated in Germany, Edinger was forced to flee because of her
Jewish heritage. She had studied at the Universities of Heidelberg
and Munich before receiving a doctorate from Frankfurt in 1921.
The topic of her dissertation was the skull and cranial cavity of
a fossil reptile, and this area of study became her life work. In
fact it is not too much to claim that she established the field of
paleoneurology and brought it to the forefront of studies in paleontology.
      From 1927 to 1938 she worked at the Senckenberg Museum
in Frankfurt as curator, without pay, of the vertebrate collection.
During this time she published one of her most important works,
Die Fossilen Gehirne (Fossil Brains). For five years after the
Nazis came to power the director managed to keep her hidden, but
in 1938 she fled and arrived at Harvard in 1940 via London. She
spent the rest of her life at Harvard's Museum of Comparative Zoology. In addition to several related research lines Edinger continued her work on fossil brains and in 1948 published her second
great work The Evolution of the Horse Brain. Edinger's recognition that evolution of the brain must be studied directly from the
fossils and that mammals' brains are uniquely suited to such study
was of great importance. She provided convincing evidence that
brain evolution occurred in a complex series rather than in the sim-
plistic straight line to perfection model. She was recognized by
important research fellowships from the Guggenheim Foundation and
the American Association of University Women. She was elected
president of the Society of Vertebrate Paleontology (1963-1964).
Wellesley College and the Universities of Giessen and Frankfurt
conferred honorary degrees on her. (See also 28.)

                                  1967

762. Anon. "Tilly Edinger Dies; Paleontologist, 69," The New
      York Times, 116 (29 May), p. 25.
      She was expelled by the Nazis and has been at the Harvard
Museum of Comparative Zoology. Her extremely productive research
program has produced two books and more than 60 papers and earned
her an honorary degree from Wellesley College.

763. A. S. R[omer]. "Tilly Edinger, 1897-1967," Society of Ver-
      tebrate Paleontology, News Bulletin (October), pp. 51-53.
      Photograph.
      A biographical sketch covering her entire career. Makes
a special point of German efforts to recognize her accomplishments
following World War II. Mentions a memorial fund being raised for
the purchase of books in her honor.

1968

764. Tobien, Heinz. "Tilly Edinger, 13.11.1897--27.5.1967,"
     Paläontologische Zeitschrift, 42 (April), pp. 1-2. In German.
     A biographical sketch which stresses her very productive re-
search career. Mentions the memorial fund being raised at Harvard.

1969

765. Hofer, H[elmut]. "In memoriam Tilly Edinger," Gegenbauer's
     Morphologisches Jahrbüch, 113, pp. 303-317. Photograph.
     In German.
     A long, detailed biography which is strong on the technical
aspects of her work. A bibliography of her work is presented by
the author and two collaborators, B. Kummel (Harvard) and H.
Tobien (Mainz).

1980

766. Gould, Stephen Jay. "Edinger, Tilly," Notable American
     Women (30), 4, pp. 218-219.
     Especially good description of the difficulties World War II
and the Nazi reign caused for scientists in Germany. Reviews
most of her career, but gives little personal insight.

GENERAL (See also 456, 540, 1149)

1929

767. [Committee of the American Home Economics Association] com-
pilers. Home Economists. Portraits and Brief Biographies
of the Men and Women Prominent in the Home Economics Movement in the United States. Baltimore: American Home Economics Association, 60 pp.
Magnificent photographs and exceptional biographical sketches
which emphasize professional interests and current involvements.
The title is explicit of the content, but does not indicate what a
beautiful book or significant tribute it is.

1945

768. Craig, Hazel T[hompson]. The History of Home Economics.
Blanche M. Stover, editor. New York: Practical Home Economics, 45 pp. Photographs.
A rich source of data on the growth of home economics from
the early years of the nineteenth century through 1945. This collection deals at length with a number of the women scientists who
were important in the American Home Economics Association, for
example, it is dedicated to Ellen Richards. Most of the biographical information is directly associated with the history of the home
economics movement. There is an especially interesting section giving annual milestones from 1909 to 1945.

1959

769. Barber, Mary L., editor. History of the American Dietetic
Association. 1917-1959. Philadelphia: Lippincott, 312 pp.
and index.
This book traces the emergence of dietetics from its primi-
tive state to its scientific state as a profession. Beginning in
World War I and leading to an emphasis on diet therapy, the history
of each area of nutrition is examined. This is a readable and informative history of the women who dedicated themselves to scientific research in nutrition and to the promotion of its importance
for society and human development. Their responsibilities in their
administrative roles are stressed.

770. MARION TALBOT
      31 July 1858--20 October 1948
      In the late 1870's it was difficult for a young, female Bos-
tonian to obtain a college preparatory education, but under the
skillful direction of her mother, Talbot overcame this barrier and
went on to complete the program of study at Boston University in
less than four years (AB, 1880). The active social life did not
seem useful enough, and she began studies at the Massachusetts
Institute of Technology. The studies were spread over the next
seven years but she did complete the work (BS, 1888).
      While at MIT Talbot worked with Ellen H. Richards, who was
doing pioneering research in the application of chemistry to practical questions such as sanitation and household science. In 1887
these two women edited the important work Home Sanitation: A
Manual for Housekeepers. Talbot and Richards continued to share
in their efforts to establish the emerging field of home economics
and to make education more available to women. As early as 1881
they had joined with other women to form the Association of Collegiate Alumnae which became the American Association of University Women. Talbot served as the first secretary and later (1895-
1897) as president of this significant organization.
      After teaching two years at Wellesley College, Talbot moved
to the University of Chicago as assistant professor and dean of
undergraduate women. She was there at the specific request of
Alice F. Palmer, and together they effectively created the program
for women. She became dean of women in 1899 and full professor
in 1905. At first she was forced to teach in the department of social science and anthropology where she was received without con-
descension. With her promotion, in 1905, she had established her
own department of household administration. In the company of
such women as Alice P. Norton, Talbot played a key role in the
establishment of Chicago's highly respected program in this new
and vigorous field. Her interests were always practical, and she
promoted both the intellectual progress and the everyday living
of her students. Outside of the university she, again with Richards, took part in the formation of the American Home Economics
Association. (See also 48.)

                                1925

771. Norton, Alice Peloubet. "Marion Talbot," Journal of Home
      Economics, 17 (September), pp. 479-482.
      At her retirement in 1925 Talbot received this very compli-
mentary review of her contributions from a long-time friend, fellow student, and colleague. The material is excellent, but it is
the warm human view of Talbot that is most apparent in these remarks.

1936

772. Talbot, Marion. More Than Lore. Reminiscences. Chicago:
      University of Chicago Press, 223 pp. Photographs.
          A priceless collection of first-person views concerning the
      growth of women's programs at Chicago. Talbot's role as dean,
      first of undergraduates and then of women, placed her in the cen-
      ter of this new university from its very beginning. Her activities
      in the home economics and university women movements place a spe-
      cial value on her thoughts for anyone interested in the beginning
      of professional opportunity for women.

1948

773. Anon. "Miss Marion Talbot," The New York Times, 98 (21
      October), p. 27.
          Obituary notice saying that she was dean at Chicago and
      taught at Wellesley.

774. Anon. "Marion Talbot, 1858-1948," University of Chicago
      Magazine (December), p. 16. Photographs.
          A lively obituary which brings out the huge contribution
      Talbot made to the University of Chicago and to women's rights.
      Underlines her characteristic humor.

1949

775. Morriss, Margaret S. "Marion Talbot, In Memoriam," Jour-
      nal of the American Association of University Women, 42 (Jan-
      uary), pp. 79-80.
          A nicely presented sketch of Talbot's career as a teacher
      and administrator. The author admits that she didn't know her
      until later in her life so she sought impressions from a variety of
      others.

776. Swain, Frances L. "Our Professional Debt to Marion Tal-
      bot," Journal of Home Economics, 41 (April), pp. 185-186.
          A short article, but written by another professional who
      knew Talbot well. An even tone and perceptive remarks about her
      role in the development of home economics at Chicago. Also speaks
      of her as a teacher and advisor to students; both with the highest
      praise.

1950

777. Anon. "Talbot, Marion," The National Cyclopaedia of American
      Biography (2), 36, pp. 425-426.
          Good outline of Talbot's education and her role in the forma-

mation of associations of women intellectuals. Gives a list of her most important books with dates of publication.

1971

778. Storr, Richard J. "Talbot, Marion," Notable American Women (30), 3, pp. 423-424.
Describes the evolution of Talbot's career and its effect on various important women's movements. Heavy concentration on her administrative duties and citation of most of her books.

1978

779. Padron, Olga. "Talbot, Marion," Biographical Dictionary of American Educators (38), 3, pp. 1266-1267.
Far too brief to cover Talbot's career; what is here is good, and there is a bibliography.

1982

780. Deegan, Mary Jo. "Marion Talbot," American Women Writers (48), 4, pp. 202-203.
Describes each of Talbot's principal works and gives them due credit as pioneering steps. Notes that some of her ideas were daring at the time and others valid even today. A limited bibliography.

781. ALICE PELOUBET NORTON
25 February 1860--23 February 1928
Norton studied at Smith College (AB, 1882). Under the leadership of Marion Talbot and Ellen Richards she organized the Sanitary Science Club as a part of the Association of Collegiate Alumnae. When her husband, Lewis M. Norton, died and left her with five children, she began to study with Richards at the Massachusetts Institute of Technology. Courses in sanitary chemistry at MIT and the Boston Normal School of Household Arts along with research on yeast led to a graduate degree from Smith (AM, 1897). During this period she taught at several schools and cared for her family.

Norton went to the Chicago Institute in 1900 and along with that institution joined the University of Chicago in 1901. Again in the company of Marion Talbot, Norton played a key role in the development of that institution's worldwide reputation for outstanding education in the growing field of home economics. In 1913, along with several other faculty, she resigned in protest over the appointment of a new head of the School of Education. Over the

next eight years she worked actively as teacher, writer, and editor
to see the establishment and growth of the American Home Economics Association. In 1921 she was chosen to form a department of
home economics at the Constantinople Women's College.

As a result of exceptional events in her life Norton's career
was unlike that of most women of her time. Having been forced
to raise five children after her husband's early death and having
felt it necessary to resign her position at Chicago, she was unable
to form a long, strong bond with a particular institution. In spite
of this apparent handicap Norton made her influence felt in the
pioneering years of the home economics movement. Her demonstrated success in raising her own family and her reputation as an
excellent teacher gained her wide respect.

1928

782. Anon. "Editorial. Alice Peloubet Norton," Journal of Home
      Economics, 20 (September), pp. 650-658. Photograph.
      Editorial comment about the value of Norton's career to the
home economics movement and short sections by her associates describing her skills in various areas. "Mrs. Norton, a Pioneer Home
Economist," Anna Barrows; "Mrs. Norton and the Journal of Home
Economics," Mary Hinman Abel; "Mrs. Norton and Constantinople
College," Mary A. Hall; and "Mrs. Norton as a Writer," [Editor?].
The last section is almost entirely selections from an earlier paper
by Norton. Difficult to read as a unit, but full of excellent material.

1971

783. Wilson, Mary Tolford. "Norton, Alice Peloubet," Notable
      American Women (30), 2, pp. 637-638.
      Makes clear the difficulties Norton overcame to establish her
outstanding career. Also describes the key role played by Richards in the life of Norton and of most of the early workers in home
economics.

1978

784. Fisher, Darlene E. "Norton, Mary Alice Peloubet,"
      Biographical Dictionary of American Educators, (38), 2, pp.
      956-957.
      Brief but generally well-organized outline of Norton's career.

785. ISABEL BEVIER
      14 November 1860--17 March 1942

Bevier's early career development as a high school language teacher was based on the success she achieved at the College (then called University) of Wooster, Ohio (PhB, 1885; PhM, 1888). However, with the tragic death of her fiancé her life took a most unexpected turn. She accepted a position in natural science at the Pennsylvania College for Women simply to be near friends in Pittsburgh. She spent the first of many summers studying chemistry at Case School of Applied Science, Cleveland. She later attended Harvard, Wesleyan, and Western Reserve Universities and finally the Massachusetts Institute of Technology. Here she became interested in food chemistry and was excited by the work being done by Ellen H. Richards.

During the years leading to the turn of the century she had been increasingly uncomfortable with the women's college setting, and when the University of Illinois invited her to join its faculty, she saw the opportunity to put into practice her concepts of the liberal education proper to women. The field of home economics was just beginning to make its appearance at American universities, and there were faculty, like Bevier, who insisted on its being taught as a rigorous scientific discipline. In several instances her standards for students and subject matter brought her into conflict with groups within and outside of the university, but she ultimately gained the respect of nearly everyone.

Under her direction the department at Illinois became a highly respected example, and she herself was widely known for her professional writing and speaking. From the very beginning in 1900 she played an active role in the formation of the American Home Economics Association. In 1910 she became that group's second president and served for three years on the editorial board of the Journal of Home Economics. Some of her contemporaries, for example, Edmund J. James then President of the University of Illinois, considered Bevier tactless, but whatever social graces she may have chosen to disregard, she was a true pioneer in the development of the home economic movement, and she contributed greatly in placing that discipline on a sound intellectual basis. She received honorary doctorates from Iowa State College (1920) and the College of Wooster (1936). The home economics building at Illinois is named for her.

1921

786. Davenport, Eugene. "Home Economics at Illinois," Journal of Home Economics, 13 (August), pp. 337-341. Photograph.
      A paper presented at a retirement "recognition service" for Bevier. What is a review of the department at Illinois is, of necessity, a biography of its founder and long-time director. There are vital personal and professional details here.

1928

787.   Bevier, Isabel. "Chapters from the Lives of Leaders. How
       I Came to Take Up Home Economics Work," Home Economist
       and American Food Journal, 6 (May), pp. 117, 136, 140.
       Photograph (cover).
       Autobiographical, of course, but more importantly this brief
article gives a deep understanding of the scientific approach, mostly chemical, taken in the early development of home economics.

1940

788.   Bevier, Isabel. "Recollections and Impressions of the Be-
       ginnings of the Department of Home Economics at the Uni-
       versity of Illinois," Journal of Home Economics, 32 (May),
       291-297.
       If only other fields of science had such documentation of
their infancy! This article should be read whether you are interested in Bevier or not. She paints all of the drama of the earliest
years of home economics at Illinois in the frankest terms.

1942

789.   Anon. "Isabel Bevier, 82; Home Economist," The New York
       Times, 91 (18 March), p. 23.
       Pays special attention to her government service in the First
World War and to her founding of the department at Illinois. Gives
a brief review of her education and says she wrote books and articles.

790.   Bane, Lita, and Anna R. Van Meter. "Isabel Bevier: Pio-
       neer Home Economist" and "Personal Recollections," Journal
       of Home Economics, 34 (June), pp. 341-344.
       A memorial to Bevier by two of her former students. Bane,
her chief biographer and successor at Illinois, writes of her career
and the high standards she set for herself and for the faculty and
students of her department. Van Meter, a member of the first class
and later Bevier's colleague, tells highly personal stories from these
two advantageous view points.

791.   Anon. "Bevier, Isabel," Current Biography Yearbook, p.
       81.
       Only a few lines and three references; one of the poorer
jobs in this generally interesting source.

1955

792.   Bane, Juliet Lita. The Story of Isabel Bevier. Peoria,
       Illinois: Charles A. Bennett, 186 pp.

Written by another professional in the field of nutrition, this book is an enjoyable reading experience for anyone interested in the pioneer days of nutrition. Isabel Bevier was a student of Ellen Richards and W. O. Atwater. This history reveals with candor the many trials both women and the profession had to endure before the women became recognized as scientific leaders, and the profession, an accepted academic discipline. Characteristic of her forthrightness was her protest in the University of Illinois daily newspaper, Illini, about the implication in the University catalog that household science "was for women only." The writing tends to be uncritical, but this is a basic source, not a balanced evaluation. There are many quotations.

1971

793. Solberg, Winton U. "Bevier, Isabel," Notable American Women (30), 1, pp. 141-142.
Gives a broad and balanced view of Bevier's career with attention to her activities beyond the University of Illinois, an area usually neglected. Shows the forceful character in the process of building a great department. An excellent but partial bibliography.

1973

794. Wilson, Mary Tolford. "Bevier, Isabel," in Dictionary of American Biography (14), supp. 3, pp. 67-69.
One of the longest and best-written biographical sketches we have seen in this fine collection. Gives a real feeling for the person of Bevier as well as the facts of her career. An excellent, critical bibliography.

1978

795. Fisher, Darlene E. "Bevier, Isabel," Biographical Dictionary of American Educators (38), 1, pp. 127-128.
Brief but worthwhile, Provides a summary with good notes on her own educational development.

796. ABBY LILLIAN MARLATT
7 March 1869--23 June 1943
After completing her education at the Kansas State Agricultural College (BS, 1888; MS, 1890), Marlatt accepted a professorship at the new Utah State Agricultural College. In Utah and later at the Manual Training High School in Providence, Rhode Island, she introduced and developed home economics courses. While at

Providence she continued her studies at Clark and Brown Universities and attracted the attention of Harry L. Russell. In 1908 Russell, then dean of the college of agriculture at the University of Wisconsin invited Marlatt to renew a failing program in home economics.

Early in this century Marlatt also took a leading role in the development of the American Home Economics Association. Along with Ellen H. Richards she participated in the forerunner of this organization, the Lake Placid Conference on Home Economics, serving as chairman (1903) and vice-president (1907). She was also vice-president of the association from 1912 to 1918. Her administrative skills also won her presidential appointments to important committees during and following World War I. Her energy was so great it was difficult for her to appreciate concerns over teaching schedules to meet the demands she made for scholarly productivity. She took charge of fund-raising drives for the American Home Economics Association, the Ellen H. Richards scholarship fund, and the establishment of home economics at the Constantinople Woman's College.

When Marlatt retired from Wisconsin in 1939, she had established a department with national standing. The graduates of this program, for whom she had a deep affection, were eagerly sought after. She was awarded two honorary degrees by Kansas State (1925) and also an honorary degree by Utah State (1938).

1931

797. Manning, Hazel. "Abby L. Marlatt," Home Economics News,
     2 (September), p. 6a. Photograph.
     A tribute recognizing her accomplishments. An outline of
major events in her career.

1943

798. Anon. "Miss Abby L. Marlatt," The New York Times, 92
     (25 June), p. 17.
     A pioneer in teaching home economics at the University of
Wisconsin. Hoover had requested that she draft a plan for food
conservation during World War I.

799. [Faculty Committee]. "Abby Lillian Marlatt. 1869-1943,"
     Minutes of the General Faculty, University of Wisconsin (4
     October).
     Text of a Faculty Resolution at her death. Gives a fairly
complete outline of her career and indicates the attitude of her colleagues concerning her contributions.

800. Jones, Nellie Kedzie. "Abby L. Marlatt," Journal of Home
     Economics, 35 (October), pp. 483-484.

A touching memorial written by Marlatt's teacher at Kansas State. Not at all sentimental, and revealing of the early development leading to later accomplishments.

801. Jones, Nellie Kedzie. "Abby Marlatt '88, Well-Known Hom Ec Director, Buried Here," [Manhattan] Kansas Industrialist (14 October).
Written in the same charming style as the more extended article (800), this is a most unusual obituary; very personal without being sentimental.

1971

802. Wilson, Mary Tolford. "Marlatt, Abby Lillian," Notable American Women (30), 2, pp. 495-497.
A nicely balanced biographical sketch which treats each of the varied aspects of Marlatt's career. Presents clear and convincing evidence of the highly scientific objectives present in the early development of the home economics department at Wisconsin. A useful bibliography.

1973

803. Weigley, Emma Seifrit. "Marlatt, Abby Lillian," Dictionary of American Biography (14), supp. 3, pp. 506-507.
A good biographical sketch with an outline of Marlatt's career and some personal stories and avocational interests.

1978

804. Dowd, M. Jane. "Marlatt, Abby Lillian," Biographical Dictionary of American Educators (38), 2, pp. 864-865.
Central facts of her career with some useful bibliography.

805. MARY DAVIES SWARTZ ROSE
31 October 1874--1 February 1941
An early leader in the field of nutrition, Rose studies at Shepardson College (BLitt, 1901), the College of Wooster, and the Rochester Mechanics Institute. In 1905 she enrolled at Teachers College, Columbia University, where she developed an outstanding career until her retirement in 1940. Following her graduation (BS, 1906) she was awarded a traveling fellowship with which she studied physiological chemistry at Yale University (PhD, 1909).

After a year at Columbia she married Anton R. Rose, a biochemist who greatly encouraged her career. That same year she was made an assistant professor in the department of nutrition

she had guided into existence the year before. In collaboration
with Henry C. Sherman of the department of chemistry she developed an extraordinary program which sought to give students
both a sound basis in science and the best teaching methods. This
department became the leading center for teaching and research
in nutrition education.

In addition to being a truly gifted teacher Rose produced
an impressive research record. Her more than 40 papers tended
to stress the practical aspects of nutrition as did her widely used
textbooks, A Laboratory Hand-book for Dietetics and The Foundations of Nutrition. She was interested in public school nutritional
programs, especially later in her career. She had written a popular book for mothers, Feeding the Family, in 1916 and in 1932 published Teaching Nutrition to Boys and Girls.

Rose also took an active interest in professional organizations.
She was a charter member of the honorary society the American
Institute of Nutrition which she served as president in 1937-1938
and as associate editor of its Journal of Nutrition from 1928 to 1936.
She was elected an honorary member of the American Dietetic Association in 1919. During World War I and in the years between
the World Wars she took part in a large number of national and
international commissions, including the Health Committee of the
League of Nations. From 1933 until 1941 she was a member of the
Council on Foods of the American Medical Association. Several in-
situtions named lectureships and scholarships in her memory. (See
also 954.)

1941

806. Anon. "Mary S. Rose Dead; Nutrition Expert," The New
      York Times, 90 (2 February), p. 46.
      Gives a record of her academic career at Columbia's Teachers
College and lists some of her books. PhD from Yale in 1921.

807. S[herman], H[enry] C. "Mary Swartz Rose. Oct. 31, 1874--
      Feb. 1, 1941. An Appreciation," Journal of Nutrition, 21
      (March), pp. 208-211. Photograph.
      Traces her career including the presidency of the Institute
of Nutrition and chairmanship at Teachers College. Rose's qualities as a gifted teacher are again strongly emphasized. Outlines
her impressive record of research contributions.

808. Sherman, Henry C. "Mary Swartz Rose, 1874-1941," Teachers
      College Record, 42 (March), pp. 544-545. Photograph.
      Traces her education and says that she began at once, after
Yale, to build an outstanding department. Rose gave her very
best as a classroom teacher, but still found time to make research
contributions in four major areas. She enjoyed an ideal family life
in the author's opinion.

809. Andrews, Benjamin R. "Mary Swartz Rose, 1874-1941," School and Society, 53 (26 April), pp. 538-539.
A brief review of her life which gives a partial list of her books and contributions to journals.

*810. [Obituary]. Journal of Home Economics, 33 (April), pp. 221-224.

811. Anon. "Mary Swartz Rose (Mrs. Anton R. Rose)," Journal of the American Medical Association, 116 (24 May), p. 2401.
Cites her as "one of the outstanding teachers of her time" and discusses her many public service activities. Mentions some of her publications and extends appreciation for her work with the Council on Foods.

812. Sherman, H[enry] C. "Mary Swartz Rose. 1874-1941," Journal of Biological Chemistry, 140 (September), 687-688.
Written by her friend and collaborator this obituary still gives a hint of the great self-discipline which characterized Rose's career.

813. Anon. "Mary Davies Swartz Rose, PhD. 1909," Yale University. Obituary Record of Graduates, 1940-41, pp. 227-228.
A detailed list of dates and places; includes education, some publications, memberships, and honors. Dry, but useful.

1971

814. Taylor, Clara Mae. "Rose, Mary Davies Swartz," Notable American Women (30), 3, pp. 196-198.
A nice presentation of Rose's career without making it the usual recitation of facts. Reads well and provides both personal and career information.

1978

815. Sorensen, Roberta. "Rose, Mary Davies Schwartz [sic]," Biographical Dictionary of American Educators (38), 3, p. 1122.
Provides a lot of facts in a very short space. Gives an exceptional bibliography.

1979

816. Eagles, Juanita Archibald; Orien Florence Pye; and Clara May Taylor. Mary Swartz Rose. 1874-1941. Pioneer in

Nutrition. New York: Teachers College Press, 172 pp.
Photograph.
Detailed and well-presented, this full-length biography is a
fine example of the scholarly yet readable studies needed for so
many of these women scientists. There are many references and
a useful bibliography.

817.   HELEN WOODARD ATWATER
       29 May 1876--26 June 1947
       At an early age Atwater was strongly influenced by her father
who, as a professor of chemistry, was an early authority on the
chemical composition and energy of food as applied to nutrition.
After his death she made a bibliography of his writings and then
joined the Office of Home Economics of the United States Department of Agriculture. During her 14 years of service to this department she wrote extensively in an effort to make rural women
aware of the importance of scientific information in food preparation.
       She left government service in 1923 to become the first full-
time editor of the Journal of Home Economics. Having received much
of her education in Europe she had a fine sense of language. With
this talent and her many personal contacts she was able to promote
high standards in both the subject matter and writing of the articles which were published. The result contributed to the growth
in stature and understanding of the very young field of home economics. Her own articles and editorials played a vital role in shap-
ing this growth. She retired as editor at the age of 65. Smith
College (BL, 1897) awarded her an honorary doctorate in 1943.

                              1941

818.   Bane, Lita; Keturah Baldwin; and Ruth Van Deman. "Salut-
       ing Helen W. Atwater. First Full-time Editor of the Journal
       of Home Economics," Journal of Home Economics, 33 (November),
       pp. 623-626.
       A trilogy of tributes to Atwater by three close friends and
associates. Her long and highly successful service to the Journal
is recognized by Bane. Baldwin gives a brief, personal view of
Atwater, again with emphasis on her editing skills. Finally, Van
Deman presents an almost poetic description of the woman herself.
This is primary source material.

                              1947

819.   A. F. W. "'97 Helen Atwater," Smith Alumnae Quarterly (No-
       vember), p. 30.
       Obituary with most of the information relating to Atwater's
association with Smith College.

1971

820. Todhunter, Elizabeth Neige. "Atwater, Helen Woodard,"
      Notable American Women (30), 1, pp. 66-67.
      An even presentation of Atwater's career. Describes her
work with her father and gives a good picture of her influence
through professional organizations.

821. KATHARINE BLUNT
      28 May 1876--29 July 1954
      Although educated as a chemist and notable as a college
president, Blunt's most memorable achievements were in home economics and nutrition. She was born in very comfortable circumstances, and until she entered Vassar College in 1894, she along
with her two sisters aspired to the finishing school education typical of their class. Following graduation (AB, 1898) Blunt was active in church and civic work, studied at the Massachusetts Institute of Technology, and taught chemistry at Vassar. In 1905 she
continued her studies at the University of Chicago (PhD, 1907).
      Blunt's career began in earnest when she joined Chicago's
department of home economics in 1913. She began to serve as the
informal chairman of the department in 1918; this position was of-
ficially recognized in 1925, the same year she was promoted to full
professor. Her scholarly publications, which made important contributions in metabolism and the effects of vitamins, continued
throughout her career. However, it is as an administrator that
Blunt made her most significant contribution. The department
grew in numbers and in stature. The faculty and the graduates
included many outstanding researchers whose work made it possible for home economics to be accepted as a valid profession and
a proper university subject. Her own writing and service on important committees served as a splendid example to students and
colleagues.
      In 1929 Blunt became the first woman president of Connecti-
cut College (then for Women). As a very young institution it
needed her administrative skill which was coupled with her lifelong
insistence on the highest standards of teaching and scholarship.
Blunt was not only wealthy and generous but a most skillful fund-
raiser. At her retirement in 1943 the college had grown in every
respect and was on a firm financial footing. She was awarded honorary degrees by Connecticut College (1943), the University of Chicago (1941), Mount Holyoke College (1937), and Wesleyan University (1936).

1927

822. Anon. "Blunt, Katharine," The National Cyclopaedia of
      American Biography (2), B, p. 385. Photograph.

An adequate review of her education and early career with
a substantial list of her memberships and offices held.

1928

823.   Blunt, Katharine.   "The Department of Home Economics,"
       Chicago University. University Record (July), pp. 187-189.
       Actually this article concerns the history of the department
at Chicago, but there is clear evidence of Blunt's own attitudes
about the proper philosophy of an academic department.

1946

824.   Anon.   "Blunt, Katharine," Current Biography Yearbook,
       pp. 57-59.   Photograph.
       An especially good review of her total career with the proper
amount of attention devoted to each phase.   While emphasizing the
magnitude and importance of her administrative contributions, her
scholarly work is treated effectively and with due weight.

1950

825.   Noyes, Gertrude.   "Katharine Blunt," Connecticut Teacher
       (January).
       A warm and personal tribute from her friend and future dean
of Connecticut College.   Noyes speaks of each aspect of Blunt's
career, but it is in her vision of the future of the struggling college that one sees most clearly the character of this strong woman.

1954

826.   Anon.   "Katharine Blunt, Educator, Is Dead," The New York
       Times, 103 (30 July), p. 17.   Photograph.
       Long obituary giving a full outline of her many contributions
and honors.   Major emphasis on her role at Connecticut College.

827.   Anon.   "Blunt, Katharine," Current Biography Yearbook,
       p. 99.
       Summary as an obituary notice.

828.   Anon.   "Katharine Blunt," Journal of Home Economics (Sep-
       tember), p. 454.   Photograph.
       A sketch noting her service to the American Home Economics
Association.   There is a nice quotation from the Hartford [Connecti-
cut] Courant of 30 July.

1978

829. Bedwell, Doree Dumas. "Blunt, Katharine," Biographical
     Dictionary of American Educators (38), 1, pp. 141-142.
     Review of Blunt's career which points out her role in the
expansion of opportunity for women's education. Useful bibliography.

1980

830. Trecker, Janice Law. "Blunt, Katharine," Notable American
     Women (30), 4, pp. 87-88.
     A readable survey of Blunt's career in science and adminis-
tration. The years at Chicago and Connecticut are both given full
exposure. Draws a clear picture of a vigorous and determined
woman. A good bibliography.

831. RUTH WHEELER
     5 August 1877--29 September 1948
     After graduation from Vassar College (AB, 1899) Wheeler
taught science and German in Pennsylvania and New York and then
went to teach chemistry at the Pratt Institute in Brooklyn. In each
of these positions she had observed the new and rapidly growing
field of home economics and especially the subdiscipline of nutrition.
In 1910 she decided to pursue a PhD program in physiological chemistry at Yale University (PhD, 1913). There followed a most important series of posts: University of Illinois (1912-1918), Goucher
College (1918-1921), and State University of Iowa (1921-1926).
     At Iowa State Wheeler was professor and head of the new
department of nutrition, an obvious reflection of her success in
the development of programs and her growing reputation. She continued to insist on a balanced program of teaching, research, and
food service. One of her most notable innovations was the internship leading to a master's degree. In 1926 she became professor
of physiology and nutrition at Vassar. She served her alma mater
until 1944 and during most of that time also directed the Vassar
Summer Institute of Euthenics, a broad-based program aimed at
improving human relations.
     From the beginning Wheeler had played an active role in her
profession. She was a charter member of the American Home Economics Association, and in 1917 she took the lead in establishing
the American Dietetic Association. As the president of the latter
organization in 1924-1926 she showed her faith and vision by establishing the Association's Journal in the face of limited funds and
the criticism of some members. During and long after World War
I, Wheeler was chairman of the committee on nutrition of the American Red Cross and published the American Red Cross Textbook
on Food and Nutrition in 1927.

832. Ross, Nelda. "Editorial. Dr. Ruth Wheeler," Journal of the
      American Dietetic Association, 24 (December), pp. 1006, 1070-
      1071.
      The first page is simply a notice of her death, but the second
entry is a nicely written biographical sketch of Wheeler's life and
career. There are several quotations from her writings which illustrate the basic philosophy she communicated to her students and
colleagues.

833. Anon. "Ruth Wheeler," Yale University Obituary Record (1
      July), pp. 143-144.
      Some family background and a detailed list of educational
dates, professional positions, memberships, and some publications.
Useful.

834. Anon. "Anna Boller Beach Receives Copher Award for 1957,"
      Journal of the American Dietetic Association, 33 (December),
      pp. 1279-1281.
      Gives the full text of Beach's acceptance speech which re-
calls her personal feelings about some of the Association's founders.
Wheeler is among those discussed.

835. Todhunter, Elizabeth Neige. "Wheeler, Ruth," Notable
      American Women (30), 3, pp. 576-577.
      Includes a detailed statement of Wheeler's career with some
feeling for the human being. Reads very well and gives the impression that she was a nice person to know as well as a talented
woman.

836. LYDIA JANE ROBERTS
      30 June 1879--28 May 1965
      Roberts entered her career rather late in life as she was
36 years old when she entered the University of Chicago (BS, 1917;
MS, 1919; PhD, 1928). The earlier years were important and productive ones in which she taught school children in Michigan, Mon-
tana, and Virginia. In these situations she developed a lifelong
interest in the relationship of diet to childhood growth.
      At this time Chicago's department of home economics under

the new chairman Katharine Blunt was at the very center of development of a strong scientific basis for research in applied nutrition. Roberts made such an impression on the faculty she was asked to join them in 1919. She remained at Chicago until her mandatory retirement in 1944. She became Blunt's successor as chairman in 1929 and proved to be a capable administrator while continuing to teach and conduct a vigorous research program.

Following her retirement she was invited to Puerto Rico where she had made an important nutrition study for the United States Department of Agriculture in 1943. She was chairman of the department of home economics at the University of Puerto Rico from 1946 to 1952. The experimental program she began there sought to combine economic and nutritional improvement and became a model for the rest of the island.

1965

837. Martin, Ethel Austin. "Lydia Jane Roberts," Journal of the American Dietetic Association, 47 (August), pp. 127-128. Photograph.
   A nicely written memorial article describing Roberts' career. Martin makes a special point of her ability to work with great intensity and at the same time to manifest a deep concern for those under her leadership.

1966

838. Martin, Ethel Austin. "The Life Works of Lydia J. Roberts," Journal of the American Dietetic Association, 49 (October), pp. 299-302.
   A most important supplement and amplification of Martin's earlier study (837). Here she examines the large corpus of Roberts' published work, seeking to determine the significant trends for both her profession and herself. A very interesting and useful approach to biography. All of the relevant bibliographic details are given.

1967

839. Bing, Franklin C. "Lydia Jane Roberts--A biographical sketch (June 30, 1879--May 28, 1965)," Journal of Nutrition, 93 (September), pp. 3-13. Drawing from a photograph.
   The title is somewhat misleading in that this excellent study is far more than a sketch. Roberts' entire life is presented in forceful, readable prose, and a detailed analysis of the significance of her contributions to nutrition emerges. An excellent start of a full biography. Even contains a lovely, unsigned poem to her.

1980

840. Ihde, Aaron J. "Roberts, Lydia Jane," Notable American
     Women (30), 4, pp. 580-581.
     Very-well developed and written in a delightful manner. One
of the best sketches in this series. Covers the whole range of
Roberts' productive career and pays special attention to her application of sound scientific principles to human needs.

841. LOUISE STANLEY
     8 June 1883--15 July 1954
     Stanley was the first woman to become a bureau chief of the
United States Department of Agriculture in 1923. She played a
major role in the development of federal programs of research and
education which showed their utility during the Depression and World
War II. Stanley was a superb administrator and organizer, but
it was her real love of people whom she considered disadvantaged
that led to her great success. This same conviction also brought
her into conflict with powerful groups in agriculture. She continued to defend the rights of consumers and all people treated
unjustly. As her career developed and her reputation grew, these
attitudes influenced policy internationally as well as at home. She
took part in the United Nations Conference on Food and Agriculture
in 1943 and the United States National Commission for UNESCO after her retirement in 1950.
     Born in Nashville, Tennessee, Stanley's parents died when
she was only four. With an inheritance she studied at Peabody
College (AB, 1903) and at the Universities of Chicago (BEd, 1906)
and Columbia (AM, 1907). She then followed the path taken by
so many of the pioneers of nutrition in those days and studied biochemistry at Yale University (PhD, 1911).
     These were the years of rapid growth of home economics and
at the University of Missouri, where she began teaching in 1907,
Stanley became department chairman from 1917 until she joined the
USDA in 1923. Her leadership was evident both within the university and in broader political spheres. As head of the legislative
committee of the American Home Economics Association she was instrumental in forcing greater federal assistance for efforts so clearly related to the improvement of the standard of life for all Americans.

1954

842. Anon. "Louise Stanley, Home Economist," The New York
     Times, 103 (16 July), p. 21.
     An internationally known authority on nutrition and home eco-
nomics. First chief of the Federal Bureau of Human Nutrition;
served from 1923 to 1943.

843.   Anon. "Dr. Stanley: Nation's No. 1 Homemaker," The Wash-
       ington Post and Times Herald, 77 (16 July), p. 24. Photo-
       graph.
       After teaching and conducting research at the University of
Missouri Stanley became the first head of the Bureau of Home Economics and served as its chief for 20 years. First woman to receive an honorary LLD from Missouri.

844.   Anon. "Louise Stanley," Journal of Home Economics, (Sep-
       tember), p. 454. Photograph.
       Obituary which gives the basic facts of her career. A nice,
but unidentified, quotation gives a feeling for the personal characteristics behind Stanley's success.

845.   Anon. "Dr. Louise Stanley," Journal of the American Die-
       tetic Association, 30 (September), p. 948.
       Notice of her death dealing mainly with her service on vari-
ous committees and commissions.

                              1962

846.   Stefferud, Alfred, editor. "After a Hundred Years," in The
       Yearbook of Agriculture 1962, pp. 30-33. Photograph.
       A comment concerning her service as chief of the USDA's
new Bureau of Home Economics. Important in that she was the
first woman to hold such a post.

                              1980

847.   Conable, Charlotte W. "Stanley, Louise," Notable American
       Women (30), 4, pp. 657-659.
       A nicely developed sketch which makes Stanley's social inter-
ests clear. Her service in the federal government not only represented an important first for women but created new and useful
programs of far-reaching significance. Mentions Stanley's interest
in and influence on young women with professional goals.

848.   GRACE ARABELL GOLDSMITH
       8 April 1904--28 April 1975
       The first physician in the United States to appreciate the
importance of nutrition in medical treatment, Goldsmith served the
Tulane University School of Medicine from 1936 until her retirement
in 1973. She graduated first in her class at Tulane (MD, 1932)
and in 1934 published the first of over 150 articles, chapters and
one book. Prior to accepting her appointment at Tulane she studied at the University of Minnesota (MS, 1936).

In New Orleans the diseases associated with vitamin deficiency were very common, and Goldsmith undertook research on vitamin C and pellagra. In 1940 the first of a long series of publications appeared, and the complex relationship between nutrition and disease became evident. As her successes grew, Goldsmith broadened her interests first to other types of disease and then to the problems of adequate community nutrition. Along with several important surveys and the development of better programs against hunger Goldsmith started at Tulane, the world's first training in nutrition for medical students. As director of the nutrition and metabolism section of the department she played a key role in the founding of the Tulane School of Public Health and Tropical Medicine. She became the first woman ever to head a school of public health as the dean of this new unit.

1964

849. Anon. "Goldsmith, Grace Arabell," The National Cyclopaedia of American Biography (2), J, p. 204. Photograph.
Detailed coverage of Goldsmith's education and career with the Department of Agriculture. A good section on her research with specific citations from several works.

1967

850. Anon. "Dr. Goldsmith Appointed Dean of Newly Created School at Tulane," Journal of the Louisiana State Medical Society, 119 (June), pp. 252-253.
Mostly about the new school of Public Health and Tropical Medicine, but since she was its creator and first dean there is biographical material here as well.

1972

851. Anon. "Tulane Nutritionist Wins Many Distinctions: Sees Hope for Solution to World's Food Problems," Tulane Report (Winter), 4 pp., unnumbered. Photographs.
A long article describing most of Goldsmith's career. Great emphasis on the world food problems, but her studies and the role of the school she directs are also fully covered. An excellent section on her work in opportunities for women.

1975

852. Anon. "Dr. Grace Goldsmith," The New York Times, 124 (29 April), p. 36.
Announces the death of the Dean emerita of the School of

Public Health and Tropical Medicine at Tulane. Cites her other administrative roles and memberships.

853. Anon. "Tulane Mourns Dr. Grace A. Goldsmith," Tulane Medicine; Faculty and Alumni (Summer), p. 23. Photograph.
Short obituary and memorial article with emphasis on Goldsmith's international reputation and honors.

854. Anon. "Grace A. Goldsmith, M.D. April 8, 1904--April 28, 1975," Nutrition Reviews, 33 (October), pp. 314-315.
An adequate coverage of her career with the greatest attention paid her research in nutrition and the honors it brought her. Some indication of the various commissions she served on and her administrative activities.

1980

855. Etheridge, Elizabeth W. "Goldsmith, Grace Arabell," Notable American Women (30), 4, pp. 283-284.
A detailed treatment of her research career and an analysis of its importance. Also directs the reader's attention to her great interest in people and her avocational activities.

GENERAL (See also 298)

1964

856. Ellsberg, H. "New Old Worlds to Conquer," Mademoiselle,
59 (June), pp. 106-108, 124, 125.
An article rich in biographical material but only for women
currently working in marine science.

857. MRS. M. BURTON WILLIAMSON
birth and death dates unknown
We know she was born in England and educated in private
schools, but other than those dim facts nothing is known of her
background. She lived in Long Beach, California, and was responsible for conducting the Zoological Department of the Summer
School of that city. In addition to her interests in the conch she
wrote a long article describing the work of a large number of
American women scientists which was published in three parts in
the Chautauquan of 1898 and 1899.

858. Williamson is cited in American Men of Science, 1906-1921.

859. ROSA SMITH EIGENMANN
7 October 1858--12 January 1947
Eigenmann had no formal training as a scientist and very
little college level education. She was a newspaper reporter in 1880
when her first scientific paper dealing with the fish of the San Diego area was published. At that time she was the recording secretary, librarian, and first woman member of the San Diego Society
of Natural History. When David S. Jordan, America's leading
ichthyologist, attended a meeting of the Society and heard her paper describing a new species she had discovered, he invited her
to study with him at Indiana University. She worked with Jordan
in his fishery survey and in 1886 met Carl H. Eigenmann, one of
his most able students.
In the six years following their marriage in 1887 the Eigen-
manns worked together and became widely known as authorities on
the freshwater fishes of South America and western North America.
While they were publishing 15 papers and monographs jointly she

was publishing 20 papers of her own and a notable monograph with
Joseph Swain on the fishes of Johnson Island in the Pacific Ocean.
     In 1891 Carl Eigenmann went to Indiana University where he
continued his scientific career. The burden of five children, including two with special needs, caused Rosa Eigenmann to restrict
her work to editing her husband's manuscripts and prevented any
further joint field studies. In spite of her short career Eigenmann
is widely recognized as the first American woman to attain prominence in ichthyology. (See also 4, 32, 40.)

1935

860. Martin, Hemme N. "San Diego Woman One of Earliest Dis-
          coverers of Pt. Loma Blindfish," San Diego Union (14 June).
      A substantial article which describes in her own words the
circumstances of her first and most famous discovery. Some general biographical detail and comments about her friendship with
David Starr Jordan.

1945

861. Raridan, W. J. "First Leaders of Natural History Society
          Recall Unit's Early Days," San Diego Union (16 January),
          p. 4. Photograph.
      Describes the association with David Starr Jordan and her
role in the development of the San Diego Society of Natural History
as members recalled it at the 70th annual meeting. Says she is
the country's only woman ichthyologist.

1947

862. Anon. "Noted Woman Expert on Fish Dies Here at 88," San
          Diego Journal (13 January), p. 14.
      Obituary which praises her scientific achievements. Discusses
her part in the development of the San Diego Society of Natural
History. Says she was the first woman reporter on the San Diego
Union newspaper.

863. Anon. "Alumni Around the World. The Emeritus Club ...,"
          Indiana University Alumni Magazine (March), p. 18.
      Obituary which lists her several "firsts."

864. Anon. "Eigenmann, Rosa Smith," Biographical Dictionary
          of American Science (40), p. 83.
      Outline of her life and career with attention limited to her
scientific accomplishments.

1971

865. Hubbs, Carl L. "Eigenmann, Rosa Smith," Notable American
      Women (30), 1, pp. 565-566.
      Very well-written story of Eigenmann's career with full atten-
tion to her personal life as well as her scientific work. Portrays
a woman having led a full, active life.

866. MARY JANE RATHBUN
      11 June 1860--4 April 1943
      As a young girl Rathbun, along with her brother, became
interested in the fish fossils they discovered in the family quar-
ries near Buffalo, New York. Her brother continued to influence
her throughout her career. He became curator of marine invertebrates at the National Museum in Washington in 1880, and the following year she accompanied him to the Woods Hole Laboratory.
Over the next few summers they worked together in sorting and
studying the huge collections of marine fauna being brought in by
the Fish Commission ships. Spencer F. Baird, head of the Commission and her brother's superior, was so impressed by her interest and talent that in 1884 he offered her a full-time position
at the National Museum.
      In the 53 years until her retirement Rathbun continued an
extensive program of self-education in marine biology in addition
to her duties of identifying and cataloging the rapidly growing collection. Her scientific publications began in 1891 and include 158
original titles dealing mostly with crustacean of the world's oceans.
One of her most elaborate works, Les Crabes d'Eau Douce, was
published between 1904 and 1906 in the Nouvelle Archives de Paris.
In 1918 the United States National Museum Bulletin published The
Grapsoid Crabs of America, a study for which George Washington
University awarded her a PhD the previous year. Her efforts in
establishing sound zoological nomenclature and her extensive collections of data provided future generations of students and scholars with vital and reliable sources from which to develop their
studies. (See also 4, 8, 11, 36.)

1943

867. Anon. "Funeral Rites Today for Dr. Mary Rathbun, Noted
      Scientist," The Evening Star [Washington, D.C.], 91 (6 April)
      p. A12. Photograph.
      Reviews her long service at the National Museum and her
many scientific contributions. The detail of her scientific work
is much greater than usual in a newspaper obituary.

868. McCain, Lucile. "Obituary. Mary Jane Rathbun," Science,
      97 (14 May), pp. 435-436.

After Rathbun retired she worked as usual for another 25 years without salary. In addition to her scientific interests she loved music and the theater.

869.   Schmitt, Waldo L. "Obituaries. Mary Jane Rathbun," <u>Journal of the Washington Academy of Sciences</u>, 33 (15 November), pp. 351-352.
   Cites her as an original member of the Academy and one who was entirely self-taught. In discussing her scientific contributions the author says, "Included in her bibliography are a number of truly monumental accounts of marine and fresh-water crabs." Expresses great admiration for her contributions to the work of the National Museum.

<u>1971</u>

870.   Schmitt, Waldo L. "Rathbun, Mary Jane," <u>Notable American Women</u> (30), 3, pp. 119-121.
   A second contribution by Schmitt to the memory of this extraordinary woman scientist. The style remains smooth and there is more detailed coverage of her career. Sadly, it is still all too short and deserves to be made into a full biography. At present this article is the best available and provides solid information.

GENERAL (See also 186, 623, 655, 662, 872, 1180, 1224)

1978

871. Green, Judy. "American Women in Mathematics--The First
      Ph.D.'s," Association for Women in Mathematics Newsletter,
      8 (April), pp. 13-15.
      A carefully researched list of American women who earned
doctorates in mathematics between 1886 and 1911. Discusses briefly each one's life and career. Gives numerous suggestions for further research. An addition and correction appeared on page 9 of
the July issue of this same publication. After Ms. Green had presented the contents of this paper to the American Mathematics Society, she received a request for a copy with the salutation "Dear
Sir."

1983

872. Whitman, Betsey S. "Women in The American Mathematical
      Society Before 1900," Association for Women in Mathematics
      Newsletter, 13 (July-December), pp. 9-13, 7-9.
      An excellent start toward a much needed study of the early
and nearly forgotten women mathematicians in the United States.
Most of the women included in the first edition of American Men
of Science are here; sadly, Scott alone is found in Notable American
Women.

873. SUSAN JANE CUNNINGHAM
      23 March 1842--23 or 24 January 1921
      In 1869 after study at Vassar College (1866-1867), Cunning-
ham joined the faculty of Swarthmore College where she spent her
entire career. She continued her studies during most of the next
20 summers to increase and keep current her knowledge of mathematics and astronomy. These intellectual activities took her to Williams College and the Universities of Harvard, Princeton, and Cambridge. Cunningham was promoted to full professor in 1874, the
post she held at her retirement in 1906. At that time she was the
only faculty member who had served the College since its founding.
In recognition of her contributions Swarthmore awarded her an honorary doctorate in 1888. (See also 9, 140, 872.)

1921

874. Anon. "De Mortuis. Susan J. Cunningham," Annual Report,
      Carnegie Foundation (7), 16, p. 162.
      Obituary listing the facts of her education and teaching ca-
reer.

875. Anon. "Cunningham, Susan Jane," The National Cyclopaedia
      of American Biography (2), unknown location.
      This biographical summary may or may not exist. It does
not appear in the often cited location, and the publisher sent us
a copy of the entry without a reference.

876. CHARLOTTE ANGAS SCOTT
      8 June 1858--8 November 1931
      Scott was the one woman of the six original faculty of Bryn
Mawr College to serve that institution for 40 years. The influence
she exerted is said to be second only to that of Bryn Mawr's first
president, M. Carey Thomas. During those formative years she
showed herself to be both a superb teacher and an internationally
recognized scholar. Her graduate students joined the faculties of
some of America's most distinguished colleges. Her undergraduates
respected the mathematical style and elegance of her lectures.
      Scott was born in England and educated at Cambridge Uni-
versity. While she and several other women won honors at Cambridge, hers in the extraordinary field of mathematics, they were
not allowed to take degrees. During the next four years (1880-
1884) she lectured at Girton College, her alma mater, and completed
her degrees at the University of London (BS, 1882; DSc, 1885).
      In addition to teaching and research Scott played an active
role in her profession. She was a founder of the New York Mathematical Society and the only woman member when it became the
American Mathematical Society in 1894-1895. After a three-year
term on the council she was elected vice-president in 1906.
      Several of her approximately 30 papers contributed to the
new field of algebraic geometry. In 1894 she published a textbook, An Introductory Account of Certain Modern Ideas in Plane
Analytical Geometry. It was most characteristic of her that she
ceased to use this book long before others because the field was
changing so rapidly. (See also 11, 25, 43, 873.)

1922

877. Anon. "Notes," Bulletin of the American Mathematical Soci-
      ety, 28 (June), p. 274.
      Brief notice that a celebration had been held in Scott's honor
and that A. N. Whitehead had given the principal address. Notes
her extraordinary record and says she should be an inspiration

to those wishing to follow a research career in mathematics, especially women.

1931

878. Anon. "Miss C. A. Scott," The Times [London] (10 Novem-
      ber), pp. 1, 16.
      Obituary which makes very favorable comments about her
work and tells the story of her undergraduate degree honors in
some detail. On page one there is a notice only.

879. Anon. [Resolutions by the Faculty of Bryn Mawr College],
      (17 December 1931 and 14 January 1932).
      Memorial statements by her colleagues, who praise her long
and important service to the College.

1932

880. Maddison, Isabel, and Marguerite Lehr. "Charlotte Angas
      Scott: An Appreciation," Bryn Mawr Alumnae Bulletin (Janu-
      ary), pp. 9-12.
      Written by former students and present colleagues, these
brief sketches make Scott's teaching and scholarship come alive.
The facts are here, but more important is the excitement conveyed
by the style and choice of words.

881. Macaulay, F. S. "Dr. Charlotte Angas Scott," Journal of
      the London Mathematical Society, 7 (July), pp. 230-240.
      A few biographical facts followed by a detailed and fairly
technical analysis of her mathematical contributions. A somewhat
weighty article, but rewarding for those who feel comfortable with
mathematics and who like a scientific presentation.

1971

882. Lehr, Marguerite. "Scott, Charlotte Angas," Notable American
      Women (30), 3, pp. 249-250.
      The perfect complement to Macaulay's article (881), this sketch
brings out all of the nontechnical and easily understood characteristics of this woman. We find not only an outstanding mathematician, but a fine teacher who has all of the human understanding
required in dealing with students (at least those who try).

1977-1978

883. Kenschaft, Pat. "Charlotte Angas Scott. 1858-1931,"
      Association for Women in Mathematics Newsletter, 7 (November-
      December), pp. 9-10 and 8 (April), pp. 11-12.

A detailed biographical sketch and a partial bibliography of Scott's works. Reveals much about Scott as a person and presents important insights on her multifaceted career. The first part deals with her education at Cambridge and the second with her influence at Bryn Mawr. The contributions of this remarkable woman are clearly presented.

1979

884. Anon. "Scott, Charlotte Angas," Biographical Dictionary of American Science (40), p. 232.
The four lines make one wonder why the editor bothered.

885. CHARLOTTE CYNTHIA BARNUM
17 May 1860--27 March 1934
Educated at Vassar College (AB, 1881), Johns Hopkins University (1890-1892), and Yale University (PhD, 1895), Barnum held a variety of positions in colleges, life insurance firms and federal government service. She taught mathematics at Smith College before beginning her work at Johns Hopkins and at Carleton College after completing her doctorate. In 1898 she held a number of positions in applied mathematics beginning with the Massachusetts and Fidelity Mutual Life Insurance Companies (1898-1901). In 1901 she joined the United States Naval Observatory and the Coast and Geodetic Survey where she applied her interest in discontinuous surface functions to the study of tides and currents. From 1908 to 1913 she was with the United States Department of Agriculture and during most of World War I she did editorial work in various departments at Yale. Her varied experience in practical mathematics more likely resulted from the lack of professional opportunity for women than personal preference. Barnum was one of the earliest members of the American Mathematical Society which she joined in 1894. (See also 11, 872.)

1933-1934

886. Anon. "Charlotte Cynthia Barnum, PhD, 1895," Yale University Obituary Record, pp. 204-205.
Gives basic facts of her education and career.

1983

887. Barnum is cited in American Men of Science, 1906-1921; and Who Was Who in America, 1, p. 59.

888.   ANNA HELENE PALMIE
        21 May 1863--12 June 1946
        Palmié studied mathematics as a fellow following her gradua-
tion from Cornell University (PhB, 1890). In 1892 she joined the
faculty of the Western Reserve University College for Women where
she rose to the rank of professor in 1895. In 1897 she became another early woman member of the American Mathematics Society and
the following year she went to Göttingen University for further
study. When Palmié retired in 1928 she expressed her love of teaching mathematics and her regret over the growth of the university
and its loss of intimacy. (See also 872.)

                            1945-1946

889.   Anon. "De Mortuis. Anna Helene Palmié," Annual Report,
        Carnegie Foundation (7), 41, pp. 118-119.
        Brief paragraph of biographical facts.

890.   Palmié is cited in American Men of Science, 1906-1921; and
        Woman's Who's Who of America, p. 619.

891.   HELEN ABBOT MERRILL
        30 March 1864--1 May 1949
        Merrill taught at her alma mater, Wellesley College (BA,
1886), from 1893 until her retirement in 1932. She had served
as department chairman since 1916 and had held an endowed
chair of mathematics. Following graduate study at the Universities of Chicago and Göttingen, she completed her formal education at Yale University (PhD, 1903). Her principal interest
was algebra, on which subject she published two textbooks.
She also attempted to popularize the subject in her Mathematical
Excursions published in 1933. She was elected vice-president of
both the Mathematical Association of America (1920) and the American Mathematical Society (1919).

                              1949

892.   Anon. "Helen A. Merrill of Wellesley, 85," The New York
        Times, 98 (3 May), p. 25.
        She received her doctorate at Yale University and taught at
Wellesley College for over 30 years. Merrill was department head
from 1916 to 1932. Several of her books are mentioned.

893.   Anon. "Helen Abbot Merrill," Yale University Obituary Rec-
        ord (1 July), p. 142.
        Outline of biographical facts.

1958

894. Anon. "Merrill, Helen Abbot," The National Cyclopaedia of
     American Biography (2), 42, pp. 171-172.
     Family background receives the greatest attention. Lists her
educational dates, professional appointments and mentions some of
her publications.

1978

895. Thomas, Janet Durand. "Merrill, Helen Abbot," Biographical
     Dictionary of American Educators (38), 2, p. 890.
     Gives a review of her education and teaching career along
with a mention of three books. Errs in saying that she is included
in Notable American Women.

896. ISABEL MADDISON
     12 April 1869--22 October 1950
     Born and educated in England, Maddison earned her under-
graduate degree at the University of London (BSc, 1893) after winning honors at both Cambridge and Oxford Universities in 1892.
Her graduate education saw the beginning of a lifelong association
with Bryn Mawr College. In 1894 she undertook a year of further
study at Göttingen University as the first recipient of the Mary
E. Garrett Fellowship designed to encourage women to study abroad.
Following her return to Bryn Mawr she completed her formal education (PhD, 1896), taught and did research in the solution of differential equations. Her most memorable service was as dean and
assistant to Bryn Mawr's first president, M. Carey Thomas, during
the formative years of that college. After her retirement in 1926
she apparently did no additional scientific or administrative work.
In 1937 she confessed "to feeling ashamed of having deserted mathematics." (See also 25, 872.)

1950

897. Anon. "Ex-Dean I. Maddison, Long at Bryn Mawr," The New
     York Times, 100 (24 October), p. 29.
     Notice of her death which deals almost entirely with her stu-
dent and administrative associations at Bryn Mawr.

1951

898. Anon. "Isabel Maddison," Bryn Mawr Alumnae Bulletin
     (Winter), p. 14.

Notice of her death and the fact that she left a large amount
of money as a pension fund for non-faculty staff at Bryn Mawr.

899.   GRACE ANDREWS
       30 May 1869--27 July 1951
       After graduation from Wellesley College (BS, 1890) Andrews
obtained her graduate education at Columbia University (AM, 1899;
PhD, 1901).   She was an assistant in mathematics at Columbia in
1901-1902 and then accepted a position as assistant treasurer at
Wesleyan University in Middletown, Connecticut.   In the 1942 alumnae record at Wellesley she reported leaving this post in October
1926.   For the rest of her life she was active in the missions service of her church and the Kosmos Club of Brooklyn.   The latter
was a social and cultural club in which she took a great interest
and served as treasurer and director of the board.

900.   Brewster, Alice L.   "Grace Andrews," unidentified clipping
       in Wellesley Archives.
       A warm, personal obituary by a classmate which outlines the
facts of Andrews' life and gives some valuable insight to her personality.
       We are indebted to Wilma R. Slaight, Archivist of Wellesley
College, for her assistance in learning about Andrews.

901.   MARY WINSTON NEWSON
       7 August 1869--December 1959
       Newson studied at the University of Wisconsin (AB, 1889)
and Bryn Mawr College (1891-1892).   After being a "fellow by
courtesy" at the University of Chicago (1892-1893) she accepted
a fellowship from the Association of Collegiate Alumnae for study
at Göttingen University (PhD, 1896).   She taught high school
mathematics in St. Joseph, Missouri, at the Kansas State Agriculture College and at Washburn College, Topeka, Kansas.   Her research interest was in differential equations.

902.   Newson is cited in American Men of Science, 1906-1921; and
       Woman's Who's Who of America, p. 596.
       We are indebted to Bernard Schermetzler, Archivist of the
University of Wisconsin, for his assistance in learning certain facts
about Newson.

903.   IDA MAY SCHOTTENFELS
       21 December 1869--11 March 1942
       Graduated from Northwestern University (AB, 1892), she
studied at Yale University where she described herself as an

honorary fellow. After earning a graduate degree at the University of Chicago (AM, 1896) Schottenfels taught at various Chicago grammar and high schools. She became an instructor at the New York Normal College in 1901 and reported that she held the chair of mathematics at Adrian College (Michigan) in 1913. A relative, Ira Schottenfels, wrote a charming letter reporting her death in which he said, "Her mind must have been on her work until the end, because the last time she was able to sit-up in bed, she traced figures on the wall drew a line & computed."

904.   Schottenfels is cited in American Men of Science, 1906.
   We are indebted to Patrick M. Quinn, University Archivist of Northwestern University, for some of these facts about her life. The records show several different birth years and we have chosen 1869, the American Men of Science entry, since she is most likely to have proofread that material.

905.   EMILIE NORTON MARTIN
   30 December 1869--1936
   Martin graduated from Bryn Mawr College (AB, 1894) and as a Mary E. Garrett fellow continued her education at Göttingen University (PhD, 1901). She began teaching at Mount Holyoke College as an instructor in 1903 and became an associate professor in 1911. She completed an index to the first ten volumes of the Bulletin of the American Mathematical Society in 1904.

906.   Martin is cited in American Men of Science, 1906-1921; and Woman's Who's Who of America, p. 543.

907.   LOUISE DUFFIELD CUMMINGS
   21 November 1870--9 May 1947
   After graduation from the University of Toronto (BA, 1895; MA, 1902) Cummings studied at the Universities of Pennsylvania and Chicago. She was a fellow in mathematics at Bryn Mawr College. Following a year of teaching in Canada, Vassar College appointed her instructor in mathematics in 1902. She returned to Bryn Mawr to complete her formal education (PhD, 1914) and continued to serve Vassar until her retirement in 1936. Cummings was interested in geometry and published a number of articles in the Transactions and the Bulletin of the American Mathematical Society. She was promoted to full professor in 1927.

1946-1947

908.   Anon. "De Mortuis. Louise Duffield Cummings," Annual Report, Carnegie Foundation (7), 42, pp. 68-69.

A longer sketch than most in this collection but still only
the most limited outline of her life and work.

1977

909. Hutchinson, Joan P. "Women in Combinatorics," Association
      for Women in Mathematics Newsletter, 7 (January-February),
      pp. 3-4.
      A review of Cummings' contributions to combinatorial analysis
and a historical perspective of the field. Includes other women
mathematicians from the early, middle, and current periods of this
century.

910. Cummings is cited in American Men of Science, 1906-1921.

911. MARY ESTHER TRUEBLOOD PAINE
      6 May 1872--19 November 1939
      Trueblood was educated at Earlham College (PhB, 1893) and
the University of Michigan (PhM, 1896). She was a fellow of the
Woman's Educational Association and studied at the University of
Göttingen in 1900-1901. As a member of the Mount Holyoke College faculty from 1902 to 1910 her scholarly work centered on the
history and philosophy of mathematics. In 1911 she married Robert Paine, a sculptor, and about 1914 joined the University of California at Berkeley where she became head of the extension department of mathematics.

1939

912. Anon. "Dr. Mary Paine of Berkeley, Dies," Los Angeles Times
      (23 November), part II.
      Obituary which speaks of her as being "regarded as one of
the ablest women mathematicians of the country." Gives a brief
outline of her career.

913. Trueblood is cited in American Men of Science, 1906-1910;
      and Woman's Who's Who of America, p. 825.
      We are indebted to Sara Beth Terrell, Archivist of Earlham
College, and Elaine D. Trehub, College History Librarian of Mount
Holyoke College, for their assistance.

914. RUTH GOULDING WOOD
      29 January 1875--unknown
      Having spent her undergraduate years at Smith College,
Wood went to Yale University as a fellow. After one year she

went to teach at Mount Holyoke College, only to return to Yale at the end of that year. After receiving her degree (PhD, 1901), she returned to Smith as instructor in mathematics in 1902 where her interests were in non-Euclidean geometry. Following a year of study at Göttingen University (1908-1909) she was promoted to full professor.

915. Wood is cited in American Men of Science, 1906-1921; and Woman's Who's Who of America, p. 900.

916. CARRIE HAMMERSLOUGH HYMES
       18 December 1875--December 1949
       Hammerslough became a private tutor in mathematics following her education at Columbia University (AB, 1896; AM, 1897). She was a Curtis Scholar in 1896-1897. She married Edward Hymes and they had two sons, Edward, Jr. and Richard.

917. Hammerslough is cited in American Men of Science, 1906.
       We are indebted to Eugene P. Sheehy, Head of Reference at the Columbia University Butler Library, for his assistance.

918. AMALIE EMMY NOETHER
       23 March 1882--14 April 1935
       Noether studied mathematics, English, and French at the Universities of Erlangen and Göttingen as a nonmatriculated auditor. In 1904 she was permitted to enroll officially at Erlangen (PhD, 1907). Her degree was awarded summa cum laude. She had already given up her early plans to teach language in favor of mathematics; she is generally considered the greatest female mathematician up to her time.
       Between 1915 and 1933 she taught at Göttingen, mostly in unofficial or honorary positions. Her work in abstract algebra led to the solution of several important problems, including the elegant mathematical formulation for several aspects of Einstein's general theory of relativity.
       When she and other Jewish professors at Göttingen were dismissed by the Nazis in 1933, she moved to Bryn Mawr College. She lectured and continued her research at Bryn Mawr and the Institute for Advanced Study at Princeton University until her early death. Her productive career advanced several areas of algebra and was an inspiration to a number of later scholars. (See also 23, 25, 43, 44, 46.)

1935

919. Anon. "Dr. Emmy Noether Dies; Noted as Mathematician," New York Herald Tribune, 95 (15 April), p. 12.

Exiled by the Nazis Noether was recognized as one of the world's greatest mathematicians. She taught at Bryn Mawr College and Princeton University.

920. Einstein, Albert. "The Late Emmy Noether," The New York Times, 84 (4 May), p. 12.
Calls her a distinguished mathematician. "In the judgment of the most competent living mathematicians she was the most significant creative mathematical genius thus far produced since the higher education of women began." Includes a discussion of his own philosophy.

921. Waerden, B. L. van der. "Nachruf auf Emmy Noether," Mathematische Annalen, 111, pp. 469-476. In German.
A detailed and technical discussion of her work dealing mostly with its philosophy and direction. There is a bibliography of her works.

922. Weyl, Hermann. "Emmy Noether," Scripta mathematica, 3, pp. 201-220.
The printed version of Weyl's memorial address at Bryn Mawr College (26 April 1935). Deals with Noether's life and personality as well as her contribution to mathematics. A fine biographical portrait emerges, and one sees her in the context of her times, particularly the years in Germany prior to World War II. Weyl makes clear the respect he had for her, "She was a great mathematician, the greatest, I firmly believe, that her sex has ever produced, and a great woman."

1962

923. Dubreil-Jacotin, Mme. Marie-Louise. "Women Mathematicians," in Great Currents of Mathematical Thought, F. Le Lionnais, editor; R. A. Hall and Howard G. Bergmann, translators. New York: Dover, 1971, vol. 1, ch. 23, pp. 268-280.
The new translation of Les Grands Courants de la Pensée Mathématique includes this review of the great women of mathematics from earliest times to Noether (pp. 277-280). While the material deals with her work, it is not phrased in technical language and the life and personality are nicely worked around the mathematics.

1970

924. Iacobacci, Rora F. "Women of Mathematics," Mathematics Teacher, 63 (April), pp. 329-337. Likeness.
Concluding a review of the contributions of women to mathematics is a nice sketch of Noether's life. Her work is described only in general terms which emphasize her methodology. There is a long quotation from Einstein's evaluation of Noether's importance.

925. Dick, Auguste. "Emmy Noether. 1882-1935." Beihefte zur
      Zeitschrift "Elemente der Mathematik." Suppléments à la
      "Revue de Mathématiques Elémentaires." no. 13, 45 pp. In
      German.
      A rich source of detailed biographical information about this
eminent mathematician. Presented are bibliography of her work,
list of significant dates, list of dissertations by graduate students,
and tributes. It is also bound together with 921 and 922.

926. Kramer, Edna E. The Nature and Growth of Modern Mathe-
      matics. New York: Hawthorn Books, pp. 656-660.
      This essential sourcebook for the history of mathematics pre-
sents a sketch which places Noether in the context of the development of algebra and calls her, "Hypatia's modern counterpart." The
section devoted to her work is followed by a reprint of Weyl's biographical paper (922).

1972

927. Kimberling, Clark H. "Emmy Noether," American Mathemati-
      cal Monthly, 79 (February), pp. 136-149.
      A start on a complete biography of Noether which reproduces
long sections of other writings about her. Some of this reprinted
material would be very difficult to find elsewhere and the overall
study is a good one. There are several particularly important parts:
her early life (mostly from Dick, 925), her contributions to physics,
and a note about her rediscovered correspondence.

1974

928. Osen, Lynn M. Women in Mathematics. Cambridge, Massa-
      chusetts: MIT Press, 185 pp.
      A series of biographical essays of outstanding women mathe-
maticians from Hypatia to Noether. There is a conclusion which
names some recent women and the current attitudes toward women
in this profession, but it is only Noether who is treated in any
biographical detail.

929. Kramer, Edna E. "Noether, Amalie Emmy," Dictionary of Sci-
      entific Biography (30), 10, pp. 137-139.
      An unusually long biography for this standard reference
source. The article does a fine job of bringing together the personal details with an introduction and evaluation of her mathematics. A brief but useful bibliography. Noether is mentioned in the
biographical sketch of her research director, Paul Albert Gordan.

1977

930. Charpentier, Debra. "Women Mathematicians," Two-Year

College Mathematics Journal, 8 (March), pp. 73-79.
A mention of Noether.

1978

931. Perl, Teri. "Emmy Noether. 1882-1935," in Math Equals.
Biographies of Women Mathematicians + Related Activities.
Menlo Park, California: Addison-Wesley, pp. 172-194.
A good biographical sketch which emphasizes her struggles
and her greatness. Presents Noether in the most interesting for-
mat by contrasting her personality and career with Sophie Kovalev-
ski, the great Russian mathematician of the preceding generation.
Of special interest are the mathematical exercises selected to illustrate Noether's work.

932. ANNA JOHNSON PELL WHEELER
5 May 1883--26 March 1966
As an undergraduate at the University of South Dakota (AB,
1903) Wheeler was encouraged by her future husband, Alexander
Pell, to continue her mathematical education. She studied at the
University of Iowa (AM, 1904) and Radcliffe College (AM, 1905).
In the following year, using the Alice Freeman Palmer Fellowship
awarded her by Wellesley College, she worked at Göttingen University and married Pell. When he accepted a position at the Ar-
mour Institute of Technology, she completed her education at the
University of Chicago (PhD, 1910).
Finding the universities closed to women faculty and faced
with the serious illness of her husband, Wheeler accepted an appointment at Mount Holyoke College in 1911. She taught and made
some research progress while caring for Pell until 1918. In that
year Wheeler began a 30-year career at Bryn Mawr College where
she established herself as teacher, scholar, and administrator.
At Göttingen Wheeler had worked with David Hilbert, who
had interested her in integral equations, an area which became central in her later research. She made extensions of Hilbert's work
and was able to achieve more general solutions in certain cases.
There was wide respect for the quality of her work, and in 1927
she became the first woman invited to deliver the Colloquium Lectures by the American Mathematical Society.
As an administrator Wheeler accomplished much in the growth
of Bryn Mawr's reputation in mathematics. She believed strongly
in the need for excellence in scholarship as well as teaching; she
herself was a master of both. She also recognized the need of faculty to have lowered teaching responsibilities if they were to follow
productive scholarly careers as well. It was through Wheeler that
the eminent mathematician Emmy Noether came to Bryn Mawr.
Wheeler believed in the necessity of a proper campus setting for
excellence in education, but she also encouraged her students to

take full advantage of professional organizations in the development
of their careers. (See also 19, 25.)

1966

*933.   [Obituary]. Evening Bulletin (Philadelphia) (29 March), p.
        70.

934.   Anon. "Dr. Anna Pell Wheeler," The New York Times, 115
        (1 April), p. 35.
        Professor emerita Wheeler made a number of contributions
to the theory of integral equations and function analysis.

935.   Oxtoby, John C., and Ruth Stauffer McKee. "Anna Pell
        Wheeler," Bryn Mawr Alumnae Bulletin (Summer), pp. 22-
        23. Photograph.
        Tributes to Wheeler by the chairman of the mathematics de-
partment and a former student at Bryn Mawr. Very important personal and professional material which helps make clear the high regard professional mathematicians had for her. Interesting notes
about the relationship between Wheeler and Noether and an amus-
ing incident involving Einstein.

1978

936.   Grinstein, Louise S., and Paul J. Campbell. "Anna Johnson
        Pell Wheeler, 1883-1966," Association for Women in Mathematics
        Newsletter, 8 (September and November), pp. 14-16.
        This short biography illustrates just what can be achieved
through persistence and self-discipline even in tragic circumstances.
A midwestern girl goes to college where she resides with her sister
at the home of one of her math professors. Encouraged by him
to continue her studies, she won a scholarship to the University
of Iowa. After her MA she won the prestigious Alice Freeman Palmer
Fellowship given by Wellesley College. A requirement for acceptance
was a promise not to marry during the award period, and having
agreed, Johnson went off to Göttingen. Meanwhile her former professor's wife died, and eventually Anna and Alexander Pell decided
to marry. Anna never revealed the true identity of her husband
who was a double agent by the name of Sergei Degaev. After their
marriage Anna pursued a PhD, first at Göttingen where she could
not get along with her mentor, Hilbert, and finally at the University of Chicago. Her husband always found a job where Anna could
do her work. Since she had already written a thesis for Hilbert
at Göttingen, where it had been rejected, she submitted it to Chicago and graduated magna cum laude in 1910. Then her struggles
became intensified, for she discovered the unacceptability of women
candidates for college or university positions. These difficulties
are presented in this paper as is the happiest part of her life, her

marriage after Pell's death in 1921 to Arthur Leslie Wheeler, a noted classics scholar at Bryn Mawr and, after their marriage, at Princeton. In September 1927 Anna Johnson took another honor; she was the only woman to be invited to give the "Colloquium Lectures" at the American Mathematical Society meeting in New York. Includes a bibliography of her works.

1978

937. Ayoub, Christine W.   "Wheeler, Anna Johnson Pell," Diction-
      ary of American Educators (38), 3, pp. 1377-1378.
      Well-organized sketch giving Wheeler's educational and pro-
fessional background and some of her honors. Makes the point
that she encouraged young faculty to be active in research and
helped them to accomplish that goal.

1980

938. Grinstein, Louise S.   "Wheeler, Anna Johnson Pell," Notable
      American Women (30), 4, pp. 725-726.
      A balanced account of Wheeler's personal life along with com-
ments on her mathematical contributions. Says that she was responsible for bringing Noether to Bryn Mawr and played other key
roles in seeing that research became an important part of the department's activities.

939. OLIVE CLIO HAZLETT
      27 October 1890--unknown
      Hazlett was educated at Radcliffe College (AB, 1912) and
the University of Chicago (MS, 1913; PhD, 1915). After two years
as an associate in mathematics at Bryn Mawr College she joined the
faculty of Mount Holyoke College in 1918. She was promoted to
associate professor in 1929. Her research interests, especially in
the linear algebras, earned her a star as one of the most distinguished mathematicians in the fourth edition of American Men of
Science (1926).

940. Hazlett is cited in American Men of Science, 1921.

941. HILDA GEIRINGER VON MISES
      28 September 1893--22 March 1973
      Von Mises was born and educated in Vienna, Austria, and
like so many Jewish intellectuals was forced to flee Europe in 1933.
At the University of Vienna (PhD, 1917) she studied pure mathematics, but her most important work was to be in applied fields,

especially probability and statistics theory. These interests began
in 1921 when she moved to the University of Berlin and began work
with her future husband, Richard von Mises, at the Institute of
Applied Mathematics. From this work evolved an equation describing the behavior of plane plastic surfaces which is named for her.

Beginning in 1934 she worked at Istanbul University and five
years later moved to Bryn Mawr College. After her marriage in
1943 and with her husband's appointment at Harvard University,
von Mises accepted the chairmanship of mathematics at Wheaton College in Norton, Massachusetts. Until her retirement in 1959 she
continued to work productively in spite of the demands of teaching
and administration. In the typical fashion of two career families,
she worked at Wheaton during the week and commuted to Cambridge
on the weekends. Her contributions in plastic theory and the mathematics of Mendelian genetics were especially important.

Following her husband's death in 1953 von Mises turned to
the task of completing several of his ideas. However, she actually
extended and improved several of his basic concepts. Her contributions to probability theory won widespread recognition. She received an honorary degree from Wheaton in 1960 and in 1956 the
University of Berlin named her professor emerita. The University
of Vienna made a special presentation on the occasion of the fiftieth
anniversary of her graduation.

1959

942. Anon. "Dr. Geiringer Retires," Wheaton College Newsletter,
     47 (September), p. 4.
     A review of her career on the occasion of her retirement.
Says she is one of the College's most distinguished faculty members and that she liked teaching the introductory course on elementary mathematics.

1973

943. Anon. "Dr. Hilda Von Mises, a Statistics Expert," The New
     York Times, 122 (24 March), p. 36.
     Engineer, mathematician, and pioneer authority on powered
flight. Follows her career from Vienna to Wheaton.

944. Anon. "Dr. Hilda von Mises, 79, mathematician at Harvard,"
     Boston Sunday Globe, 203 (25 March), p. 95. Photograph.
     Traces her flight from Germany and notes the high points
of her research and honors.

945. Anon. "Obituaries. Hilda Geiringer von Mises," Wheaton
     College Newsletter, 60 (April).
     Obituary which stresses her research, especially with under-
graduates, and notes that she preferred to be called Mrs. Geiringer
at Wheaton.

<u>1980</u>

946.   Richards, Joan L.   "Geiringer, Hilda," <u>Notable American</u>
       <u>Women</u> (30), 4, pp. 267-268.
       This fine article gives more attention to her life in Europe
and is noteworthy for its description of her philosophy of research.

947.   MARGARET LOYD JARMAN HAGOOD
       26 October 1907--13 August 1963
       One of the earliest workers in the application of mathematics
to the study of social problems, Hagood made fundamental contributions to the developing fields of sociological statistics and demog-
raphy.   After graduation from Queen's College in Charlotte, North
Carolina (AB, 1929) she continued her education in mathematics
at Emory University (AM, 1930).
       In the mid-1930's she, along with a group of vigorous young
scholars, joined the Institute for Research in Social Science headed
by Howard Odum at the University of North Carolina.   Her intense-
ness of purpose and her skill in mathematics made Hagood a key
figure in this pioneering group.   Each of her studies over the next
few years made an important contribution to the growing application
of complex statistical methods to the study of social problems.   Published in 1941 as <u>Statistics for Sociologists</u>, this book in its first
and later editions, has strongly influenced the development of sociological methodology.
       After she finished her doctoral dissertation at North Carolina
(PhD, 1939), she was appointed in the department of sociology as
a research associate at the Institute.   Her first study, entitled
<u>Mothers of the South</u>, was published in 1939.   This human and un-
derstanding record of the poor southern farmer in the great depression remains one of her most important contributions.
       Between 1942 and her retirement in 1962 Hagood worked in
the United States Department of Agriculture.   First, in the Bureau
of Agricultural Economics and after 1952 as head of the Farm Population and Rural Life Branch of the Agricultural Marketing Service.
In both of these positions Hagood continued her work in the application of statistics to the analysis of population and economic
information.   Her development of the "level-of-living index" was
considered an important step in providing useful data for policy-
making decisions.   These contributions won her election as president of the Population Association of America in 1954 and of the
Rural Sociological Society in 1956.

<u>1963</u>

948.   Taeuber, Conrad.   "Margaret Jarman Hagood, 1908-1963,"
       <u>American Statistician</u>, 17 (October), p. 37.
       This memorial article describes Hagood's contribution to

statistics and service to the Department of Agriculture. Her colleague at the Bureau of the Census speaks of her as a warm and
energetic person whose intellectual talents were fully devoted to
her work.

1964

949. Eldridge, Hope T. "Margaret Jarman Hagood. 1907-1963,"
     Population Index, 30 (January), pp. 30-31.
     The author describes Hagood's career with special attention
to her contributions to sociologists. Interesting comments on the
style of her writing saying, "the whole book [Statistics for Sociolo-
gists] bears the imprint of her personality--its patience, its gentle-
ness, its glint of humor, its sweetness."

950. Taylor, Carl C. "Margaret J. Hagood (1907-63)," Rural So-
     ciology, 29 (January), pp. 97-98.
     Traces her life by referring to each of her most important
publications. Says that her most lasting contribution will be "like
[that of] every other top professional ... what she has done to
help develop other top professional persons."

1980

951. Scott, Anne Firor. "Hagood, Margaret Loyd Jarman," Notable
     American Women (30), 4, pp. 297-298.
     Scott gives a fine picture of Hagood's career and deals with
her most important research contributions as an integral part of
her personal life. Makes an important point in regard to her work
for the government. Her responsibility included establishing methods
for making comparisons and for insuring their validity. Stresses
Hagood's serious concern for the people whom she wished to aid
through her research.

(See also 580)

952. MARY BLAIR MOODY
8 August 1837--1919
In the 1906 and 1910 editions of American Men of Science
Moody reports that her "departments of investigation" are medicine
and languages. It is clear from her list of "chief subjects of research" that her efforts were far ranging indeed, including these
in addition to general medicine: natural science, household economics, rearing, education, necessities, and rights of children.
Her "in progress" research involved the flora of California and bird
life in the United States.

Moddy was educated at the University of Buffalo (MD, 1876)
and was the founder and senior physician at the Women's and Children's Dispensary in Buffalo from 1882 to 1886. She gives no other
positions or dates and apparently moved to New Haven, Connecticut, prior to 1906. She was associated with two serials, the Buffalo Medical and Surgical Journal as a book reviewer and the Bulletin of the Buffalo Natural Field Club as associate editor. The
latter publication may have been related to environmental concerns
since she was a member of the Forestry Association and the Association [for the] Protection of Adirondacks. Moody was also a member of the American Association for the Advancement of Science.

While the small evidence in hand suggests that Moody was
not a scientist as we understand the term, it is interesting that
she thought of herself as one, and Cattell allowed her to be included
in his biographical directory. Did she actually complete and publish any of the several projects listed?

953. ANITA NEWCOMB McGEE
4 November 1864--unknown
McGee had a long and highly acclaimed career in military
medicine. She served as acting Assistant Surgeon of the United
States Army during the Spanish-American War (1898-1900) when
she was the founder of the Army Nurse Corps. She also served
through the Philippine insurrection and the Boxer campaign. She
was an officer in the Japanese army during the war with Russia
in 1904. Her duties included organizing and training nurses, in-
specting hospitals in Japan and Manchuria, and serving as supervisor of nurses at Hiroshima and on board the principal hospital
ships. For her efforts she received a number of decorations,

including the Imperial Order of the Sacred Crown and special decorations from the Emperor and Empress of Japan.

She speaks of her father, Professor Simon Newcomb, USN,
as a distinguished astronomer and her husband, W. J. McGee, as
a scientist. Her preparatory education was in private schools and
Europe. She took her medical degree at Columbian (George Washington) University in 1892 following her marriage in 1888. The
McGees had two children: a daughter, Klotho, and a son, Eric
Newcomb.

With regard to her scientific interests she reports very little. In the third edition of American Men of Science she says she
is interested in heredity in humans, but nothing is given in the
two earlier editions. She reports that she was a fellow of the
American Association for the Advancement of Science and secretary
of section H in 1897. In 1911 McGee was a lecturer in hygiene at
the University of California in Berkeley and a "contributor to magazines." Here is a subject for some research in who was a scientist
in the first decades of the century. (See also 4.)

1936

954.   Barnard, Eunice Fuller. "Women Microbe Hunters," Inde-
       pendent Woman, 15 (December), pp. 379, 396-397. Photo-
       graphs.
       Article noting several women in medical research. The cen-
tral theme is the progress women are making in professional roles.

1937

955.   Anon. "Science Opens Its Doors to Women," Literary Digest,
       124 (10 July), pp. 17-18. Photographs.
       The subtitle is especially interesting: "But Pay Still Lags
Behind That of Males." There is a bit of career information on
a few women in medicine but the paper deals mostly with salary
inequities and the colleges which are providing education for
women.

1949

956.   Anon. "Centennial of a Trailblazer," Journal of the American
       Medical Women's Association, 4 (March), pp. 125-127. Photo-
       graphs.
       Hobart and William Smith Colleges present citations to several
outstanding women physicians on the centennial of Elizabeth Blackwell's graduation.

957.   Snelgrove, Erle E. "The First Woman Doctor," Hygeia, 27
       (August), pp. 534-535, 567. Photographs.

In commemoration of the 100th anniversary of Elizabeth Blackwell's graduation, Hobart and William Smith Colleges made special
citations to 12 leading women doctors. Biographical notes.

1953

958. Anon. "Blackwell Awards of the New York Infirmary,"
      Journal of the American Medical Women's Association, 8
      (June), pp. 210-212. Photographs.
      Several women physicians are recognized on the centennial
of the first American woman's graduation with a medical degree.
There is a short biographical sketch of each woman honored.

1957

959. Lovejoy, Esther Pohl. Women Doctors of the World. New
      York: Macmillan, index. Photographs.
      A history of women's contributions to medicine. There is a
short introductory chapter on the beginning of medicine, but emphasizes the period during which women fought to gain acceptance
as physicians. The book treats the history of women's participation in all parts of the world. Among those in American medicine
we find mention of Cori, Hamilton, L'Esperance, and Sabin, along
with a number of others who receive limited comment. Some non-
physicians are included. Even where the discussion is biographical
the details are limited to women's role in the development of educational and professional opportunities for women in medicine.

1964

960. Corner, George W. A History of the Rockefeller Institute.
      1901-1953. Origins and Growth. New York: Rockefeller
      Institute Press, index.
      This detailed history of an unusual research and educational
institution written by an equally unusual research scientist and
medical historian is a most valuable source for anyone interested
in the development of American medical research. Although John
Rockefeller had discussed (for three years) the idea of an institution devoted to medical research, it was the death of his first grand-
child at three years of age which catapulted the idea into reality.
In addition to his teaching career at several distinguished medical
schools, Corner spent five years as historian at the Rockefeller
Institute. Several women scientists are mentioned briefly in connection with various research activities, but Sabin is the only woman
member whose career is treated in detail.

(See also 1040)

961. FLORENCE RENA SABIN
      9 November 1871--3 October 1953
      Sabin's desire to become a research physician may have been
influenced by her father who was not able to reach that goal, but
in any event it was certainly fostered at Smith College where she
earned a BS in 1893. Still there was a need to earn the money
to follow her interests, and she taught mathematics in Denver and
zoology at Smith before becoming the first woman to enroll at The
Johns Hopkins Medical School and its first woman graduate in 1900.
In 1902 she became the first woman member of the Hopkins faculty
and in 1917 its first woman full professor.
      For twenty-five years she taught at Hopkins and conducted
extensive research in blood cells and the lymph vessels. She made
several fundamental contributions and became noted for her extremely careful work and constant search for more precise methods. She
devoted herself to teaching, making students discover for themselves
rather than simply memorizing. When one of her students was appointed chairman of the department, she was disappointed, but continued to be an active, generous member for another eight years.
      In 1925, the same year she was elected to the National Acad-
emy of Sciences and in the midst of her two-year term as president
of the American Association of Anatomists, she accepted an appointment at the Rockefeller Institute for Medical Research. All three
of these events mark a first for a woman. For 13 years she led
a group working on the pathology and biochemistry of tuberculosis.
      After she was made emeritus at Rockefeller, Sabin retired
to her native Colorado. Six years later she began what is in many
ways the most exciting aspect of her distinguished career. She
was asked by the governor to help make an assessment of the state's
health status. The results of her work were shocking to the people, and largely through her efforts eight Sabin health bills were
made law in 1947. (See also 8, 11, 12, 19, 23, 33, 41, 42, 43,
46, 954, 955, 956, 957, 958.)

1920

*962. Howell, W. H. "Presentation to the University of the Por-
       trait of Dr. Florence Rena Sabin," Bulletin Johns Hopkins
       Hospital, 31, p. 151.

1925

963. Anon. "Academy of Sciences Elects First Woman," The New
      York Times, 74 (30 April), p. 9.
      Sabin becomes the first woman elected to the National Acad-
emy of Sciences in its 62 year history. The others elected with
her are listed and her notable research with blood cells is described briefly.

964. Walker, Harold. "Academy of Sciences Opens to a Woman,"
      The New York Times, 74 (17 May), sect. 4, p. 6. Painting.
      Describes Sabin's work as a "Romantic Adventure." Con-
cerns the present state of her research.

1929

965. Anon. "Woman Doctor Wins Prize for Research," The New
      York Times, 79 (16 November), p. 19. Photograph.
      Sabin wins the annual Pictorial Review award. A list of the
distinguished men and women on the selection committee and her
description of her work.

966. Anon. "A Feminine 'First,'" The New York Times, 79 (19
      November), p. 30.
      Sabin has been selected by "a highly competent committee
as 'the American woman who has made the most distinctive contribution to American life in the fields of arts, letters or the sciences.'" Reports that she received a $5,000 award from the Pictorial
Review and is the first woman to be elected to the National Academy of Sciences.

1930

967. Anon. "Sabin, Florence Rena," The National Cyclopaedia
      of American Biography (2), C, pp. 288-289. Photograph.
      Article gives family background and educational history, and
concludes with a recitation of Sabin's many honors. Of interest
is the informative discussion of her research in nontechnical language.

1943

968. Yost, Edna. American Women of Science (21), pp. 62-79.
      While there is a tone of how easily opportunities came to
Sabin there is also a great appreciation of how well she used them.
Pays special attention to Sabin's modesty and to the high regard
her students and colleagues had for her.

1945

969. Anon. "Sabin, Florence Rena," Current Biography Yearbook,
      pp. 527-529. Photograph.
      An important biography of Sabin using a substantial number
of excellent quotations from her and about her. The emphasis is
on her relationship with other people and her attitude toward humanity as expressed in her life and work.

1947

970. Maisel, Albert Q. "Dr. Sabin's Second Career," Survey
      Graphic, 36 (November), pp. 138-140. Photograph.
      Tells of her active work for better health laws in Colorado.

1948

971. Sapieha (Peterson), Virgilia; Ruth Neely; and Mary Love
      Collins. "Florence Rena Sabin," in Eminent Women Recipients
      of the National Achievement Award. Menasha, Wisconsin:
      Banta Publishing, ch. 1, pp. 1-12. Photograph.
      Written on the occasion of the presentation of this presti-
gious award, the story is devoted almost entirely to a review of her
studies from the time she entered The Johns Hopkins Medical School.
There is little technical detail and emphasis is on her devotion to
the work and her humane philosophy. There are a few notes about
her interests outside of science.

1953

972. Anon. "Florence R. Sabin, Scientist, 81, Dies," The New
      York Times, 103 (4 October), p. 89. Photograph.
      A long obituary which mentions some of her publications and
honors including being the first woman elected to the National
Academy of Sciences and her teaching at Johns Hopkins. States
that she had worldwide fame for her lymphatic research. Gives
several quotations from her Rockefeller colleagues.

973. Anon. "Obituaries. October 3. Florence Rena Sabin," Wilson
      Library Bulletin, 29 (December), p. 328.
      Cites some of her "firsts" and notes her biography of Frank-
lin P. Mall.

1955

974. Anon. "Sabin, Florence Rena," The National Cyclopaedia
      of American Biography (2), 40, pp. 12-13.

A longer, updated version of the biography published during
her lifetime (967). Lists many of her honors and presents a chronology of her research with little comment.

1959

975. Andriole, Vincent T. "Florence Rena Sabin--Teacher, Scien-
      tist, Citizen," Journal of the History of Medicine, 14 (July),
      pp. 320-350.
      This major study of Sabin's life and career is taken from
Andriole's doctoral thesis at Yale University School of Medicine.
The nicely balanced and readable account is carefully documented.
We are indebted to the author for a great amount of research ef-
fort. Much of Sabin's own writing is also cited.

976. Bluemel, Elinor. Florence Sabin, Colorado Woman of the
      Century. Boulder, Colorado: University of Colorado Press,
      238 pp.
      The biography of the "first woman to receive a full profes-
sorship at Johns Hopkins University [and] the first woman to be
made a member of the Rockefeller Institute for Medical Research."
Florence Sabin was a woman of great courage, dignity, and warmth,
and this work emphasizes each of these attributes. Her humanitarian interests are reflected in her divergent activities as a dedicated scientist and a firm suffragette.

1960

977. McMaster, Philip D., and Michael Heidelberger. "Florence
      Rena Sabin," Biographical Memoirs, National Academy of Sci-
      ences, 34, pp. 271-319. Photograph.
      The very fine writing in surprisingly nontechnical language
describes her scientific contributions in a most pleasant fashion.
The same can be said of the authors' attention to her teaching,
political activities, and social talents. In the standard manner of
these memoirs there is a detailed and exhaustive bibliography
of Sabin's published work and a good chronology of her life.
Necessary reading for any serious study of Sabin and a possible
model for future short biographies of women scientists.

1961

978. Kubie, Lawrence S. "Florence Rena Sabin, 1871-1953," Per-
      spectives in Biology and Medicine, 4 (Spring), pp. 306-315.
      In many ways this article represents the complement to the
National Academy Memoir (977) in that it deals primarily with the
social and personal side of Sabin's life. There are charming and
unforgettable stories of times spent with friends as well as moments

of pain and disappointment. A very human and significant contribution.

1964

979. Corner, George W. A History of the Rockefeller Institute
      (960), pp. 238-242 and index. Photograph.
      Corner refers to Sabin's earlier work at Johns Hopkins Uni-
versity and deals at length with her studies of tuberculosis at the
Rockefeller Institute. Her "painstaking, accurate observations"
are clearly demonstrated. Corner sums up by saying, "her great
talents were more fully displayed to her medical students and--
surprisingly--in public life than in a relatively cloistered environment like that of the Institute laboratories of her day."

1969

*980. Phelan, Mary Kay. Probing the Unknown: The Story of
       Dr. Florence Sabin. New York: Crowell, 176 pp.
       A biography for younger readers.

1970

981. Talbott, John H. "Florence Rena Sabin (1871-1953)," in A
      Biographical History of Medicine. New York: Grune and
      Stratton, pp. 1181-1183. Sketch.
      A short biography showing her place in the development of
modern medicine.

982. Stoddard, Hope. "Florence Sabin," in Famous American
      Women. New York: Thomas Y. Crowell, pp. 360-369.
      Photograph.
      A well-written story which deals with Sabin's activities in
teaching, research, and public service. The human qualities of
this remarkable woman are warmly portrayed. Includes a short
list of books for further reading.

1975

983. Brieger, Gert H. "Sabin, Florence Rena," Dictionary of
      Scientific Biography (29), 12, pp. 48-49.
      Rather short considering the subject, but well written.
Strictly an overview of her scientific work. A limited bibliography.

1977

984. Corner, George W. "Sabin, Florence Rena," Dictionary of
      American Biography (14), supp. 5, pp. 600-601.
          Corner who as the historian of the Rockefeller Institute had
      an advantageous position to view Sabin's career. He writes with
      strength about his fellow scientists and is able to supplement the
      general biography with his critical judgment. His appreciation of
      the relative merits of various studies makes this reference essential.

985. Rossiter, Margaret W. "Florence Sabin: Election to the
      N.A.S.," The American Biology Teacher, 39 (November),
      pp. 484-486, 494. Photograph.
          Quickly traces the early history of women in science and
      gives excellent biographical detail for Sabin. A brief presentation
      of the National Academy of Science and Mme. Curie when she visited
      the United States. Some choice remarks by members about the elec-
      tion of Annie J. Cannon. The Academy is treated very fairly, but
      does not come out looking like a group of gentlemen. A must for
      those who think women have been treated with respect by their
      colleagues.

1978

986. O'Meara, Carol. "Sabin, Florence Rena," Biographical
      Dictionary of American Educators (38), 3, pp. 1135-1137.
          A short sketch with emphasis on the high points of Sabin's
      career. Limited bibliography.

1980

987. Brieger, Gert H. "Sabin, Florence Rena," Notable American
      Women (30), 4, pp. 614-616.
          A much more colorful and interesting sketch than that prob-
      ably forced by editorial demands in item 983. The clarity of the
      exposition is noteworthy. A more personalized picture of Sabin
      the woman emerges.

988. Levin, Beatrice S. Women and Medicine (46), pp. 116-120.
      Photograph.
          Sabin is discussed at some length in connection with the num-
      ber of remarkable women who studied at The Johns Hopkins Medical
      School. Remarks on her professional attitude and personal life-
      style.

989. MARGARET ADALINE REED LEWIS
      9 November 1881--20 July 1970

Lewis graduated from the Women's College of Baltimore, later renamed Goucher College (AB, 1901), and studied at a number of universities in Europe including Zurich, Paris, and Berlin. She worked as an assistant to Thomas H. Morgan at Bryn Mawr College and later at Columbia University. In 1910 she married Warren Harmon Lewis. She lectured in a variety of schools until 1915 when she became a collaborator at the Carnegie Institution of Washington in Baltimore. In 1927 she was promoted to research associate, a position she held until 1946 when she was made a member of the Wistar Institute of Anatomy and Biology of Philadelphia. From 1958 until 1964 she held emeritus status at Wistar.

Her earliest work concerned regeneration in crayfish and the embryology of amphibia along with cytology of living cells and the nature of ultramicroscopic viruses. Soon after their marriage the Lewises developed tissue culture techniques which became widely used. She had been interested in this area of research since her work in Berlin where she may have conducted the first known successful in vitro mammalian tissue culture experiment. In the decade 1910-1920 the Lewises worked to discover the optimum conditions and the range of cells which could be successfully grown. Their interest in microscopic studies led them to develop clear solutions on special slides. The technique became known as the Lewis culture and the medium the Locke-Lewis solution. As early as 1915 they were able to provide a reasonably complete morphological description of a number of living cells. By 1917 they had begun to determine some physiological activities, and at the Carnegie Institute she added important studies of the effects of acidity on these processes. In later years they studied the chemotherapy of dyes in cancer.

As author and coauthor, often with her husband, Lewis presented nearly 150 scientific papers. They received jointly the William Wood Gerhard Gold Medal of the Pathological Society of Philadelphia and an honorary degree from Goucher College in 1938. She was an honorary life member of the Tissue Culture Society and earned a star as one of the most important anatomists in the sixth edition of American Men of Science (1937).

1979

990.   Anon. "Lewis, Margaret Adaline Reed," The National
        Cyclopaedia of American Biography (2), 58, pp. 142-143.
        A nicely written account of Lewis' career which pays special attention to the work she and her husband shared. Discusses the scientific work in reasonably nontechnical language, but with sufficient detail to be understandable. Presents her educational background and gives an extensive list of their honors.

991.   ELIZABETH CAROLINE CROSBY
       25 October 1888--unknown

Crosby was educated at Adrian College (BS, 1910) and the University of Chicago (MS, 1912; PhD, 1915). After five years as principal and school superintendent in Petersburg, Michigan, she joined the department of anatomy at the University of Michigan where she was promoted to full professor in 1936. Her studies of the comparative neurology of vertebrates was recognized by the Achievement Award of the American Association of University Women, the Distinguished Faculty Achievement Award of the University of Michigan and the Cajal Society Citation of the American Association of Anatomists. She earned a star as one of the leading anatomists in the seventh edition of American Men of Science (1943).

1955

992. Anon. "Education. Roses for Anatomy," Newsweek, 46 (11 July), p. 54.
Notes the banquet given to recognize her selection as the Michigan teacher who had contributed the most to medical education. Also mentions her achievement award from the American Association of University Women. Excellent quotations.
We are indebted to Paul Hart of State College at Brockport for finding this article and bringing it to our attention.

1958

993. Anon. "Education. Goodbye, Messrs. Chips," Time, 72 (21 July), p. 64. Photograph.
The topflight neuroanatomist is retiring after having become the first woman full professor at the University of Michigan.

MEDICAL SCIENTISTS: GENETICISTS

(See also 1033, 1435, 1444, 1451)

994. MAUD CAROLINE SLYE
   8 February 1869--17 September 1954
   One of the most important earlier contributors to the study of genetics in cancer, Slye had the nearly impossible disadvantage of having neither a medical nor graduate degree. She began her education at the University of Chicago in 1895, but three years of supporting herself as a secretary resulted in a nervous breakdown. She completed her education at Brown University (AB, 1899) and taught at the Rhode Island State Normal School until 1905.
   In 1908 she was invited to become a graduate assistant in biology at the University of Chicago. Her first studies involving a nervous disorder in mice led to her lifelong interest in the role heredity plays in cancer. After joining the new Sprague Memorial Institute in 1911 Slye's career began to develop, and by 1913 she had completed her first paper for publication. She had carried out breeding experiments on 5,000 mice and found that 298 spontaneously developed cancers.
   These experiments led to her appointment as director of the Cancer Laboratory of the University of Chicago in 1919 and her promotion to associate professor of pathology in 1926. From that beginning until her retirement in 1944 she bred, raised, and studied over 150,000 mice. In the early years she accomplished this without assistance, and for most of her career she refused to take a vacation fearing to leave her priceless "mouse Utopia" to anyone else. Her earliest hypothesis that cancer was the result of a single Mendelian character was modified and still proved to be oversimplified, but the extensive data she obtained under the most carefully controlled conditions firmly established the importance of heredity in cancer susceptibility.
   Slye received numerous honors from such organizations as the American Medical Association (gold medal, 1914), the American Radiological Society (gold medal, 1922), the University of Chicago (Ricketts Prize, 1915), and Brown University (honorary DSc, 1937). (See also 23, 954, 955.)

1933

995. Menaugh, John A. "Rearing Mice to Save Men," Minneapolis Sunday Journal (5 February). Photographs.
   A popular account of her mouse breeding experiments. The

empLasis is on how concerned Slye is for her mice and the care
she takes to be certain of the methodology she employs. Good general description of cancer and her approach to its study and prevention.

996.   Jaffe, Bernard. "Cancer," in Outposts of Science (17),
       ch. 4, pp. 129-160. Photograph. This chapter appeared
       in condensed form in Reader's Digest, 28 (March 1936), pp.
       77-80.
       Begins with a general description of the nature of cancer
and the problems in its study. The detailed presentation of her
work reads like a detective story of the very best type but without
easy solutions. The work being carried on in other laboratories
is also reported and carefully integrated with that of Slye. The
opposition she faced on a variety of fronts is told in a manner which
centers attention on the problems and resolutions rather than on
the melodramatics. In conclusion Jaffe reprints one of the poems
Slye writes for relaxation.

997.   Anon. "Medicine. Mouse Matching," Time, 28 (16 Novem-
       ber), pp. 77-78. Photograph.
       Centers on the debate between Slye and Clarence C. Little
over the importance of heredity in cancer susceptibility.

998.   Anon. "Medicine. If Mice Were Men," Time, 28 (31 August),
       p. 24. Photograph.
       A discussion of Slye's theory of the inheritance of cancer
susceptibility in mice and the implications for treating cancer in
humans.

999.   Anon. "Science. Cancer," News-Week, 9 (9 January), pp.
       38-39.
       A brief review of Slye's long work with mice in seeking the
required data relative to cancer as a heredity problem. Strong
statements by her about the desirability of selection in human reproduction.

1000. Anon. "Science. Researcher: Dr. Slye Lays Cancer Plans
       for Mice and Men," News-Week, 9 (10 April), pp. 26-28.
       Photographs.
       An interesting and overly popularized account of Slye's
claims that cancer could be bred out in a few human generations

if romance didn't get in the way.   Reports that she had modified
her original theory in the light of new evidence.

1001.   Anon.   "Twelve Women from Various Walks of Life Who Set
        a Pace in Science, Education, Law, the Arts," Senior Scho-
        lastic (Teacher Edition), 30 (15 May), p. 11.   Photograph.
        Notes her efforts and success in mouse breeding experiments
concerning cancer.

1938

1002.   Frazier, Corinne Reid.   "Does She Hold the Key to Cancer?"
        Current History, 49 (September), pp. 35-36.
        As the winning essay in a contest held by the Women's Press
Club of New York, it is obviously written to produce the greatest
dramatic effect.   Coincidentally, however, it comes close to captur-
ing the equally dramatic effect of Slye's work and her intense belief in it.

1940

1003.   Jaffe, Bernard.   "Science in a Democracy.   Some Reasons
        Why Science Thrives in an Atmosphere Where the Spirit of
        Free Research Is Unhampered," Senior Scholastic (Teacher
        Edition), 36 (11 March), pp. 17-19, 24.   Photograph.
        A play for a school assembly, the narrator introduces vari-
ous outstanding American scientists who tell their story and suggest that this is the land of opportunity.   Interesting comments
on the subjects of war and opportunities for women in science.

1004.   Anon.   "Slye, Maud," Current Biography Yearbook, pp.
        743-745.   Photograph.
        This article tells the familiar story, but in a very pleasant
manner and with important emphasis on the great amount of dedication and sacrifice Slye's work demanded of her.   The problems
of human breeding, autopsies, and romance are all treated in a dig-
nified fashion.   A useful bibliography.

1954

1005.   Anon.   "Maud Slye, 75, Noted Cancer Expert, Dies," Chicago
        Daily Tribune, 113 (18 September), p. 1.   Photograph.
        Review of her career with discussion of her controversial
theory.   Notes her 38 years of effort and the honors which came
to her.

1006.   Anon.   "Dr. Maud Slye, 75, Pathologist, Dies," The New
        York Times, 104 (18 September), p. 15.

Her devotion to research has involved hundreds of thousands
of mice and shown that cancer can be bred out of the race. Says
that in retirement she has been preparing a statistical compilation
of her work. Cites her books of poetry, Songs and Solaces and
I in the Wind.

1977

*1007. McCoy, Joseph J. The Cancer Lady: Maud Slye and Her
        Heredity Studies. Nashville, Tenn.: T. Nelson.

1980

1008. Parascandola, John. "Slye, Maud Caroline," Notable American
       Women (30), 4, pp. 651-652.
       A balanced treatment. Emphasizes her difficulties in get-
ting the proper authorities to respect her work. Shows her wil-
lingness to modify her theory when new data required it.

1009. MADGE THURLOW MACKLIN
       6 February 1893--14 March 1962
       Throughout her 38 years of pioneering research in the field
of medical genetics, her term for the field she created, Macklin
carried on a one-woman, highly successful campaign to include genetics in the standard medical school curriculum. On the basis
of her work many of her colleagues came to realize the clinical importance of family history. Her controversial views on eugenics
probably contributed to the fact that she was promoted only once,
to the rank of assistant professor, by the University of Western
Ontario. She was not allowed to teach anything except embryology
for first-year students.
       Following her education at Goucher College (AB, 1914) and
The Johns Hopkins Medical School (MD, 1919) and marriage in 1918,
Macklin moved to London, Ontario, with her husband where they
collaborated on some studies in histology. She developed a passion for carefully controlled experiments and data analysis. The
contributions she made in the application of sound statistical techniques to genetics at the very beginning were of great significance.
She demonstrated, with compelling evidence, that both environmental and hereditary factors play a role in such specific cancers as
those of the stomach and the breast. Her human studies comple-
mented the mice experiments of Maud Slye. She was especially interested in physicians making use of these data to be watchful for
early signs of tumors.
       In 1945, after years of one-term appointments, she was noti-
fied that it would not be renewed, and she moved to the Ohio State
University as a National Research Council associate. In spite of

the difficulty of her husband remaining in London, she continued
a productive career until she retired in 1959. She received an honorary degree from Goucher College (LLD, 1938), the Elizabeth Blackwell Medal of the American Medical Women's Association (1957), and
was elected president of the American Society for Human Genetics
in 1959.

1952

1010. Anon. "Ohio State Researcher's Work Is Basis of Article
          on Cancer," Columbus Dispatch (27 March).
          Report on the appearance of an article in the popular maga-
zine Redbook based on Macklin's studies. There are a number of
quotations both from the article and from Macklin stressing the importance of heredity considerations in preventing cancer.

*1011. [Macklin's Cancer Studies], Redbook.

1962

1012. Soltan, Hubert C. "Madge Macklin--Pioneer in Medical Ge-
          netics," The University of Western Ontario Medical Journal,
          38 (October), pp. 6-11.
          The review of her life and education is cursory, and most
of the paper deals with her efforts to introduce genetics into the
medical school curriculum and the application of sound statistical
methods in genetic studies. Both of these concerns are illustrated
with her lifelong work on the prevention of cancer. There are many
quotations from her writings.

1977

1013. Barr, Murray L. A Century of Medicine at Western. A
          Centennial History of the Faculty of Medicine, University
          of Western Ontario. London, Ontario: The University of
          Western Ontario, pp. 359-361. Photograph.
          The entire history of the Medical School at the University
of Western Ontario which includes Macklin's contributions. There
is a brief, but adequate description of her education and research
interests. Noteworthy is the frank admission that "Dr. Madge Macklin did not receive from Western the recognition that her contributions deserved." The whole matter is put in a reasonable context
by pointing out that she was rather outspoken and the times did
not favor husband-wife teams.

1980

1014. Mehler, Barry. "Macklin, Madge Thurlow," Notable

American Women (30), 4, pp. 451-452.
A well-told story which brings together the difficulties and
the successes of a strong-willed person and a two-career family.
The description of her research is not overly technical and her
involvement in controversial causes is presented in a balanced fashion.

1015. MARGARET LEWIS NICKERSON
8 December 1870--unknown
Nickerson was educated at Smith College (AB, 1893) and took a graduate program at Radcliffe College (AM, 1897) as a fellow of the Association of Collegiate Alumnae. Following her medical training at the University of Minnesota (MD, 1904), she taught histology and embryology in the medical department of that university until 1912. Her work in histology earned her a star as a scientific leader in American Men of Science (1906).

1016. Nickerson is cited in American Men of Science, 1906-1921.

1017. MARY ANN ALLARD BOOTH
    8 September 1843--15 September 1922
    A very early expert in the application of the techniques of
photography to the microscopic study of disease-bearing parasites,
Booth was self-educated and conducted her research at home.   In
1907-1908 she came to national prominence by assisting in the successful campaign against the bubonic plague in San Francisco. Her
large collection of slides and photomicrographs of parasites was given
to the National Museum upon her death.
    Booth was a popular lecturer on scientific uses of the micro-
scope and illustrated her talks with stereopticon slides which she
prepared from her collection. She was a member of the American,
New York, and Royal Microscopical Societies. From its beginning
she was the editor of Practical Microscopy. (See also 4.)

1914

1018. Anon. "Booth, Mary Ann Allard," The National Cyclopaedia
    of American Biography (2), 15, p. 107.
    Not a very long article, but still gives a fairly good indica-
tion of Booth's research interests. Her lecturing and editing activities receive special praise. Lists her professional memberships.

1922

1019. Anon. "Mary A. Booth," The New York Times, 71 (16 Sep-
    tember), p. 15.
    Announcement of her death saying she had international
fame, especially for her work on the bubonic plague.

1020. GLADYS ROWENA HENRY DICK
    18 December 1881--21 August 1963
    After obtaining her undergraduate education at the Univer-
sity of Nebraska (BS, 1900) it took an additional three years before Dick was able to persuade her mother to permit a medical education. At The Johns Hopkins University following her graduation
(MD, 1907), and in Berlin in 1910, Dick was introduced to her
life's work in biomedical research.
    At the University of Chicago she worked with her future
husband and collaborator George F. Dick. They were married in

1914 and after a brief time in private practice she joined her husband at the McCormick Memorial Institute for Infectious Diseases. Their close collaboration resulted in important new knowledge, techniques, and materials in efforts to bring scarlet fever under control. In 1923 they showed convincingly that the true cause of the disease is the hemolytic streptococci. In a surprisingly short time they had isolated the toxin produced and developed methods of treatment, diagnosis, and prevention of the disease. In 1925 they were considered for the Nobel Prize in medicine, but none was given.

The Dicks were criticized strongly for taking patents on the toxin and its methods of manufacture. They claimed that they received no financial benefit from them and that their only wish was to insure the quality of the product. Gladys Dick brought a suit against the Lederle Laboratories for improper manufacturing procedures. With the introduction of antibiotics during World War II the issue was closed, but there can be little doubt of the significance of their work in the preceding 20 years. They received the Cameron Prize of the University of Edinburgh and the Mickel Prize from the University of Toronto (1933). She received honorary degrees from the Universities of Nebraska, Northwestern, and Cincinnati, all in the late 1920's, but there is some confusion as to the exact dates and which were awarded jointly.

1927

1021.   Anon. "Scarlet Fever Conquerors," Science News Letter,
        12 (22 October), p. 259. Photograph.
        The article states that five years ago very little was known
about scarlet fever and now it is both understood and treatable.
Gives a brief summary of their work and the application of the Dick
test.

1963

1022.   Anon. "Gladys Dick, Scarlet Fever Expert, Dies," Chicago
        Tribune, 116 (23 August), p. 1A, 2.
        Says that while she lived in California for the past few
years she did most of her research on the Dick vaccine in Chicago
during the 1920's. At that time she was affiliated with the McCormick Institute for Infectious Diseases.

1023.   Anon. "Deaths. Dick, Gladys Rowena Henry," The Journal of the American Medical Association, 186 (28 December),
        p. 1186.
        An interesting paragraph which emphasizes her work with
her husband and their joint prizes.

1969

1024. Anon. "Dick, Gladys Rowena Henry," The National Cyclopaedia
       of American Biography (2), 51, p. 107.
       Gives a brief review of her education and research along
with a description of the work she did with her husband. There
is a list of honors the Dicks received.

1980

1025. Rubin, Lewis P. "Dick, Gladys Rowena Henry," Notable
       American Women (30), 4, pp. 191-192.
       After a good presentation of Dick's early life and education
Rubin discusses the development of the Dick test and the criticism
of their taking patents on it. His discussion is objective and fair.
His treatment of their family life is excellent.

1026. ELIZABETH LEE HAZEN
       24 August 1885--24 June 1975
       Overcoming the disadvantages of birth on a Mississippi farm
and the death of her parents before she was four, Hazen established herself as an important figure in the diagnosis and treatment of viral and bacterial infections. She began her education
at the Mississippi Industrial Institute and College which became the
Mississippi University for Women (BS, 1910). It was to be a long
path to a graduate education at Columbia University (MS, 1917;
PhD, 1927), but one which produced rich rewards for humanity.
       Hazen began her independent studies at the Columbia Uni-
versity Mycology Laboratory where she was excited by the recent
discovery of penicillin. Her search for an antifungal antibiotic was
soon to bring her into a lifelong collaboration with the chemist Rachel
Brown of the New York State Central Laboratory. In 1948 they
discovered fungicidin, which is better known as nystatin (named
for the New York State Department of Health). The range of uses
for this antibiotic is extraordinary and includes combating mold in
human and animal food as well as yeast infections of the vagina,
intestine, skin, and mucous membranes. It was used to restore
murals and manuscripts in Florence following the 1966 flood.
       The very large amounts of money generated by this dis-
covery played a key role in the support of research in mycology
in the nearly 30 years between the discovery and termination of
the Brown-Hazen Fund in 1978. Under the direction of the Research Corporation half of the more than 13 million dollars went
to a fund for the support of research in their field of interest and
the other half for the support of other grant programs. Hazen took
an active part in the direction of the grant programs. Both she
and Brown encouraged some use of the monies for the support of
educational opportunities for women.

Hazen's life was changed very little by the discovery. She was devoted to her work and very reluctant to make public appearances. The Squibb Award in Chemotherapy was awarded jointly to Hazen and Brown in 1955 and they were the first women to receive the Chemical Pioneer Award of the American Institute of Chemists in 1975.

1975

1027. Anon. "Elizabeth Lee Hazen--1886-1975" and "Brown and Hazen Receive A.I.C. Award," Research Corporation Quarterly Bulletin (Summer), p. 4. Photograph.
A summary of Hazen's career alongside a short article about the presentation of the Chemical Pioneer Award from the American Institute of Chemists. Emphasis is on the discovery of nystatin, the important antifungal drug.

1028. Anon. "In Memoriam. Dr. Elizabeth Lee Hazen," The Stethoscope (September), p. 6. Photograph.
The announcement of a special meeting at the Columbia-Presbyterian Medical Center in honor of Hazen. Most of the note concerns the arrangements and list of speakers.

1029. Anon. "Dr. Elizabeth L. Hazen," Mississippi University for Women Alumnae News (Fall), p. 43. Photograph.
A few highlights of her career.

1976

1030. Bacon, W. Stevenson. "Elizabeth Lee Hazen, 1885-1975," Mycologia, 68 (September-October), pp. 961-969.
Written by a member of the Staff of the Research Corporation which directed the use of the monies resulting from the sale of nystatin for the support of research, this biography shows the woman behind those vitual funds. The entire career is traced and each of Hazen's research successes recounted. The numerous honors are cited, but it is her intense desire to learn and to help others to learn that is most impressive.

1980

1031. Rubin, Lewis P. "Hazen, Elizabeth Lee," Notable American Women (30), 4, pp. 326-328.
Careful research coupled with a smoothly written article. The drama of the discovery of nystatin is nicely contrasted with the use of the royalties for the support of new research. Note the often repeated errors in Hazen's date and place of birth.

1981

1032. Baldwin, Richard S. The Fungus Fighters. Two Women
       Scientists and Their Discovery. Ithaca, New York: Cor-
       nell University Press, 212 pp. Photographs.
       Describes well the lives and collaboration of the microbiolo-
gist and the chemist. Since Baldwin was associated with Research
Corporation there is a great deal about the Hazen-Brown Fund and
the research activities it supported. An interesting view of two
fine people.

1033. HATTIE ELIZABETH ALEXANDER
       5 April 1901--24 June 1968
       Unlike many successful women scientists, Alexander did not
show great drive and desire for success as an undergraduate at
Goucher College (AB, 1923). It was after three years in the Public Health Services of the United States and Maryland that she established an outstanding record in the Johns Hopkins School of Medicine (MD, 1930). During her internship at the Harriet Lane Home
in Baltimore she became interested in the disease influenzal meningitis which became her principal career research area. She then
accepted an additional intern year at Babies Hospital of the Columbia-
Presbyterian Medical Center followed by appointment in the department of pediatrics. She became full professor in 1958 and professor emerita from 1966 until her death.
       Under her directorship the microbiological laboratory became
widely acknowledged as an excellent example to other services. In
addition to her research and administrative duties Alexander was
an active teacher, and while she disliked the usual lecture mode
of instruction, she was known for the high quality of her bedside
teaching. Her students were forced to back up their judgments
with convincing evidence.
       At the time Alexander began her research the usual treat-
ment of influenzal meningitis was essentially useless. By skillfully
blending the discoveries in theoretical biology with medical practice she, along with the immunochemist Michael Heidelberger, was
able to develop a rabbit serum capable of a complete cure of infants ill with this previously fatal disease. She was among the
first to recognize that genetic mutation lay behind the often observed resistance of bacteria to antibiotics. Building on reports
from the Rockefeller Institute showing that DNA was able to change
genetic characteristics, she and Grace Leidy showed similar changes
with DNA obtained from their Hemophilus influenzae. These experiments played an important role in overcoming the skepticism which
greeted the first reports of this exciting new area of biological research.
       Alexander received many awards and honors, including the
E. Mead Johnson Award for Research in Pediatrics (1942), the Stevens Triennial Prize for the best essay on a medical subject (1954),

and the Oscar B. Hunter Memorial Award of the American Thera-
peutic Society (1961). She was the first woman to be elected president of the American Pediatric Society (1964).

1962

1034. Turner, Lenore. "From C Student to Winning Scientist,"
       Goucher Alumnae Quarterly (Winter), pp. 18-20. Photo-
       graph.
       The theme is her outstanding success in spite of an early
lack of self-discipline. With some slight exaggeration the article
makes clear the long hours of difficult work and the years of dedication. Good reading and technically sound.

1964

1035. Anon. "Alexander, Hattie Elizabeth," The National Cyclopaedia
       of American Biography (2), J, pp. 106-107. Photograph.
       A comprehensive biographical sketch. There is so much
information that it does not read well, but it is a rich source of
facts on positions, publications, and honors.

1968

1036. Anon. "Dr. Hattie Alexander, 67, Dies; Columbia Research
       Pediatrician," The New York Times, 117 (25 June), p. 41.
       Photograph.
       Alexander won international recognition for her research
leading to the first effective antiserum for meningitis. She became one of the few women to head a major medical group when
she was elected president of the American Pediatric Society in 1964.

1037. Singewald, Charlotte Stout. "Hattie E. Alexander. Died
       June 24, 1968," Goucher Alumnae Quarterly (Fall, pp. 35-
       36. Photograph.
       An obituary which carries personal insights from student
days. A lovely tribute from the mother of a child her work had
saved.

1038. McIntosh, Rustin. "Hattie Alexander," Pediatrics, 42 (Sep-
       tember), p. 544.
       A letter to the editor by a colleague describing Alexander's
scientific objectivity and her courage. In both cases several specific examples are cited. A valuable document.

1980

1039. Dubos, René. "Alexander, Hattie Elizabeth," Notable

American Women (30), 4, pp. 10-11.
A well-balanced sketch with proper attention given to the professional and personal aspects of Alexander's life. The discussion of her research and accomplishments is particularly appealing. A good bibliography.

(See also 993)

1040. LYDIA MARIA ADAMS DE WITT
      1 February 1859--10 March 1928
      De Witt was 40 years old before her career in medical re-
search began. For most of her adult years preceding graduation
from the University of Michigan (MD, 1898; BS, 1899), she had
taught in a number of Michigan schools. While obtaining her medical education she had demonstrated skill in research, and for the
next 11 years she worked at Michigan in the areas of anatomy, histology, and pathology. She studied in Berlin in 1906.
      In 1912 she was invited to join the Sprague Memorial Institute
at the University of Chicago. Here De Witt made a long series of
studies in which she applied the method used so successfully by
Paul Ehrlich in the treatment of syphilis. De Witt examined the
effects of dyes linked to such metals as copper, gold, and mer-
cury on tuberculosis. In the end all of these efforts failed to produce the cure sought, but there were positive outcomes. She demonstrated with her meticulous experiments that the positive results
reported by other laboratories could not be reproduced. Of even
greater significance were the papers she wrote over the years since
they became the model upon which later workers achieved success
using other chemical compounds.
      De Witt's professional stature was recognized by the respect
of her colleagues at the Sprague Institute, her appointment as an
associate professor of pathology at the University of Chicago (1918),
and her election as president of the Chicago Pathological Society
(1924-1925). She received an honorary degree from the University of Michigan in 1914.

1927

1041. Anon. "De Witt, Lydia M. Adams," The National Cyclopaedia
      of American Biography (2), B, pp. 457-458. Photograph.
      Biographical facts and an impressive list of positions held
and publications. A good source.

1928

1042. Anon. "Deaths. Lydia M. De Witt," The Journal of the
      American Medical Association, 90 (24 March), p. 996.

A paragraph which describes her education and lists her professional positions.

1971

1043. Long, Esmond R. "De Witt, Lydia Maria Adams," Notable American Women (30), 1, pp. 468-469.
A well-written description of her younger life, her education, and professional career. The evaluation of the significance of De Witt's contributions is most welcome.

1044. ALICE HAMILTON
27 February 1869--22 September 1970
She never thought of herself as a social reformer, and yet Hamilton had a large effect on the way most American workers are treated by their employers. After earning an MD at the University of Michigan in 1893 (she took only a few science courses and no undergraduate degree) and studying bacteriology and pathology in Ann Arbor, Baltimore, Leipzig, and Munich, she accepted a teaching position at Northwestern University. In Chicago she joined Jane Addams at Hull House where she was exposed to the poverty of the city and to the conditions in which people really live and work. After ten years of trying to bring together her emotional and scientific needs she happened to read some discussions of the medical problems in British industry. She read extensively, and in 1908 she was appointed to the Illinois Commission on Occupational Diseases, and in 1910 she was named supervisor of the first statewide survey of industrial poisons. This position gave her the opportunity to combine her laboratory and field work and to develop practical applications.
The results of her studies, especially of the lead industries, and the state law which they brought about, are landmarks in industrial toxicology and the prevention of needlessly dangerous industrial conditions. In 1919 she was invited to become head of Harvard's Department of Industrial Medicine where she remained until her retirement in 1935. At Harvard, where she insisted on a half-time appointment so she could continue her field work, she greatly expanded the breadth of studies in dangerous industrial materials and practices. Her basic method remained the same, i.e., to learn the industry in every detail, preferably from firsthand experience, and to attempt to induce the management to institute changes for their own benefit as well as for their workers'. After retirement Hamilton conducted still another important study of the new rayon industry and wrote her autobiography, Exploring the Dangerous Trades. (See also 23, 33, 42, 48, 955, 956, 957, 958.)

1930

1045. Evans, Elizabeth Glendower. "People I Have Known. Alice
       Hamilton, MD, Pioneer in a New Kind of Human Service,"
       The Progressive, 2 (29 November and 20 December), p. 3.
           A two part article which gives a great deal of insight to
the character of Hamilton and the nature of the service she is making available in the interest of better working conditions. Comments
on her reasons for entering medicine and calls her one of the nation's most notable women.

1943

1046. Yost, Edna. American Women of Science (21), pp. 44-61.
           Hamilton is presented as a woman of great courage as well
as high scientific standards. An especially good treatment of her
efforts to obtain support for improvements from the industrialists
rather than simply to press for laws.

1047. Hamilton, Alice. Exploring the Dangerous Trades. The
       Autobiography of Alice Hamilton, M.D. Boston: Little,
       Brown, 433 pp. Charcoal sketches.
           Upon reading this book, one finds it easy to understand
how Hamilton was able to obtain cooperation from so many people
and accomplish so much in one lifetime. The scenes are not attractive, but the person and the work are. All the way from the
apt title to the delicate use of language this is a book that will make
anyone reexamine the question of social responsibility.

1946

1048. Anon. "Hamilton, Alice," The National Cyclopaedia of
       American Biography (2), G, pp. 107-108. Photograph.
           Traces her educational background and gives a complete
description of her research. Cites many of Hamilton's publications
and relates them to the growth of an awareness of the dangers of
industrial hazards. Mentions some of her honors.

1049. Anon. "Hamilton, Alice," Current Biography Yearbook, pp.
       234-236. Photograph.
           An important article in that it explores both the scientist
and the social reformer. After a brief introduction noting her early
life and her education, Hamilton's research method and results are
discussed. This scientific material is followed by a careful outline
of her effective efforts to promote desirable change in the working
conditions in the industries she studied. A partial list of her significant publications is given with the year they appeared.

*1050. Ellis, Sally. Boston Post (2 September).
        See item 1051.

1051.   Anon. "Alice Hamilton, MD," Industrial Medicine, 15 (No-
        vember), pp. 664, 666.
        Includes a quotation taken from the Boston newspaper arti-
cle cited above and reviews Hamilton's activities in industry.

1947

1052.   Woolf, S. J. "Triumphs of a Pioneer Doctor," The New York
        Times Magazine, 97 (9 November), pp. 20, 70-71. Drawing
        by the author.
        This feature article appeared at the time Hamilton received
the Lasker Award. The interview covered every topic from her
ideas about polution to her tastes in fashion.

1053.   Anon. [Lasker Awards for 1947], The American Journal
        of Public Health, 37 (December), pp. 1612-1616. Photo-
        graph.
        Hamilton is cited "for an inspiring life of public service."
The awards are designed to recognize those "whose efforts have
contributed to, or will in time result in, the vastly improved health
status of the peoples of the earth."

1948

1054.   Sapieha (Peterson), Virgilia; Ruth Neely; and Mary Love
        Collins. Eminent Women Recipients of the National Achieve-
        ment Award. Menasha, Wisconsin: George Banta Publishing,
        ch. 5, pp. 57-72. Photograph.
        Most of the ordinary biographical material is given only
passing attention in this tribute to Hamilton's accomplishments. Relates clearly the terrible conditions she discovered and the ingeni-
ous methods she employed. Stresses her deep conviction of the
need to take an active part in seeing that improvements were made.
This forceful article portrays a remarkable woman.

1956

1055.   Anon. "Medicine. Woman of the Year," Time, 68 (19 No-
        vember), p. 91. Photograph.
        An interesting comparison in the fact that Upton Sinclair
was working on The Jungle only five miles from where Hamilton
was beginning her move toward social progress. Mentions several
of her celebrated cases. Written on the occasion of being named
woman of the year in medicine by her colleagues in the American
Medical Women's Association.

1957

1056.   Anon.   "Woman of the Year--Alice Hamilton," Industrial Medicine and Surgery, 26 (February), p. 72.   Photograph.
Hamilton is selected as New England's Woman of the Year.
This article notes that coincidentally she and Upton Sinclair were
working on social problems at the same time and in nearly the same
place.

1959

1057.   Anon.   [Alice Hamilton], Industrial Medicine and Surgery,
28 (May), pp. 224-225.
A review of her pioneering efforts in recognition of her
90th birthday.

1058.   Anon.   "Harvard Honors Dr. Alice Hamilton," The Social
Service Review, 33 (June), p. 170.
As a 90th birthday present Hamilton's friends and former
students established a scholarship and lecture fund in her honor
at the Harvard School of Public Health.   Says that no social worker
should fail to read Exploring the Dangerous Trades.   There is a
long quotation from one of her colleagues at the time of her retirement.

1961

1059.   Johnstone, Rutherford T.   "Editorials.   Climate for Exploration," Archives of Environmental Health, 3 (November), pp.
559-561.   Photograph.
A touching tribute to the person who single-handedly created so much awareness of industrial problems and worked so hard
towards their solution.

1060.   Morris, Sarah I.   "A Tribute to Dr. Alice Hamilton," Archives of Environmental Health, 3 (November), 562.   Photograph.
Significant note written by one of Hamilton's teachers.

1962

1061.   Anon.   "A Hall of Fame of Occupational Disease Investiga-
tors," Industrial Medicine and Surgery, 31 (March), pp.
130-131.   Photograph.
Notes that Hamilton is the first to be selected for this honor.
The bulk of the article consists of a translation of the biographical
sketch by Franz Koelsch which appeared in German in the Handbüch
der gesamten Arbeitsmedizin.

1965

1062. Hamilton, Alice. "Edith and Alice Hamilton. Students in Ger-
      many," The Atlantic, 215 (March), pp. 129-132.
      The serious but funny trials of two brilliant young women
trying to study in Germany. Lots here to enjoy and still more to
think about seriously. Hamilton's final visit is interesting in that
she believes she sees progress made for women in the person of
her old friend Tilly Edinger.

1969

1063. Anon. "People," Time, 93 (7 March), p. 40. Photograph.
      Everyone talks about the "good old days" except Dr. Hamil-
ton. On her 100th birthday she says the country is really much
better for most people now than it was when she started studying
industrial medicine.

1970

1064. Anon. "Hamilton, Alice," Current Biography Yearbook, p.
      463.
      A supplement to the 1946 article cited in 1049.

1065. Anon. "Alice Hamilton, 101, Physician, Teacher," The New
      York Times, 120 (23 September), p. 50.
      Calls her a pioneer in occupational medicine and says she
wrote many books. She worked in factories, mines, and munitions
plants to study firsthand the causes of the workers' problems.
Notes that she was the first woman to hold faculty rank at Harvard.

1972

1066. Hardy, Harriet L., editor. "Alice Hamilton, M.D.," Jour-
      nal of Occupational Medicine, 14 (February), pp. 97-114.
      Photographs.
      A special issue dedicated to Hamilton and containing all man-
ner of articles in her honor. Each of the entries contributes to
posterity's understanding of her. A "posthumanous [sic] salutation on the 102nd anniversary of the birth of Dr. Alice Hamilton."
      Hamilton, Alice. "What Price Safety," pp. 98-100.
      McCord, Carey P. "Alice Hamilton," p. 101.
      Mayers, May R. "Alice Hamilton," pp. 102-104.
      Johnstone, Rutherford T. "One of America's Great Physi-
cians," p. 105.
      Felton, Jean Spencer. "Alice Hamilton, M.D.--A Century
of Devotion to Humanity," pp. 106-110.
      Reznikoff, Paul. "The Grandmother of Industrial Medicine,"
p. 111.

Goldwater, Leonard J. "Alices and Hatters," pp. 112-113.
Drinker, Philip. "Alice Hamilton," p. 114.

1974

1067. Slaight, Wilma Ruth. Alice Hamilton. First Lady of Indus-
     trial Medicine. Dissertation, Case Western Reserve Univer-
     sity, 229 pp.
     A carefully researched and documented biography whose
central purpose is "to indicate that her thoughts and actions outside of her chosen profession were as important in gaining an accurate picture of Alice Hamilton as was her work in the field of
industrial medicine." In spite of the several difficulties which
Slaight describes, the task is well performed and a much clearer
picture emerges.

1980

1068. Sicherman, Barbara. "Hamilton, Alice," Notable American
     Women (30), 4, 303-306.
     A lengthy biography for this series, it examines Hamilton's
long and exciting career. Treats social aspects along with the
medical problems in a well-developed expository style. Particularly important is the attention given to Hamilton's political ideas. Her
evaluation of Russia and Germany and her views on pacificism make
interesting reading.

1982

1069. Levy, Ilise. "Alice Hamilton," American Women Writers (48),
     2, pp. 226-227.
     Presents the essentials of Hamilton's career and makes clear
the continuing importance of her work and writings. An important
bibliography.

1070. DOROTHY REED MENDENHALL
     22 September 1874--31 July 1964
     After receiving her earliest education at home, Mendenhall
entered Smith College (BL, 1895) where a biology course helped
her decide on a career in medicine. She took some courses in chemistry and physics at the Massachusetts Institute of Technology before beginning her medical education at The Johns Hopkins Medical
School (MD, 1900). Mendenhall spent two more years at Hopkins
as an intern and fellow in pathology. During that brief period she
earned an international reputation for her recognition of the Reed
cell as the distinctive characteristic of Hodgkin's disease. She
refused to be reappointed at Hopkins because she saw little oppor-

tunity for women to advance there. In New York she became the
first resident physician at the Babies Hospital, and in 1906 moved
to Madison, Wisconsin, where her husband was professor of physics. The next eight years were spent in the care of her family.

In 1914 she returned to professional life but in a new career
field. As a field lecturer for the department of home economics
of the University of Wisconsin, she began to study several questions
in the area of child welfare. Among these concerns were infant
mortality, nutrition, and public health. Her extraordinary ability
in organizing in a useful fashion the work of different government
agencies proved to be most beneficial. Her extensive studies of
the height and weight of young children and the work of the mid-
wife in Denmark made an important impact on childbirth and growth;
for example, in 1937 Madison was recognized as having the lowest
infant mortality of any American city.

Mendenhall's name is honored, along with her classmate and
fellow medical student Florence Sabin, in Sabin-Reed Hall at Smith
College.

1964

1071. Anon. "Dr. Dorothy Mendenhall, Famed Pediatrician, Dies,"
       Capital Times (Madison, Wisconsin) (31 July), pp. 1, 8.
       Photograph.
       An obituary which gives some facts about her career, es-
pecially as they relate to Madison.

1072. Anon. "Obituaries. Dr. Dorothy R. Mendenhall, 89, Noted
       Pediatrician, Dies," Wisconsin State Journal (1 August), p.
       6. Photograph.
       An obituary which cites her as the first fellow at Johns Hop-
kins. Gives special attention to her sons who are well known educators.

1971

1073. Wilson, Edmund. "Dorothy Mendenhall," in Upstate. Rec-
       ords and Recollections of Northern New York. New York:
       Farrar, Straus and Giroux, ch. VI, pp. 59-71. Drawing.
       Wilson, Reed's cousin, writes of her life and of the people
she knew. As a celebrated author, his treatment of her years at
the Hopkins Medical School and of her relationship with her husband is especially sensitive and revealing.

1974

1074. Corea, Gena. "Lost Women. Dorothy Reed Mendenhall:
       'Childbirth Is Not a Disease,'" Ms (April), pp. 98-104.
       Photographs.

Gives details of Mendenhall's career with some emphasis on the death of her daughter and her own injuries during the badly handled birth. However, the article is not sensationalized and deals fairly with her career, family, and accomplishments.

1976

1075. Bergman, Jean. "Dorothy Reed Mendenhall (1875-1964),"
Famous Wisconsin Women, 6, pp. 48-53. Photographs.
Deals mostly with her education and the difficulty of the birth of her daughter. A sound article.

1980

1076. Robinton, Elizabeth D. "Mendenhall, Dorothy Reed,"
Notable American Women (30), 4, pp. 468-470.
A well-balanced article which gives attention to Mendenhall's early work on Hodgkin's disease as well as her later and more publicized work with childbirth. There is also mention of her deep interest in proper nutrition among children.

1077. ELISE STRANG L'ESPERANCE
January 1878?--21 January 1959
Surprisingly little is known of L'Esperance's early life in view of the public nature and wide recognition of the significance of her work. She was educated at the Woman's Medical College of the New York Infirmary for Women and Children (MD, 1900). After a year of internship at New York Babies Hospital and seven years of private practice in Detroit and New York she decided to turn to research and to fight for the improvement, and in some instances the creation, of proper clinical resources.

At the Cornell University Medical College she worked on the pathology of malignant tumors from 1910 until 1932. Her publications show useful contributions to the knowledge of several tumors and Hodgkin's disease. L'Esperance began her academic association with Cornell as an instructor in 1912, and she became the first woman to hold the rank of assistant professor at the Medical College when she was promoted in 1920. After an absence of a decade she returned to Cornell in 1942 and was promoted to full professor in 1950.

While L'Esperance did good work in these basic research areas, her efforts to promote the early detection and treatment of cancer are most lasting. She and her sister, May Strang, founded the Kate Depew Strang Tumor Clinic at the New York Infirmary in 1933. The clinic offered complete physical examinations to apparently healthy women and provided referral service for any sign of cancer. L'Esperance saw that the clinic was staffed entirely by women physicians and that an extensive campaign of public

education was conducted. In time other clinics were opened and
the service expanded to men and children. Other groups in other
cities built upon this model, and the value of early detection became more widely accepted both by the public and the medical profession. Several important new techniques were developed at the
Strang clinics, for example, the "Pap" smear for the diagnosis of
cervical cancer.

L'Esperance was especially concerned that opportunity for
women in medicine be maintained and expanded. She was president
of the Women's Medical Society of New York State (1935-1936) and
of the American Medical Women's Association (1948-1949). She served
as editor of the Medical Woman's Journal from 1936 to 1941 and as
the first editor of the Journal of the American Medical Women's Association from 1946 to 1948. Of the many awards and honors she
received perhaps the most prestigious was the Albert Lasker Award
of the American Public Health Association in 1951. (See also 956,
957.)

1943

*1078. Medical Woman's Journal, 50 (14 January).

1947

*1079. New York World Telegram (11 January), p. 8.

*1080. Country Life, 1 (May), p. 41.

1948

1081. Crawford, Mary M. "Medical Women in the News. Elise S.
        L'Esperance, MD," Journal of the American Medical Women's
        Association, 3 (July), pp. 310-311.
        Described as a natural leader on the occasion of her elec-
tion as president of the American Medical Women's Association. Article notes her energy and the intellectual vigor of her approach
to problems.

1949

*1082. Medical Woman's Journal, 56 (23 March).

1950

1083. Anon. "Medicine. Prevention Is Her Aim," Time, 55 (3
        April), pp. 78-79. Photograph.

Written on the occasion of her promotion (at about 70) to
full professor. Gives extensive biographical detail as well as treating the main theme of her life's work in early cancer detection and
treatment.

1084.   Anon. "L'Esperance, Elise (Depew Strang)," Current
         Biography Yearbook, pp. 340-341. Photograph.
         Reports on L'Esperance's career in good detail and uses a
number of quotations from other writings about her. Also cites
some of her own publications and lists her honors.

1952

1085.   Gross, Miriam Zeller. "Men of Medicine. 'For Significant
         Contributions to Medicine,'" Postgraduate Medicine (August),
         pp. 187-190.
         The rather strange title of this article about L'Esperance
is something of an honor. Actually, the article is a fine presentation of her efforts to establish clinics for the early detection of
cancer and the wonderfully rapid growth they enjoyed. Gives some
biographical details and a few personal glimpses.

1958

1086.   Day, Emerson. "Elise Strang L'Esperance," Necrology of
         the Faculty of Cornell University, (1958-1959), pp. 16-18.
         A memorial containing personal and professional information.
Points out that much of her work was educational and that one
measure of her success is the lessened fear of cancer found in the
public mind.

1959

1087.   Anon. "Dr. L'Esperance, Specialist, Dead," The New York
         Times, 108 (22 January), p. 31.
         The founder of several cancer clinics and the breeder of
race horses. At first she was a pediatrician, but then became interested in the early detection of cancer. Lists her honors and
other professional activities.

1088.   Reid, Ada Chree. "Elise Strang L'Esperance, MD," Journal
         of the American Medical Women's Association, 14 (May), pp.
         432-433. Photograph.
         Following a review of her education and medical work, the
author presents details on the relationship between L'Esperance
and James Ewing of the Department of Pathology at the Cornell University Medical Center. She was the first woman to attain profes-
sorial status at that institution.

1980

1089. Dwork, Deborah. "L'Esperance, Elise Strang," Notable
       American Women (30), 4, pp. 417-419.
       Describes her career with emphasis on the clinics and the
ever increasing demands placed upon them and L'Esperance. Mentions some of her activities in promoting equality for women in medicine. Data on her education, honors received, and a fine bibliography are all here.

1090. LOUISE PEARCE
       5 March 1885--10 August 1959
       Pearce was educated at Stanford University (AB, 1907),
Boston University School of Medicine, and The Johns Hopkins University School of Medicine (MD, 1912). Following her year of internship at Johns Hopkins she went to the Rockefeller Institute
for Medical Research where she remained until her retirement in
1951.
       Just before she began her work at Rockefeller Paul Ehrlich
had shown that an organic compound containing arsenic was effective in treating syphilis. The director of the laboratory, Simon
Flexner, assigned Pearce, Wade H. Brown, W. A. Jacobs, and Michael Heidelberger to combine their skills in chemistry and pathology in an effort to find a similar drug useful in the treatment of
sleeping sickness. In 1919 a promising compound had been found
and Pearce went to the Belgian Congo to test it in a carefully
planned treatment of actual cases. Within days she had very exciting results, and within weeks the disease not only seemed to
be completely gone, but general health restored. The years following this initial success proved also to be ones of great accomplishment. Pearce and Wade studied syphilis in rabbits, which
closely resembled the human variety, and the results proved of
genuine benefit. During the progress of these studies they found
a tumor which was capable of being grown, and the Brown-Pearce
tumor was studied by cancer laboratories worldwide. Their breeding program and studies led them to isolate a virus similar to human smallpox when an epidemic of rabbit pox nearly destroyed their
carefully developed colony.
       In addition to her research and writing for scientific jour-
nals Pearce took an active interest in the advancement of women
in science. She was a director of the American Association of University Women and an honorary member of the board of the Journal
of the American Medical Women's Association. She was twice decorated by the Belgian government for her work on sleeping sickness.

1913

1091. Anon. "Woman Aid to Flexner," The New York Times, 62
       (11 August), p. 6.

When Pearce was appointed as assistant to the brilliant Simon Flexner of the Rockefeller Institute it caused quite a stir. She is quoted as saying, "I just think it's ripping."

1948

1092. Anon. "Louise Pearce, MD. Medical Woman of the Month," Journal of the American Medical Women's Association, 3 (December), p. 523. Photograph.
A good review of her accomplishments.

1959

1093. Anon. "Dr. Louise Pearce, Physician, 74, Dies," The New York Times, 108 (11 August), p. 27. Photograph.
An obituary which develops her career in some detail. Cites her work on sleeping sickness as an associate member of the Rockefeller Institute. Pearce was a visiting professor at the Peiping University in China.

1094. Fulton, J. D., "Obituaries. Dr. Louise Pearce," Nature, 184 (22 August), pp. 588-589.
A standard obituary citing the accomplishments and honors, but presenting nothing new.

1960

1095. Baumann, Frieda. "Memorial to Louise Pearce, M.D. (1885-1959)," Journal of the American Medical Women's Association, 15 (August), p. 793. Photograph.
Biographical facts with some hints about Pearce's social life. Interesting for its suggestion that she had broad reading interests.

1961

1096. Fay, Marion. "Louise Pearce, 5th March 1885--9th August 1959," Journal of Pathology and Bacteriology, 82 (October), pp. 541-551. Photograph.
Highlights of Pearce's career is followed by an apparently exhaustive bibliography of her publications.

1967

1097. Benison, Saul. Tom Rivers. Reflections on a Life in Medicine and Science. Cambridge, Massachusetts: Massachusetts Institute of Technology Press, pp. 82-85.
This Oral History Memoir allows Rivers, who knows he is

nearing the end of his life, to reminisce about his years at the Rockefeller Institute and be candid about his colleagues. He praises
Pearce and her work.

1980

1098. Corner, George W. "Pearce, Louise," Notable American
       Women (30), 4, pp. 531-532.
       Corner, the official historian of the Rockefeller Institute
and himself a scientist, is in a particularly good position to present and evaluate Pearce's work. He does it well, without being
over technical nor neglecting the little personal material available.

1099. DOROTHY HANSINE ANDERSEN
       15 May 1901--3 March 1963
       Andersen was educated at Mount Holyoke College (AB, 1922)
and Johns Hopkins Medical School (MD, 1926). Even before she
finished her degree, two papers, completed under the direction
of Florence Sabin, had been accepted for publication. Refused a
residency at Strong Memorial Hospital following her internship at
the University of Rochester, she accepted an appointment in pathology at the College of Physicians and Surgeons of Columbia University. In 1935 her research on reproduction and the endocrine
glands earned her a research degree from Columbia (DMedSc), and
she moved to Babies Hospital at the Columbia-Presbyterian Medical
Center where she worked until her death. Andersen began a lifelong study of infant heart defects which contributed to several later
important medical advances. In her very first year she made an
observation which, following careful analysis of the literature, clearly demonstrated the previously unrecognized disease she named cystic fibrosis. Her publication of these results won the E. Mead Johnson Award in 1938.
       While her career developed in the usual fashion to outward
appearances--assistant attending pediatrician (1945), chief of pathology (1952), and full professor (1958)--Andersen was always a
controversial person in the hospital. Much of the criticism stems
from her recognition of the true importance of her discovery and
her insistence on following it beyond pathology and developing
methods for its diagnosis and treatment. She acquired the chemical and clinical skills on her own and in the 1940's presented important results on the use of chemotherapy in the treatment of
cystic fibrosis. Later she began to publish on the more general
questions of the genetics of this hereditary disease.
       When the new field of open-heart surgery emerged during
World War II, her knowledge and large collection of cardiac defects
came to be of great importance. Cardiologists at Babies Hospital
and others were trained by the program she developed in the anatomy and embryology of the heart. She was so highly regarded

at Babies that no surgeon was allowed to operate before completing
her course. Later in her life she published a number of papers
on cardiac malformations and continued her work on cystic fibrosis.
Her last major paper on this subject described the condition, thought
to be found only in infants, in young adults.

1963

1100. Anon. "In Memoriam. Dr. Dorothy Andersen," The Stethoscope (April).
An obituary giving details of her career. Centers on her
service at Columbia-Presbyterian Medical Center. Lists her honors.

1101. Anon. [Dorothy H. Andersen], The Journal of the American
Medical Association, 184 (25 May), p. 670.
A single paragraph listing some of her professional activities.

1964

1102. Damrosch, Douglas S. "Dorothy Hansine Andersen," The
Journal of Pediatrics, 65 (October), pp. 477-479. Photograph.
An exceptional memorial article. The writing is clear and
concise and the choice of material excellent. A vital source which
makes delightful reading and provides an example to be followed.

1980

1103. Machol. Libby. "Andersen, Dorothy Hansine," Notable
American Women (30), 4, pp. 18-20.
A well-written and nicely balanced account of Andersen's
life and career. Machol is especially good in her description of
the determination Andersen showed in the face of professional dis-
approval.

(See also 989)

1104. CAROLINE WORMELEY LATIMER
       28 March 1859?--between 1930 and 1935
       Educated at the Woman's Medical College of Baltimore (MD,
1890) and Bryn Mawr College (AB, ?; AM, 1896), Latimer began
her career as an instructor in biology at the Woman's College of
Baltimore in 1897. In the second edition of American Men of Science
(1910) she is shown as still teaching at the renamed Goucher College. She described her professional position as a literary assistant
to Drs. H. A. Kelly and L. F. Barker, probably of Johns Hopkins,
in the period through 1920. In 1915 she was an associate editor
of Appleton's Medical Dictionary. She was interested in the fatigue
of nerves of cold-blooded animals and the toxic effects of the trans-
fusion of blood from one animal to another. The Register of Graduate Students at Bryn Mawr gives her birthdate as 28 March 1859.

1105. Latimer is cited in American Men of Science, 1906-1910.
       We are indebted to Lucy Fisher West, College Archivist of
Bryn Mawr, for her assistance in learning about Latimer.

1106. IDA HENRIETTA HYDE
       8 September 1857--22 August 1945
       Hyde attracted more attention and received more support in
Europe than in her home country. In spite of the title of her autobiographical article, "Before Women Were Human Beings," and largely on the strength of her determination, she was invited to study
at the University of Strasbourg in 1893 after two productive years
in the Bryn Mawr College laboratory of Jacques Loeb. She had
obtained her undergraduate education at the Universities of Illinois
and Cornell (BS, 1891).
       Hyde's work in zoology was, in the judgment of some faculty,
worthy of a doctoral degree, but the opposition of others caused
her to move to the University of Heidelberg. There, after having
successfully overcome the opposition, she became the first woman
to earn a doctorate (PhD, 1896). She returned to the United States
after additional research at Naples and the University of Bern.
       In 1898 she joined the faculty at the University of Kansas
where she remained until her retirement in 1920. Her teaching and
research reputation grew both in the new department of physiology,
where she was promoted to full professor in 1905, and in the School

of Medicine. She was known for her stimulating teaching and published a textbook, Outlines of Experimental Physiology (1905) and
Laboratory Outlines of Physiology (1910). She completed most of
the requirements for a medical degree summers at the Rush Medical
College of Chicago and continued to work in Europe.

As a research scientist Hyde's interests were broad and her
work precise. She studied both vertebrate and invertebrate animals with respect to circulation, respiration and nervous systems.
At a very early stage of its development she applied micro methods
to the study of individual cells. These activities were recognized
by her election as the first woman member of the American Physiological Society in 1902 and her service as chairman of the Women's
Commission of Health and Sanitation of the State Council of National
Defense during the First World War. (See also 23, 43.)

1927

1107. Anon. "Hyde, Ida Henrietta," The National Cyclopaedia of
       American Biography (2), B, pp. 146-147. Photograph.
       Sketch of her education and professional career. It is most
useful for its list of her memberships in scientific organizations
and a partial bibliography with dates of publication.

1938

1108. Hyde, Ida H. "Before Women Were Human Beings," Journal
       of the American Association of University Women, (June),
       pp. 226-236.
       The autobiographical account of Hyde's adventures in a Ger-
man laboratory when she was the 1893 fellow of the Association of
Collegiate Alumnae. This article is required reading for anyone
interested in the development of American women scientists; it is
also a pleasure to read. Hyde not only lived the events, but wrote
of them with the same accuracy and taste that characterized her
scientific publications.

1945

1109. Anon. "Ida H. Hyde, Pioneer," Journal of the American
       Association of University Women, (Fall), p. 42.
       An obituary notice which draws attention to her work in
Germany under the Association of Collegiate Alumnae fellowship.

1110. Anon. "Recent Deaths. Ida Henrietta Hyde," School and
       Society, 62 (8 September), p. 154.
       Well-presented outline of her life. Says that she established
a scholarship for women studying science.

1971

1111. Deyrup, Ingrith J. "Hyde, Ida Henrietta," Notable American
Women (30), 2, pp. 247-249.
       The full story of Hyde's pioneering studies in Germany along
with a very nice description and evaluation of her scientific contributions. An important paragraph is devoted to her concern for
the status of women and her efforts to improve the situation.

1112. EDITH JANE CLAYPOLE
       1 January 1870--27 March 1915
       Claypole was born in England and moved with her family to
the United States when she was two years old. Following her undergraduate education at Buchtel College, Akron, Ohio (PhB, 1892),
she studied at Cornell University (MS, 1893) and the Massachusetts
Institute of Technology. She taught zoology at Wellesley College
and served as acting department head from 1896 to 1898. She went
with her father to the Throop Polytechnic Institute in Pasadena,
California, in 1898. After a year she began the study of medicine
at the University of Southern California (MD, 1904). She then worked
as a pathologist in Los Angeles while writing a book entitled Blood
of Necturus and Cryptobranchus and several articles in scientific
journals. (See also 4.)

1906

1113. Anon. "Claypole, Edith Jane," The National Cyclopaedia
of American Biography (2), 13, pp. 259-260.
       This sketch provides most of the limited biographical data
available. Gives facts of her life only till the turn of the century.

1915

1114. Anon. [Obituary], Science, 41 (9 April), pp. 527, 754.
       A research associate in pathology at the University of Cali-
fornia, Claypole was well known as a teacher and investigator in
biology. Cites her work on immunization against typhoid fever.
The second reference notes a resolution by the Science Club of
Wellesley College which recognizes that she died as a result of an
infection incurred while preparing typhoid vaccine for the army.

1115. ANNE MOORE
       10 August 1872--25 September 1937
       Moore was educated at Vassar College (AB, 1896; AM, 1897)
and the University of Chicago (PhD, 1901). She was an assistant
in biology at Vassar during 1898-1899 and went to the State Normal School in San Diego, California, in 1901 where she became head
of the department of biology. She was interested in the effects

of electrolytic solutions on muscle tissue and wrote a book entitled
Physiology of Man and Other Animals. Later in her life Moore seems
to have turned away from science. She became interested in the
theater, worked as a drama critic, and joined Eva La Gallienne's
experiment at the Civic Repertory Theater. Moore also wrote two
books of poems: Children of God and Winged Things and A Misty
Sea.

1116. Moore is cited in American Men of Science, 1906-1910.
        We are indebted to Lisa Browar, Curator of Rare Books,
and Terri O'Shea, Associate Director Alumnae of Vassar College,
for their help in discovering most of the information about Moore.

1117. JUDITH GRAHAM POOL
        1 June 1919--13 July 1975
        Pool made significant contributions to the treatment of hemo-
philia as a result of her research in blood coagulation. The process
of cryoprecipitation allows the preparation of a fraction of blood
plasma containing the antihemophilic factor used in the treatment
of hemophilia. The material and the means of obtaining it have
become the standard of blood bank and industrial methods.
        Pool began her education at the University of Chicago (BS,
1939; PhD, 1946). During these same years she held a teaching
post at the Colleges of Hobart and William Smith in Geneva, New
York, and had two sons. She went with her husband to Stanford
University and returned to the laboratory in 1950 as a member of
the staff of the School of Medicine. Here she was to spend the
rest of her brief life.
        During her dissertation research Pool had been the first
to determine the electrical potential of a single muscle fiber. Her
subsequent research in blood coagulation was equally careful and
productive. She was especially interested in an inhibitor of the
antihemophilic factor which causes some cases to grow worse with
further transfusions. She published several important papers on
this subject.
        The significance of Pool's research was widely recognized
and she was invited to give a number of lectures, including the
Paul M. Aggeler Memorial Lecture in 1974. She was a member of
the national scientific advisory committee for both the National Institutes of Health and the American Red Cross Blood Program. She
received the Murray Thelin Award of the National Hemophilia Foundation (1968), the Elizabeth Blackwell Award from Hobart and William Smith (1973), and the Professional Achievement Award from
the American Association of University Women. (See also 42.)

1975

1118. Anon. "Dr. Judith G. Pool, Hemophilia Expert," The New
        York Times, 124 (15 July), p. 36.

A noted researcher who discovered a simple method of obtaining the protein needed by hemophiliac patients. Gives a brief educational vita.

1976

1119. Brinkhous, K. M. "Judith Graham Pool, Ph.D. (1919-1975). An Appreciation," Thrombosis and Haemostasis, 35 (30 April), pp. 269-271. Photograph.
   A memorial which pays attention to Pool's human warmth and devotion to people as well as to her professional contributions.

1980

1120. Brinkhous, K. M. "Pool, Judith Graham," Notable American Women (30), 4, pp. 553-554.
   Longer and more detailed than his earlier article (1119) this biographical sketch, too, is well written and presents the flavor of an interesting woman who was also a fine scientist. The two articles complement one another nicely. A good bibliography.

ORNITHOLOGISTS

GENERAL (See also 1389, 1395, 1410, 1459)

1933

1121. Anon. American Ornithologist's Union. Fifty Years' Progress of American Ornithology 1883-1933. Lancaster, Pennsylvania: The American Ornithologist's Union, 239 pp.
A book of essays on various ornithological topics. Nice's article, "The Theory of Territorialism and Its Development," is included (pp. 89-100). Even the article, "American Ornithological Literature, 1883-1933" by Witmer Stone, mentions only one American woman's work: Bailey's Handbook of the Birds of the Western United States.

1955

1122. Welker, Robert Henry. Birds and Men. American Birds in Science, Art, Literature, and Conservation, 1800-1900. New York: Atheneum, pp. 187-191.
The contribution of nineteenth-century Americans to the study of birds lies both in the fields of ornithology and science writing. Four outstanding women are treated in this book which places them squarely in the context of a rapidly growing emphasis on education about birds. Bailey is included in this section; Miller, Wright and Doubleday are found in the section devoted to science writers.

1123. FLORENCE AUGUSTA MERRIAM BAILEY
8 August 1863--22 September 1948
Bailey belongs both to the serious writers and popularizers of natural history and to the science of ornithology. It is true that she made no new discoveries, but her extensive and exact observations coupled with her extraordinary writing make works like Handbook of Birds of the Western United States standards of their type.
At the newly founded Smith College Bailey studied for four years but took no degree. In recognition of her accomplishments Smith awarded her a degree in 1921. She had begun to publish articles in the Audubon Magazine during her last year, and these pieces formed the basis of her highly successful Birds Through

an Opera Glass in 1889. After two years of social work in Chicago
she developed tuberculosis and went west for the better climate.
There followed a succession of books, including one of the first
popular American bird guides, Birds of Village and Field in 1898.
    Returning to the East, she married Vernon Bailey in 1899
and began a series of field trips in California, New Mexico, Ari-
zona, Texas, and the Pacific Northwest. For the next 30 years,
as her husband became chief field naturalist for the United States
Biological Survey, Bailey studied and recorded countless observations. In 1928 she published the first comprehensive study of bird-
life in these areas. Birds of New Mexico won for her the honor
of being the first woman to receive the Brewster Medal of the American Ornithologists' Union (1931) and an honorary degree from the
University of New Mexico (LLD, 1933). (See also 4, 8, 43, 48,
1121, 1122.)

1904

1124. Anon. "Bailey, Florence (Merriam)," The National Cyclopaedia
       of American Biography (2), 12, pp. 263-264.
       Examines her developing interest in birds and gives a list
of her publications with the dates they appeared. There are useful comments on her method and writing style.

1950

1125. Oehser, Paul H. "Florence Merriam Bailey: Friend of Birds,"
       Nature Magazine, 43 (March), pp. 153-154. Photograph.
       A nicely constructed life story of Bailey which discusses
her interest in birds and its place in the science of ornithology.
Special notice of her literary style and the close collaboration between husband and wife which was such an important part of her
life.

1952

1126. Oehser, Paul H. "In Memoriam: Florence Merriam Bailey,"
       The Auk, 69 (January), pp. 19-26.
       This longer and more scientifically oriented biography still
retains the pleasant, familiar style of the earlier work (1125).
Bailey's entire career is covered and each of her more important
publications discussed. Once again Oehser takes pains to evaluate
her place in American ornithology and in American literature.

1971

1127. Oehser, Paul H. "Bailey, Florence Augusta Merriam,"
       Notable American Women (30), 1, pp. 82-83.

This third in a series of biographical sketches by the same author is distinctive in spite of covering the same ground. The writing continues to be smooth and informative, but it presents Bailey as a more complete person. There is a discussion of her early interest in social work and of her love of the rugged out-of-doors life. A central theme is, as before, the warm, close comradeship between husband and wife. These three sketches should form the basis of a full biography.

1982

1128.   Seaton, Beverly. "Florence Augusta Merriam Bailey," American Women Writers (48), 1, pp. 91-93.
        Covers both her principal writings about birds and her book about Mormon life. Especially strong in placing Bailey in context of her times. Bibliography.

1129.   FANNIE PEARSON HARDY ECKSTORM
        18 June 1865--31 December 1946
        Eckstorm used the vast store of information and experience she obtained from her family, especially her father, to become a recognized authority on both the wildlife and the people of Maine. In a lifetime spent in the wilderness and with a rare scientific skill, she preserved for the future an understanding of that state's history and beauty. These accomplishments are most easily recognized in her writings (for example, The Bird Book and The Penobscot Man), but her political efforts to save the Maine forests and to protect the rights of the inhabitants deserve equal tribute.
        Following her education at Smith College (AB, 1888), she took the first of several long canoe trips with her father into areas probably never before seen by a white woman. She used the memories and the detailed scientific notes for many later books on the North Woods. She served as superintendent of the Brewer schools for two years, but failing to persuade the town to provide the money required to raise standards, she spent a year in Boston reading scientific manuscripts for D. C. Heath, publishers. While in Boston she married the Rev. Jacob Andreason Eckstorm.
        Later in her life Eckstorm collaborated with several people interested in the Maine ballads. Music which would have vanished was preserved in several highly regarded books, and she was awarded an honorary degree by the University of Maine (MA, 1929). Eckstorm's interests and energy extended to the history and legends of the Indians, and she published a series of articles and a monograph, Indian Place-Names of the Penobscot Valley and the Maine Coast. She was widely recognized for the quality of her scholarship and for her generosity to serious scholars. (See also 48.)

1910

1130. Anon. "Sudden Death of Manly Hardy," The Bangor [Maine]
       Daily News (10 December).
       A long obituary of Eckstorm's father says very little about
his daughter, but his influence on her life and career was so great
the material is of unusual importance.

1947

1131. Anon. "Noted Authority on Maine Indians Dies in Brewer,"
       The Bangor [Maine] Daily News (1 January), pp. 1, 4.
       Photograph.
       Obituary cites her studies of Maine Indians and says she
was an ornithologist of prominence. Traces her life and career
in amazing detail for a short article.

1953

1132. Ring, Elizabeth. "Fannie Hardy Eckstorm: Maine Woods
       Historian," New England Quarterly, 26 (March), pp. 45-
       64.
       This study fails to mention Eckstorm's work in ornithology
and is primarily concerned with her interests in the people of the
wilderness, the Indians and the woodsmen. Ring discusses her
contributions in detail, but criticizes her sharply. Says that she
stated strong opinions about the correctness of a particular thesis
before all the data were collected. Ring admits, however, that in
the collections of ballads this shortcoming was actually an asset.

1974

1133. Smith, David C. "Eckstorm, Fannie Hardy," Dictionary of
       American Biography (14), supp. 4, pp. 248-249.
       A brief but key source in that Smith treats each aspect of
her varied contributions. Eckstorm's publications in all fields are
discussed, and the overall judgment is that her collections are important basic sources of material for scholars.

1971

1134. James, Janet Wilson. "Eckstorm, Fannie Pearson Hardy,"
       Notable American Women (30), 1, pp. 549-551.
       James treats each of Eckstorm's interests and evaluates her
importance in a balanced, precise and well-written account of a
complex subject. There is a wealth of material packed into an all
too short article.

1982

1135. McFadden-Gerber, Margaret. "Fannie Pearson Hardy Eck-
      storm," American Women Writers (48), 1, pp. 573-575.
      A well-written essay which reviews fully the development of
Eckstorm's career. Maintains that her careful research has left
an important mark in several areas. Excellent bibliography.

1136. MARGARET MORSE NICE
      6 December 1883--26 June 1974
      A true amateur, Nice was initially interested in languages
as a student at Mount Holyoke College (AB, 1906) and psychology
at Clark University (AM, 1915). She actually published 18 articles on child psychology from observations of her own children.
She never held an appointment at any university or scientific laboratory, and yet it has been said that she made "the outstanding
contribution of the present quarter century to ornithological thinking in America."
      After more than two years of research Nice published The
Food of the Bob-white, which showed both her extraordinary patience and her interest in behavior. She went with her husband
to the University of Oklahoma where they had five daughters.
There Nice began her research which, after 35 articles, resulted
in the publication The Birds of Oklahoma which she and her husband
wrote in 1924. With the constant support of her husband, Nice
wrote 250 research reports in her career which moved from early
listings of frequency and distribution to some extremely important
studies of bird behavior. These later studies involved her recognition that it was essential to study individual birds to obtain a
valid life history. During the 1930's in Columbus, Ohio, she conducted studies which resulted in the Studies in the Life History
of the Song Sparrow. These efforts made her one of the most highly respected ornithologists. She has been said to have, "almost
single-handedly, initiated a new era in American ornithology."
      The skill Nice possessed in languages also made a fine con-
tribution as she produced a large number of reviews of the works
of leading European publications. In 1955, at her fiftieth reunion,
Mount Holyoke presented her an honorary DSc. She was the first
woman to become president of a major American ornithological group
when she was elected to that position by the Wilson Ornithological
Society in 1938.

1974

1137. Parkes, Kenneth C. "The President's Page. Margaret
      Morse Nice, 1883-1974," The Wilson Bulletin, 86 (Septem-
      ber), 301-302.
      Nice was long associated with the Wilson Ornithological

Society for which she served as president. It is thus important
to read the thoughts of her closest scientific associates. The spirit
of the amateur is clear as is the respect she gained among the pro-
fessionals. An especially interesting comment concerning the current sensitivity about the gender of scientists. Includes a review
of some of her more important studies.

1138.   Editor [David W. Johnston]. "Obituary. Margaret Morse
        Nice (1883-1974)," Bird-Banding, 45 (Autumn), p. 360.
        Stresses Nice's contributions, service, and honors.

1975

1139.   Stresemann, Erwin. Ornithology. From Aristotle to the
        Present. Hans J. and Cathleen Epstein, translators. Cam-
        bridge, Massachusetts: Harvard University Press, pp. 359,
        381.
        In this American edition Nice is mentioned most favorably
in an added epilogue. Emphasizes the importance of her example
which was widely followed.

1977

1140.   Trautman, Milton B. "In Memoriam: Margaret Morse Nice,"
        The Auk, 94 (July), pp. 430-441. Photograph.
        This is certainly the most detailed biography of Nice and it
is a very good one. The author obviously knew her well and had
a great respect for her work and her person. All of the biographical facts are here, but they are secondary to the story of her remarkably productive career. There are some charming personal
insights not to be found elsewhere.

1141.   Beecher, W. J. "The Song Sparrow Lady," Chicago Acad-
        emy of Sciences Newsletter, 1 (1 December), pp. 1-4.
        Photograph.
        A true portrait of Nice, much of it is told in her own words.
This sketch makes good reading and contributes to our understanding of a remarkable person. The style is warm and the facts are
given, but it is the depth of feeling and unbelievable energy that
are most clear.

1979

1142.   Nice, Margaret Morse. Research Is a Passion with Me.
        Foreword by Konrad Lorenz. Toronto: The Margaret Nice
        Ornithological Club and Consolidated Amethyst Communica-
        tions, 322 pp.
        A fascinating autobiography of a woman who recalls, "The

most cherished Christmas present of my life came in 1895--Mabel
Osgood Wright's **Bird Craft (1895).** For the first time I had col-
oured bird pictures." She was then 12. Notably Mr. Whitmer Stone
in his article "American Ornithological Literature 1883-1933" in Fifty
Years Progress of American Ornithology (1121) fails to mention this
woman who published consistently in Bird-Lore and who was instrumental in encouraging one of America's greatest ornithologists. This
book would interest anyone wishing to combine family and career,
and for bird-lovers it is a treasure. From the days at Mount Holyoke to her travels throughout her married life, to the people like
Konrad Lorenz (whom she came to know so well), to her academic
lectures and scientific observations, and the news about the Wilson
Ornithological Club founded in 1888, the book is as lively and interesting as its author must have been.

1980

1143.   Trautman, Milton B. "Nice, Margaret Morse," Notable
        American Women (30), 4, pp. 506-507.
        Not as long or detailed as his earlier biography (1140), yet
the article is able to convey both the scientific importance of Nice's
work and the deep love she had for nature.

(See also 569, 911, 1241, 1254)

1144. CORA AGNES BENNESON
10 June 1851--unknown
An interesting subject for future study would be why and
how Benneson found her way into <u>American Men of Science</u> in 1906.
She lists herself as being a student of the "science of government,"
and the few biographical details readily available indicate that she
was a political scientist. She entered the University of Michigan
in 1875, five years after it first admitted women (AB, 1878). She
was the first woman editor of the <u>Chronicle</u>, the college paper.

The Harvard Law School refused her admission on the grounds
that "the equipment was too limited to receive women," and she
returned to Michigan. She was one of two women in a class of 175
and claims she studied with one of the strongest law faculties in
America. Immediately after completing her studies (LLB, 1880; AM,
1883) and being admitted to the bar in Michigan and Illinois she
spent two years and four months in a world tour. In her travels
she "made it a point to visit the law courts of all the principal civilized countries of the world as well as their governing assemblies."

After she returned, armed with this extensive knowledge
of foreign government operations, she gave lectures in Quincy,
Illinois, St. Paul-Minneapolis and most of the major cities in the
East. She held a fellowship in history at Bryn Mawr College in
1887-1888 and then made her home in Cambridge, Massachusetts.
She was admitted to the bar of that state in 1894.

She appears to have written no books, but her many articles were published in a wide variety of journals and reviews.
She frequently read papers before the American Association for
the Advancement of Science. She was elected a fellow of that organization after two major presentations in 1898 and 1899, "Execu-
tive Discretion in the United States" and "Federal Guarantees for
Maintaining Republican Government in the States."

1927

1145. Anon. "Benneson, Cora Agnes," <u>The National Cyclopaedia
of American Biography</u> (2), 17, pp. 398-399.
Biographical detail of Benneson's career and family background. Notes her being refused admission to Harvard. Lists her
publications.

1146.   Benneson is cited in <u>American Men of Science</u>, 1906; <u>Who</u>
        <u>Was Who in America</u>, 1, p. 830.

1147.   CELESTIA SUSANNAH PARRISH
        12 September 1853--7 September 1918
        Parrish was educated at the Roanoke (Virginia) Female Col-
lege, the State Normal School of Virginia and Cornell University
(PhB, 1896). She taught in the public schools of Virginia, the
State Normal School of Virginia, Randolph-Macon Woman's College,
and the State Normal School of Georgia. These varied positions
were held prior to, during, and following her own college years.
In 1911-1912 she served as State Supervisor of Schools in Georgia.
In <u>American Men of Science</u> she gives her professional area as philosophy, but in other biographical dictionaries she is listed as an
educator. It seems probable that she was in educational psychology
since she states that she "Established the first psychological laboratory and taught the first child study class in the South." She
also belonged to a number of educational societies and published
articles in the <u>American Journal of Psychology</u> and <u>The Educational</u>
<u>Review</u>. In addition to her work in education she was apparently
an active member of the Association of Collegiate Alumnae and the
Southern Association of College Women. Here we have a fine example of a woman demanding further study.

1148.   Parrish is cited in <u>American Men of Science</u>, 1906; <u>Who Was</u>
        <u>Who in America</u>, 1, p. 938; <u>Woman's Who's Who of America</u>,
        p. 623.

1149.   JULIA HENRIETTA GULLIVER
        30 July 1856--25 July 1940
        A splendid teacher of ethical philosophy and biblical litera-
ture and a distinguished president of Rockford College, Gulliver
does not appear to have done any work in what we should call the
philosophy of science. She does indicate an interest in the psychology of dreams and as president of Rockford, she introduced
a pioneering program in home economics.
        Gulliver was a member of the first class of Smith College
(AB, 1879), and her senior thesis on dreams was accepted for publication in the <u>Journal of Speculative Philosophy</u> (April, 1880). She
continued her study independently and presented her thesis on
the philosophies of Plato, Comte and Spencer for Smith's second
doctorate (PhD, 1888). She became professor and department head
at Rockford Female Seminary in 1890 and continued her studies at
the University of Leipzig in 1892-1893. There she, in the company
of over 200 men, came under the influence of Wilhelm Wundt and
translated Part One of his <u>Ethics</u>.

In 1902 she was selected as Rockford's president. The College was typical of the struggling institutions of that day, and for the next 14 years she made a heroic and successful effort to place it on a sound intellectual and fiscal basis. Under her direction important additions were made to the stature of the faculty; the library was greatly expanded, and the size of the student body and endowment increased. She introduced courses in home economics and secretarial studies for both practical and philosophical reasons. She was a firm believer in women retaining their traditional influence in the home and at the same time playing an ever increasing role in the community. She was determined that educated women cease to be "social parasites."

In addition to her heavy responsibilities as president, Gulliver continued to teach and to mold young women by giving them, "their first concepts of the nature and destiny of man and of the Bible as organic evolution." In 1908 the French government made her an Officier d'Académie and in 1910 Smith College awarded her an honorary LLD. (See also 48.)

1940

1150.   Anon. "Julia H. Gulliver, Educator, Is Dead," The New
        York Times, 89 (28 July), p. 27.
        Talks about the great progress of Rockford College under
her leadership and notes that she received an honor from the
French government. Some family and educational background.

1151.   E. N. H. "In Memoriam. Julia Henrietta Gulliver 1879,"
        Smith Alumnae Quarterly (November), p. 41. Photograph.
        A general curriculum vitae and some personal insights.

1947

1152.   Church, Lorena M. "Julia Henrietta Gulliver, 1902-1919,"
        in Profiles of the Presidents. Rockford, Illinois: Rockford
        College, pp. 18-20.
        While the major intent of this article is to describe Gulliver's presidency of Rockford College, there are valuable pieces
of biographical data. An especially good balance between the high
moral tone of her New England background and the practical ways
in which the College prospered under her guidance.

1971

1153.   Robbins, Michael W. "Gulliver, Julia Henrietta," Notable
        American Women (30), 2, pp. 104-105.
        A complete, if limited, picture of the philosopher, teacher,
administrator at her best. The effect Gulliver must have had on

her colleagues and her students comes through clearly in this very readable account.

1982

1154.   Poland, Helene Dwyer. "Julia Henrietta Gulliver," American Women Writers (48), 2, pp. 200-202.
        Outlines Gulliver's education and career. Shows that she herself represented an example of her convictions in action. A clear description of her views on women's place in society.

1155.   ANNA ALICE CUTLER
        24 January 1864--1957
        Cutler was educated at Smith College (AB, 1885; AM, 1898) and Yale University (PhD, 1896). She taught for a year at Rockford College and returned to Smith where she spent the rest of her career. She rose to the rank of full professor in 1905. Her scholarly interests included esthetics and their influence on Kant's "theory of knowledge."

1156.   Cutler is cited in American Men of Science, 1906; Who Was Who in America, 3, p. 204.

1157.   ELLEN BLISS TALBOT
        22 November 1867--25 January 1968
        For 36 years Talbot served Mount Holyoke College as professor and for 32 years as chairman of philosophy. She was educated at the Ohio State University (AB, 1890) and Cornell University (PhD, 1898). She taught at Emma Willard's Troy Female Seminary for two years before going to Mount Holyoke. Her scholarship concerned the philosophy of Fichte. She does not seem to have dealt specifically with scientific topics.

1968

1158.   Anon. "Ellen Talbot, 100, Taught Philosophy," The New York Times, 118 (26 January), p. 47.
        Notice of her death giving her dates at Mount Holyoke and saying she was the first appointment made by Mary E. Woolley.

1159.   Talbot is cited in American Men of Science, 1906; Who Was Who in America, 4, p. 1067.

1160. GRACE NEAL DOLSON
       13 February 1874--15 May 1961
       Following her undergraduate education at Cornell University
(AB, 1896), Dolson studied at Cornell and the Universities of Jena
and Leipzig (1897-1898). She returned to Cornell to expand her
studies of Renouvier and his school in nineteenth-century philosophy (PhD, 1899). Beginning in 1900 she was professor of philosophy at Wells College in Aurora, New York. In a Cornell University register of Alumni Biographical Information dated 19 June
1952 she gives her name as Sister Hilary, C.S.M. and states that
since 1929 she has been superintendent of St. Mary's Hospital for
Children. In that same document Sister Hilary says that she has
published "a good many magazine articles." At some point she became assistant superior of St. Mary's Convent in Peekskill, New
York, where she died.

                              1961

1161. Anon. "Sister Hilary," The New York Times, 110 (17 May),
       p. 3.
       Only a few lines giving the names of her mother and father
and time of the Requiem.

1162. Dolson is cited in American Men of Science, 1906.
       We are indebted to Kathleen Jacklin, Archivist of Cornell
University, for her assistance.

1163. MARY CHILTON NOYES
        13 January 1855--13 September 1936
        Noyes was educated at the Universities of Iowa (PhB, 1881;
AM, 1884), Cornell (MS, 1894) and Western Reserve (PhD, 1895).
From 1886 to 1900 she taught mathematics, physics, and astronomy
at Lake Erie College. After 1900 she was an instructor in these
same subjects at the Minneapolis Academy. The Cornell University
Alumni Records show that she was retired in Pasadena, California,
and that she died there. Her scholarly interests concerned the
relationship between heat and elasticity.

1164. Noyes is cited in American Men of Science, 1906. That pub-
        lication gives her doctoral degree as Cornell in 1896.
        We are indebted to Kathleen Jacklin, Archivist at Cornell
University, for her assistance.

1165. MARCIA ANNA KEITH
        10 September 1859--29 December 1950
        Keith taught in the Massachusetts public schools and at the
Michigan Seminary prior to enrolling at Mount Holyoke College (BS,
1892). She taught mathematics at Mount Holyoke from 1885 to 1888
and was head of the department of physics from 1889 to 1905. During the year 1897-1898 she studied at the University of Berlin. She
taught at the Lake Erie College in 1905 and from 1906 to 1918 was
an assistant to a consulting engineer.

1951

1166. E. R. L. "1883. Marcia Ann [sic] Keith," [Mount Holyoke
        Alumnae Bulletin?] (May).
        This unidentified clipping gives information quite different
from that of American Men of Science. For example, her class,
middle name and dates at Mount Holyoke. Of greater significance
is the statement that she was the first teacher of physics (1885-
1903) and the first to give individual laboratory work. She started
the physics colloquium and was a charter member of the American
Physical Society.

1167. Keith is cited in American Men of Science, 1906-1921.
        We are indebted to Elaine D. Trehub, Mount Holyoke Col-
lege History Librarian, for her assistance in locating this information.

1168. MARGARET ELIZA MALTBY
       10 December 1860--3 May 1944
       When she graduated from Oberlin College (BA, 1882), Maltby
was undecided about her career choice and went to New York City
to study at the Art Students' League. After a year, however, she
returned to Ohio where she taught high school for four years. During this time a new talent in science emerged, and she soon found
herself neglecting all other interests. In 1887 she entered the Massachusetts Institute of Technology (BS, 1891). Oberlin awarded
her an MA in that same year. From 1889 to 1893 she taught physics at Wellesley College. She continued to teach and began graduate work at MIT. In 1893 with a traveling fellowship she was at
Göttingen University where she became the first American woman
to earn its doctorate (PhD, 1895). The quality of her work so impressed the eminent German physicist Friedrich Kohlrausch that
he invited her to continue with him for an additional year and to
return in 1898-1899 when he had become president of the
Physikalisch-Technische Reichsanstalt in Charlottenburg.
       As the holder of one of the few German doctorates (certain-
ly the only one in physics) Maltby taught at Wellesley, where she
was head of the department, and at Lake Erie College. In 1900
she accepted an appointment in chemistry at Barnard College of
Columbia University. She soon moved to physics where she became associate professor and department chairman in 1913. Her
demands on herself and her students coupled with the extra help
she gave them freely, left little time for research. Still, the published record of her earlier work in high electrical resistance measurement and the conductivity of aqueous salt solutions was recognized as being of fundamental significance. In the first edition
of American Men of Science (1906) she won a star indicating that
her peers ranked her among the 150 most outstanding physicists
in America.
       In additon to these professional activities Maltby played an
active role in development of career opportunities for women. She
was chairman of the fellowship committee of the American Association of University Women from 1913 to 1924 and influenced the development of selection standards in that important source of funds
for advanced study. She published the History of Fellowships
Awarded by the American Association of University Women, 1888-
1929 describing the accomplishment of the fellows. In 1926 the
AAUW established a fellowship in her honor. (See also 23, 32, 40,
43.)

                              1927

1169. Ferris, Helen, and Virginia Moore. Girls Who Did. Stories
       of real girls and their careers. Illustrated by Harriet Mon-
       cure. New York: E. P. Dutton, pp. 213-226.
       A series of essays written by women who have worked to-
ward and achieved successful careers in art, literature, business,

and education. The last chapter deals with the young girl who
is thinking about the future. It poses problems, asks pertinent
questions, and speaks directly to the teenager. Maltby's section
is partly in the form of a dialogue and much of it is autobiographical. She outlines the difficulties and joys which lie before a young
woman who seeks a scientific career.

1944

1170. Anon. "Dr. M. E. Maltby, Long at Barnard," The New
York Times, 93 (5 May), p. 19.
A review of Maltby's education and her 31 years at Barnard
College. She is said to have introduced the first course in the
physics of music.

1171. Anon. "Editorials. Margaret E. Maltby, Pioneer," Journal
of the American Association of University Women, 37 (Summer), pp. 245-246.
Maltby served the Association in a number of very practical
ways and this brief tribute pays special attention to some of the
more significant ones. There is also some limited general biography. Notes the Maltby Fellowship established in 1926.

1960

1172. Barr, E. Scott. "Maltby, Margaret Eliza," American Journal of Physics, 28 (May), pp. 474-475. Photograph.
An unusual memorial. Following the standard biography is
a lengthy quotation from a letter by Mrs. Philip Randolph, the wife
of Maltby's adopted nephew. They obviously had a long and close
relationship and the insight to the personality of Maltby is invalu-
able.

1971

1173. Wiebusch, Agnes Townsend. "Maltby, Margaret Eliza,"
Notable American Women (30), 2, pp. 487-488.
Maltby's life and work woven into a well-written, readable
story. Tells of her pioneering educational adventure in Germany
and puts into a clear chronology the complicated early days when
she seemed to be several places at once. There is a good section
dealing with her efforts to secure assistance for women wanting
to enter a scientific career.

1979

1174. Anon. "Maltby, Margaret Eliza," Biographical Dictionary
of American Science (40), p. 167.

Five lines which contribute nothing beyond recognition of her existence.

1175. JESSIE ISADORE SPAFFORD
       3 January 1862--23 September 1952
       After graduation from Vassar College (AB, 1884) Spafford became head of the department of mathematics and physics at the Rockford Seminary, later Rockford College, where she remained until 1906. She had advanced studies at the Universities of Zurich (1891-1892) and Chicago (1896). There is no evidence that she took an advanced degree, and we have no specific information about her professional interests. She was something of an educational pioneer when she introduced required laboratory work in physics. She also raised the money to obtain the needed equipment. After her retirement she was very active in business and social organizations.

1952

1176. Anon. "Miss Spafford Dies: Business, Civic Leader,"
       Rockford (Illinois) Morning Star (24 September), pp. 1-2A.
       Photograph.
       A memorial article which emphasizes Spafford's position as a vice-president of the Third National Bank. There is a section on her teaching career which mentions that Rockford had the first X-ray equipment in the area through her efforts.

1177. Spafford is cited in American Men of Science, 1906-1910;
       Woman's Who's Who of America, p. 788.
       We are indebted to Lisa Browar, Curator of Rare Books, and Terri O'Shea, Associate Alumni Director of Vassar College, for their assistance in obtaining this information.

1178. ISABELLE STONE
       18 October 1868--unknown
       After completing her undergraduate education at Wellesley College (AB, 1890), Stone moved to the University of Chicago (MS, 1896; PhD, 1897). She taught at the Preparatory School of Bryn Mawr College for one year before going to Vassar where she was instructor in physics until 1906. Along with her sister she directed a School for American Girls in Rome, Italy, from 1907 to 1914. In 1923 the Misses Stone moved their school to Washington, D.C. From 1916 to the opening of their school, Isabelle had been head of the physics department at Sweet Briar College.
       Stone's scholarly interests were in the electrical properties of thin films and methods of depositing such films in a vacuum.

Some of this work was carried out at Columbia University where she also studied the colors of platinum films.

1179. Stone is cited in <u>American Men of Science</u>, 1906-1921; <u>Who Was Who in America</u>, 5, p. 698.

1180. FANNY COOK GATES
26 April 1872--24 February 1931
Gates began her education at Northwestern University (AB, 1894; AM, 1895) and held fellowships in physics and mathematics at Bryn Mawr College, McGill, Cambridge, Göttingen, Zurich, and Chicago Universities before completing it at the University of Pennsylvania (PhD, 1908). Her studies in Europe were financed in part by the Association of Collegiate Alumnae.

From 1898 to 1911 she was head of the department of physics at the Woman's College of Baltimore (Goucher College) where she continued her studies of the radioactive properties of chemical compounds including the effect of heat on them. In 1911 she became dean of women and professor of physics at Grinnell College in Iowa and in 1916 at the University of Illinois. (See also 19.)

1905

1181. Anon. [Returns from England], <u>Science</u>, 22 (3 November), p. 574.
Gates, having been at the Cavendish laboratory, has resumed her duties as head of the physics department at the Woman's College of Baltimore.

1182. Gates is cited in <u>American Men of Science</u>, 1906-1921; <u>Who Was Who in America</u>, 1, p. 444.

1183. ELIZABETH REBECCA LAIRD
6 December 1874--26 March 1969
Born in Canada, Laird received her undergraduate education at the University of Toronto (AB, 1896) and continued her studies at Bryn Mawr College (PhD, 1901) and the Universities of Berlin and Cambridge. After having taught a year at the Ontario Ladies' College and her year in Berlin, she joined the faculty of Mount Holyoke College where she became head of the department of physics in 1903 and professor in 1905. She retired in 1940. Her research interests were in the vibration of solids in liquids, magnetic lag, and spectral analysis.

1901

1184. Laird, Elizabeth R. "The Absorption Spectrum of Chlorine,"
       The Astrophysical Journal, 14 (September), p. 86.
       An autobiographical sketch published with the paper taken
from her thesis.

1185. "Physics. Laird, Elizabeth Rebecca," unidentified clipping
       from Mount Holyoke.
       Taken from a kind of technical biographical dictionary, the
article gives basic information followed by a long bibliography of
professional publications.

1186. Laird is cited in American Men of Science, 1906-1921.
       We are indebted to Elaine D. Trehub, Mount Holyoke Col-
lege History Librarian, for her assistance in learning about Laird.

1187. KATHARINE BURR BLODGETT
       10 January 1898--unknown
       Blodgett has many "firsts" in her career, including her
position among the first widely respected industrial scientists in
the United States. While an undergraduate at Bryn Mawr College
(AB, 1917) she visited the General Electric Research Laboratories
where her father had worked as a patent attorney. Her guide was
Irving Langmuir, the Nobel Prize winner in chemistry, with whom
she was to collaborate during her long and productive career with
GE. His advice was to follow her interest in physics in spite of
the limited opportunity for women in that field.
       Following her graduation from Bryn Mawr (AB, 1917), Blod-
gett earned a graduate degree in chemistry at the University of
Chicago (MSc, 1918). The war time shortage of scientists and Langmuir's belief in her ability opened a rare path for her in his laboratory. For the next six years they worked closely on problems of
electrical flow, but he recognized her need for further education
and urged her to go abroad. At the Cavendish Laboratories she
studied with another Nobel Laureate, Ernest Rutherford, and became the first woman to earn a doctorate in physics from Cambridge
University (PhD, 1926).
       She continued to work with Langmuir, but in 1933 she be-
gan the research which led to her first major, independent discovery. While following up his discovery of monomolecular layers
of oil on water she found that it was possible to coat these very
thin films on solids and that the colors reflected by different numbers of layers gave a useful measure of their thickness. This led
to the development of a practical, and simple, gauge for such measurements. The utility of such a device in chemistry, biochemistry,
physics, and metallurgy was quite clear. Blodgett employed this
discovery in the development of an invisible or nonreflecting glass.
After she and her assistants showed how to make such films more

stable, the invention became widely used in a variety of optical
instruments and windows.

Blodgett received deserved recognition for these and other
discoveries. She has been given honorary degrees by Elmira (1939),
Western (1942) and Russell Sage (1944) Colleges, and Brown University (1942). The American Chemical Society presented her its
Garvan Medal for distinguished work by a woman in 1951. She
earned a star as one of the 1,000 most distinguished American scientists in the seventh edition of American Men of Science (1943).
(See also 23, 28, 43.)

1939

1188. Anon. "New Inventions," Time, 33 (9 January), 33. Photo-
       graph.
       Gives a fairly detailed description of the theory behind the
"invisible" glass along with several possible applications. The intense competition between productive scientists is mentioned.

1189. McLaughlin, Kathleen. "Creator of 'Invisible Glass' Woman
       of Many Interests," The New York Times, 89 (24 Septem-
       ber), sec. D, p. 4. Photograph.
       From the multiplication table to the bridge table Blodgett
is easy to meet, though not so easy to know. She likes chopping
wood, gardening, and now has the problem of how to toughen her
thin-films. She will "put it to stew."

1940

1190. Arthur, Julietta K. "Women of 1939," Independent Woman,
       19 (January), pp. 3, 29. Photograph.
       Notes her selection as a member of a group of outstanding
women representing various fields.

1191. Anon. "Blodgett, Katharine Burr," Current Biography
       Yearbook, pp. 90-91. Photograph.
       Good notes about Blodgett's work and her personality. A
useful, popular bibliography.

1941

1192. Kerr, Adelaide. "Women in Science. Eyeglasses That Are
       'Invisible.' Dr. Katharine Blodgett's Discovery," New York
       Post (4 June). Photograph.
       A technically correct presentation for the lay reader with
several interesting quotations. Makes the point that her "acciden-
tal" discovery only happened after years of very exacting work.

1193. MacLennan, Nancy. "Women Inventors Steal the Show at
       G-E Party," The Bridgeport [Connecticut] Post (24 March).
       Photograph.
       Two outstanding inventors, Blodgett and the electrical en-
gineer Edith Clarke, are asked questions ranging from mathematics
to opportunities for women. Their "off-the-cuff" remarks make
interesting reading and may be valuable if the reporting is accurate.

                              1943

1194. Yost, Edna. American Women of Science (21), pp. 196-213.
       A remarkably clear explanation of the path to and an ap-
preciation of the thin-film research of Blodgett and Langmuir. Her
determination and scientific skill are clearly described. Yost makes
a strong point of Blodgett's blance between basic research and practical application.

                              1944

1195. Burleigh, Ida L. "Today's Women. Sees Place for More
       Women in Research Laboratories," The Christian Science
       Monitor, 36 (24 October), p. 8. Photograph.
       Traces her career with emphasis on the nonreflecting glass
and long hours of work during the war. Says women who wish
to enter some field of science must like to solve problems. If they
do, there is a good chance they will be successful since they seem
to have the necessary power of concentration and are often enthu-
siastic about their work.

                              1946

1196. Goff, Alice C. Women Can Be Engineers (634), pp. 177-
       182.
       Another in the series of biographies of women who are en-
gineers or, as in this case, in a field closely related to engineering. The intent is to provide good examples for young women who
might consider a career in engineering, and Goff makes a most appealing example of Blodgett. The biographical facts are smoothly
worked around a carefully presented description of the theory and
practice of the research leading to the nonreflecting glass.

                              1947

1197. Chamberlin, Jo. "Woman of Science. Mistress of the Thin
       Films," Science Illustrated, 2 (December), pp. 9-11. Photo-
       graph.
       Gives Blodgett's biography and some detail of her experi-

ments. Most interesting is the description of her colleagues and
their work showing that most science is not done in isolation. Good
description of her more recent studies.

1951

1198. Anon. "G.E. Research Scientist Wins Chemistry Medal,"
       The New York Times, 100 (15 March), p. 33. Photograph.
       Tells of her work at Cambridge, the "invisible glass" and
gives the title of her 1952 Garvan Medal address.

1199. Anon. "Problem-Solver Katharine Blodgett Wins Garvan
       Medal," Chemical and Engineering News, 29 (9 April), p.
       1408. Cover photograph.
       An excellent portrait that stands out from the scientific
material. Gives her New England background credit for her ability to take on hard problems. Talks about her avocational interests and the research which led to the award.

1200. Anon. "Look Applauds, Dr. Katharine Burr Blodgett,"
       Look, 15 (28 August), p. 19. Photograph.
       Written on the occasion of winning the Garvan Medal. Ar-
ticle cites her as the first doctorate in physics from Cambridge and
calls her one of the country's foremost women scientists.

1952

1201. Anon. "Blodgett, Katharine Burr," Current Biography
       Yearbook, pp. 55-57. Photograph.
       Gives standard biographical data, but really updates the
earlier article (1191). Especially good on her work during World
War II. Additional bibliography.

1202. ELDA EMMA ANDERSON
       5 October 1899--17 April 1961
       The field of health physics was very young when Anderson
went to Oak Ridge, Tennessee, in 1949; when she died 12 years
later, it was well on its way to maturity. Much of the credit for
such a rapid change must be given to her, since both personally
and through her students she worked to encourage full professional status for this vigorous young field. She was a founding
member of the Health Physics Society and served as president from
1959 to 1960. In that year she helped to establish the American
Board of Health Physics which she also served as chairman until
her death.
       Anderson came to health physics with a broad, practical back-
ground, and she was deeply committed to what she felt was a field

of lasting significance. In 1941, while on sabbatical leave from her teaching and administrative duties at Milwaukee-Downer College, she accepted a position with the Office of Scientific Research and Development at Princeton University. This work led to the Manhattan Project and the Los Alamos Scientific Laboratory where she was present at the "Trinity event," the first atomic explosion. Her contribution to the frantic search for the atom bomb was in the area of spectroscopy and the determination of the neutron cross-section of atoms vital to its construction. The same work was later useful in the construction of reactors for peaceful applications of atomic power. Following the excitement of those days in the New Mexico desert, her life as a college teacher and department chairman was less attractive.

Her appointment at Oak Ridge was as the first chief of education and training. She was primarily responsible for the development and implementation of the training program, but she taught and advised graduate students as well. In collaboration with faculty from Vanderbilt University in Nashville she designed a program in health physics leading to the Master of Science Degree. At the same time she and her students were producing research results of general benefit. Most of their results were published as articles in the scientific journals of physics and chemistry. She also wrote a book in 1950, Manual of Radiological Protection for Civil Defense.

Anderson was educated at Ripon College (AB, 1922) and the University of Wisconsin (AM, 1924; PhD, 1941). She taught physics, mathematics, and chemistry at a junior college and high school before joining Milwaukee-Downer. The Health Physics Society created an award for accomplishment by a young scientist in her honor.

1961

1203.   Anon. "Obituary. Elda Anderson, Pioneer of Health Physics in the Atomic Energy Program, Dies at 61," Health Physics, 5 (June), p. 244. Photograph.
Notes the establishment of a memorial scholarship in honor of Anderson. Reviews her contributions to this new field of physics.

1204.   Anon. "Obituaries. Elda E. Anderson," Physics Today, 14 (July), p. 68. Photograph.
More personal than most obituaries and gives the mechanism for making contributions to a Memorial Scholarship Fund.

1968

1205.   Anon. "Anderson, Elda Emma," The National Cyclopaedia of American Biography (2), 50, pp. 281-282. Photograph.

Gives Anderson's educational background and professional positions. There is some description of her scientific interests and honors.

1206. Sanders. S. Marshall, Jr. "Elda Emma Anderson," Health Physics, 15 (September), pp. 217-218.
The text of a talk given when the author accepted the Anderson Award of the Health Physics Society. A particularly valuable article since it consists of personal recollections for the benefit of "a new generation of health physicists who will never know Dr. Anderson."

1969

1207. Mills, William A. "Elda Emma Anderson," Health Physics, 17 (September), pp. 403-404.
Another winner of the Anderson Award speaking fondly of his former teacher. Especially interesting in that he makes some attempts to guess what she would think of the way health physics is going.

1974

1208. Kathren, Ronald L., and Natalie E. Tarr. "The Origins of the Health Physics Society," Health Physics, 27 (November), pp. 419-428. Photograph.
Since she played a key role in the foundation of this Society, she and her contributions are often mentioned. There is a fine tribute entitled, "In Memory of Andy" (p. 427).

1980

1209. Kathren, Ronald L. "Anderson, Elda Emma," Notable American Women (30), 4, pp. 20-21.
A biography, yes, but also the story of Anderson's life imbued with unusual vitality. The reader gets a feeling for just how influential Anderson was in the early development of this field.

1210. MARIA GERTRUDE GOEPPERT MAYER
28 June 1906--20 February 1972
The typical university town of Göttingen in the 1920's held probably the greatest collection of scientific talent the world had ever seen. The results in mathematics and physics were daily shaking the foundations of our understanding of how the elements of the universe are constituted. It was here that the third woman to win a Nobel Prize in science lived and was educated. Mayer's

father, Friedrich Goeppert, like five generations before him was
a university professor; his daughter, overcoming the great difficulties of being a woman displaced from her home by the war, would
carry on that tradition.

Mayer entered the University of Göttingen in 1924 to study
mathematics, but after her father's death in 1927 she turned her
interest to physics and particularly quantum mechanics, the description of very small, very energetic atomic particles. After a term
on a fellowship at Cambridge University she completed her dissertation (PhD, 1930) and married an American postdoctoral fellow,
Joseph E. Mayer.

In the United States there followed a long succession of reasonable positions for Joseph, but very little recognition for his at
least equally talented wife. Mayer was accepted and recognized
by most of her peers, however, and together with her own belief
in her work she was able to raise a family, put up with the academic snobbery, and continue to produce extraordinary research.
Her work dealt with what must be recognized as one of the most
fundamental questions of all: What causes the stability of certain
atoms and the instability of others? The growing body of knowledge on this subject was particularly mysterious and intriguing.
A series of "magic numbers" was clearly associated with these questions. It was the model of the nucleus and the explanation of the
numbers for which Mayer was awarded the Nobel Prize in 1963. (See
also 35, 39, 43.)

1954

1211. Fermi, Laura. Atoms in the Family. Chicago: University
       of Chicago Press, pp. 170-171.
       The first meeting of Enrico Fermi (the author's father) with
the Mayers in Ann Arbor in 1930. They made charmingly naive
plans to sail to the South Seas if the United States moved toward
becoming a Nazi state.

1963

1212. Anon. "5 Scientists Share in 2 Nobel Awards. Woman
       Laureate to Get Her Wish," The New York Times, 113 (6
       November), pp. 1, 46. Photograph.
       A few biographical and scientific notes with a note on her
statement that she "always wanted to meet a monarch."

1213. Anon . "US Nobel Prize Winners in Europe for Ceremonies,"
       The New York Times, 113 (9 December), p. 42.
       Notes that Mayer is the first American woman to win a Nobel
Prize.

1214. Anon. [Nobel Awards], The New York Times, 113 (11

December), p. 20. Photograph.
A long discussion of Linus Pauling which mentions Mayer.

1964

1215. Harrington, Mary. "An American Mother and the Nobel Prize--
       A Cinderella Story in Science," McCall's (July), pp. 38,
       40, 124. Portrait.
       In spite of its popular tone this article describes in some
detail and in appropriate language the basic concept of Mayer's research. There is also the full picture of Mayer the woman and the
loving family life she enjoyed.

1972

1216. Anon. "Maria Mayer, 65, a Nobel Physicist," The New York
       Times, 121 (22 February), p. 40. Photograph.
       Some description of the work leading to the Nobel Prize as
well as personal data. Points to Enrico Fermi's contribution and
makes a good point of her difficulties in gaining acceptance of her
ideas.

1217. Anon. "Dr. Maria Mayer, Nobel Prize Winner," The Wash-
       ington Post and Times Herald, 95 (22 February), sec. C,
       p. 6. Photograph.
       Her theory explained the structure of the atomic nucleus
and greatly extended basic concepts of the physical world.

1218. Anon. "Biography. Maria Goeppert Mayer," in Nobel Lec-
       tures (Physics), 1963-1970. New York: Elsevier, pp. 38-39.
       Biographical remarks presented as a part of the Nobel Prize
ceremony.

1973

1219. Dash, Joan. "Maria Goeppert-Mayer," in A Life of One's
       Own. Three Gifted Women and the Men They Married. New
       York: Harper and Row, pp. 229-346, 368-369. Photograph.
       A rich, personal biography which not only gives the facts
of Mayer's career, but presents it all in a fully developed story.
The person is the subject rather than the list of vital statistics.
There are some thought-provoking comments on what talented women
do in science and why. Reveals the "inside" information on the
lives of great physicists and discusses their often-mentioned love
of humor. Presents much information and analysis of the migration
of scientists to the United States before World War II. Finally,
the support Mayer received from her husband and their full, happy
life together is beautifully told.

1978

1220. Opfell, Olga S. "Madonna of the Onion. Maria Goeppert-
       Mayer," in The Lady Laureates (39), pp. 194-208, 255-256.
       Photograph.
       A highly personal sketch of Goeppert-Mayer, her life and
work. The facts are all here, but they are secondary to the love
of life shown by this woman who explored nature's innermost secrets.

1979

1221. Sachs, Robert G. "Maria Goeppert Mayer. June 28, 1906--
       February 20, 1972," in Biographical Memoirs of the National
       Academy of Sciences, 50, pp. 310-328. Photograph.
       The usual tightly written, largely scientific biography of a
member of the National Academy. There is little personal information here, but the description of her career is well done. Detailed
bibliography of her published research.

1980

1222. Dash, Joan. "Mayer, Maria Gertrude Goeppert," Notable
       American Women (30), 4, pp. 466-468.
       This condensed biography (see 1219) still presents a well-
rounded person with both personal and professional interests. The
article reads well and retains the flavor of her earlier work. Especially strong are the descriptions of Mayer's relationships to the
other distinguished physicists of her generation.

GENERAL (See also 296, 1136)

1982

1223. Stevens, Gwendolyn, and Sheldon Gardner. The Women of
Psychology: Pioneers and Innovators, vol. 1; Expansion
and Refinement, vol. 2. Cambridge, Massachusetts: Schenk-
man. Photographs.
An impressive start toward making biographical material on
women available in at least one scientific field. This detailed study
presents the stories of the individuals and relates them to the growth
and development of the various subdivisions of psychology. Many
excellent photographs.

1224. CHRISTINE LADD-FRANKLIN
1 December 1847--5 March 1930
In the days when women were openly denied admissions to
lectures and degrees, Ladd-Franklin made her presence felt in the
scientific world. In the first edition of American Men of Science
(1906) she earned a star as one of the 1,000 most important scientists in the country. Her early education was at Vassar College
(AB, 1869) where there she was interested in physics.
Since there were no laboratories open to women, she taught
school and wrote educational articles on mathematics. She sought
graduate work at Johns Hopkins University, and since she was
known through her writing to one of the mathematics professors,
she was granted admission and held a fellowship from 1879 to 1882.
She completed the requirements for a doctorate, but it was not
awarded until much later (PhD, 1926).
After her marriage to the mathematician Fabian Franklin she
began a vigorous career devoted to research and publication. At
first she worked in mathematics, but moved more to the area of
symbolic logic. Later she combined her interests in physics and
mathematics with the young field of psychology, where she made
her most lasting contributions. While her husband was on sabbatical leave she studied in the laboratories at the Universities of
Göttingen and Berlin where she became familiar with the theories
of color vision. She rejected the two major ideas in this area and
developed her own, which attempted to use the strongest aspects
of the other two theories. As with all scientific theories hers has
been modified and expanded upon, but it did represent an important contribution in its time.

Ladd-Franklin was a vigorous, determined woman who succeeded in her career without any regular or continued academic
appointment and in the face of considerable opposition to her presence in research laboratories. She was recognized for the importance of her work by being asked to present papers at several international meetings and to write or edit parts of standard works
in psychology. Vassar awarded her an honorary degree (LLD, 1887).
(See also 4, 11, 1223.)

1918

1225. Anon. "Ladd-Franklin, Christine," The National Cyclopaedia
       of American Biography (2), 26, pp. 422-423.
       A detailed sketch which talks about and gives a bibliography
of her most important works. Mentions her honors and treats her
education and early career in a thoughtful manner. This is one
of the best examples in this comprehensive but uneven biographical
source.

1930

1226. Anon. "Dr. Ladd-Franklin, Educator, 82, Dies," The New
       York Times, 79 (6 March), p. 23.
       A distinguished scientist who was a pioneer in helping other
women obtain an education.

1227. Woodworth, R. S. "Obituary. Christine Ladd-Franklin,"
       Science, 71 (21 March), p. 307.
       She was remarkable for the brilliancy of her achievements.
There was a strong element of feminism in her motivation.

1932

1228. Anon. "Ladd-Franklin, Christine," The Psychological
       Register, 2 and 3, pp. 134-135, 290-291.
       Biographical facts and an extended bibliography of profes-
sional publications. The 1929 issue (volume 2) is identical to this
one.

1933

1229. R[obert] S. W[oodworth]. "Ladd-Franklin, Christine,"
       Dictionary of American Biography (14), 10, pp. 528-530.
       The variety and depth of her life, her professional activi-
ties, and her interest in educational opportunity for women are expressed in succinct terms.

1971

1230. Hurvich, Dorothea Jameson. "Ladd-Franklin, Christine,"
       Notable American Women (30), 2, pp. 354-356.
       A well-written biography which reveals something of her
personality and examines her various professional interests. Offers a balanced assessment of the importance of her work.

1976

*1231. [Christine Ladd-Franklin], Association for Women in Mathematics
        Newsletter (Summer).

1232. LILLIEN JANE MARTIN
       7 July 1851--26 March 1943
       Widely recognized for her contributions, Martin worked in a
large number of areas, for example, personality, hypnotism, aesthetics, and the subconscious. Her work in private consultation in
mental hygiene together with her active role in founding clinics
made an important impact of the lives of many people. However,
she deserves the highest praise for her work in gerontology. Her
own example played a central role here. She traveled alone to Russia at 78, she made a transcontinental auto tour at 81 and spent
six months seeing South America at 87.
       At Vassar College (AB, 1880), she showed special talent
in science and for the next 14 years taught at a number of high
schools. She also became a senior administrator at the Girls' High
School in San Francisco in 1889. In spite of her fine work and
growing reputation she decided at the age of 43 to begin the study
of psychology and went off to the University of Göttingen for four
years of study (PhD, 1898). She returned to Germany several
times for additional research periods and became better known in
international circles than at home. She received the distinction
of an honorary degree from the University of Bonn (PhD, 1913).
       In 1899 she was appointed assistant professor at Stanford
University. She became full professor in 1911 and, in 1915, the
first woman department head. After her retirement in 1916 she
began her work in private practice. She moved to San Francisco
and became very active in the mental hygiene clinics she founded
at the Polyclinic and Mount Zion Hospitals. Her clinic at the latter hospital is probably the first one to deal with normal preschool
children. Martin earned a star as one of the 1,000 most distinguished American scientists in the second edition of American Men
of Science (1910). (See also 1223.)

1937

1233. Anon. "Martin, Lillien Jane," The National Cyclopaedia of

American Biography (2), 16, p. 153.

A sketch outlining Martin's education and giving a list of her publications. Discusses the importance of her research and clinical work.

1942

1234. Anon. "Martin, Lillien J(ane)," Current Biography Yearbook, pp. 575-577. Photograph.

A good biography with a large number of quotations by Martin. Emphasizes her positive outlook in solving problems. The biographical facts are interestingly presented and a few references are given.

1943

1235. Anon. "Lillien Martin, 91, Psychologist, Dies," The New York Times, 92 (28 March), p. 25. Photograph.

As a prolific writer and consultant Martin led a very full life. She was a pioneer in the rehabilitation of older people. Cites some of her books.

1236. Ruess, Christopher. "Lillien J. Martin," American Sociological Review, 8 (June), pp. 350-351.

A short obituary full of praise for the founder of "three new professions after her retirement at 65." Gives an indication of each of these new ventures: consulting psychologist, founder of child guidance clinics, and gerontologist. A poem to her by a former student and fellow worker is reprinted.

1237. Fenton, Norman. "Lillian Jane Martin, 1851-1943," The Psychological Review, 50 (July), pp. 440-442.

A discussion of her many professional contributions along with brief notes about her education. Mentions several of her publications and pays special attention to her vigorous life in old age.

1238. Merrill, Maud A. "Lillien Jane Martin: 1851-1943," The American Journal of Psychology, 16 (July), pp. 453-454.

"She [Martin] lived nearly 92 years and never grew old." Places her in the context of the growth of psychology during her life time and especially in relation to the outstanding women psychologists who were her contemporaries.

1948

1239. Ford, Miriam Allen de. Psychologist Unretired. The Life Pattern of Lillien J. Martin. Stanford, California: Stanford University Press, 127 pp. Photographs.

A highly personal view of Martin written by an admiring colleague. The book also contains two chapters (on Germany and Stanford) written by J. Harold Williams who had been Martin's student. There emerges a clear picture of Martin as a determined and capable psychologist who made use of the latest methods and equipment. Beyond this technical skill de Ford shows that Martin exerted a most beneficial influence on a large number of people.

1971

1240. Burnham, John Chynoweth. "Martin, Lillien Jane," Notable American Women (30), 2, pp. 504-505.
    A well-balanced account of Martin's career with emphasis on her training and the huge number of people she influenced. As in all treatments of her life there is a strong feeling of wonder at her extraordinary "retirement."

1241. MARY SOPHIA CASE
    2 March 1854--1 February 1953
    When she died Case was the oldest member of the faculty at Wellesley College which she had served for 40 years. She joined that faculty, following her graduation from the University of Michigan (AB, 1884), as an instructor in Latin. Soon her interests changed, and she was promoted to associate professor of psychology and the history of philosophy in 1890. She was promoted to full professor in 1914. Her publications were all articles published in the philosophical literature. In her youth she was crippled by polio and used a wheelchair at Wellesley, but in spite of this handicap and her deafness she played an active role in the early development of the social and intellectual life of the college.

1953

1242. Anon. "Miss Mary S. Case of Wellesley, 98," The New York Times, 102 (2 February), p. 21.
    Tells of her long service and many contributions to Wellesley. Brief mention of her career.

1243. Anon. "Mary Sophia Case," School and Society, 77 (7 February), p. 92.
    Notes her long service to Wellesley and the variety of subjects she taught.

1244. MARGARET KEIVER SMITH
    1856--1934

Smith was born in Canada and received her first collegiate education at the Oswego New York Normal School (Diploma, 1883). After several years of study at the Universities of Jena, Thuringen, and Göttingen in Germany she completed her graduate work at Zurich (PhD, 1900).

She joined the State Normal School at New Paltz, New York, in 1901 as professor and director of psychology and geography. Her scholarly interests were broad including the psychology of rhythm and work, reaction-time as a measure of physical condition and the value of Latin as a normal school subject.

1245. Smith is cited in American Men of Science, 1906-1921; Woman's Who's Who of America, pp. 761-762.

1246. MILICENT WASHBURN SHINN
15 April 1858--13 August 1940
A most interesting person, Shinn does not seem to have made the best use of what appeared to be considerable talents in both literature and science. She took her undergraduate education at the University of California (AB, 1880), and before it was completed she was a member of the editorial staff of the San Francisco Commercial Herald. There and in other publications she contributed both prose and poetry. She also did a great deal of editorial work, particularly on the Overland Monthly.

Her second career brought her attention from both the scientific and the intellectual world. When her niece was born in 1890 she kept an extensive and carefully designed set of notes on the growth and development of the little girl. The publication of these observations formed the basis of her doctoral dissertation at the University of California (PhD, 1898). These were one of the very limited sets of such systematic studies of infants and brought her widespread attention. She also wrote the material in a popular form which was widely read.

In her early 40's Shinn retired to her family's ranch. She taught her brother's children, did no further scientific work and wrote very little. She seemed so capable, but represents such a marked contrast to the women scientists who continued their careers for their entire lifespan. (See also 1223.)

1902

1247. Greene, Charles S. "Memories of an Editor," Overland Monthly, 40 (September), pp. 264-270. Photograph.
An important source of information on her work as an editor. In tracing the history of Overland Greene says she had, "editorial ability of the highest sort" and "was a tower of strength."

1940

1248. Anon. "Milicent W. Shinn, a Psychologist, 82," The New
York Times, 89 (15 August), p. 19.
A long obituary which describes and praises her work on
infant behavior. Notes about her book being recognized by other
psychologists and printed in many languages.

1942

1249. Hinkel, Edgar J., and William E. McCann, editors. "Shinn,
Milicent Washburn," Biographies of California Authors and
Indexes of California Literature, 1, pp. 195-196.
A bibliography of her writings which is almost certainly in-
complete.

1971

1250. Burnham, John Chynoweth. "Shinn, Milicent Washburn,"
Notable American Women (30), 3, pp. 285-286.
A good story of her varied life which leaves many questions
waiting for answers. While pointing out her talents, Burnham concludes, perhaps sadly, that, "Neither in literature nor in science
had she sustained her early promise."

1251. THEODATE LOUISE SMITH
9 April 1860--16 February 1914
Smith began her education at Smith College (AB, 1882; AM,
1884) and then taught at seminaries in Brooklyn and Washington
until 1893. She completed her education at Yale University (PhD,
1896). At various times she studied at Cornell, Clark, and Berlin Universities.
She made her rather brief career at Clark where she began
as a research assistant to the president, G. Stanley Hall. The
last five years of her life she was lecturer and librarian of the
Children's Institute and head of the Department of Child Welfare
at Clark. Her personal library of literature on child welfare along
with her extensive writings formed a valuable resource for scholars
in that area.

1914

1252. Anon. "Theodate Louise Smith," Yale University Obituary
Record (1 June), p. 712.
A summary of Smith's life. Her birth date is given as 11
April 1859.

1253.   Smith is cited in American Men of Science, 1906-1910;
        Woman's Who's Who of America, p. 764.

1254.   MARY WHITON CALKINS
        30 March 1863--26 February 1930
        Following her graduation from Smith College (AB, 1885; AM
1887) Calkins joined the faculty of Wellesley College as an instructor in Greek. She served that College until her retirement 42 years
later. She was promoted through the ranks to full professor in
1898.
        In 1890, after a year of additional study at Clark and Har-
vard Universities, Calkins moved from Greek to psychology and
philosophy by invitation. She continued to work in the Harvard
laboratories and in 1895 passed the oral examination and submitted
a monograph on association. This piece had evolved out of her
work with Hugo Münsterberg for her doctoral degree. The Harvard Corporation refused the recommendation of the department
that she be awarded the degree, and when Radcliffe College offered to confer it several years later, she refused since all of her
work had been done at Harvard.
        While Calkins did not think of herself as an experimentalist,
she established one of the earliest psychology laboratories in the
United States and the first at a women's college. She also did good
experimental research in emotion, dreams, memory, and related areas. Her true interest in both psychology and philosophy was in
finding the best expression of the self. She felt that the study
of ideas apart from people was too abstract. She published approximately 68 papers in psychology and 37 in philosophy. Her
books The Persistent Problems of Philosophy and A First Book in
Psychology were published in 1907 and 1909, and both saw several
subsequent editions.
        Several honors came to Calkins including honorary degrees
from Columbia University (LittD, 1909) and Smith College (LLD,
1910). She was the first woman elected president of the American Psychological Association (1905) and of the American Philosophical Association (1918). She was made an honorary member of the
British Psychological Association in 1928. In the first edition of
American Men of Science (1906) she was starred as one of the 1,000
most distinguished American scientists. (See also 8, 36, 1223.)

                                    1906

1255.   Anon. "Calkins, Mary Whiton," The National Cyclopaedia
        of American Biography (2), 13, p. 75.
        A brief sketch early in her career which already shows her
productivity and hints at her future importance.

1930

1256. Anon. "Death in Newton of Prof. Mary W. Calkins," Boston Transcript, 101 (27 February), sect. 2, p. 1.
Mostly about her many honors with references to her books and long service to Wellesley College.

1257. Anon. "Dr. Mary Calkins Dies, Noted Philosopher," The New York Times, 79 (27 February), p. 24.
Calkins taught at Wellesley for 40 years and is the foremost American woman philosopher. In 1928 she became the first woman elected to the British Psychological Association.

1258. Anon. [Dr. Mary Wilton Calkins], The Philosophical Review, 39 (May), p. 323.
A resolution by a committee of the Pacific Division of the American Philosophical Association. Gives her high praise as a teacher and scholar.

1259. Brightman, Edgar Sheffield. "Mary Whiton Calkins, Her Place in Philosophy," Wellesley Alumnae Magazine, 14 (June), pp. 307-311. Photograph.
The text of an address given in a memorial chapel service on 13 April. Brightman sees Calkins as the most prominent pupil of Josiah Royce but not just as his follower. In listing several of her most important contributions he shows her originality of thought.

1260. Vincent, Helen Cook. "Miss Calkins as a Teacher," Wellesley Alumnae Magazine, 14 (June), pp. 311-313. Photograph.
A talented, inspiring teacher who tolerated no slipshod thinking.

1261. Procter, Thomas H. "Miss Calkins as a Colleague," Wellesley Alumnae Magazine, 14 (June), pp. 313-314. Photograph.
An able leader who always asked, "What is the right thing to do?"

1262. Calkins, Mary Whiton. "The Philosophical Credo of an Absolutistic Personalist," in Contemporary American Philosophy vol. 1, George P. Adams, editor. New York: Russell & Russell, pp. 199-217.
A technical, but vital, source which describes in vivid terms exactly how Calkins saw her position in philosophy. The careful attention to detail and exact definitions which characterize Calkins are evident.

1931

*1263. Calkins, Raymond. In Memoriam, Mary Whiton Calkins, 1863-1930.

Contains a biographical sketch by her brother and tributes from several colleagues. From <u>Notable American Women</u> (1266).

1944

1264. Bussey, Gertrude C. "Calkins, Mary Whiton," <u>Dictionary of American Biography</u> (14), supp. 1, pp. 149-150.
A fine sketch which discusses Calkins' contributions to both psychology and philosophy. A good point is made about her social interests and the role she played in supporting what she felt were just causes. There is a minor error in the bibliography where the series of articles in the <u>Wellesley Alumnae Magazine</u> are in volume 15.

1961

1265. Calkins, Mary Whiton. "Mary Whiton Calkins," in <u>A History of Psychology in Autobiography</u>. vol. 1, Carl Murchison, editor. New York: Russell and Russell, pp. 31-62.
Here is the perfect complement to her autobiographical statement on philosophy (1262). Since Calkins made outstanding contributions to both fields, we are most fortunate to have her personal feelings so beautifully and precisely described. Once again the language is technical and the argument highly organized, but it is well worth the effort required as a means of appreciating this extraordinary person.

1971

1266. Onderdonk, Virginia. "Calkins, Mary Whiton," <u>Notable American Women</u> (30), 1, pp. 278-280.
A very smoothly written biography which treats each aspect of Calkins' long career. Notes her great self-discipline and points out her faith and personal contentment.

1972

*1267. Heidbreder, Edna. "Mary Whiton Calkins: A Discussion," <u>Journal of the History of the Behavioral Sciences</u>, 8, pp. 56-68.

*1268. Strunk, Orlo. "The Self-psychology of Mary Whiton Calkins," <u>Journal of the History of the Behavioral Sciences</u>, 8, pp. 196-203.

1977

1269. Kuklick, Bruce. The Rise of American Philosophy. Cambridge, Massachusetts, 1860-1930. New Haven, Connecticut: Yale University Press, pp. 590-594.

A history of the development of a strong faculty in philosophy at Harvard. There is an appendix (4) entitled, "Women Philosophers at Harvard," which is mostly about Calkins and the dispute over her degree. Author says, "Harvard was never kind to women."

1978

1270. Dowd, M. Jane. "Calkins, Mary Whiton," Biographical Dictionary of American Educators (38), 1, pp. 229-230.

A readable sketch of Calkins' life citing a representative sample of her work and honors. Limited bibliography.

1979

1271. Furumoto, Laurel. "Mary Whiton Calkins 14th President of the American Psychological Association," Journal of the History of the Behavioral Sciences, 15, pp. 346-356.

An analysis of the reasoning behind her refusal to accept the Radcliffe degree. Discusses the plight of women's education, especially in psychology, in the 1890's. There is biographical information and an indication of Calkins' contributions to psychology.

1980

1272. Furumoto, Laurel. "Mary Whiton Calkins (1863-1930)," Psychology of Women Quarterly, 5, pp. 55-68.

A fine paper which reviews Calkins' entire life and career. Recalls her notable refusal to accept the PhD from Radcliffe College when it became clear that Harvard would not award it. Extensive bibliographic references.

1273. ANNA JANE McKEAG
13 March 1864--23 November 1947

In 1892 McKeag went to Wilson College where she completed her undergraduate education (AB, 1895). She then taught at Wilson while taking her graduate education at the University of Pennsylvania (PhD, 1900).

In 1902 she joined the faculty of Wellesley College and advanced to full professor in 1909. She became president of Wilson College in 1912 but returned to Wellesley three years later. She remained at Wellesley until she retired in 1932. McKeag was very active in the scholarly and professional life of educational psychology in New England and the Nation. She presented papers at international symposia in London and Paris, was a collaborator on the Journal of Educational Psychology, and was three times president of the New England Society of College Teachers of Education. (See also 1223.)

1947

1274. Anon. "Anna J. McKeag," The New York Times, 92 (24 November), p. 23.
       Notice that she was professor emerita of education at Wellesley College.

1275. Anon. "Anna Jane McKeag," School and Society, 66 (6 December), p. 442.
       A list of dates of professional appointments.

1276. Anon. "De Mortuis. Anna Jane McKeag," Annual Report, Carnegie Foundation, 43, p. 102.
       An obituary noting her professional positions and memberships in professional organizations. States that McKeag was a prominent educator.

1277. KATHLEEN CARTER MOORE
       14 November 1866--1920
       Moore's education began at the University of Pennsylvania (Certificate, 1890). After teaching and studying there and at Barnard College of Columbia University, she completed her work at Pennsylvania (PhD, 1896). She became head of the Bardwell School of Philadelphia about 1900. Her scholarly interests concerned childhood psychology.

1278. Moore is cited in American Men of Science, 1906-1910.

1279. ELEANOR ACHESON McCULLOCH GAMBLE
       2 March 1868--30 August 1933
       One of the notable faculty members of Wellesley College, Gamble was associated with the college from her undergraduate years (AB, 1889) until her death. She studied at the Universities of Cornell (PhD, 1898) and Göttingen (1906-1907). Her scholarly interests were in the processes of memorization and the exhaustion of the sense of smell. She was the editor of the second volume of Wellesley College Studies in Psychology and the author of several technical articles. At the beginning of her career she

taught Greek and Latin at the Western Female College and the Platts-
burgh New York Normal School. (See also 1223.)

1280. Gamble is cited in American Men of Science, 1906-1921; Who
       Was Who in America, 1, p. 437; Woman's Who's Who of America,
       p. 314.

1281. MARY PARKER FOLLETT
       3 September 1868--18 December 1933
       A thoughtful student of what has come to be known as group
psychology, Follett had the personal charm and sincere interest
in people which made one feel he had her complete attention. She
began her studies at Radcliffe College (AB, 1898) where she was
especially interested in political economy and history. Prior to her
graduation she had studied at Newnham College, Cambridge University, and published her first book, The Speaker of the House of
Representatives.
       Most of her early work was in the establishment of organiza-
tions for the improvement of community life. She was active in
the foundation of the Roxbury League of Boston which for the first
time demonstrated that school facilities could be used after hours
as community centers. Her work in the area of vocational guidance
for schoolchildren accomplished much and led the Boston city school
board to establish other evening centers built on her model.
       These activities influenced her second book, The New State.
She developed her lifelong view that the organization and integration of community groups as individuals was superior to the conven-
tional view that true democracy required majority rule. With the
growth of the questions of labor-management relationships Follett
began an even broader application of her ideas. Her third book,
Creative Experience, again stressed the need for integration. By
insisting on an active role for the individual she saw that conflict
was neither the best nor the necessary route to solving the problems of differing interests. From this basis it was a short step
to her finest work which was in industrial management. She began an extensive program of lectures and writings. Since her life
paralleled the growth of the supreme importance of business in our
society, she played a vital role in the development of a practical
philosophy to deal with its many social concerns.

                                 1934

1282. Cabot, Richard C. "Mary Parker Follett, an Appreciation,"
       The Radcliffe Quarterly (April), pp. 80-82.
       A rather long memorial piece which traces the development
of Follett's interest in the full use of school resources. Cabot relates the evolution of Follett's interests and activities which led
to the formulation and practice of an entire philosophy. Follett's

experiences and productive life work resulted in the publication
of two major books. A nice concluding section.

1943

1283. Ginn, Susan J. "Mary Parker Follett," in The Women's Mu-
       nicipal League of Boston. A History of Twenty-five Years
       of Civic Endeavor. Dorothy Worrell, editor. Boston: By
       the League, pp. 207-208.
       Consists mainly of quotations from Cabot's Appreciation
(1282), but adds that her service to the League was greatly valued.

1971

1284. Crawford, Dawn C. "Follett, Mary Parker," Notable American
       Women (30), 1, pp. 639-641.
       A rich biography which synthesizes the details of Follett's
varied activities. Both the theory and the practice leading to Follett's success as a writer and lecturer in group psychology are described as is her practical contributions to community life.

1285. CARRIE RANSON TAYLOR SQUIRE
       27 January 1869--24 April 1952
       Squire taught at normal schools in Alabama, Montana, and
Wisconsin from the beginning of the twentieth century. She was
interested both in the scholarly aspects of certain areas of psychol-
ogy--such as fatigue, rhythm and esthetics--and in the practical
questions of industrial education. She was educated at the Universities of Hamline (PhB, 1889), Minnesota (MS, 1898), and Cornell
(PhD, 1901). She also studied at the Universities of Leipzig and
Würzburg. Following her teaching and administrative activities she
sought to apply her ideas in the practical world of business.

1286. Squire is cited in American Men of Science, 1906-1910;
       Woman's Who's Who of America, p. 772.
       We are indebted to Muriel McEachern of the Research and
Records Office at Hamline University and Kathleen Jacklin, Archivist at Cornell University, for their assistance.

1287. ALICE HAMLIN HINMAN
       20 December 1869?--28 October 1934
       Following her education at Wellesley College (AB, 1893) and
Cornell University (PhD, 1897) Hinman joined the faculty of Mount
Holyoke College. After only one year there she married Edgar L.
Hinman, chairman of the department of philosophy and psychology

at the University of Nebraska, and moved to Lincoln. She taught psychology and ethics at the University and other schools of the area at various times, but it was in public service to education that she made her most important contributions. From 1907 to 1919 she served on the Lincoln board of education and as its chairman in 1910. During this period, and largely through her influence, the public school system grew from being rather backwards to a model for progressive education. She was active in a wide range of local, national, and international service organizations. She had scholarly interests in memory, hypnotism, and infant psychology and wrote several articles and reviews in the <u>American Journal of Psychology</u>. She also contributed to a book on hypnotic phenomena.

1918

1288.   Anon.   "Hinman, Alice Hamlin," <u>The National Cyclopaedia</u>
        <u>of American Biography</u> (2), 26, pp. 269-270.   Photograph.
        After an introductory note about her education the article
relates Hinman's active participation in the public affairs of Lincoln, Nebraska. Mentions several of her publications and lists her memberships. Makes a particular point of her great skill in dealing with people and how ably she used this talent to better the community.

1289.   Hinman is cited in <u>American Men of Science</u>, 1906-1921; <u>Who</u>
        <u>Was Who in America</u>, 1, p. 563; <u>Woman's Who's Who of America</u>,
        p. 391.

1290.   MARGARET FLOY WASHBURN
        25 July 1871--29 October 1939
        In reading Washburn's autobiographical article "Some Recollections" one cannot fail to be impressed by her sense of humor and perceptive remarks on fashions in American education. Her own training, she recalls, began on the 5th birthday when she discovered that "thinking about myself was agreeable." Memories of her schooling, both private and public, were not however quite so pleasant. Born in Harlem, the family moved later to Walden, New York, where, she says, "I learned very little," and finally to Kingston where she found that Regents exams "are below contempt." As a counterbalance to an intellectually dull life at school, she read constantly and made several attempts, about age ten, to write literary pieces, for which she admits she had no talent. It was at Vassar College (AB, 1891) that she developed an interest in chemistry and French.
        Wishing to study with James M. Cattell at Columbia, she persisted until she was allowed to attend his lectures, but it was not on an equal basis with the male students but as a "hearer," or, to put it more bluntly, as an inferior. After receiving a graduate

degree in philosophy from Vassar (AM, 1893), Washburn went on
to Cornell University to study with Edward B. Titchener (PhD,
1894). Following her dissertation she spent six years at Wells College as professor of philosophy. It was not until 1903, after another
two year stint at Cornell and one year at the University of Cincinnati that Vassar became her permanent home. A scholarly, but
stimulating lecturer, she attracted many students, and her encouragement of undergraduates to take an active role in research was far-
sighted and productive. Her practice of publishing the results
jointly with these neophyte scholars shocked those research directors who continued to take all the credit for their projects.

Two books suggest the stature of her scholarship. The Animal Mind (1908) is a pioneering effort "to organize the literature
on the patterns of animal consciousness and to argue that they
are both open to and worth investigation." Then in 1916 she published Movement and Mental Imagery, which she saw as an attempt
"to interpret the experimentally obtained data on the higher mental
processes by the motor principles." Her early interest in chemistry is reflected here in a desire to align psychology with the physical sciences.

Such rich accomplishments were accompanied by several honors. The second woman to be elected president of the American
Psychological Association (1921), she became coeditor of the American Journal of Psychology in 1925, which published an entire issue
honoring her third of a century of scholarship in 1927. She earned
a star in the first edition of American Men of Science (1906) as
one of the 1,000 most distinguished American scientists. Finally
in 1931 she was elected to the National Academy of Sciences, the
second woman to achieve that high honor. Of greatest value was
her life full of devotion to her discipline and her students. (See
also 32, 43, 1223.)

1927

1291. "Washburn Commemorative Volume," The American Journal
       of Psychology, 39, 442 pp. Photograph.
       Thirty-two technical papers each of which in some way re-
lates to Washburn's teaching and research interests. Includes a
bibliography of her writings. The dedication reads: "To Margaret
Floy Washburn. Teacher, Author, Scientist. Twenty-five years
Professor of Psychology at Vassar College and Editor of the American Journal of Psychology. This Volume is Dedicated by your Colleagues in Recognition of Thirty-three Years of Distinguished Service to Psychology."

1932

1292. Washburn, Margaret Floy. "Some Recollections," in A His-
       tory of Psychology in Autobiography, vol. 2. Carl Murchi-

son, editor. Worcester, Massachusetts: Clark University
Press, pp. 333-358. (Pages from the 1961 edition, New York:
Russell and Russell.)
   A delightfully told story of the early years of psychology
in America by a modest and literate woman. The autobiography is
enlightened by an abundance of small details available only from
a willing as well as talented writer. The discussion of her research
also reveals special insights, for as a contributor to research publications and as an editor of one of them, she was in a unique position. She was able to observe and describe the advance of psychological studies and the schools of thought they represented,
a task she carried out with wisdom, fairness, and obvious good
humor.

1939

1293.   Anon. "Dr. M. F. Washburn of Vassar Faculty," The New
        York Times, 89 (30 October), p. 17.
   Unusual detail covering her personal life and her professional career. Considers noteworthy her capabilities as both a teacher and a scholar.

1940

1294.   Macurdy, Grace Harriet. "Memories of Margaret Floy Wash-
        burn. July 25, 1871--October 29, 1939," Vassar Alumnae
        Magazine (January), pp. 2-4. Photograph.
   Washburn had a great interest in Classical literature, thus
it is entirely appropriate that the chairman of the Greek department at Vassar wrote this memorial article. Brief as the story is,
the fullness of the long friendship of these colleagues is clear as
is the personality of the subject. This is essential reading.

1295.   Langfeld, Herbert S. "Tribute of a Colleague," Vassar Alum-
        nae Magazine (January), p. 4. Photograph.
   Just a note, but since it represents the view of her closest
professional colleague it is most valuable. Pictures Washburn as
an "idea experimenter" who "never acknowledged defeat." Says
that students respected her scholarship and teaching ability, but
were somewhat afraid of her.

1296.   MacCracken, Henry Noble. "Tribute of a Friend," Vassar
        Alumnae Magazine (January), p. 5. Photograph.
   A penetrating sketch by the president of Vassar who says:
"We differed on many subjects, but were always the closest of
friends." A brief but detailed picture of Washburn as a human
being and a professional. This same page describes the Washburn
Memorial Fund and plans for a memorial service.

1297. Hincks, Elizabeth M. "Tribute of a Former Pupil," Vassar
       Alumnae Magazine (January), p. 6. Photograph.
       Presents the view of Washburn as a brilliant lecturer and a
fair, but demanding teacher. An especially interesting note on
the changed view Hincks had of Washburn when they met many
years later, "I realized before that she had had no short comings
as a teacher, but now I knew she would be unequalled as a friend."

1298. Dallenbach, Karl M. "Margaret Floy Washburn, 1871-1939,"
       The American Journal of Psychology, 53 (January), pp. 1-
       5. Photograph.
       A biographical sketch which is notable for the amount of
and careful attention to detail.

1299. Martin, Mabel F. "The Psychological Contributions of Mar-
       garet Floy Washburn," The American Journal of Psychology,
       53 (January), pp. 7-18.
       A scholarly article loaded with useful documentation. Tech-
nical but vital for understanding Washburn's professional career.

1300. Kambouropoulou, Polyxenie. "A Bibliography of the Writ-
       ings of Margaret Floy Washburn: 1928-1939," The American
       Journal of Psychology, 53 (January), pp. 19-20.
       A detailed and carefully organized list.

1301. Pillsbury, W[alter] B. "Margaret Floy Washburn (1871-
       1939)," The Psychological Review, 47 (March), pp. 99-109.
       Written by Washburn's fellow graduate student under Titchen-
er at Cornell, this memorial tribute emphasizes the significance of
her research and contains important material on the development
of her views as a student and professor. Pillsbury adds perspective to her own account (1292), for their long and cordial association allows him to present a balanced, though admiring portrait.

                              1943

1302. Anon. "Washburn, Margaret Floy," The National Cyclopaedia
       of American Biography (2), 30, p. 248. Photograph.
       Some family background and educational record followed by
a presentation of her scientific output. Several significant publications are cited. Includes a few personal glimpses and mentions
her contributions to professional organizations.

                              1949

1303. Woodworth, Robert S. "Margaret Floy Washburn. 1871-
       1939," Biographical Memoirs of the National Academy of Sci-
       ences, 25, pp. 275-295. Photograph.
       A beautifully written and informative article. While Wood-

worth places major emphasis on Washburn's scientific work, he introduces personal detail in a most charming fashion. There are some
quotations from her writing and an unprejudiced evaluation of the
importance of her studies. An ample bibliography of both Washburn's publications and writings about her.

1958

1304.	Woodworth, Robert S. "Washburn, Margaret Floy," Dictionary
	of American Biography (14), suppl. 2, pp. 698-699.
	A biography emphasizing Washburn's professional career.
Discusses her contributions as a scholar and as a teacher, particularly her influence on students. Reviews the nature of her scholarly work, especially her pioneering efforts at involving undergraduate students in meaningful, publishable research.

1971

1305.	Boring, Edwin G. "Washburn, Margaret Floy," Notable
	American Women (30), 3, pp. 546-548.
	This biography underscores the magnitude and importance
of Washburn's scholarly contributions. It describes her philosophy
regarding the schools of psychological thought current during her
lifetime, and it points out the extent to which she involved her
undergraduate students in her research. This article has much
of the personal flavor of her own autobiographical memoir (1292).

1978

1306.	Harper, Betty S. "Washburn, Margaret Floy," Biographical
	Dictionary of American Educators (38), 3, pp. 1352-1353.
	Limited biographical information and a useful but incomplete
bibliography. Lists several of her publications with dates.

1980

1307.	Goodman, Elizabeth S. "Margaret F. Washburn (1871-1939):
	First Woman Ph.D. in Psychology," Psychology of Women
	Quarterly, 5, pp. 69-80.
	Fully documented and smoothly written, this article covers
Washburn's entire life and career. Asks some questions about her
motivation for staying at a small, undergraduate college when she
was one of the most highly respected people in the field; offers
exciting possibilities for future research on women in science.

1308. ETHEL DENCH PUFFER HOWES
       10 October 1872--unknown
       Howes taught mathematics at Smith College for three years
following her graduation (AB, 1891) and then studied at the Universities of Berlin and Freiburg. Upon her return she taught psychology at Radcliffe College while completing her education (PhD,
1902).
       During the next five years she taught psychology at Sim-
mons and Wellesley Colleges and was promoted to associate professor at the latter school. She was interested in the psychology of
symmetry and esthetics. She earned a star in the second edition
of American Men of Science (1910) as one of the 1,000 most distinguished American scientists.

1309. Howes is cited in American Men of Science, 1906-1921;
       Woman's Who's Who of America, p. 409.

1310. FLORENCE MacLEAN WINGER BAGLEY
       7 January 1874--12 August 1952
       Bagley was educated at the University of Nebraska (AB,
1895; AM, 1898). She studied at Cornell University in 1900 where
she was interested in the esthetics of color and published an article in the American Journal of Psychology on Fechner's color rings
in 1902. The previous year she married William C. Bagley, a noted
educational psychologist, at Teachers College of Columbia University.

1311. Bagley is cited in American Men of Science, 1906-1910;
       Woman's Who's Who of America, p. 65.
       We are indebted to Joseph G. Svoboda, Archivist of the Uni-
versity of Nebraska, for his help in trying to learn more about
Bagley.

1312. HELEN BRADFORD THOMPSON WOOLLEY
       6 November 1874--24 December 1947
       Woolley was educated at the University of Chicago (PhB,
1897; PhD, 1900). Her dissertation was published under its original title, Psychological Norms in Men and Women and later as The
Mental Traits of Sex. She continued her studies in Paris and Berlin before joining the faculty at Mount Holyoke College. She taught
for only three years before her marriage to the pathologist Paul G.
Woolley. With him she spent several years in the Orient where she
worked in the Philippines Bureau of Education for a short time.
       From 1911 to 1921 the Woolleys lived in Cincinnati, and she
was appointed director of the Bureau for the Investigation of Working Children. In that position she was able to make numerous comparisons of working and school children and to publish a series of

reports and the important monograph <u>Mental and Physical Measure-</u>
<u>ments of Working Children</u>. The results of these researches were
important in her successful drive to induce the Ohio legislature
to pass the Bing Law for regulating compulsory school attendance
and child labor practices.

In 1922 Woolley became associate director of the Merrill-
Palmer School in Detroit. Here she organized one of the first nursery schools in the country. Her extraordinary skill in observing
children and in interpreting their motivation enabled her to make
good use of the laboratory aspects of this new psychological tool.
Her publications rapidly became classics and led to the development
of the Merrill-Palmer Scale of Mental Tests. Woolley's skill as .a
speaker and her ability to write for the layperson contributed greatly to the growing movement for broader interest in child development. These contributions were especially evident in her work with
the American Association of University Women of which she was vice-
president in 1923-1925.

Woolley was particularly able when it came to the difficult
task of integrating different fields of research. She was an important figure in the application of education, welfare, and social legislation to improve the lives of women and children. This characteristic is well illustrated by her last major publication, a chapter
on "Eating, Sleeping and Elimination" in <u>A Handbook of Child Psy-</u>
<u>chology</u>. Here she brought together research in nutrition, pedi-
atrics, education, psychiatry, and psychology in a constructive
view of the child as a whole. Woolley earned a star in the third
edition of <u>American Men of Science (1921)</u> as one of the 1,000 most
distinguished American scientists. (See also 1223.)

1935

1313. Fowler, Cedric. "They Train the Young Idea," <u>New Out-</u>
       <u>look</u>, 165 (February), pp. 32, 35.
       Woolley is included in a presentation of the leaders in the
development of the nursery school movement. Examines her fundamental contributions to this educational innovation and places them
in the context of the times.

1948

1314. Anon. "Laureate Members--In Memoriam. Helen Bradford
       Thompson Woolley," <u>Educational Forum</u>, 12 (May), pp. 506r-
       506s.
       Notes the death of a member elected in 1925. Mentions her
educational and professional background and several of her books.

1971

1315. Zapoleon, Marguerite W., and Lois Meek Stolz. "Woolley,

Helen Bradford Thompson," <u>Notable American Women</u>, (30),
3, pp. 657-660.

A long and well-written biography which blends together all
of the varied facets of Woolley's personality and career. In the
development of such a novel concept as the early education movement, the leading people bring together such diverse activities that
they are difficult to describe in a limited space. The authors have
done a remarkable job and their collaborative product reads smoothly. The bibliography is unusually useful.

<u>1978</u>

1316.   Wertheim, Sally H.   "Woolley, Helen Bradford Thompson,"
        <u>Biographical Dictionary of American Educators</u> (38), 3, pp.
        1438-1439.

        Provides biographical data and lists Woolley's most signifi-
cant professional positions and publications. Points out her active
role as a community leader.

1317.   JUNE ETTA DOWNEY
        13 July 1875--11 October 1932

        Downey made her entire career at the University of Wyom-
ing (AB, 1895) and played a key role in the growth and development of that small and remote university. Originally her interests
were in Classics, and she majored in Latin and Greek. After a
year of teaching, however, she became excited about the relationship between psychology and esthetics. She began study at the
University of Chicago (AM, 1898) and returned to Wyoming as instructor in English. She spent a sabbatical leave back at Chicago
(PhD, 1908) and her dissertation, <u>Control Processes in Modified</u>
<u>Handwriting</u>, was published in the monograph series of the <u>Psy-</u>
<u>chological Review</u>.

        Wyoming promoted Downey to professor in 1905, the first
woman to head a department of psychology in a state university.
She had few graduate students and a heavy teaching load, but her
own determination and her skillful use of undergraduate collaborators resulted in an impressive research bibliography. In addition
to her 76 scientific publications listed in the <u>Psychological Register</u>
she wrote 29 literary books and articles. Perhaps the most interesting and difficult of these publications was <u>Kingdom of the Mind</u>;
her effort to present experimental psychology to children.

        Downey worked in many different areas of psychology: cre-
ativity, voluntary and involuntary motor controls, imagery, and
esthetics. Her design of experiments was often imaginative. Her
interest in the analysis of personality through handwriting is probably her best known research and led to the Will-Temperament Test
also closely associated with her. This work, which has been shown
to have serious limitations, is still regarded as a pioneering venture

and did stimulate a great deal of later research by Downey and others.

The contributions she made were recognized in several ways, for example, she was the first woman elected to the Society of Experimentalists and served on the council of the American Psychological Association (1923-1925). She earned a star in the fourth edition of American Men of Science (1926) as one of the 1,000 most distinguished American scientists. (See also 1223.)

1932

1318. Uhrbrock, R[ichard] S[tephen]. "Obituary. June Etta Downey," Science, 76 (23 December), pp. 585-586.
    Describes her career as a researcher and notes several of her most outstanding books. Say she was "an indefatigable worker [and] kind, generous and human." Some information is given of her educational background.

1933

1319. Anderson, John E. "June Etta Downey: 1875-1932," American Journal of Psychology, 45 (April), pp. 362-363.
    Almost entirely devoted to her contributions to psychology this memorial, while specialized, is most useful. The sequential development of her professional career is carefully outlined.

1320. Uhrbrock, Richard Stephen. "June Etta Downey," Journal of General Psychology, 9, pp. 351-364. Photograph.
    In addition to descriptions of Downey as a person and teacher this article deals extensively with her research. Each of her several interests is carefully developed and their part in her total professional career outlined. The bibliography is drawn from the complete one prepared by Lillian Portenier and shows the literary side of Downey's writings.

1934

*1321. In Memoriam, June Etta Downey, 1875-1932.
    The basic source of biographical information [from Notable American Women (1322)].

1971

1322. Burnham, John Chynoweth. "Downey, June Etta," Notable American Women (30), 1, pp. 514-515.
    A nicely balanced account of Downey's career without neglecting the biographical details. An especially strong description

of her method of research and an evaluation of the value of her contributions.

1323. NAOMI NORSWORTHY
       29 September 1877--25 December 1916
       While her career was tragically brief, Norsworthy made important contributions to our understanding of the feebleminded. She received her first education from the Trenton State Normal School (Diploma, 1896) and taught in the public school of Morristown until 1899. She began graduate work at Teachers College of Columbia University (PhD, 1904) and remained there for the rest of her life. Norsworthy's dissertation, The Psychology of Mentally Deficient Children, provided convincing evidence that the feebleminded are not a type, but the condition is a matter of degree. Her work was a forecast of the basic concept of mental age. She wrote other books, two of which were completed and published by her colleagues after her death. However, it was as an inspiring and demanding teacher that she made her most profound contribution. (See also 1223.)

1916

1324. Anon. "Dr. Naomi Norsworthy Dies," The New York Times, 66 (26 December), p. 11.
       Cites her two most important books and her teaching at Teachers College.

1917

1325. Anon. "College News and Departmental Notes. Service in Memory of Professor Norsworthy," Teachers College Record, 18, pp. 85-91. Photograph.
       A short biography, tributes, and remarks by the dean and two colleagues. The Chaplain's prayer is included.

1918

*1326. Higgens, Caldwell. The Life of Naomi Norsworthy. Boston.

1934

1327. M[ary] T. W[hitley]. "Norsworthy, Naomi," Dictionary of American Biography (14), 13, pp. 557-558.
       Gives her high praise as a teacher with great feeling for students but, "conscientious to an extreme degree [and] scorning

superficiality." Discusses her contributions and concludes that
she did pioneering work in several fields, but did not go far in
them.

1978

1328. Johnsen, Gary C. "Norsworthy, Naomi," Biographical
       Dictionary of American Educators (38), 2, p. 951.
       Cites her outstanding public speaking ability. A useful
bibliography.

1329. KATE GORDON
       18 February 1878--unknown
       Gordon was educated at the University of Chicago (PhB,
1900; PhD, 1903). Following a year of study as a fellow of the
Collegiate Alumnae Association, she joined the faculty of Mount Holyoke College in 1904 where she was promoted to associate professor
the following year. Gordon spent a year at Columbia University's
Teachers College and four years on the faculty of Bryn Mawr College. She was appointed at the Carnegie Institute of Technology
in 1916 and rose to associate professor in 1919. Her scholarly interests centered on the areas of memory, attention, and the esthetics of color. She was also interested in the development of mental
tests for children.

1330. Gordon is cited in American Men of Science, 1906-1910.

1331. MABEL CLARE WILLIAMS KEMMERER
       6 November 1878--1981?
       Kemmerer was a member of the faculty of the University of
Iowa, where she was educated (PhB, 1899; PhD, 1903), until her
marriage to Theodore W. Kemmerer in 1924. She continued to have
responsibilities for correspondence courses until her retirement in
1936. She was the first woman to receive a doctoral degree from
Iowa. Her interests were chiefly in the areas of early memories,
color vision, and visual illusions. She published a book entitled
Some Psychology in 1930 in which she refers to herself as "sometime associate professor of psychology." She was promoted to that
rank in 1921.

1332. Williams is cited in American Men of Science, 1906-1921.
       We are indebted to Earl M. Rogers, Curator of Archives at
the University of Iowa, for his efforts to help us learn about
Williams-Kemmerer.

1333.   AUGUSTA FOX BRONNER HEALY
        22 July 1881--11 December 1966
        One of the true pioneers in the study and counseling of
juvenile delinquents, Healy and her husband, William Healy, provide an excellent example of teamwork. In fact one of their most
important contributions was the introduction of the team approach
in which the social worker and psychologist met on an equal basis
with the physician in conferences for diagnosis and treatment.
After Healy finished the program of the Louisville Normal School
in 1901, she taught for two years and then entered Teachers College of Columbia University (BS, 1906; AM, 1909). In these and
later years she studied with both the theoretically inclined psychologists of Columbia and the more practical group at Teachers College. During this same period and continuing until 1911 she taught
English at her old Louisville Girls' High School. Throughout her
career she had a special feeling for and ability to work with children, especially young girls.
        She completed her studies at Columbia (PhD, 1914.)
Her dissertation, published as A Comparative Study of the Intelligence of Delinquent Girls, is considered a standard work. Its appearance at the very beginning of the serious use of mental testing by psychologists is noteworthy. The previous summer she had
attended a series of lectures given by William Healy at Harvard.
He was just beginning an extensive research program on the motivation of juvenile offenders in Chicago. When he recognized the
interest and talent Bronner displayed, he offered her a position
in the Chicago Juvenile Psychopathic Institute. Thus, began the
joint career which contributed so largely to this new field.
        The team moved to Boston in 1917 to open the Judge Baker
Foundation, later renamed the Judge Baker Guidance Center. The
major reason for this relocation was their desire to extend their
research activities by also being involved in the follow-up treatment
of their cases. Successful in this objective, theirs became a model
for many other similar groups. While it is true that Bronner limited
herself by electing to stay in Healy's shadow, together they accomplished a great deal in an extraordinarily difficult area. Bronner
was president of the American Orthopsychiatric Association in 1932.
(See also 1223.)

                                1934

1334.   Stevenson, George S., and Geddes Smith. Child Guidance
        Clinics. A Quarter Century of Development. New York:
        The Commonwealth Fund, index.
        This book traces the origins and development of child guid-
ance clinics, their cases, services, and usefulness in research.
It should be noted that in 1919 there were only seven clinics na-
tionwide, and the charts show an astonishing increase explained
by the succeeding chapters. Bronner is mentioned as Healy's assistant and as a member of an advisory committee "to formulate a

plan for work in child welfare" for the Commonwealth Fund, and
as the co-author of two books.

1948

1335. Healy, William, and Augusta F. Bronner. "The Child Guid-
       ance Clinic, Birth and Growth of an Idea," in Orthopsychia-
       try, 1923-1948. Retrospect and Prospect. Menasha, Wis-
       consin: George Banta Publishing Co.
       The second part of this section, "The Later Years," involves
Bronner's contribution and deals with the Judge Baker Foundation
in Boston in 1917 to "investigate the problems of delinquency." A
discussion of their methods, findings, and "teaching ventures" is
followed by a summary and bibliography.

1966

1336. Anon. "Obituaries. Mrs. A. B. Healy," The Boston Globe,
       690 (12 December), p. 36.
       Says she was a researcher at Yale and cites several of her
books.

1980

1337. Burnham, John C. "Bronner, Augusta Fox," Notable American
       Women (30), 4, pp. 108-110.
       Included with the standard biographical details is a nice de-
scription of the ways in which this husband-wife team organized
their individual contributions. The story of the development of
the child guidance clinics is well told.

1338. LETA ANNA STETTER HOLLINGWORTH
       25 May 1886--27 November 1939
       At college Hollingworth was most interested in writing, but
decided to be practical and obtain a teaching certificate as well.
She did teach for two years following graduation from the University of Nebraska (BA, 1906). When she moved to New York with
her husband, a graduate student and later professor at Columbia
University, she found that there were no openings in the school
system for married women and no markets for her writing.
       After their financial situation improved, Hollingworth took
graduate work at Columbia (MA, 1913) and worked in clinical testing and psychology in conjunction with Bellevue Hospital. She completed her education at Columbia (PhD, 1916) and the following year
helped in the founding of the American Association of Clinical Psychology. She also accepted a position on the faculty of Teachers

College where she remained for the rest of her life. She was promoted to professor of education in 1929. Hollingworth's first area
of research was the alleged sex difference of women. Her doctoral
dissertation showed no difference in the mental and motor skills
of women near or in the menstrual period as compared with similar
tests of men. Her views were not in accord with the views of some
of her eminent colleagues, but her reputation among scientists was
unquestionable and was one result of her carefully documented research. Her stimulating lectures made her popular in feminist circles. She and her husband marched together in suffrage parades,
but it was in the reform of attitudes, rather than in political reform, that she saw hope for the future of women.

Later, in the 1920's and 1930's, Hollingworth shifted her
interests to the exceptional child. She made lasting contributions
with her studies of gifted children. At Teachers College she established a Guidance Laboratory to carry out testing and counseling, and she worked as a consultant to school systems to obtain
research data. She was a key person in the establishment, in 1936,
of the Speyer School for children with exceptionally high I.Q.'s.
Her books, Gifted Children and Children Above 180 I.Q. published
in 1926 and posthumously in 1942 were often cited and represent
very significant contributions to this emerging field. She developed
the concept of "optimum intelligence" in which she felt that the best
total adjustment occurred in the narrow Stanford-Binet range of
125 to 155 I.Q.

The Hollingworths received joint honorary degrees from the
University of Nebraska in 1938, and a conference on the education
of the gifted child was held in her honor at Teachers College in
1940. (See also 23, 48, 1223.)

<u>1939</u>

1339. Anon. "Mrs. Hollingworth of Columbia Staff," The New York
       Times, 89 (28 November), p. 25.
       Outlines her education and states her position as head of
the Speyer School.

1340. Anon. "Dr. Leta Hollingworth, 53, Dies; Experimental Edu-
       cation Leader," New York Herald Tribune, 99 (28 November),
       p. 18.
       Founder of the Speyer School devoted to finding the best
methods to educate exceptional children. Gives a biography and
several titles of her books.

<u>1940</u>

1341. Gates, Arthur I. "Obituary. Leta S. Hollingworth,"
       Science, 91 (5 January), pp. 9-11.
       A detailed, useful biography. Author says Hollingworth

had a deep faith in the power of honest scientific work to promote
human welfare.

1342. Poffenberger, A. T. "Leta Stetter Hollingworth: 1886-1939,"
      The American Journal of Psychology, 53 (April), pp. 299-
      301.
      Treats her professional career in detail saying that there is
a constant thread of interest in individual and group differences.
She was an active supporter of the feminist movement and, "an ardent champion of the superior child."

1943

1343. Hollingworth, Harry L. Leta Stetter Hollingworth. A Biog-
      raphy. Lincoln, Nebraska: University of Nebraska Press,
      204 pp. Photographs.
      A biography by a loving husband and a devoted colleague.
Many heavily edited quotations from her letters. The author has
an ambivalent attitude about publishing any of her words at all.
He wrote about her early life by piecing together odd bits of information, except for the first year when her mother kept a detailed account. Some of her poetry is reprinted, which is important, but one wishes her husband hadn't been quite so fearful.
Limited bibliography.

1344. [Devoted to Papers Honoring Leta S. Hollingworth], Teachers
      College Record, 42 (December), pp. 183-238.
      The Foreword entitled, "Education and the Individual," is
by Arthur I. Gates (1341) and the Introduction is by Harry L.
Hollingworth (1343). The six articles are written by her former
students and each deals with a subject on which she lectured,
taught, wrote, or conducted research. In effect each of the papers examines to some extent Hollingworth's contribution to that
subfield. This is an extremely valuable collection.

1971

1345. Roemele, Victoria S. "Hollingworth, Leta Anna Stetter,"
      Notable American Women (30), 2, pp. 206-208.
      The author is a good storyteller and Hollingworth's life is
a good story. She brings together the close, loving relationship
between this couple who apparently shared their lives completely.
The interplay between academic psychological research and feminist
action is well presented.

1975

1346. Shields, Stephanie A. "Ms. Pilgrim's Progress. The

Contributions of Leta Stetter Hollingworth to the Psychology of Women," American Psychologist, 30 (August), pp. 852-857.

A detailed and scholarly review of her work but also a good biographical introduction. Illustrates Hollingworth's careful documentation with relevant literature. She always had faith that the conflicts she saw so clearly would be resolved.

1347. Benjamin, Ludy T., Jr. "The Pioneering Work of Leta Hollingworth in the Psychology of Women," Nebraska History, 56 (Winter), pp. 493-505. Photograph.
       A well-documented study with much biographical detail.

1978

1348. Schimizzi, Ned V. "Hollingworth, Leta Anna Stetter," Biographical Dictionary of American Educators (38), 2, p. 660.
       A career summary outlining the general direction of her research interests. Cites several books and gives a short bibliography.

1982

1349. Kuenhold, Sandra. "Leta Stetter Hollingworth," American Women Writers (48), 2, pp. 315-317.
       Gives a short, but balanced picture of Hollingworth's several career interests. Mentions her book of poetry. A limited bibliography.

1350. FLORENCE LAURA GOODENOUGH
       6 August 1886--4 April 1959
       Following her graduation from the Normal School in Millersville, Pennsylvania (BPd, 1908), Goodenough taught in various schools of Pennsylvania and New Jersey. She was especially interested by her work at the Vineland (New Jersey) Training School which served retarded children. During this same time she was continuing her education at Columbia University (BS, 1920; AM, 1921). She then moved to Stanford University (PhD, 1924) where she worked with Lewis M. Terman who was starting his exciting studies of mental measurements of gifted children.

       Goodenough became chief psychologist at the Minneapolis Child Guidance Clinic in 1925 and the following year was appointed to the Institute of Child Welfare of the University of Minnesota. She continued as research professor at this institution until her retirement in 1947. From the time of her doctoral dissertation, Measurement of Intelligence by Drawings, she argued convincingly against the narrow study of single behavior units and for the study of individual differences in reactions to a variety of environmental and developmental growth stages. This position brought her square-ly into the center of the great nature-nurture debates of the 1930's and 1940's.

Through her extensive and penetrating writings Goodenough made major contributions to the growth and usefulness of tools for the measurement and interpretation of intelligence in children. Her Handbook of Child Psychology first published in 1931 and her crea-tion of the Minnesota Preschool Scale for the early estimation of mental ability were both widely recognized as important contribu-tions. Perhaps her most important, and constantly held, theme was the serious error of thinking that I.Q. is a constant with the result that children were placed in unchangeable boxes at an early age.

The importance of Goodenough's work is evident in the es-teem in which she was held by her peers. She was president of the National Council of Women Psychologists in 1942, but hoped for its "early demise" and the elimination of sexual differences in her profession. She was also president of the Society for Research in Child Development in 1946-1947 and Division 7 of the American Psy-chological Association in 1947. In the sixth edition of American Men of Science (1937) she earned a star as one of the 1,000 most distinguished American scientists. (See also 1223.)

1959

1351. Harris, Dale B. "Florence L. Goodenough, 1886-1959,"
Child Development, 30, pp. 305-306. Photograph.
Details of her birth and education. Author calls her one of the most distinguished scholars of her time. She was rigorous and exacting as a scholar; human and humane as a teacher; a lover of birds, flowers and music; a bibliophile and a noteworthy amateur photographer.

1980

1352. Wolf, Theta Holmes. "Goodenough, Florence Laura,"
Notable American Women (30), 4, pp. 284-286.
A detailed picture of the development of Goodenough's in-terest in and contributions to psychology. Wolf is especially good in describing exactly the position she took in the debates over I.Q. measurement. An important bibliography since so little has been published on her career.

1353. MARIE GERTRUDE RAND FERREE
29 October 1886--30 June 1970

Rand began her education at Cornell University (AB, 1908) and continued at Bryn Mawr College (AM, PhD, 1911). Her research director, Clarence E. Ferree, urged her to continue their work, and she remained at Bryn Mawr as a postdoctoral fellow and later as a research associate until 1927. Rand and Ferree were married in 1918 and worked in close collaboration until his death in 1942.

Rand's dissertation and much of the subsequent work she and Ferree carried out dealt with the color sensitivity of the retina. From these studies they developed the Ferree-Rand perimeter which became an important tool for the diagnosis of vision problems. Later, at the Wilmer Ophthalmological Institute of the Johns Hopkins University School of Medicine and the Research Laboratory of Physiological Optics in Baltimore, Rand and Ferree conducted a number of important studies as industrial consultants. One of their most notable projects was the illumination of New York's Holland Tunnel.

After her husband's death Rand became a research associate at the Knapp Foundation of the Columbia University College of Physicians and Surgeons where she began again to study color vision. In collaboration with Legrand Hardy and M. Catherine Rittler she developed the Hardy-Rand-Rittler plates which allowed ophthalmologists and psychologists to determine the type and degree of the vision defects they studied.

Rand was recognized by her colleagues as having made truly important contributions to her field. She was the first woman elected a fellow of the Illuminating Engineering Society in 1952 and received the Society's Gold Medal in 1963. She was the first woman to receive the Edgar D. Tillyer Medal of the Optical Society of America in 1959. (See also 23.)

1946

1354.   Anon.   "Rand, Gertrude," The National Cyclopaedia of
        American Biography (2), G, p. 480.
        The essential biographical facts: family background, education, research interests, publications, and honors.

1959

1355.   Ogle, Kenneth N.   "Gertrude Rand.   Edgar D. Tillyer
        Medalist for 1959," Journal of the Optical Society of America,
        49 (October), pp. 937-941.   Photograph.
        Actually the text of the citation read at the presentation of this medal to Rand.   A nice biographical sketch, but centers on her research contributions.   A detailed but selected bibliography of her publications.

1963

*1356. Lighting News (August and November).

1970

1357. Anon. "Dr. Gertrude Rand, 84, Dead; Researcher on Human Vision," The New York Times, 119 (2 July), p. 35.
She and her husband often worked jointly and they held
several patents. Her research in vision was both theoretical and
practical. Mentions some of her honors.

1980

1358. Garber, Elizabeth. "Rand, Marie Gertrude," Notable American
Women (30), 4, p. 565.
Provides a good picture of Rand's life and career, but leaves
you wishing a little more detail had been added.

1359. CHARLOTTE BERTHA BÜHLER
20 December 1893--3 February 1974
Bühler studied first at the University of Freiburg and completed her undergraduate education at the University of Berlin in
1914-1915. She refused the great honor of an assistantship with
Carl Stumpf because she recognized that her own interests in thought
processes were quite different from his interests in feelings. Instead she moved to the University of Munich where she met, and
later married, Karl Bühler. Following her graduation (PhD, 1918)
they began a 20-year period of productive and highly original work.
At the Dresden Institute of Technology, where she became
the first woman privatdozent in 1920, they shifted from the currently fashionable emphasis on physics to a biological approach to
psychology. When Bühler returned to Europe after a year of study
with Edward Thorndike at Columbia University on one of the first
Rockefeller Exchange fellowships, she joined her husband at the
University of Vienna. They founded a psychological institute, and
she was made head of a child psychology department which proved
most innovative. It was during this time in Vienna that Bühler
developed the approach of studying life biography using her collection of adolescent diaries.
As World War II became inevitable the happy productive days
in Vienna came to an end and, like so many other Jewish scholars,
the Bühlers were forced to flee. After two years in Oslo they came
to the United States and faced a long succession of non-positions
and lack of research opportunity. Bühler refused to be overcome
by these difficulties and began a private practice of psychotherapy
and continued to publish widely, including one of her most important

works, Psychologie im Leben unserer Zeit. She also played a key
role in arranging the Old Saybrook Conference and later became
president of the new Association for Humanistic Psychology. (See
also 1223.)

1972

*1360. Bühler, Charlotte B. [Autobiographical statement], in
Psychologie in Selbsdarstellungen. Ludwig J. Pongratz,
editor. Berne. pp. 9-42. In German.

1973

*1361. Anon. "The Discoverer of the Child," Die Welt (20 Decem-
ber). In German.

1974

1362. Havighurst, Robert J. "Charlotte Bühler," Human Development, 17, pp. 397-398.
    Makes a point of the good fortune American psychology had
when the Nazis drove out so many intellectuals. Calls her an "in-
domitable woman." Quotes her on advice to the woman's movement,
"do your best and ask no favors."

1363. Massarik, Fred. "Charlotte Bühler: A Reflection," Journal
of Humanistic Psychology, 14 (Summer), pp. 4-6. Photograph.
    The warmth of this highly personal tribute can be sensed
in the words of the author, "Charlotte Bühler has made a difference in my life as a psychologist--but more importantly as a human
being." Leaves the technical detail of her professional career to
others and treats the spirit of her life's work.

1980

1364. Allen, Melanie. "Bühler, Charlotte Bertha," Notable American
Women (30), 4, pp. 119-121.
    A smooth reading and descriptive biography with the appro-
priate technical detail. Still the human drama of the refugee family and the upheaval caused by war are clear. In spite of these
difficulties Bühler carries on her career to the end and makes important contributions. A good biographical sketch.

1365. CAROLINE BEAUMONT ZACHRY
       20 April 1894--22 February 1945

One of the leaders of the progressive education movement, Zachry strongly influenced efforts to make schools more concerned with the social development of the child. She graduated from Teachers College of Columbia University (BS, 1924) and taught for two years in the experimental Lincoln School. Her graduate education was also at Teachers College (MA, 1925; PhD, 1929). Her dissertations reveal that she was already deeply interested in the ways in which psychology could influence teachers. A rare opportunity to spend a year in Vienna with Carl Jung confirmed beyond doubt her interest and ability in psychology. The educational question of new teaching methods was replaced by a serious examination of the development of school children.

Fortunately she was also a talented administrator and could see to the implementation of the results of psychological research in the schools. In this role she made a truly great impact. She directed a study of adolescence for the Commission on Secondary School Curriculum of the Progressive Education Association from 1934 to 1939. The results were published as Emotion and Conduct in Adolescence; her best-known book. As director of the Institute for the Study of Personality Development, which was later renamed the Caroline B. Zachry Institute of Human Development, she continued this work until 1942 when Fiorello La Guardia appointed her director of the Bureau of Child Guidance of the New York City Board of Education.

Zachry's emphasis on social development as the school's chief responsibility has been used perhaps excessively, but it also played a role in deemphasizing the equally excessive child-centered philosophy. There can be little doubt that she influenced later workers such as Elizabeth Irwin and Benjamin Spock, both of whom spoke of her importance in their development. In spite of the fact that she was not a psychiatrist, she was elected a fellow of the American Orthopsychiatric Association.

1945

1366. Anon. "Caroline Zachry, Psychologist, 50," The New York Times, 94 (24 February), p. 11. Photograph.
Notes that she was the first woman to head the Bureau of Child Guidance and that she organized and directed the Mental Health Institute.

1971

1367. Graham, Patricia Albjerg. "Zachry, Caroline Beaumont," Notable American Women (30), 3, pp. 701-702.
A thoughtful description of how Zachry moved from the traditional psychology of her time to an interest in the role that discipline could play in the teaching process. There are undeveloped hints about her being "moderately successful as a teacher" and her "much greater success in working with prospective

and practicing teachers." One might wish to see this theme developed.

1368. ELSE FRENKEL-BRUNSWIK
       18 August 1908--31 March 1958
       Frenkel-Brunswik was educated at the University of Vienna
(PhD, 1930) and remained there until 1938. She was always an
active participant in psychoanalysis, a field of which the intellectual capital was certainly Vienna. This aspect of her life together
with her association with the "Vienna Circle" became the source
for her productive career in the United States. It was also in this
group which developed the logical positivism approach that she met
her future husband, Egon Brunswik.
       After their marriage at the University of California in Berke-
ley, she became a research psychologist at the Institute of Child
Welfare where she remained for the rest of her career. She published the results of her studies in Vienna, Mechanisms of Self De-
ception, based on her psychoanalysis. Soon after, in 1940, she
began publishing on the relationship of psychoanalysis to the psychology of personality. These works came at just the right time
since her background in psychoanalysis and logical positivism was
necessary for the growing American interest in clinical psychology.
She played an influential role by bringing some balance between
the competing forces of behaviorism which insisted on tying concepts tightly to measurement and the more speculative forms of psychoanalysis.
       After 1942 she, along with Nevitt Sanford, Daniel Levinson
and, later, Theodor Adorno, began major studies of anti-Semitism.
The work which resulted, The Authoritarian Personality, has been
considered a major and lasting influence in the study of prejudice.
This work has also been sharply criticized for flaws of several kinds,
but it is still considered a classic effort in social science. Following the suicide of her husband she was never able to regain the
research momentum of her earlier career. (See also 1223.)

                              1968

1369. Levinson, Daniel J. "Frenkel-Brunswik, Else," Internation-
       al Encyclopedia of the Social Sciences. David L. Sills, edi-
       tor, vol. 5, pp. 559-562.
       A brief, but detailed biographical study with a careful eval-
uation of the methodology and results of her research.

                              1980

1370. Smith, M. Brewster. "Frenkel-Brunswik, Else," Notable
       American Women (30), 4, pp. 250-252.

A full and readable discussion of her training and scientific contributions. There is a fine presentation of the difficulties faced by women in the academic community. Smith also presents Frenkel-Brunswik's unique position relative to the development of interest in psychoanalysis in the United States.

SCIENCE WRITERS AND ARTISTS

(See also 215, 328, 413, 415, 681, 1123)

1371. MARIA MARTIN
       3 July 1796--27 December 1863
       Nothing is known of Martin's education, but her art and
correspondence show that she was well educated and drawn to intellectual questions. She lived most of her life in the home of her
sister, the wife of John Bachman. It is possible that he influenced
her interest in natural history, and it is certainly through him that
she became the collaborator of James Audubon.
       Audubon visited the Bachmans in Charleston in 1831 and
encouraged Martin's development of her artistic talent. He taught
her to paint birds, and she began to prepare the background for
his watercolors of American birds. He had high praise for her work,
and she contributed many of the backgrounds for his Birds of America printed in England and later for the American editions.
       After her sister's death Martin married Bachman, and they
worked together in his collaboration with Audubon and his sons
on The Viviparous Quadrupeds of North America. Later she made
drawings of some reptiles of Carolina for the North American Her-
petology of John E. Holbrook.
       Martin, one of America's best nineteenth-century nature art-
ists, continued her friendship and correspondence with Audubon
until his death in 1851. He clearly respected her and appreciated
her talent; he named a particular woodpecker for her.

1917

1372. Herick, Francis Hobart. Audubon the Naturalist. A His-
       tory of His Life and Time. New York: D. Appleton, index.
       Several interesting notes on Martin, some in the words of
Audubon from a diary he kept on visits to Charleston.

1960

1373. Coffin, Annie Roulhac. "Maria Martin (1796-1863)," Art
       Quarterly, 23 (Autumn), pp. 281-300.
       A fine contribution to our knowledge of Martin. Good schol-
arship and a large number of reproductions of her paintings.

1962

1374. Hollingsworth, Buckner. "Maria Martin. 1796-1863. Audubon's 'Sweetheart'--and a Fine Botanical Artist," in Her Garden Was Her Delight. New York: Macmillan, pp. 54-66.
Develops the part Martin played in Audubon's bird paintings along with a highly personal insight to her life of devotion and patience. Describes the contributions she made to her future husband's (John Bachman) work, The Viviparous Quadrupeds of America. Hollingsworth sums up her scientific career, "She was no great genius but hers was a sturdy talent worthy of all gratitude and respect."

1375. Hollingsworth, Buckner. "Maria Martin--Audubon Called Her Sweetheart," Audubon Magazine, 64 (July--August and September--October), pp. 197-199, 266-269.
Related to the chapter in her book (1374), but expanded and with a large collection of fine examples of her work. Not only the birds and plants she did with and for Audubon, but flowers and insects as well.

1965

1376. Coffin, Annie Roulhac. "Audubon's Friend--Maria Martin," The New York Historical Quarterly, 49 (January), pp. 28-51.
The general biographical material leads into a detailed study of the various paintings which are said to be Martin's, Audubon's, or their combined work. Presents evidence to help resolve these questions. Though a scholarly article, it reads well. Of special interest is the large number of Martin's paintings which are published for the first time. This is part of a full biography in preparation at that time.

1971

1377. Coffin, Annie Roulhac. "Martin, Maria," Notable American Women (30), 2, pp. 505-506.
Building on the earlier paper (1376) Coffin gives us the full story of Martin as well as it can be pieced together from the fragments available. It does not appear that her projected biography has yet appeared, but these two small samples make one hope it will.

1980

1378. Durant, Mary, and Michael Harwood. On the Road with John James Audubon. New York: Dodd, Mead, pp. 338-344.

The authors followed many of Audubon's travels using his
voluminous journals as a guide. What he said is clearly distinguished from their reactions. An unusual biographical form makes
this book enjoyable even though not much of it pertains to Martin.

1379. ELIZABETH CABOT CARY AGASSIZ
       5 December 1822--27 June 1907
       After her marriage to the naturalist Louis Agassiz, she be-
came his constant collaborator in scientific and educational efforts.
Several of the latter, such as the Anderson School of Natural History on Penikese Island, were of special importance in the education of women scientists. She kept records of most of his expeditions and the published accounts are, in large measure, the result
of her literary skill.
       After his death she collected his works and published Louis
Agassiz: His Life and Correspondence. Then she turned her ener-
gies to the cause of education for women where she showed a great
deal of tact and farsightedness. She became the president of the
Harvard Annex and later of its successor, Radcliffe College. She
insisted on equal treatment of the women in terms of the rigor and
quality of subject matter and teaching. (See also 1, 4, 9, 37, 48,
718.)

1902

1380. Anon. [Fund for Radcliffe], Science, 16 (26 December),
       p. 1039.
       In honor of Agassiz's 80th birthday $116,000 has been
raised for the construction of a students' house.

1904

1381. Anon. "Agassiz, Elizabeth Cabot (Cary)," The National
       Cyclopaedia of American Biography (2), 12, p. 46. Like-
       ness.
       Almost no mention of her scientific work or even of her
contributions to that of her husband. Deals largely with her work
in education and cites several publications.

1907

1382. Anon. "Obituary," Science, ns 26 (5 July), p. 3.
       Says she worked closely with her husband, Louis Agassiz,
and was president of Radcliffe College.

*1383. Gilman, Arthur. "Elizabeth Cary Agassiz: First President of
        Radcliffe College," Harvard Graduate's Magazine (September).

1919

1384. Paton, Lucy Allen. Elizabeth Cary Agassiz. A Biography.
Boston: Houghton Mifflin, 423 pp. Photographs.
This biography, written some ten years after Agassiz's death,
is rich in quotations and memories of her colleagues. The central
theme is her contributions to Radcliffe College, but it contains much
of interest with respect to her scientific accomplishments. There
are selected examples of her correspondence which the author admits are not representative for several reasons. Much of the correspondence was lost or too personal for publication. The author
also makes the significant point that Agassiz had such a close family life that she wrote to a very limited circle other than those in
Germany and Switzerland. This book is an important resource.

1928

1385. D[onald] C. P[eattie]. "Agassiz, Elizabeth Cabot Cary,"
Dictionary of American Biography (14), 1, p. 114.
Short. Makes one comment about her interest in natural
history; "her service to science as Agassiz's amanuensis and biographer cannot be exaggerated."

1971

1386. Hawkins, Hugh. "Agassiz, Elizabeth Cabot Cary," Notable
American Women (30), 1, pp. 22-25.
A good biography; like most in this series, it attempts to
present the whole person. A number of excellent quotations, some
attention to Agassiz's contribution to science and more detail on
her role at Radcliffe.

1978

1387. Bredemeier, Nancy. "Agassiz, Elizabeth Cabot Cary,"
Biographical Dictionary of American Educators (38), 1, pp.
14-15.
Pays more attention to her scientific accomplishments than
the others. Mentions the Anderson School and her book First Les-
sons in Natural History. Is in error on her date of death.

1982

1388. Smith, Susan Sutton. "Elizabeth Cabot Cary Agassiz,"
American Women Writers (48), 1, pp. 23-24.
While pointing out that Agassiz never considered herself
a scientist, Smith makes it clear that her ability to describe

scientific results was impressive. Notes her other major accomplishments. Some bibliography.

1389. OLIVE THORNE MILLER
       25 June 1831--25 December 1918
       Since her family moved a great deal during her childhood,
Miller's education was both limited and varied. As a girl she wrote
a great deal, but during the early years of her marriage to Watts
T. Miller she devoted herself to their family. In the late 1860's
she began writing again and discovered that stories and books for
children sold. While most of her early work is just more of the
massive output of nineteenth-century children's stories, the same
cannot be said of her nature sketches.
       Her second book, Little Folks in Feathers and Fur, and
Others in Neither, suggests the breadth of her interest in presenting nature to children. Birds, insects, fish, reptiles, and
many others are described factually but with lightness appropriate
to her audience. This book is the result of research rather than
observation, and most of the errors of fact are the fault of reports in the literature.
       In 1880 Miller began the serious observation of birds which
resulted in some of her most important work. Her first book, Bird-
Ways, was written for adults and shows her interest in humanizing
this aspect of natural history. She began to travel extensively
and, in spite of her natural shyness, to lecture. Two of her best
books, A Bird-Lover in the West and With the Birds in Maine, published in 1894 and 1904 respectively, show her growing skill and
her basic philosophy that nature represents a refuge from urban
pressures.
       Miller continued writing until late in life, and her work was
respected by professional naturalists. She combined a genuine
sensitivity with the strength required to make a successful career.
The accuracy of her observations and her skill in reaching young
and lay readers was widely recognized. (See also 4, 8, 11, 48,
1122.)

1918

1390. Anon. "Olive Thorne Dies at 87," The New York Times,
       68 (27 December), p. 11.
       A noted writer on birds and bird life. Several of her books
are cited and it is said she wrote many magazine articles. There
is no direct reference to her scientific contributions.

1919

1391. Bailey, Florence Merriam. "Mrs. Olive Thorne Miller," The
       Auk, 36 (April), pp. 163-169. Photograph.

Written by another member of the group of important women working in the late nineteenth and early twentieth centuries, this memorial presents a vivid picture of Miller's great productivity. Bailey tells how Miller became interested in birds after her earlier difficulties and successes as a writer. There is a great deal of information which is otherwise unobtainable.

1930

*1392. Tracy, Hency C. American Naturalists.

1971

1393. Welker, Robert H. "Miller, Olive Thorne," Notable American Women (30), 2, pp. 543-545.
A well-balanced biographical sketch which traces Miller's writing career along several different lines. Says that her nature writing, unlike her stories for children, is not fiction and makes a distinctive contribution to the type of literature it represents. There are some excellent personal notes.

1982

1394. McFadden-Gerber, Margaret. "Harriet Mann Miller," American Women Writers (48), 3, pp. 183-185.
Miller, an early conservationist, was popular and influential. Her children's books are not particularly noteworthy, but her nature writing deserves to be read today. She was concerned with women expanding their horizons. "Harriet Mann" is a pseudonym.

1395. MABEL OSGOOD WRIGHT
26 January 1859--16 July 1934
How Wright became interested in nature is not known, but sometime after her marriage to James O. Wright in 1884 she began writing popular nature studies for newspapers. The first of these, "A New England May Day," was published in the New York Evening Post in 1893. In 1894 she published this and other stories in The Friendship of Nature and a year later Birdcraft: A Field Book of Two Hundred Song, Game, and Water Birds. The second book has been called "one of the first and most successful of the modern bird manuals."
Like these first efforts all of Wright's books show a deep respect for nature and a concern for accurate description. She was constantly participating in activities to preserve nature and to inhibit the destruction of natural resources. In collaboration with the naturalist Elliott Coues she wrote Citizen Bird in 1897 and, as sole author, Gray Lady and the Birds in 1907. She was a founder

of the Connecticut Audubon Society and served as its president
for many years. She was elected to the American Ornithologists'
Union in 1895 and made a full member in 1901.

Wright appears to have taken a great deal of pride in her
romances which now have a limited value as reflections of social
change in her time. She did contribute an advanced view of what
she called the "new woman" who, of necessity, appeared about the
time of the Civil War and pursued new educational, social, and even
sexual recognition and identity. While she herself was, to some
extent, a career woman, Wright also voices loud attacks on feminism.

Her book My New York, published in 1926, is autobiographical as well as being a strong social commentary. There is surprisingly little mention of her contributions to nature study and conservation which occupied 30 years of her life. (See also 48, 1122.)

1904

1396.   Anon. "Wright, Mabel Osgood," The National Cyclopaedia
        of American Biography (2), 12, p. 545.
        Traces the development of her career as an author. Men-
tions each of her books and her service in professional and amateur
ornithological societies. Notes her refusal to lecture in public (see
1398).

1926

1397.   Wright, Mabel Osgood. My New York. New York: Macmil-
        lan, 276 pp.
        A delightful, charming tale of the New York City of Wright's
youth. As she says in her opening chapter, "pray be mellow-
hearted in judgment, and above all things do not seek to prison
me between dates, or try to prove that it rained on a particular
day when I said the sun was shining."

1934

1398.   Anon. "Mabel O. Wright, Naturalist, Dies, 75," The New
        York Times, 83 (18 July), p. 17.
        The founder and first president of the Audubon Society of
Connecticut, Wright began writing as a girl. She has published
a long list of books on animals and bird life. Comments that she
is well known as a lecturer (see 1396).

1399.   F[rank] M. C[hapman]. "Mabel Osgood Wright. 1859-1934,"
        Bird-Lore, 36 (July-August), p. 280.
        Wright was a constant contributor to this review and served
it from the beginning in various capacities. This issue with her
obituary also carries her last article. There is a good description

of her many contributions to the popular knowledge and understanding of birds.

1400. F[rank] M. C[hapman]. "Obituaries. Mrs. Mabel Osgood Wright," The Auk, 51 (October), pp. 564-565.
In this obituary the author supplements his earlier description of Wright (1399) and deals with her interest in conservation as well as bird life. Assesses her character and attitudes toward her vocation.

1971

1401. Welker, Robert H. "Wright, Mabel Osgood," Notable American Women (30), 3, pp. 682-684.
A discussion and analysis of Wright's work coupled with the usual facts makes this an extremely important biographical sketch. Welker sees her as something of a social critic and as an important early advocate of the "new Woman." For both of these ideas she should be read more fully.

1982

1402. Seaton, Beverly. "Mabel Osgood Wright," American Women Writers (48), 4, pp. 469-471.
An important nature writer who was unable to make the transition to fiction. Wright contributed to the popular understanding of nature with her charming, nostalgic style. A good bibliography of her work.

1403. MARY MORRIS VAUX WALCOTT
31 July 1860--22 August 1940
Walcott had no formal training in art or in science, and yet she made some widely respected wildflower watercolors. This activity represents her most lasting contribution, but she was also active in geography, mineralogy, glaciology, exploration, and horticulture.
Her early interest was probably the result of summer vacations spent in the Canadian Rockies. There, under the influence of an uncle, she and her brother became active observers of a variety of natural subjects. It was also in that region where a botanist urged her to paint flowers rather than the landscapes she had been doing since childhood. The new activity took hold of her imagination and she made many trips on horseback in search of new and interesting specimens.
After her marriage to Charles D. Walcott, secretary of the Smithsonian Institution, they continued to spend summers in the Canadian Rockies and she continued her painting. Walcott's major

work, North American Wild Flowers, appeared in five volumes in
1925. She has been called the "Audubon of American wild flowers"
and was invited to lecture many times, including before the Royal
Society of Canada. She continued an active life in natural history.
At 75 she contributed 15 paintings to Illustrations of North American Pitcher-plants.

1938

1404. Lincoln, Bab. "Careers: Famous Painter of Wild Flowers
      Young for Years," The Washington Times (17 December),
      p. 8. Photograph.
      At 78 Walcott is proud of the fact that she still rides over
the mountain trails in search of new wildflowers. An exhibition
of her paintings is about to open at the National Museum. Claims
that her health is the result of never having smoked or touched
alcoholic drink. There is a brief description of her method of painting and her publications.

1939

1405. Berryman, Florence S. "Wild Flower Water Colors Display
      All Varieties," The [Washington] Sunday Star (15 January),
      pt. 5, p. 5.
      A report of the current display of Walcott's paintings with
some detail about them and the artist.

1406. Smith, Gretchen. "Woman Geographers' Head Is Wild Flower
      Authority," The [Washington] Sunday Star (26 February),
      pt. 3, p. 11.
      On the occasion of her election as president of the Society
of Woman Geographers this article devotes much of its attention
to her numerous travels. Says that she is also a photographer
and has presented lectures illustrated with her own work.

1940

1407. Anon. "Mrs. Walcott, Widow of Former Head of Smithsonian,
      Dies," The [Washington] Evening Star, 88 (23 August), p.
      12A. Photograph.
      Says that she was a writer as well as an artist, but cites
only her paintings. Emphasizes her extensive travel in rugged
country.

1408. H[elen] W[alcott] Y[ounger]. "Obituary. Mary Vaux Wal-
      cott," Science, ns 92 (25 October), pp. 372-373.
      An extraordinary woman; the first to climb Mt. Stephen and
had a mountain in the Canadian Rockies named for her. She lived

a "completely rounded life." Her published wild flower paintings, which she claimed were her hobby, were widely recognized as artistically and scientifically fine.

1971

1409.   Shetler, Stanwyn G. "Walcott, Mary Morris Vaux," Notable American Women (30), 3, pp. 525-526.
Describes Walcott's varied career and evaluates the importance of her artistic contributions. Makes a good point of her skill in using her connections with the Smithsonian to promote the broader understanding of scientific research.

1410.   NELTJE BLANCHAN DE GRAFF DOUBLEDAY
        23 October 1865--21 February 1918
        One of the group of important popular writers on birds, Doubleday is best remembered for her alleged role in attempting to reduce the circulation of Theodore Dreiser's first novel, Sister Carrie. Of far greater importance were her published works making interest in the natural history of birds more widely appreciated.
        After the publication of her first book in 1889, which concerned Indians, Doubleday began serious work on birds that produced Bird Neighbors in 1897. The naturalist John Burroughs wrote in his introduction that the book was "reliable" and "written in the vivacious strain by a real bird lover." The book was reliable in the sense that it was drawn from published reports rather than observation, and one ought to be generous to the author; Doubleday's love of her subject is complete.
        A shortcoming of several of her later books lies in the fact that Doubleday never fails to express her attitude towards certain species; for example, she is in favor of killing off all sharp-shinned and Cooper's hawks. A related problem exists in her books on flowers where she assumes that her reader has land, money, and hired hands as did the author. Still she reveals her knowledge and love of aspects of nature beyond the birds. In her last book, Birds Worth Knowing, she says to a young audience that an "immense wave of interest in birds [has] recently swept over the country [making] the ultimate passage of protective laws in every state of the Union a foregone conclusion." She should be given credit for an important contribution to this movement. (See also 48, 1122.)

1906

1411.   Anon. "Doubleday, Neltje Blanchan De Graff," The National Cyclopaedia of American Biography (2), 13, p. 400.
Half of this note is devoted to the exploits of her ancestors, but it does say that her "scientific facts, gathered by personal observation, are treated in her books with a poetic feeling."

1918

1412.   Anon.   "Mrs. F. N. Doubleday Dead," The New York Times,
        67 (23 February), p. 12.
        States that she was in China with her husband on a mission
for the American Red Cross and that she wrote nature books under
the pen name Neltje Blanchan.   There is a brief note on 17 March
simply stating the facts about funeral services.

1971

1413.   Welker, Robert H.   "Doubleday, Neltje Blanchan De Graff,"
        Notable American Women (30), 1, pp. 508-509.
        Although she was later than most of the nature writers of
her time, Doubleday did have a large following and did contribute to the growth of interest and knowledge of wildlife.   The
article presents a well-rounded picture of her and treats each of
the several activities in which she was interested.

1982

1414.   Seaton, Beverly.   "Nellie [sic] Blanchan De Graff Doubleday,"
        American Women Writers (48), 1, pp. 536-538.
        The author of several popular bird and nature books,
Doubleday was a part of the conservation movement.   She was interested in gardening and Indian lore.   She was a minor figure
in spite of having a wide readership.   The bibliography is poorly
done.

1415.   RACHEL LOUISE CARSON
        27 May 1907--14 April 1964
        Rachel Carson and Silent Spring are too much a part of our
lifetime to be fully appreciated.   We have her own word that she
wanted to be a writer, but became a zoologist in order to have
something to write about.   It seems undeniable that she is one of
the most talented science writers who ever lived; whether she is
one of the best nonfiction writers of the twentieth century is still
an open question.   While she did indeed redirect the world's thinking about our relationship with and responsibility towards nature,
just how important her contribution is must await future judgment.
        After graduation from Pennsylvania College for Women (AB,
1929) she won a scholarship at the Johns Hopkins University where
she studied zoology (AM, 1932).   She taught for three years at
the University of Maryland and spent her summers at Woods Hole,
Massachusetts.   In 1935 family responsibilities forced her to seek
other employment, and she became one of the first two women to
obtain professional positions with the United States Bureau of
Fisheries.
        In the traditional mold of the writer who must work full time

to support her writing, Carson produced Under the Sea-Wind in
her spare time and saw it become an artistic success but a financial
failure because of unfortunate timing. The Sea Around Us was
also written under the intense pressure of full-time job responsibilities, but this time she found the world-acclaim she deserved.
Her later writings retained this early promise and led to Silent
Spring. The influence of this little book will not be fully appreciated for years to come, but in the words of one editor, "A few
thousand words from her, and the world took a new direction."
(See also 32, 33, 42, 43, 48.)

1964

1416.   Anon.   "Rachel Carson, Dies of Cancer; 'Silent Spring'
          Author Was 56," The New York Times, 113 (15 April), pp.
          1, 25.
          A long, detailed article which deals with both the person
and the importance of her writing.

1972

1417.   Brooks, Paul.   The House of Life.   Rachel Carson at Work.
          Boston: Houghton Mifflin, 350 pp.
          A nicely written biography by one clearly sympathetic and
appreciative of her influence on our lives.   There are many quotations from her unpublished work.

1980

1418.   Brooks, Paul.   "Carson, Rachel Louise," Notable American
          Women (30), 4, pp. 138-141.
          A long and highly readable account of this modern woman
who believed so strongly in her mission.   The growth of her skill
as a writer under trying circumstances is very well portrayed.
There is a great deal of information and insight here about the person, her philosophy and her method.

1982

1419.   Gartner, Carol B.   "Rachel Carson," American Women Writ-
          ers (48), 1, pp. 301-306.
          A very long article in this important series.   Gartner deals
with Carson's career in general and with each of her books in detail.   There are selected quotations from other writers about the
significance of Carson's work.   This is a most important treatment
and makes one hope for more.

ZOOLOGISTS

GENERAL (See also 721, 722, 1415)

1944

1420. Lillie, Frank R. The Woods Hole Marine Biological Laboratory. Chicago: University of Chicago Press, index. Photograph.
Anyone interested in marine biology and the history of marine laboratories will find this book essential. It traces the growth and development of the Woods Hole Laboratory, discusses the research undertaken during the first 20 years, and contains a chapter about the marine laboratories in both Europe and America. "A very beautiful study of Katharine Foot on fertilization of the earthworm" is mentioned, but there is no photograph. Cornelia Clapp's contributions are also mentioned, and her picture is included in the photograph of the 29 Trustees of which she is the only woman.

1421. CORNELIA MARIA CLAPP
17 March 1849--31 December 1934
Clapp was for over 40 years one of the central figures in the development of Mount Holyoke Seminary and College. She taught Latin for one year following graduation from the Seminary in 1871 and returned to South Hadley. At first she taught mathematics and gymnastics, but her association with the gifted science teacher Lydia Shattuck soon brought her into the study of natural history. A second important influence was her selection for Louis Agassiz's Anderson School of Natural History on Penikese Island. During that summer of 1874 with his admonition to "study nature, not books" she entered a new domain which she quickly established at Mount Holyoke.

Clapp's ability to make students serious nature lovers was a talent admired by all who knew her. Neither a formal lecturer nor a publishing research scholar, she was responsible for influencing hundreds of young women through her teaching techniques and personal enthusiasm. Students were taught the arts of patient, accurate observation rather than sterile memorization. Clapp herself continued an active scholarly life, with many summers at Woods Hole. When that laboratory opened in 1888 Clapp was the first to be given a problem to work on. Unfortunately her dislike of writing prevented much of this work from ever being published.

As Mount Holyoke moved towards becoming a college, Clapp took the lead in meeting the greater demands of faculty qualifications. At the beginning of the 1880's she studied with outstanding young teachers like William T. Sedgwick at the Massachusetts Institute of Technology and E. B. Wilson at Williams College. She took degrees by examination at Syracuse University (PhB, 1888; PhD, 1889). The following year she began a three-year leave for further study at the University of Chicago (PhD, 1896).

In addition to her influence at home Clapp took an active part in gaining opportunities for women to study science. This was especially true at Woods Hole where she not only continued her own work but served as teacher, librarian, corporation member, and trustee. Her influence in scientific circles outside of Mount Holyoke is evident in the fact that she was one of six women who earned one of the 150 stars given zoologists in the first edition of American Men of Science (1906). (See also 4, 11, 32, 37, 40, 1420.)

1935

1422.   Anon. "Cornelia H. Clapp, Educator, 85, Dies," The New
        York Times, 84 (2 January), p. 25.
        An associate of Louis Agassiz and a pioneer in the development of Mount Holyoke. "Several years ago wide tribute was paid to her as a woman not only of some scientific genius but also one who stood among the foremost in the country in the ability to impart her knowledge and her interest to her students."

1423.   Morgan, Ann H. "Cornelia Maria Clapp. March 17, 1849-
        December 31, 1934. An Adventure in Teaching," Mount Holyoke Alumnae Quarterly, 19 (May), pp. 1-3. Photograph.
        A detailed description of Clapp's innovative teaching methods told by a colleague who understood the significance of these demanding techniques.

1424.   Lillie, Frank R. "[Clapp] At Woods Hole," Mount Holyoke
        Alumnae Quarterly, 19 (May), pp. 3-4. Photograph.
        A brief note concerning Clapp's contributions to the marine biology laboratory. Only her administrative work is discussed.

1425.   Wallace, Louise Baird. "A Tribute to Dr. Clapp," Mount
        Holyoke Alumnae Quarterly, 19 (May), pp. 4-5. Photograph.
        A student, now a successful zoologist, recalls with vivid memory her impressions of Clapp and expresses her admiration and gratitude.

1426.   Anon. "Glimpses of Dr. Clapp," Mount Holyoke Alumnae
        Quarterly, 19 (May), pp. 5-7. Photograph.
        Recollections of moments they shared and of Clapp's character. Two are actually signed: "Summer, 1934, Woods Hole" by Abby H. Turner and "A Tribute from Mt. Dora" taken from the remarks of Rev. D. B. Spencer at her funeral in Mount Dora, Florida.

1427. Morgan, Ann; Abby H. Turner; and Mary E. Woolley. "Res-
       olution Adopted by the Faculty of Mount Holyoke College,"
       Mount Holyoke Alumnae Quarterly, 19 (May), p. 8. Photograph.
       Suggests the high regard in which Clapp was held by her
colleagues.

1428. Anon. "Chronology," Mount Holyoke Alumnae Quarterly,
       19 (May), pp. 8-9. Photograph.
       A list of the significant events of her many years of service
to Mount Holyoke.

1936

1429. Carr, Emma Perry. "One Hundred Years of Science at Mount
       Holyoke College," Mount Holyoke Alumnae Quarterly, 20,
       pp. 135-138. Photograph.
       The current head of the department of chemistry describes
the growth of science and pays respect to Clapp's important role
in that process.

1971

1430. Haywood, Charlotte. "Clapp, Cornelia Maria," Notable
       American Women (30), 1, pp. 336-338.
       A well-written summary of Clapp's career. Brings out a
number of her personal characteristics and shows the development
of a truly splendid teacher.

1978

1431. Flowers, Evelyn Patricia. "Clapp, Cornelia Maria,"
       Biographical Dictionary of American Educators (38), 1, pp.
       267-268.
       Provides essential facts of her career.

1979

1432. Anon. "Clapp, Cornelia Maria," Biographical Dictionary of
       American Science (40), p. 53.
       Four lines with nothing new.

1433. ANNIE PARKER HENCHMAN
       22 March 1852--1926?
       Henchman studied at Radcliffe College during the period
from 1884 to 1890, but apparently did not take a degree. She

worked as a teacher and as a laboratory assistant in Cambridge, Massachusetts. Later she was at the Station for Experimental Evolution at Cold Spring Harbor on Long Island, New York. Her interest was in the nervous system of Limax maximus and the development of hooks in Pectinatella.

1434.   Henchman is cited in American Men of Science, 1906-1910.

1435.   KATHARINE FOOT
        14 October 1852--1944?
        Foot is a prominent member of the large group of meritorious but neglected woman zoologists. In spite of the fact that she earned a star in the first edition of American Men of Science (1906) as one of the 1,000 most distinguished scientists in the country, there does not appear to be a single article about her. Her death was announced in 1944, but no obituary could be found. She lists her education as being at private schools and her address (in 1906) as 80 Madison Avenue, New York City.
        In The National Union Catalog Pre-1956 Imprints there are 23 entries which are mostly reprints from her papers. Most of these research publications were written jointly with Ella Church Strobell. Several of the papers are noted as being related under the general title "Cytological Studies [by] Foot and Strobell, 1894-1917." Part 23 of this series appeared in the May 1917 issue of the Biological Bulletin. The Foot-Strobell work centered on genetics and the interpretation of modern studies of chromosomes. It appears that these two were in the thick of the current scientific debates since several of their papers end with a review, and a gentle but often pointed remark, about the published conclusions of other scientists. In the third edition of American Men of Science (1921) Foot is still starred and shown to be working for Morgan Harjes Company, Paris, France. (See also 4, 1420.)

1436.   Foot is cited in American Men of Science, 1906-1921.

1437.   KATHARINE JEANNETTE BUSH
        30 December 1855--19 January 1937
        Bush spent her entire career at Yale University in the zoological laboratories of the Peabody Museum. She obtained what amounts to an undergraduate education through her association with Addison E. Verrill. Yale College didn't admit women at the time. In his memoir as a member of the National Academy of Sciences she is cited in the following terms, "For more than thirty years [Verrill] had the faithful assistance of Dr. Katharine J. Bush, co-author of several of his papers on mollusks and annelids, whose accuracy and ability are reflected in nearly all of Professor Verrill's publications during that period."

She began in 1879 in the capacity of "completing the cata-
logues, and writing labels," but in 1883 she published her first
original paper in the Proceedings of the United States National Museum. In 1885 she was a special student in Yale's Sheffield Scientific School, and in 1901 she was awarded the first doctorate in
zoology given a woman by Yale.

When Bush was paid, it was from grants by the United
States Fish Commission which supported the systematic classification of the large collections of sea animals obtained by government
and private expeditions in the late nineteenth century. Her thesis
and published papers are a rich store of careful descriptions and
accurate drawings of marine invertebrates, especially mollusks, annelids and echinoderms.

Like so many women scientists of her time Bush's contributions were far more significant than the brief mention of her life
found in the standard biographical dictionaries. The evidence lies
deeply buried in the tributes to or of male colleagues and the original research literature. (See also 4, 8.)

1977

1438. Remington, Jeanne E. "Katharine Jeannette Bush: Pea-
       body's Mysterious Zoologist," Discovery, 12, pp. 3-8.
       A well-written biography put together by diligent research
in the Peabody Museum. While some of the evidence for details
of Bush's life are circumstantial, the overall portrait is convincing
and attractive. Would that other papers could be so enjoyable!

1439. MARY ALICE WILCOX
       24 April 1856--5 June 1953
       Wilcox taught school in Boston after her undergraduate edu-
cation at Newnham College of Cambridge University. She joined
the faculty at Wellesley College in 1883 and became emerita professor of zoology there in 1910. In 1896 she studied at the University of Zurich (PhD, 1898) and about that time did research
at the Naples Station. Her scholarly interests were in the comparative anatomy of mollusks and Acmaeidae. (See also 8.)

1440. Anon. "Mary A. Wilcox of Wellesley, 97," The New York
       Times, 102 (7 June), p. 84.
       A brief description of her education. Calls her a pioneer
in the teaching of zoology and embryology in women's colleges.

1441. Anon. [Obituary], School and Society, 77 (13 June), p.
       383.
       Lists a few places she taught.

1442. HARRIET RANDOLPH
       27 October 1856--1927?
       Randolph studied at Bryn Mawr College (AB, 1889) and the
University of Zurich (PhD, 1892). For reasons that demand investigation she is listed in the 1920 Bryn Mawr Calendar as a graduate
student, demonstrator in biology, and reader in biology all in the
general period 1892-1913. In 1915 she was a graduate student at
the University of California and in 1917-1918 at Columbia University.
She was interested in the Annelids and Protozoa and genesis in insects.

1443. Randolph is cited in American Men of Science, 1906-1910.
       We are indebted to Lucy Fisher West, College Archivist at
Bryn Mawr, for her assistance.

1444. NETTIE MARIA STEVENS
       7 July 1861--4 May 1912
       The early years of Stevens' life are a mystery, and it was
not until she was 31 years old that she began her education. First
at the Normal School (Westfield, Massachusetts) and then at Stanford University (BA, 1899; MA, 1900) she prepared herself to teach.
During the years in California she spent summers in the Hopkins
Seaside Laboratory at Pacific Grove, and her first scientific paper
was published in 1901. She had already begun further graduate
work at Bryn Mawr College (PhD, 1903), which she completed after
a year of study at the Zoological Laboratories in Naples and at the
University of Würzburg. Her work at the latter school under the
direction of Theodor Boveri was made possible by a fellowship. In
1908 after having been notified of winning the Ellen Richards Research Prize, she returned to the United States.
       Stevens continued her research at Bryn Mawr where she
spent her entire career. Her thesis and first research interest
was in the morphology and taxonomy of the ciliate protozoa; by
1903 she had published nine papers in the scientific literature. She
then turned her attention to cytology and the regenerative processes.
With her colleague, Thomas H. Morgan, she carried out important
studies showing that these recently discovered abilities were not
found in all organisms and that they were already seriously re-
stricted in the two- and four-cell stages of embryo development.
       The interest in genetics created by the rediscovery of Men-
del's heredity laws together with Boveri's important studies of chromosomes attracted Stevens. She and Edmund B. Wilson, who was
working independently, were the first to demonstrate that the sex
of an organism was determined by a particular chromosome. This
work on the male's X and Y chromosomes represents well her scientific approach which consisted of precise observation and cautious
interpretation. She had a great enthusiasm for science which she
was able to convey to her students. In the second edition of

American Men of Science (1910) she won a star as one of the 1,000
most distinguished American scientists. (See also 32.)

1912

1445. I.M. and M.M., '08. "In Memoriam. Nettie Maria Stevens,"
       The Bryn Mawr Alumnae Quarterly (June), pp. 124-126.
       Rather brief tribute to Stevens. An unusual commentary
on what a distinguished zoologist she was and how unlikely her
students were to have known that. Gives the text of a memorial
resolution passed on 6 June by the Alumnae Association.

1446. Morgan, T[homas] H[unt]. "The Scientific Work of Miss
       N. M. Stevens," Science, 35 (11 October), pp. 468-470.
       It is rare for one to begin so late in life and yet to attain
such a high rank. Her devotion to the work and the great precision with which she carries it out are matched by the terse clarity
of her prose. Her publications sometimes approach meagerness.

1447. Anon. "The Death of Nettie Maria Stevens," Science, 35
       (17 May), p. 771.
       The published text of a resolution passed by the Bryn Mawr
faculty. There are some facts and a deep sense of appreciation
by her colleagues. They note her "faithfulness; responded to every
call."

1913

1448. Anon. [Resolution on Stevens' Death], Science, 37 (7 Feb-
       ruary), p. 215.
       The text of a resolution of the American Society of Zoolo-
gists giving her a "very high place among cytologists" and prais-
ing the fundamental character of her work.

1971

1449. Ris, Hans. "Stevens, Nettie Maria," Notable American Women
       (30), 3, pp. 372-373.
       A full and balanced presentation of Stevens' research. Ris
has high praise for the precision of her work, the brevity of her
writing and her talent as a teacher. He says that her discovery
of the X and Y chromosomes and their relationship to sex determination was of profound importance.

1978

1450. Bush, Stephen G. "Nettie M. Stevens and the Discovery

of the Sex Determination by Chromosomes," Isis, 69 (June),
pp. 163-172. Photograph.
  A scholarly study which looks into the question of priority
in the discovery of the X and Y chromosomes and their role in sex
determination. A fundamental study which can be read by the nonspecialist. Generally finds that the literature is rather confused
about who should get the credit, but Stevens' case is stronger than
usually suggested.

1451. ELLA CHURCH STROBELL
        26 June 1862--unknown
        Strobell's story, or more properly non-story, is very simi-
lar to her close collaborator, Katharine Foot. She was educated
in private schools and worked, and perhaps lived, at 80 Madison
Avenue, New York City. Over the years 1894 to 1917 these women
published at least 23 papers which seem to be at the center of certain debates over the sex determination by chromosomes. Since
essentially nothing was written about either of these women, it is
a mystery why, unlike Foot, Strobell did not earn a star in American Men of Science and why, in fact her entry was dropped from
the third edition in 1921.

1452. Strobell is cited in American Men of Science, 1906-1910.

1453. EMILY RAE GREGORY
        1 November 1863--18 January 1946
        Gregory taught at a variety of schools during her career
with the longest single appointment being at Wells College (Aurora,
New York) from 1901 to 1909. She took an undergraduate degree,
with an emphasis in music, at Wellesley College (AB, 1885), and
after seven years of teaching at various girls' schools went to the
University of Pennsylvania (AM, 1896). She completed her education at the University of Chicago (PhD, 1899); she also studied
at the Woods Hole and Naples Laboratories.
        Her scholarly interests were in the origin of the pronephric
duct in selachians and the development of the excretory system
in turtles. Following her years at Wells she taught for two years
at the Constantinople College for Women and remained active in promoting that school through the American Association of University
Women.

                                    1946

1454. Anon. "Miss Emily Rae Gregory," The New York Times,
        95 (20 January), p. 42.
        A notice of her death which lists several memberships and

says she taught and lectured in biology at Wells College. Mentions
that she had an interest in preventive medicine.

1455. GERTRUDE CROTTY DAVENPORT
       28 February 1866--1946?
       Davenport was educated at the University of Kansas (BS,
1889) and studied at Radcliffe College until her marraige in 1894.
She accompanied her husband, Charles B. Davenport, to his post
as director of the Carnegie Station for Experimental Evolution at
Cold Spring Harbor, New York, where she worked on microscopic
methods in the biological laboratory. She was interested in the
embryology of the starfish of that region of Long Island Sound.

1456. Davenport is cited in American Men of Science, 1906-1921;
       Woman's Who's Who of America, p. 230.

1457. LOUISE BAIRD WALLACE
       21 September 1867--21 January 1968
       Wallace was a graduate of Mount Holyoke College (AB, 1898)
and served on its faculty from 1899 until 1912. In that year she
joined the faculty of Constantinople College where she became dean
of faculty in 1913. Her graduate education was obtained at the
University of Pennsylvania (AM, 1904; PhD, 1908), and she also
studied at the Woods Hole and Naples Laboratories.
       In addition to her teaching and administrative duties Wallace
wrote often on the toadfish and spiders. She was especially interested in the role of chromosomes and in spermatogenesis in the spiders.

1458. Wallace is cited in American Men of Science, 1906-1921;
       Woman's Who's Who of America, p. 848.
       We are indebted to Elaine D. Trehub, College History Li-
brarian of Mount Holyoke College, for her help in learning about
Wallace.

1459. MARION ELIZABETH HUBBARD
       31 August 1868--24 February 1956
       In 1937, when she retired, Hubbard had been a member of
the faculty of Wellesley College for 33 years. As chairman of the
zoology department for 17 of those years she was given major credit for rebuilding the department after a serious fire in 1914. Six
years of her own research was lost in that fire.
       Hubbard graduated from Mount Holyoke College (AB, 1889)
and continued her education at the University of Chicago (BS,
1894). That year she joined the Wellesley faculty and became full

professor in 1917. Her research interests were in heredity, and she conducted studies at Woods Hole, the University of California, and the San Diego Marine Biological Laboratory. In addition to significant publications on protective devices in salamanders she also contributed studies of the bluebird.

1937

1460. Anon. "June Marks Retirement of Valued Members. Marian E. Hubbard," The Wellesley Magazine (June), p. 369. Photograph.
Highlights of her career at Wellesley. Cites several of her publications.

1956

1461. Anon. [Obituary press release]. Typed and undated, 2 pp.
Details of birth, death, service to the college (33 years), memberships, and research interests. Dry as sandpaper.
We are indebted to Wilma R. Slaight, Archivist of Wellesley College, for these items and other information on Hubbard.

1462. CAROLINE BURLING THOMPSON
27 June 1869--5 December 1921
Prior to completing her education at the University of Pennsylvania (BS, 1898; PhD, 1901), Thompson taught at several private schools. She joined the faculty of Wellesley College in 1901 as instructor of zoology and rose to full professor in 1916.
As a teacher Thompson was both original and thorough. In both teaching and research she had splendid training but was never biased by her background. Instead of remaining tied to the current fashions, she explored new fields and brought her own excitement home to her students.
Her principal research work concerned such social animals as the termite and the honey bee. She carried out careful experiments which demonstrated the inadequacy of certain widely accepted ideas of the reasons for termite behavior and set research in that area off in new and productive directions. Her results with the honey bee were incomplete at the time of her death.

1922

1463. T.E.S. "Caroline Burling Thompson, 1869-1921," Science, 55 (13 January), pp. 40-41.
An obituary which is, in effect, a full biographical sketch.

Discusses her research work and, while the language is technical,
the basic ideas are clear to the lay reader.

1464.   HELEN DEAN KING
        27 September 1869--7 March 1955
        King spent 40 years at the Wistar Institute of the Univer-
sity of Pennsylvania where she bred rats through 150 generations.
From this data base she discovered a wide variety of new types
which were later of use in research with laboratory animals. One
of the most interesting of these types was the "waltzing rat" which
travels in circles and is related to the similar type of mice bred
by Maud Slye.
        After completing her undergraduate studies at Vassar Col-
lege (AB, 1892), King served as an assistant in the biology laboratory before going to Bryn Mawr where she took her graduate degrees (AM and PhD, 1899). She began teaching science at Miss
Baldwin's School in Bryn Mawr. In her last year there (1906-1907)
she was also a university research fellow at Pennsylvania. In 1908
she joined Wistar as an assistant in anatomy. By her retirement
in 1948 she was assistant professor of embryology and had served
on the Institute's advisory board.
        In addition to the new types of rats King's research also
shed light on some important areas of heredity. Through careful
inbreeding experiments with brother and sister rats she demonstrated the capacity to improve the strain. This knowledge has
been applied to other animals, including race horses. King was
vice-president of the American Society of Zoologists and earned
a star as one of America's 1,000 most distinguished scientists in
the first edition of American Men of Science (1906).

                                1955

1465.   Anon. "Dr. Helen King, 85, Noted Zoologist," The New
        York Times, 104 (10 March), p. 27.
        Obituary noting that her special interest was the inbreed-
ing of rats and that in 40 years she had studied 150 generations.
Some biography.

1466.   AGNES MARY CLAYPOLE MOODY
        1 January 1870--unknown
        Although she earned a star as one of America's 1,000 most
distinguished scientists in the first edition of American Men of
Science (1906) Moody's life and career are completely unstudied.
She was born in England and took her undergraduate education
at Buchtel College, Akron, Ohio (PhB, 1892). At Cornell University (MS, 1894) she continued to study the same courses as her

twin sister, Edith Jane Claypole; she completed her education at the University of Chicago (PhD, 1896).

Moody taught zoology at Wellesley College (1896-1898) and histology at Cornell (1898-1900). It was said that she was the first woman to teach in laboratory and recitation courses which Cornell required of all students. At that time she joined her father and sister at the Throop Polytechnic Institute in Pasadena, California, where she taught zoology and geology. Later she became interested in the public education system and served on the board of Pasadena. She was associated with Mills College after 1918. (See also 4.)

1906

1467.   Anon. "Claypole, Edith Jane," The National Cyclopaedia of American Biography (2), 13, pp. 259-260.
Primarily about her twin sister, but gives some facts about Agnes.

1468.   Moody is cited in American Men of Science, 1906-1921; Woman's Who's Who of America, p. 571.

1469.   MARY ALICE BOWERS HALL
2 October 1871--August 1950
Bowers was educated at Smith College (BL, 1895) and Radcliffe College (AM, 1898). She became an instructor in zoology at Wellesley College in 1899. She lists her scholarly interest as the peripheral distribution of the cranial nerves of Spelerpes bilineatus. She married R. H. Hall.

1470.   Bowers is cited in American Men of Science, 1906.
We are indebted to Eleanor M. Lewis, Research Associate at the Smith College Archives, for her assistance.

1471.   ANNAH PUTNAM HAZEN
22 September 1872--May 1962
In the first two editions of American Men of Science (1906-1910) Hazen reports that she is a high school biology teacher in New York City, and in the third (1921) that she is a bacteriologist at the Base Hospital, Camp Lee, Virginia. Suggests that she served during the First World War.

Hazen was a scholar and fellow at Bryn Mawr College from 1897 to 1899 following her education at Smith College (BL, 1895) and Dartmouth College (MS, 1897). Her scholarly interests were in the development of the coxal gland in Limulus and regeneration of sea-anemones.

1472.   Hazen is cited in <u>American Men of Science</u>, 1906-1921;
        <u>Woman's Who's Who of America</u>, p. 375.
        We are indebted to Eleanor M. Lewis, Research Associate at
the Smith College Archives, for her assistance.

1473.   MARY LOUISE NICHOLS
        19 February 1873--22 February 1953
        Nichols studied at the University of Pennsylvania (PhD,
1901) after completing a certificate in Biology (1893). During these
years she spent some time at the Woods Hole Laboratory (probably
summers). She was the author of a number of scientific works dealing with such diverse topics as comparative studies of Crustacen
spermatogenesis, development of pollen in Sarracenia and nesting
habits of the burrowing bee. From 1895 to 1905 she was a teacher
of zoology and geography at the Philadelphia Normal School.

1474.   Nichols is cited in <u>American Men of Science</u>, 1906-1921;
        <u>Woman's Who's Who of America</u>, p. 598; <u>American Women 1935-
        1940</u>, p. 659.
        We are indebted to Francis James Dallett, Archivist of the
University of Pennsylvania, for his assistance.

1475.   AUGUSTA RUCKER
        24 May 1873--unknown
        Rucker changed her career rather dramatically about 1900
when she no longer indicates an affiliation with the University of
Texas where she had been an instructor in zoology. She took a
medical degree at the Johns Hopkins University (MD, 1911) and
became attending physician in pediatrics at the New York Infirmary
for Women and Children.
        Her earlier education had been at Texas (AB, 1896; AM,
1899). She lists her scholarly interests as the Texan Koeneia, especially its anatomy and position among the Arachnida.

                                 1919

1476.   Anon. "Augusta Rucker--An Appreciation" and "Who's Who
        at Texas. Augusta Rucker, '96," <u>The Alcalde</u> (April).
        Photograph.
        Two biographical sketches telling of Rucker's career as a
physician in New York City. The editor says the "appreciation"
is taken from a letter by a New York doctor who has known her
personally and professionally for some years. Both articles speak
of her service to babies and mothers in her new position.

1477.   Rucker is cited in <u>American Men of Science</u>, 1906.

We are indebted to William H. Richter, Assistant Archivist of the University of Texas, for his assistance.

1478. FLORENCE PEEBLES
        3 June 1874--1958?
        During her career Peebles taught at a number of schools and colleges; for example, between 1899 and 1919 she was associated with Miss Wright's School, Bryn Mawr College, Goucher College, Newcomb College, and Chapman College. In several of these situations she accepted administrative duties in addition to her teaching and research. Her own education was obtained from two of these schools, Goucher, then called the Woman's College of Baltimore, (AB, 1895) and Bryn Mawr (PhD, 1900).
        It isn't much wonder that she didn't have time to establish a lifelong career at one place when you learn that during these same years she studied at the Universities of Munich, Halle, Bonn, Würzburg, Freiburg, and at the Berlin Koch Institute. Between 1898 and 1927 she worked five times at the Naples Zoological Station and between 1895 and 1924 ten times at the Woods Hole Marine Laboratory. Much of this activity was supported by fellowships resulting from her recognition as an important contributor to the scientific literature.
        She wrote extensively for various scientific journals such as the Biological Bulletin and the Journal of Experimental Zoology as well as a number of longer monographs. She was interested in questions of embryology and regeneration, especially those related to hydroids, Haematococcus and acoelous flatworms. Peebles' extensive research earned her a star as one of America's 1,000 most distinguished scientists in the first edition of American Men of Science (1906). (See also 19.)

1951

1479. Hogue, Mary Jane. "The Contributions of Goucher Women to the Biological Sciences," Goucher Alumnae Quarterly (Summer), pp. 13-22. Photograph.
        A brief description of Peebles' career, her service to Goucher and to several other schools and organizations after her formal retirement in 1942.

1480. Peebles is cited in American Men of Science, 1906-1921; Woman's Who's Who of America, p. 634; American Women 1935-1940, p. 698.

1481. HARRIET RICHARDSON SEARLE
        1874?--28 March 1958

Richardson was a Collaborator of the Smithsonian Institution from 1901. She was educated at Vassar College (AB, 1896; AM, 1901) and Columbia University (PhD, 1903). Her chief interests were in the Isopoda with which she did systematic work.

1482. Richardson is cited in American Men of Science, 1906-1910; Woman's Who's Who of America, p. 686.
We are indebted to Lisa Browar, Curator of Rare Books, and Terri O'Shea, Associate Director Alumnae Association, both of Vassar College, for their able assistance.

1483. AMELIA CATHERINE SMITH CALVERT
        23 February 1876--24 December 1965
        Calvert was educated at the Philadelphia Normal School, Bryn Mawr College and the University of Pennsylvania (BS, 1899). Her scientific interests were in structure and parasitism of Aphyllon uniflorum and reactions of Allolobopora foetida. She married Philip P. Calvert in 1901, and they were joint authors of the book A Year of Costa Rican Natural History published in 1917.

1484. Calvert is cited in American Men of Science, 1906-1921; American Women 1935-1940, p. 141.
We are indebted to Francis James Dallett, Archivist of the University of Pennsylvania, for his help in learning about Calvert.

1485. ANN(A) HAVEN MORGAN
        6 May 1882--5 June 1966
        Morgan studied at Wellesley College before moving to Cornell University (AB, 1906). She taught zoology for three years at Mount Holyoke College and then returned to Cornell for graduate Study in biology (PhD, 1912). At about this time she dropped the final "a" from her first name. She had great enthusiasm for her subject, and her published works include not only the careful studies of aquatic insects for which she first received recognition, but several more popular books. In the latter publications her writing, drawing, and photography played an important role in making the subject of ecology clear to a wider audience.
        From 1912 until her retirement in 1947 Morgan was a member of the Mount Holyoke faculty. She was a full professor in 1918 and chairman of the department from 1916. Several summers were spent in research at the Woods Hole Marine Laboratory and the Tropical Laboratory in Kartabo, British Guiana. Beyond the technical studies, especially of mayflies, she continued to broaden her interests. In 1930 she published Field Book of Ponds and Streams: An Introduction to the Life of Fresh Water which has been the source of information on collecting and preserving specimens for many amateur naturalists. Nine years later her book Field Guide of Ani-

mals in Winter described the fundamental ideas of animals in their
relationship to their ecological environment and was made into an
educational film in 1949.

Later in her career Morgan became more and more interested in the questions of biological education. She continued to
write and to give lectures and workshops for teachers of geography, zoology, and sociology. She was especially concerned with
the preservation of the wilderness. Her scientific accomplishments
were recognized when she won a star as one of the 1,000 most distinguished American scientists in the fifth edition of American Men
of Science (1932). (See also 16, 43.)

1966

1486. Anon. "Prof. Ann Morgan, Taught Zoology at Mount Holy-
      oke," The New York Times, 115 (6 June), p. 41.
      Obituary which calls Morgan a conservationist and an author-
ity on water zoology. Cites her books and the film she helped prepare.

1487. Anon. "Deaths. Dr. Ann Haven Morgan, Prominent Con-
      servationist, Dies at 84," Holyoke [Massachusetts] Transcript-
      Telegram (6 June) p. 14. Photograph.
      A long memorial article which cites several of her books and
says she was in great demand as a lecturer. Notes that she was
selected as one of three woman in the 250 scholars named as the
most distinguished scientists.

1967

1488. Alexander, Charles P. "Ann Haven Morgan, 1882-1966,"
      Eatonia (15 Feburary), pp. 1-2.
      This issue is dedicated to Morgan, a true pioneer, and
Willis C. Day, an astute amateur. A nicely presented biographical sketch is followed by a bibliography of her books and papers
on the mayflies.

1489. Blaisdell, Muriel. "Morgan, Ann Haven," Notable American
      Women (30), 4, pp. 497-498.
      A fully developed sketch which describes Morgan's work
along with very interesting notes of a more personal nature. An
especially nice treatment of the interest she had in the emerging
concern for the environment.

1490. ESTELLA ELEANOR CAROTHERS
      4 December 1882--unknown
      Carothers studied at the University of Kansas (BA, 1911;

MA, 1912) before coming East to complete her education at the University of Pennsylvania (PhD, 1916). She remained at Pennsylvania until 1933 when she joined the University of Iowa as a research associate. She won the Ellen Richards Research Prize in 1921. Her scholarly interests centered on the cytology, genetics, and effects of X-rays on chromosomes. She won a star in the fourth edition of American Men of Science (1926) as one of America's 1,000 most distinguished scientists.

1491. Carothers is cited in American Men of Science, 1906-1921; American Women 1935-1940, p. 149.

1492. ETHEL BROWNE HARVEY
        14 December 1885--2 September 1965
        In the 1930's Harvey showed that cells of the sea urchin eggs from which the nuclei had been carefully removed could divide and form collections of up to 500 cells. Scientists recognized that current theory demanding chromosomes to direct the process of cell division was no longer completely valid. The popular press announced that she had created life without parents. Her own evaluation was much more cautious and centered on the importance of the cytoplasm in the cell division process with the genes contributing to later stages where they controlled more specialized growth.
        Harvey's interest in these topics of biology began with her graduate studies at Columbia University (AM, 1907; PhD, 1913) in which she examined the male germ cells of the aquatic insects of the Notonecta. She had completed her undergraduate education at the Woman's College of Baltimore (AB, 1906). Between these two periods of formal education, and many summers afterwards, she worked at the Woods Hole Marine Laboratory. The Sarah Berliner Fellowship, one of several awards she won, was to have taken her to Germany, but World War I caused her to use it at the Hopkins Marine Station of the University of California.
        When she returned from California she worked as a laboratory assistant at Cornell University and in 1916 married Edmund N. Harvey, a Princeton biologist. The Harveys shared a deep interest in biology, but each worked independently. It was characteristic of her time that almost the only support she received for her work was office space at Princeton and a share of her husband's space at Woods Hole. She did receive one grant from the American Philosophical Society in 1937. Harvey published about 100 papers in the biological literature and the important book The American Arbacia and Other Sea Urchins, published in 1956.
        Harvey received many honors for her work including an honorary degree from her alma mater now known as Goucher College (DSc, 1956). She was the second woman to be a trustee of the Woods Hole Laboratory, elected a half century after Cornelia Clapp. She was elected to membership in several foreign societies, such as the Institut International d'Embryologie and the Societa

Italiana de Biologia Sperimentale. She won a star as one of America's 1,000 most distinguished scientists in the sixth edition of American Men of Science (1937).

1935

1493. Anon. "Half-Cells Without Nuclei Develop to Many-Celled Stage," Science News Letter, 28 (12 October), p. 227.
Reports the experiments which Harvey used to demonstrate the process of cell division without the presence of any nucleus. This work may require some "revolutionary changes in biology's fundamental concepts."

1937

1494. Anon. "New Life Is Created Without Sex," Life, 3 (13 September), pp. 70-72. Photograph.
A popular and accurate account of the essential concept and technique developed by Harvey to demonstrate the importance of the cytoplasm of cells in the reproductive process. There is a detailed sequence of photographs showing the key steps in the experiments.

1495. Laurence, William L. "Life Is Created Without Parents," The New York Times, 87 (28 November), pp. 1, 41.
A long feature article with many quotations. Says that her work, reported at the American Philosophical Society meeting, requires a new mechanism for the development of life. Also points out that it suggests "brave new World."

1496. O'Neill, John J. "Life Produced in Eggs Without Either Parent, " New York Herald Tribune, 97 (28 November), pp. 1, 32.
The report by Harvey of Princeton to the American Philosophical Society meeting poses a problem for geneticists. A long article which states the cells grew without inheritance characteristics of either parent.

1497. Anon. "Science. Birth Without Parents: Woman's Findings Add to Doubt on Accepted Genetics Theory," Newsweek, 10 (6 December), pp. 36-37.   .
At the fall meeting of the American Philosophical Society Harvey presented the results of her experiments with the eggs of the sea urchin and showed one of the limits in current genetic theory. A brief presentation of her experiments, results and conclusions.

1498. Anon. "Parthenogenetic Merogony," Time, 30 (6 December), p. 32.

A paragraph in a report of the Philadelphia meeting of the American Philosophical Society describes Harvey's results.

1951

1499.   Hogue, Mary Jane. "The Contribution of Goucher Women to the Biological Sciences," Goucher Alumnae Quarterly (Summer), pp. 13-22. Photograph.
The section devoted to Harvey gives personal data from college days and describes briefly her research.

1956

1500.   Thomas, Christine Dann. "An Alumna Sees Her Daughter Graduate," Goucher Alumnae Quarterly (Summer), pp. 6-8. Photograph.
When Thomas' daughter graduated from Goucher College in 1956, Harvey was awarded an honorary Doctor of Science degree. In giving the citation which accompanied the presentation Thomas adds a thoughtful biographical sketch.

1957

1501.   Anon. "The Year 1957. Dr. Ethel Browne Harvey," Bryn Mawr Alumnae Bulletin, 14, p. 9. Photograph.
Notes that Harvey has been elected the outstanding alumna of 1957. Some biography.

1965

1502.   Anon. "Dr. Ethel Harvey, Biologist, Was 79," The New York Times, 114 (3 September), p. 27.
An obituary which treats in some detail her experiments with reproduction without nuclei.

1967

1503.   Butler, E. G. "Memorials. Ethel Browne Harvey," The Biological Bulletin, 133 (August), pp. 9-11.
An important article for its description of the work done at Woods Hole and especially her love for that laboratory. Includes some nice personal remarks.

1980

1504.   Haraway, Donna J. "Harvey, Ethel Browne," Notable

American Women (30), 4, pp. 319-321.

In writing about Harvey's life and career, the over-worked and popularized theme of life without sex is replaced by a very level and sound description. The author also attempts successfully to show just how difficult the life of a woman in a two career marriage can be and how well Harvey met these problems.

1505. LIBBIE HENRIETTA HYMAN
       6 December 1888--20 August 1969
       Hyman earned degrees at the University of Chicago (BS, 1910; PhD, 1915) and remained there for another 16 years. She tried botany and chemistry before finally becoming excited about zoology and especially the invertebrates. Her research director, C. M. Child, influenced her greatly, and most of her early publications were made jointly with him.

In 1931 Hyman was able to leave the University. Using the small income from two rather successful texts, she began the detailed study which resulted in the six-volume The Invertebrates. In the years 1940 to 1967 she worked at the American Museum of Natural History as a research associate. While she had no salary, the Museum provided an office, a small laboratory, and a fine library. From the start this work was recognized as being of fundamental importance. At its 50th anniversary the University of Chicago selected her as one of two women in a group of 35 to receive honorary doctorates. At that time only one volume had been published. In the preface she states with characteristic modesty, "... it is obviously impossible for any one person to have a comprehensive first-hand knowledge of the entire range of the invertebrates, and consequently a work of this kind is essentially a compilation from the literature." Others disagree, "... The Invertebrates is more than a compilation: it incorporates incisive analysis, judicious evaluation and masterly integration of information."

Hyman lived a quiet, private life and was especially fond of her flowers. She received several honorary degrees and gold medals in recognition of the magnitude and significance of her work. She was a member of the National Academy of Sciences. (See also 16, 43.)

1943

1506. Yost, Edna. American Women of Science (21), pp. 122-138.
       With characteristic pleasure, Yost retells Hyman's story and her unusual career. We see the influential research director, C. M. Child; the importance Hyman gave to her work; and the warm person who was capable of meeting and overcoming any difficulty.

1960

1507. Anon. "Scientists in the News. Libbie H. Hyman," Science,
      131 (27 May), p. 1599. Photograph.
      Notes her being awarded the Gold Medal of the Linnean
Society. For the past 30 years she has been working on The Invertebrates which will be the most comprehensive work in English
in its field.

1508. Anon. [Interview], New Yorker, 36 (27 August), pp.
      21-22.
      A very folksy tone in an interview at the time she received
the Gold Medal of the Linnean Society. Chats about how she got
started in science by roaming around in the woods and a scholarship to Chicago.

1969

1509. Anon. "Dr. Libbie Hyman, Zoologist, Dead," The New York
      Times, 118 (5 August), p. 37. Photograph.
      Tells of her huge work and the honors that have come to
her. A good general review of her life and career.

1510. Anon. "Dr. Hyman, Zoologist," The Washington Post, 92
      (6 August), p. C5.
      One of the nation's foremost authorities on invertebrate
zoology. Her classic work won the American Museum's Gold Medal
last April.

1970

1511. Anon. "Obituaries. Dr. Libbie Henrietta Hyman," Nature,
      225 (24 January), pp. 393-394. Photograph.
      The plan of her great work, the six volumes of The Inver-
tebrates is described along with her other publications and the honors which came to her. There are some valuable personal notes.

1512. Corliss, John O. "In Memoriam. Libbie Henrietta Hyman
      (1888-1969)," Transactions of the American Microscopical
      Society, 89 (April), p. 196.
      A brief tribute in which the author says, "Much fuller ac-
counts ... will surely be appearing elsewhere; my purpose here
is purely to record the passing of an unusually dedicated and productive scientist." This he does beautifully.

1513. Blackwelder, Richard E. "In Memoriam ... Libbie Henrietta
      Hyman, 1888-1969, Her Life ...," The Journal of Biological
      Psychology, 12 (October), pp. 3-12. Photographs.
      Perhaps one of the strangest and most valuable memorials

ever published. Blackwelder simply puts on paper all of the thoughts
that come to him. It is terrible writing, but it was never meant
to be prose. This is a true goldmine of background for anyone
wishing to learn about Hyman. The main article is well supplemented by similar, but more polished, recollections by James V.
McConnell (the editor of this Libbie H. Hyman Memorial Issue),
pp. 1-2; Taku Komai, p. 13; and Masaharu Kawakatsu, pp. 14-
15. The whole is concluded with a fine bibliography by William K.
Emerson.

1974

1514. Stunkard, Horace W. "In Memoriam. Libbie **Henrietta** Hy-
      man, 1888-1969," in Biology of the Tubellaria (Libbie H.
      Hyman Memorial Volume). New York: McGraw-Hill, pp.
      ix-xiii.
      Another good biography which brings out Hyman's warm
personality as well as the extraordinary productivity Hyman demonstrated. This article is followed by another bibliography of her
works by William K. Emerson (1513) and a series of technical papers presented in her honor.

1980

1515. Winsor, Mary P. "Hyman, Libbie Henrietta," Notable American
      Women (30), 4, pp. 365-367.
      This biographical sketch deals with her huge scientific out-
put, but it also brings together the personal qualities and tells
much more of her life story. Places less emphasis on the technical material.

1516. AMY ELIZABETH ADAMS
      28 March 1892--15 February 1962
      Adams began her education at Mount Holyoke College (AB,
1914) where she was to spend her professional career, rising to
full professor in 1928. She continued her education at Columbia
University (AM, 1918) and Yale University (PhD, 1923). She published reports of her research in such scientific periodicals as the
Anatomical Record, the Journal of Experimental Zoology and the
Journal of Experimental Biology. In addition to her scientific work
she should be remembered as one of the group of women at Mount
Holyoke who became proficient in the vital chore of obtaining small
grants to make research at a liberal arts college possible. She was
recognized for the importance of her scientific studies by winning
a star in the sixth edition of American Men of Science (1937).

1962

1517. Anon. "A. Elizabeth Adams," The New York Times, 111
       (16 February), p. 29.
       The well-known embryologist was formerly a professor of
zoology at Mount Holyoke College.